Dynamic Repetition

The Tauber Institute Series for the Study of European Jewry

JEHUDA REINHARZ, General Editor
CHAERAN Y. FREEZE, Associate Editor
SYLVIA FUKS FRIED, Associate Editor
EUGENE R. SHEPPARD, Associate Editor

The Tauber Institute Series is dedicated to publishing compelling and innovative approaches to the study of modern European Jewish history, thought, culture, and society. The series features scholarly works related to the Enlightenment, modern Judaism and the struggle for emancipation, the rise of nationalism and the spread of antisemitism, the Holocaust and its aftermath, as well as the contemporary Jewish experience. The series is published under the auspices of the Tauber Institute for the Study of European Jewry—established by a gift to Brandeis University from Dr. Laszlo N. Tauber—and is supported, in part, by the Tauber Foundation and the Valya and Robert Shapiro Endowment.

For the complete list of books that are available in this series, please see www.brandeis.edu/tauber

Dynamic Repetition
History and Messianism in Modern Jewish Thought

GILAD SHARVIT

Brandeis University Press

WALTHAM, MASSACHUSETTS

Brandeis University Press
© 2022 by Gilad Sharvit
All rights reserved

Manufactured in the United States of America
Typeset in Bennet by Richard Lipton

For permission to reproduce any of the material in this book, contact
Brandeis University Press, 415 South Street, Waltham MA 02453,
or visit brandeisuniversitypress.com

LIBRARY OF CONGRESS CATALOGING-IN-PUBLISHING DATA
Names: Sharvit, Gilad, author.
Title: Dynamic repetition : history and messianism in modern Jewish
    thought / Gilad Sharvit.
Description: Waltham, Massachusetts : Brandeis University Press, [2022] |
    Series: The Tauber Institute series for the study of European Jewry |
    Includes bibliographical references and index. | Summary: "Dynamic
    Repetition proposes a new understanding of modern Jewish theories of
    messianism across the disciplines of history, theology, and philosophy.
    This book explores how ideals of repetition, return, and the cyclical
    occasioned a new messianic impulse across an important swath of late
    nineteenth and early twentieth century German Jewish thought" —
    Provided by publisher.
Identifiers: LCCN 2022006506 | ISBN 9781684581030 (paperback) | ISBN
    9781684581047 (ebook)
Subjects: LCSH: Messiah—Judaism—History of doctrines—20th century. |
    Philosophy, German—20th century. | Jewish philosophy—20th century. |
    Jewish philosophy—Germany.
Classification: LCC BM615 .S457 2022 | DDC 296.3/36—dc23/eng/20220222
LC record available at https://lccn.loc.gov/2022006506

5 4 3 2 1

To Shiri, Roni, Adi, and Shakked

If some frail, consumptive equestrienne in the circus were to be urged around and around on an undulating horse for months on end without respite by a ruthless, whip-flourishing ringmaster, before an insatiable public, whizzing along on her horse, throwing kisses, swaying from the waist, and if this performance were likely to continue in the infinite perspective of a drab future to the unceasing roar of the orchestra and hum of the ventilators, accompanied by ebbing and renewed swelling bursts of applause which are really steam hammers—then, perhaps, a young visitor to the gallery might race down the long stairs through all the circles, rush into the ring, and yell: Stop! against the fanfares of the orchestra still playing the appropriate music.

FRANZ KAFKA, "Up in the Gallery," D, 436

Contents

Acknowledgments

This book has profited immensely from the support, help, comments, suggestions, and insights of friends and colleagues near and far. My deepest gratitude goes to Joe Albernaz, Robert Alter, Steven Aschheim, David Biale, Agata Bielik-Robson, Jose Brunner, Arie Dubnov, John Efron, Jonathan Garb, Noam Gil, Willi Goetschel, Shai Hazkani, Martin Jay, Elad Lapidot, Niklaus Largier, Vivian Liska, James Martel, Ghilad Shenhav, and Elliot Wolfson. Above all, I am grateful for the ongoing support and friendship of Karen Feldman, Eyal Bassan, and Ori Rotlevy. Their kind and attentive comments on the manuscript and the inspiring conversations we had were foundational to my work process.

I could not have completed this project without the support of the Center for Jewish Studies and the Townsend Center for the Humanities at the University of California, Berkeley; the Leo Baeck Institute Jerusalem for the Study of German-Jewish History and Culture; and the Richard Koebner Minerva Center for German History at the Hebrew University of Jerusalem.

I would like to thank Brandeis University Press for supporting this project. The encouragement and counsel of Eugene Sheppard were invaluable. Sylvia Fried navigated the publication process in a steady hand. Sue Berger Ramin, Ann Brash, and Natalie Jones have been professional and a pleasure to work with. I would also like to thank Elizabeth Thompson and Roni Sharvit for their help with an earlier version of the manuscript.

Earlier versions of portions of some of the chapters have appeared in the following publications: "Freud on Ambiguity: Judaism, Christianity, and the Reversal of Truth in Moses and Monotheism," in *Telos* 188 (2019): 127–51; "History and Eternity: Rosenzweig and Kierkegaard on Repetition," in *Jewish Studies Quarterly* 26, no. 2 (2019): 162–98; and "The Production of Exile: Rosenzweig's Translations of Jehuda

Halevi," in *The Germanic Review* 93, no. 1 (2018): 19–29. I thank the journals and their editors for permission to reprint that material here.

This book is dedicated to my wife, Shiri, and my daughters, Roni, Adi, and Shakked. They are the loves of my life and the inspiration to my work.

Abbreviations

Walter Benjamin

AP   *The Arcades Project*, trans. Howard Eiland and Kevin McLaughlin (Cambridge, MA: Belknap Press of Harvard University Press, 1999).

C   *The Correspondence of Walter Benjamin, 1910–1940*, ed. Gershom Scholem and Theodor W. Adorno, trans. Manfred R. Jacobson and Evelyn M. Jacobson (Chicago: University of Chicago Press, 1994).

CS   Walter Benjamin and Gershom Scholem, *The Correspondence of Walter Benjamin and Gershom Scholem 1932–1940*, ed. Gershom Scholem, trans. Gary Smith and Andre Lefevere (New York: Schocken Books, 1989).

GSB   *Gesammelte Schriften*, 6 vols., eds. Rolf Tiedemann und Hermann Schweppenhäuser (Frankfurt am Main: Suhrkamp, 1991).

OT   *The Origin of German Tragic Drama*, ed. John Osborne (New York: Verso, 1998).

SW   *Walter Benjamin: Selected Writings*, 4 vols., ed. Marcus Bullock and Michael W. Jennings (Cambridge, MA: Belknap Press of Harvard University Press, 1996–2003).

Sigmund Freud

SE   *The Standard Edition of the Complete Psychological Works of Sigmund Freud*, 24 vols., ed. and trans. James Strachey (London: Hogarth Press, 1953).

Franz Kafka

D   *The Diaries of Franz Kafka*, 2 vols., ed. Max Brod, trans. Joseph Kresh (vol. 1) and Martin Greenberg with the cooperation of Hannah Arendt (vol. 2) (New York: Schocken Books, 1948–49).

L   *Letters to Friends, Family, and Editors*, trans. Richard and Clara Winston (New York: Schocken Books, 1977).

ST   *The Complete Stories*, ed. Nahum N. Glatzer (New York: Schocken Books, 1971).

Søren Kierkegaard

R   *Repetition and Philosophical Crumbs*, trans. M. G. Piety (Oxford: Oxford University Press, 2009).

FTR *Fear and Trembling; Repetition*, ed. and trans. Howard V. and Edna H. Hong (Princeton, NJ: Princeton University Press, 1983).

Franz Rosenzweig

GSR *Der Mensch und sein Werk: Gesammelte Schriften*, 4 vols. (Haag: Martinus Nijhoff, 1976–1984).

JH   "Jehuda Halevi: Ninety-Two Hymns and Poems," in *Franz Rosenzweig and Jehuda Halevi: Translating, Translations, and Translators*, trans. Barbara E. Galli (Montreal: McGill-Queen's University Press, 1995).

SR   *The Star of Redemption*, trans. Barbara E. Galli (Madison: University of Wisconsin Press, 2005).

Dynamic Repetition

Introduction
Scenarios of Repetition

In the famous tale of the Messiah at the Gate of Rome, the Babylonian Talmud recounts Rabbi Yehoshua ben Levi's meeting with the prophet Elijah.[1] According to Jewish tradition, Elijah foretells the Messiah's arrival, and so R. Yehoshua takes this singular opportunity to ask Elijah, "When will the Messiah arrive?"[2] Elijah's response is, however, unorthodox: he instructs R. Yehoshua to go and ask the Messiah Himself, at the gate of Rome, where He is sitting among the poor and the lepers. When R. Yehoshua asks how he might recognize the Messiah, Elijah replies that while the others at the gate undress all their wounds at once, the Messiah changes his bandages one after the other, in order to be ready at every moment "to serve to bring about the redemption." R. Yehoshua indeed goes to find the Messiah and asks Him about the timing of His arrival. To this, the Messiah replies laconically, "Today." The story continues, and R. Yehoshua returns to Elijah to inquire about the exchange. The Messiah evidently did not come that day. Could it be, R. Yehoshua wonders, that the Messiah lied? Elijah, however, refutes R. Yehoshua's accusation. He interprets the Messiah's "today" with a quotation from Psalms: "Today, if you will listen to his voice."[3]

The tale of the Messiah at the Gate of Rome appears in the Talmud in the context of a debate among the sages about the different ways to calculate the coming of the Messiah and the end of time. The tale therefore evokes the central theme of this book, namely the models of time and history that shape Jewish representations of messianism in modernity. And as is customary with the Talmud, the story may be seen as representing two opposing ways to understand the temporality and historical conditions of the messianic "today."[4] The prevalent interpretation of the story is that the coming of the Messiah happens at the end of time, as the *completion of history*. The implication of this

I

reading is that His coming is dependent upon us and our devotion. As Elijah explains to R. Yehoshua, if we listen to His voice, the Messiah will come today. The second, less common interpretation suggests that even for the Messiah Himself, the time of His coming is unknown. The Messiah is waiting for the end of time just like the rest of humanity, full of expectation, but uncertain when it will happen. It could happen on any "today," for which reason he must treat his wounds one after the other, ready to be called at each moment. The notion that any moment could become the time of the Messiah's arrival sheds a completely different light on the "end of time." If time could end at any moment, on any "today," then history's end is not a completion so much as a breaking off. What is more, in this interpretation of the tale, the coming of the Messiah would be unrelated to our actions. It may happen at any time, which means there is no human action that can affect it.

The various models of messianism in Judaism seem to be positioned at one of these two poles. In some versions, the arrival of the Messiah is dependent on the continual efforts of humankind. This model goes along with an understanding of history as an ongoing succession of events in which the present is causally generated by the past, and thus the efforts of humankind accumulate and generate further results. Here, the study of the Torah (*limud Torah*) and acts of kindness (*gemilut hasadim*) change the course of history and bring the Messiah, as R. Elazar explains to his students a few lines after the end of the Talmudic story. In some mystical versions of apocalyptic messianism, however, history is ended abruptly by divine forces in a catastrophic event. Here, human actions are meaningless or at best irrelevant. History is ever the same, and true change in reality is beyond human comprehension.

Still, there is one point on which both versions agree: both seem to focus on the *endpoint* of history. Whether abruptly or as a result of human endeavors, the Messiah arrives, and His arrival heralds an end to time. A closer reading of the tale, however, offers another model of temporality in connection with the Messiah, which, as I argue in this book, deeply informs modern Jewish theories of history and messianism. The tale portrays a unique form of messianic temporality, one best described in terms of *repetition*. This is demonstrated, first, by the repetitive outline of the story, in that R. Yehoshua meets Elijah twice. Second, and more importantly, the Messiah Himself experiences repetition while He treats his wounds one after the other: He unties his bandage, then treats the wound, and then ties the bandage again, one wound after the other, again and again, in an endless cycle of repetition. The lepers, in contrast, undress their wounds all at once—a one-time, dramatic, and vulnerable exposure. The same rhythm of repetition defines the promise of His coming: The Messiah could come today, as He was supposed to come every day before that, day after day after day. Rather than offering a story either about linear history or abrupt messianic interventions in history, the Talmud tale appears to depict messianic time differently. The Messiah, it seems, enacts a different form of time. The Messiah experiences time in and through repetition. In the following pages, I show how similar to the messianic enactment of repetition in this famous Talmudic tale, ideals of repetition restructured the possibility of redemption in the early twentieth-century German Jewish thought.[5] Instead of depicting the figure of a messiah as achieving an arrival of an ending, several models of messianism emerged in which redemption came to be described in drastically different terms. That is, a temporal model of repetition, rather than a succession of events, came to be associated with the end of time and redemption.

To understand the interconnections of redemption and repetition in modern Jewish thought, the following chapters focus on the works of Franz Rosenzweig, Franz Kafka, Walter Benjamin, and Sigmund Freud. To be sure, my choice to focus on this group of thinkers and authors is not meant to be exhaustive. We find concerns with structures of repetition in the German Jewish world in many more writers and thinkers, from Gershom Scholem's vision of tradition and revelation in Kabbalah to Georg Simmel's explorations of Nietzsche's eternal return in *Schopenhauer und Nietzsche* (1907). The purpose of this work is rather to uncover the constitutive role of repetition in formulations of messianism in modern German Jewish thought and to connect these models with a larger interest in repetition in modern philosophy.

In many works on German Jewish thought, the horrors of the First World War, the collapse of the social and political infrastructure of the

Weimar Republic and the ensuing antisemitism, and the deterioration of the Jewish tradition due to processes of assimilation and secularization are mentioned as primary reasons for the radicalization of Jewish intellectuals in the early twentieth-century German-speaking world.[6] These thinkers (such as the religious/mystical group of Gershom Scholem, Martin Buber, Franz Rosenzweig, and Hans Kohn; the group of anarchists/Marxists of Gustav Landauer, Georg Lukács, Ernst Bloch, Erich Fromm, and Walter Benjamin; and a group of writers including Kurt Hiller, Salomo Friedlaender, and Franz Kafka) had a worldview which, despite decisive differences, shared what Steven Aschheim defines in *Culture and Catastrophe* (1996) as a "post-*Bildung* conceptual framework."[7] Disillusioned with the promises of progress made by German Enlightenment, worried about rising fascism across Europe, and highly critical of the European political institutions, this generation cultivated radical theories of politics and history that borrowed much from Jewish messianic traditions. Their messianic thought, however, did not participate in the confidence in a Jewish renewal offered by Jewish orthodoxy or Zionism but demanded a complete repudiation of the world and the construction of a radically different society. *In the Shadow of Catastrophe* (1997), Anson Rabinbach captures this moment clearly: "This new Jewish spirit, a product of the 'post-assimilatory Renaissance,' can be described as a modern Jewish messianism: radical, uncompromising, and comprised of an esoteric intellectualism that is as uncomfortable with the Enlightenment as it is enamored of apocalyptic visions—whether revolutionary or purely redemptive in the spiritual sense."[8] In what follows, I use the peculiar modern model of dynamic repetition as my point of entry into discussions on messianism in Jewish modernity. However, instead of offering traditional theological discussions of the Messiah as the redeemer or political theology discourses on messianism and the law, I investigate the function of structures of repetition in messianic thought. This shift in focus allows me to identify a messianic drive in various instances in Jewish modernity and propose a markedly broader model of modern Jewish messianic thought than the apocalyptic messianism that sees redemption as a singular event at the end of history.

To understand how the idea of repetition came to be a mode or source for German Jewish messianic thought, we first need to see how the Jewish idea of dynamic repetition—the focus of this book—differs from usual understandings of the term. In an everyday way, we think of repetition as the duplication of an event. We recognize repetition as taking place when the same thing or experience reoccurs. This prevalent notion involves consistency and sameness, as reflected in the common identity of discrete events in time or different objects in reality. Historically, this model of repetition informed much of the logic governing the archaic world. Rather than conceiving history as an ongoing transition of events, archaic culture believed cycles of repetition regulated both cosmos and human reality. As Mircea Eliade famously showed in *The Myth of the Eternal Return* (1954), for archaic man and woman, the fact that the sun will shine again tomorrow, the moon will be full, and fall will follow summer were signs of order in what was considered a chaotic world. The eternal repetition of days, months, and seasons guaranteed stability, order, and safety. It allowed archaic society to recognize patterns of natural law and thereby safeguarded its members from the dangers of historical change, from what they perceived as anarchy.

The modern Jewish thinkers I investigate took, however, their cues from the ways repetition is understood in modern philosophy. The modern philosophical formulation of repetition originated in a small and "whimsical"[9] book by Søren Kierkegaard entitled *Repetition* (*Gjentagelse*), published in October 1843 on the same day as his celebrated *Fear and Trembling*. At odds with the ancient paradigm, and seemingly paradoxically, Kierkegaard sees in repetition an opportunity for the generation of *newness*. Briefly put, Kierkegaard focuses on repetition as a special return to one's past. Not a simple return as envisioned in archaic society in which the past is identical to the present, but a return in which one reappropriates the past—that is, a return which allows one to relive the past in the present in different ways. This return, he argues, generates a different understanding of the present and, consequently, a different future. In experiencing the present as a repetition of the past, Kierkegaard further claims, one transcends the limits of one's personal history.

Repetition is what Kierkegaard calls a "recollection forward." In contradistinction to the focus of the archaic world on that which is the same in repetition, Kierkegaard notes the differences between repetitions. "The dialectic of repetition is easy," he writes in *Repetition*, "because that which is repeated has been, otherwise it could not be repeated; but precisely this, that it has been, makes repetition something new."[10] This insight is crucial to Kierkegaard's existential philosophy. The nucleus of a "web of fundamental Kierkegaardian concepts,"[11] repetition underscores a mode of *expectancy*: it generates a difference in homogenous personal reality and thereby a possibility for a different future. This logic, I argue, was amplified in modern Jewish thought to the extent that it founded a new messianic impulse. This paradigmatic shift was possible partly because Freud, Benjamin, Rosenzweig, and Kafka demonstrated the power of modern repetition as a *collective* experience, while modern philosophy focused almost exclusively on *individual* experiences of repetition.

In the history of modern philosophy, Kierkegaard's evocation of repetition is often mentioned as a point of origin for a new philosophical interest in repetition. Together with Nietzsche's fascination with the eternal return, Kierkegaard's *Repetition* inaugurated a tradition in modern philosophy that developed the metaphysical, political, and even literary aspects of repetition, as detailed in Gilles Deleuze's work on the ontological preeminence of difference and Martin Heidegger's investigations of Dasein's modes of temporality. The modern philosophical meditations on repetition provide a framework for understanding significant formulations of messianism and the representation of history in early twentieth-century German Jewish thought. Given that history is commonsensically perceived as an ongoing succession of events in which the present is a result of events in the past, the Jewish thinkers who are the focus of this book were able to think of ways to radically change the present by focusing on historical repetitions. In contrast to the archaic world, in a modern Jewish imagination, structures of dynamic repetition do not produce stability and sameness, but a much-needed opportunity for a radical transformation of self and world. Strange to say, repetitions prove history *is* dynamic, something that can be wrested from deterministic models.

In the tale of the Messiah at the Gate of Rome, repetition is experienced in two opposing ways, represented by the Messiah and R. Yehoshua. The Messiah experiences repetition firsthand: He continuously changes his bandages. In this sense, repetition defines his temporal orientation. R. Yehoshua, however is asked to *"listen* to His voice." Rather than experiencing repetition, R. Yehoshua needs to develop a special kind of a listening, a unique recognition of repetition. A certain attentiveness is required. This duality reverberates with modern Jewish theories of history and messianism. Benjamin, Kafka, Freud, and Rosenzweig believed that a change in the present is possible only when the present is understood as a repetition of the past, a repetition that highlights differences crucial for radical intervention in the present. Their models of history and repetition are, however, different. For Benjamin and Kafka, the *exposure* of repetitive structures preconditions the possibility of redemption; that is, a listening, or, better said, an attention to patterns of repetition opens up the present to the messianic intervention. In contrast, in Freud and Rosenzweig, the *actual experience* of cyclical time or of repetition has redemptive qualities.

To offer a first approximation of what this means, in Benjamin's understanding of history in the 1930s, the recognition of a historical repetition of a certain moment of the past in the present illuminates other possibilities for the present and the future. A messianic change depends on images of "redeemed life"[12] evoked by such repetition: the discovery of a dynamic repetition of the past in the present, which produces what Benjamin terms "constellation," provides an urgently needed opportunity to disrupt the causal connections of linear history and to interrupt an otherwise homogenous reality; it thereby creates, in Benjamin's theory, the *conditions* for bringing an "end" or producing something "new." These repetitive relations constitute the possibility of redemption, that is, the end of the history as "one single catastrophe"[13] and the establishment of that which is "beyond the sphere of thought."[14] Similarly, Kafka, in a 1921 letter on the figure of Abraham, formulates a model of repetition that illustrates other messianic possibilities within one and the same present. The letter, which details three alternative accounts of the story of the *Akedah*, or the Binding of Isaac, suggests a model of literary discovery of repetition. However, for Kafka, repetition is not enacted between events in history but between different versions of the same plot. This narrative structure found in many of Kafka's works provides a model for seeing the historical moment as already encompassing concrete different histories, thereupon anticipating Benjamin's messianic thought.

In contrast, in Freud's *Moses and Monotheism* (1939) a series of repetitive murders is seen as redirecting *in actu* the course of history. These historical events create distinct, individual periods of history with specific social, ethical, and religious formations, like Judaism and Christianity. The analysis of the interrelations between these historical periods uncovers an indirect yet significant revelatory impulse in Freud's last work on the origins of the Jewish people. Lastly, in *The Star of Redemption* (1921) Rosenzweig's version of a dynamic repetition is introduced to explain the role of the Jewish people in the linear historical movement toward world redemption. Here, repetition is framed as the cyclical repetition of the Jewish calendar, and it is said to constitute the temporal orientation of the Jewish people. According to Rosenzweig, the *actual* Jewish experience of cyclical repetition produces the conditions for the Jews' "eternal life" in the present.[15]

With a model of dynamic repetition best understood in the lineage of Kierkegaard and Nietzsche, we are able to expand previous conventions in the study of Jewish modernity and gain a better grasp of the complexities of Jewish messianic thought. Freud's theory, for example, is seldom considered to deal with redemption, and Rosenzweig and Benjamin are usually perceived as having very different, even opposing, visions of redemption. The focus in the present study on repetition also allows us to revisit the question of the Jewishness of each of the four writers—another theme that has been extensively studied and may initially seem to have been exhausted. I do not suggest the four figures have the same messianic vision in mind or share an understanding of what "Judaism" entails; nor do I assert their work relates to categories such as "Jewish literature" or "Jewish theory," or if even such relations are desired. The differences between Freud's psychoanalysis, Benjamin's literary, political, and philosophical insights, Rosenzweig's *New Thinking*, and Kafka's poetics are far too great for such analysis. Instead, the following pages open a conversation between them based on their mutual interest in repetition with a view to uncovering the diverse visions of messianic thought in Jewish modernity.

To be clear, my use of the term *dynamic repetition* involves different shadings. In particular, I identify two interconnected trajectories of repetition in modern philosophy: the "repetition-as-recollection forward" trajectory of Kierkegaard and Heidegger and the "repetition-as-difference" trajectory of Nietzsche and Deleuze. The first underscores a constant movement from the past to the future through the present: repetition is seen as a vehicle for injecting change and dynamism into individual experience by reformulating an individual's understanding of his or her past. In the second, repetition affords a deeper, clearer understanding of the world; it allows an individual to recognize the "fullness" of the object and its "dynamic" nature, and is based on producing difference rather than identity. At the risk of oversimplifying things, in the first trajectory, repetition is constructive, while in the second, it is elucidatory: in Heidegger and Kierkegaard, repetition constitutes a possibility for a different present and thereby a new future; in Nietzsche and Deleuze, it is like a "wheel, endowed with a violent centrifugal movement,"[16] providing a particular clarification or illumination of existence. The pages to follow narrate how Rosenzweig, Benjamin, Freud, and Kafka intervene in these figurations of repetition and time in the context of the messianic tradition. The chapters on Rosenzweig focus on his model of repetition and its interrelations with Kierkegaard's work, those on Benjamin highlight similarities first with Nietzsche and then with Heidegger, while the short intermezzo on Kafka focuses on his response to Kierkegaard but unravels a model of repetition closer to Deleuze, as does the chapter on Freud. However, as in modern philosophy, the Jewish focus on repetition did not produce one distinct model: there is no unified vision of repetition. Rather, repetition functions differently and produces different temporal and ontological effects fitting the overall philosophical worldview of each thinker.

This book thus allocates Jewish thought on dynamic repetition its rightful place in the philosophical tradition, between the nineteenth-century philosophy of repetition of Kierkegaard and Nietzsche and post–Second World War work on repetition in French poststructuralism, with a goal of offering a rereading of Jewish messianic thought within the basic trajectories of twentieth-century philosophy. In bringing together Jewish thought and modern philosophy, the book draws out the *messianic* implications of a modern model of dynamic repetition, a model disregarded by twentieth-century philosophy. Primarily, Jewish messianic thought exposes the disruptive potential of repetition understood in differentiating, dynamic terms. This is possible because of a shift in the framework of theories of repetition in Jewish thought. As I argue in the following chapters, one of the fundamental attributes of repetition in Jewish thought is its *intersubjectivity*. While repetition applies to individuals and their understanding of reality in most formulations of repetition in modern philosophy, Freud, Benjamin, and Rosenzweig were interested in historical and social configurations of repetition. This shift in their intellectual focus allowed them to refigure repetition in messianic terms, but also, and equally importantly, to illustrate the communal dimensions of the modern notion of repetition. Their work established the constitutive role of repetition in the construction of communal experiences, laying the groundwork for modern debates on community.

The book's first two chapters comprise a theoretical and historical introduction to the concept of repetition and its history in the German Jewish context. The first chapter starts with a presentation of the role of repetition of the same in the archaic world, as analyzed in Eliade's *The Myth of the Eternal Return*. It then sets the context for a modern philosophy of repetition, with a short presentation of major contributions, including Kierkegaard's *Repetition*, Nietzsche's idea of the eternal recurrence, Deleuze's *Difference and Repetition* (1968), and Heidegger's *Being and Time* (1927). These philosophical works serve as a theoretical framework for the ensuing investigation of the role of dynamic repetition in modern Jewish thought.

The second chapter offers a historical context for the growing interest in models of repetition in the modern German Jewish world. The point of entry to the argument is the concern of many in the early twentieth-century German Jewish community with the eradication of traditional Jewish ways of life due to tendencies of secularization and assimilation in the *fin-de-siècle* Jewish world. These tendencies motivated various attempts to reconstitute a modern Jewish communal life by what was perceived as a return to or repetition of a mythologized Jewish past. The interest in an imagined collective past was mirrored, for example, in the Zionist project that aimed to reestablish the Jewish identity by returning to supposedly ancient forms of Jewish nationality; it also captured the imagination of those who admired the "authentic" Jewish life of East European Jewish communities and who wanted to repeat or reclaim it as a foundation for a new Jewish tradition. My argument is that the growing fascination with such notions of return and repetition prior to and during the interwar period was fertile soil for their application to messianic thought in Jewish modernity.

The third chapter examines the messianic thought of Rosenzweig in his monumental *The Star of Redemption*. Its argument centers on the role of the cycles of days, weeks, and annual festivals in the temporal orientation of the Jewish people. Against previous attempts to read Rosenzweig as following an archaic model of return of the same, the chapter demonstrates a fundamental affinity between Rosenzweig's theory of history and modern notions of dynamic repetition, focusing on Søren Kierkegaard's theory of time and eternity in *Repetition*. The analogy explains how, for Rosenzweig, repetition interrupted homogenous time and brought about a heightened consciousness that restructured the Jewish people's relations to time and history.

The fourth chapter investigates the application of Rosenzweig's theory of repetition in his book of translations of Jehuda Halevi's poems and hymns. Halevi's poems, usually sung and read at important events of the Jewish calendar, played a significant role in concretizing a peculiar Jewish cyclical temporality to the Jewish community. The chapter explores a series of literary maneuvers that Rosenzweig employs in his book of translations to manifest this experience of dynamic repetition to his readers. These measures endow his translations with a messianic purpose.

Next, in a short intermezzo on Kafka and repetition, I look at a 1921 letter by Kafka in which he discusses Abraham and the story of the *Akedah*. Kafka wrote about Abraham in a letter to his friend Robert Klopstock, in a great measure as a response to Kierkegaard's *Fear and Trembling*. This short letter showcases the different ways Kafka deployed a model of dynamic repetition to rupture identity and transgress against sameness. In thinking of the symbolic position of the biblical patriarch as the point of origin of Jewish history, I point to the messianic gesture in Kafka's Abraham letter.

The fifth and sixth chapters focus on Benjamin's models of dynamic repetition and their unique place in Benjamin's understanding of modernity. I argue that repetition has a dual meaning and function in Benjamin's oeuvre. First, repetition of the same is seen as a constitutive feature of hellish modern experience; second, and at the same time, Benjamin's model of dynamic repetition, which I term "repetition of opposites" is part of the solution to this problem.[17] That is, repetition (of the same) mirrors modern, painful reality, while repetition (of opposites) has the potential to change this reality. In the fifth chapter, I use different examples to show how in Benjamin's analysis of modernity in the early 1930s, the rise of industrial capitalism, processes of urbanization, and the eradication of traditional ways of life results in a phantasmagoria of eternal return. The chapter closely traces Benjamin's investigations of archaic eternal return vis-à-vis several conceptual frameworks—for example, the dreaming collective, and his work on Baudelaire, Nietzsche, and the French political activist Auguste Blanqui—to make the argument that Benjamin's explorations of the modern eternal return laid the foundation for his ideas about the redemptive qualities of dynamic repetition.

The sixth chapter shows, in different contexts, Benjamin's own model of "repetition of opposites." I start by unravelling several threads of Benjamin's early theory of origin (*Ursprung*) in his work on the German mourning play. I focus on his investigation of structures of repetition of "unique and extreme"[18] objects in the book's famous Epistemo-Critical Prologue (*Erkenntniskritische Vorrede*) to claim that his repetition of opposites offers an intervention into the modern discourse of dynamic repetition. Exploring an important affinity between Benjamin's notion of the idea and his mystical theories of language as grounded in biblical narrative, I argue that his model of repetition of opposites complicates the basic dichotomies of sameness and difference, singularity and historical connections that inform the modern discourse on repetition. In the last section of the chapter, I return to Benjamin's later theory of history in the *Passagenwerk* and "On the Concept of History" to illuminate how he merged the discontinuities and differences emphasized by modern philosophy of repetition with the insights gained from his explorations of Jewish mystical theories of language to conceptualize the messianic interruption of historical time.

The seventh and last chapter of the book probes the psychoanalytical dimension of the idea of repetition in German Jewish thought. For many, Freud is the hero of Jewish assimilation and a defender of liberal values and morals. However, the chapter uncovers a messianic impulse that governs Freud's last monumental work, *Moses and Monotheism*. I draw on recent works by Edward Said and others to recover a radical theory of history from Freud's ruptured and idiosyncratic work. My claim is that analogous to the role of dynamic repetition in messianic thought in Jewish modernity, the historical repetition in *Moses and Monotheism* constitutes a critical tool in the Freudian battle against reason and progress. In psychoanalytic terms, *Moses and Monotheism* offers a kind of "messianic therapy," in which the recognition of structures of historical repetition is intended to free humanity from its blind desire for eternal, absolute truths. In this reading, Freud defines in psychological terms that which Benjamin's unique version of historical materialism hopes to achieve. I also argue that Freud's conceptual work in *Moses and Monotheism* anticipates, to a certain degree, Deleuze's *Difference and Repetition*. The chapter ends with a discussion of the connections between Freud's new theory of history and Benjamin's early theory of origin in order to argue for a weak form of messianism in Freud.

In his influential book *The Logic of Sense* (1969), Deleuze declares: "Psychoanalysis, it is true, taught us that we are ill from repetition, but it also taught us that we are healed through repetition."[19] In the next pages, I argue that it is not only in psychoanalysis that we are healed through repetition. To make my case, I discuss Rosenzweig's rumination on the Jewish calendar and its impact on the temporal orientation of the Jewish people and his literary maneuvers in his book of translations of the poems of Halevi; Kafka's poetical production, especially his 1921 letter on Abraham; Benjamin's early model of origin and later model of history; and Freud's model of historical return of the repressed. As I go on to show, they all represent the diverse and fascinating ways repetition informed a significant messianic impulse in the early twentieth-century German Jewish world. For these thinkers and writers, repetition negates the horrors of history; through repetition, they believed, we are all to be healed.

I · Preliminaries

CHAPTER I

From Eternal Return to Modern Repetition

The story goes that the idea of the eternal return of the same (*die ewige Wiederkehr des Gleichen*) came to Friedrich Nietzsche in a flash of inspiration. The life-changing event happened in August 1871, during his visit to the Sils-Maria area in Switzerland. Approaching the Surlej boulder, on one of his daily walks around the lake of Silvaplana, Nietzsche had a revelation that came to define his philosophical project. The experience had an immediate effect on Nietzsche, which he carefully documented in a notebook entry, in an unusually exhilarated, albeit enigmatic, tone: "6,000 feet above the ocean and far higher still above all things human!"[1] Years later, in a section on *Thus Spoke Zarathustra* in *Ecce Homo* (1908) Nietzsche described this experience in greater detail: "Does anyone, at the end of the nineteenth century, have a clear idea of what poets in strong ages called inspiration? If not, then I'll describe it. With the slightest scrap of superstition in you, you would indeed scarcely be able to dismiss the sense of being just an incarnation, just a mouthpiece, just a medium for overpowering forces. The notion of revelation . . . provides a simple description of the facts of the matter."[2] In later years, says Julian Young in his recent Nietzsche biography, "Nietzsche would fall silent when walking with a companion past the pyramidal stone, as if entering a holy precinct. The arrival of the thought had, for him, the character of a visitation."[3]

Nietzsche's revelation near the Surlej boulder marked the modern revival of the eternal return. Through Nietzsche, the idea of eternal return that defined much of the experience in archaic societies became a modern philosophical principle. This chapter begins by portraying this history of the eternal return in the archaic world and its afterlife in Judaism. The focus of the discussion is on the production of sameness and timelessness in these formulations of repetition, which widely differ from the modern concept of repetition. This history of ideas of cyclicality and repetition will provide a counterimage to works on repetition in early twentieth-century German Jewish thought.

Despite Nietzsche's foundational importance to the intellectual interest in repetition in modernity, the modern formulation of repetition appears first in Kierkegaard's *Repetition* (*Gjentagelse*). The book was the first to offer a new understanding of repetition, one that differed from the archaic one. In contrast to the paradigm of the return of the same, Kierkegaard found inspiration and provocation in an idea of repetition that produces differences. This new understanding found its definitive form in twentieth-century philosophy through Heidegger and Deleuze; it later informed Hans-Georg Gadamer's work on tradition, Jacques Derrida's work on the logic of alterity, and Paul de Man's interest in repetition as a textual and literary phenomenon, to give some notable examples. My intention in the second part of the chapter is to introduce the reader to the landscape of modern philosophy of dynamic repetition and its contribution to radical thought. I focus first on the model of "repetition-as-difference" shared by Nietzsche and Deleuze. I then turn to the model of "repetition-as-recollection forward" of Kierkegaard and Heidegger. To clarify, the modern fascination with repetition takes many forms and is based on several ontological and epistemological assumptions from diverse philosophical frameworks which are too far apart to support any attempt to suggest a unified conceptual field. My aim is, rather, to extricate several key characteristics from the modern discussion on repetition that illuminate the mechanisms of the messianic thought of Benjamin, Freud, Rosenzweig, and Kafka. In the next chapters, we will see how the modern works on repetition discussed herein, some of which appeared only after the Second World War, form a conceptual framework to investigate representations of history and messianism in modern German Jewish thought. Specifically, we will see how the differences and disruptions that modern philosophy identified in repetition were utilized to think of *historical* differences and disruptions, that is, to think of *messianic* interventions in history.

The History of the Idea of Eternal Return
Eternal Return in the Archaic World

Mircea Eliade, the Romanian-born historian of religion, probably contributed most to the modern understanding of the archaic notion of eternal return in his foundational *The Myth of the Eternal Return*.[4] The point of entry to Eliade's argument is his claim that in archaic society, the profane world was consistently conceived as valueless or without meaning. The significance of a thing was not embedded in the physical presence of the object but established through its relations to a sacred transcendence. In Eliade's words, "reality is acquired solely through repetition or participation; everything which lacks an exemplary model is 'meaningless.'"[5] Archaic societies had several ways in which they were able to reconnect profane reality with such a meaning: religious rituals and rites were structured to repeat divine archetypes that the gods modeled in myths (for example, rites of marriage had divine models in the union of gods); cities, houses, and objects were built following mythic prototypes that validated them; and the organization of social and material space imitated celestial or cosmological examples. In this society, myths were especially important because they presented a lively, detailed, and concrete, primarily cosmogonic, narrative that archaic civilizations could repeat to make their reality sensible. Indeed, the loyalty to divine models was so pervasive that, according to Eliade, "the archaic world [knew] nothing of 'profane' activities: every act which has a definite meaning—hunting, fishing, agriculture; games, conflicts, sexuality—in some way participates in the sacred."[6]

To put the relations of the sacred and the profane in terms of repetition, the archaic world is composed of endless repetitions of myths and archetypes. Human acts, objects, and artifacts repeat divine examples to become real and meaningful. I term this form of repetition "archaic repetition" or "recollection," following Kierkegaard's definition in *Repetition*. In archaic repetition, acts and objects return or recollect a higher ahistorical model of meaning, which usually resides in the beginning of time or before creation. These acts of imitation are successful when the imitation is flawless, when the profane seems to be identical with the sacred. This similarity or identity allowed archaic society to generate meaning (back) into history. In archaic repetition, to add, the only meaningful connection is consequently between the profane and the divine: in each moment of repetition, the profane is affiliated with the divine, but there are no similar relations between different moments of repetition. Repetition applies to the relations between this world and the divine, not to different events or objects in profane reality. The individual phenomenon imitates the mythic model, *not* other profane phenomena, or, put otherwise, acts or objects repeat each other only in as much as they all repeat the same transcendent model.

In Eliade's analysis, this archaic form of repetition changed an individual's relations to historical time: "All sacrifices are performed at the same mythical instant of the beginning; through the paradox of rite, profane time and durations are suspended. And the same holds true of all repetitions, i.e., all imitations of archetypes; through such imitation, man is projected into the mythical epoch in which the archetypes were first revealed."[7] It is not too much of a stretch to say that repetition changed the ontological and temporal matrix of archaic societies. Unlike Platonic ontology, which manifested many basic principles of archaic practices but did not presume to imply a change in the temporal orientation of those who had the knowledge of Plato's theory of Forms, the repetition in archaic society "projected" man and woman into mythic reality. Rather than simply copying mythic reality in an individual's life or relating her to the mythic form, repetition changed that individual's relations to time. A rite did not connect man and woman *with* sacred reality but delivered them *to* sacred reality: it dislocated archaic man and woman from profane history and introduced them to a timelessness outside history which Eliade famously termed mythical time, or *in illo tempore* (Latin for "in that time").[8] Mythical time, to briefly explain, represented the time at which myth happened, or the time of the origins of the world, "the extratemporal instant of the beginning."[9] In archaic society, the transition to this mythical time implied "an implicit abolition of profane time, of duration, of 'history'"[10] by which the individual evaded the flow of time and enjoyed a meaningful eternity.

The cyclical repetition of the year had a special place in the archaic wish to negate time. In most societies, the new year was celebrated in rituals of purification or cleansing. During these festivals, the disasters, faults, and mistakes of the last year were revoked so that the coming year could enjoy a new beginning (the rituals usually involved a dramatic play presenting a struggle between good and evil). However, these rituals signified a wish to reject more than the concrete past. The beginning of the year was important because it represented "primitive man's need to free himself from the recollection of sin, i.e., of a succession of personal events that, taken together, constitute history."[11] That is, in relinquishing the evils of the past year, archaic society intended to relinquish history altogether. The beginning of the year, repeated every year, provided an opportunity for intentional forgetfulness: at that point in time, history was erased from consciousness and thereby annulled.

More importantly, cyclical time *in itself* came to be fundamental to the negation of time. The cycles of the moon, the sun, and the seasons symbolized cycles of generation and destruction, of birth and death, which, when considered seriously, proved that changes in nature were superficial and insignificant. The moon was destined to regain its full form despite periodic changes. Nature was eternal even when winter took the place of fall. Archaic society applied this cyclical motion of nature to its understanding of the cosmos. Myths of cyclical time predominated the archaic world whereby endless time was divided into periods or epochs during which the cosmos enacted a complete cycle of creation, destruction, and recreation. These cycles were the earliest forms of the idea of the eternal return, an extremely effective way to suspend time. In this early version of the eternal return, the past was identical to the future, and nothing new ever truly happened. "This eternal return reveals an ontology uncontaminated by time and becoming," writes Eliade, "no event is irresistible and no transformation is final. In a certain sense, it is even possible to say that nothing new happens in the world, for everything is but the repetition of the same primordial archetypes."[12] On their own, rituals and rites had immediate but limited influence. After the rite was over, the individual returned to historical life. The eternal return, however, secured every moment from the evil touch of history, since history was negated *in principle* in the eternal return.

For present purposes, note that the eternal return functioned according to the same logic as the archaic repetition return. In archaic society, the infinite return of the same reality essentially converted each and every instance in history into a model or prototype, by essentializing an historical and thus meaningless transiency into a long series of *types of events*: "If all moments and all situations of the cosmos are repeated *ad infinitum*, their evanescence is, in the last analysis, patent; *sub specie infinitalis*, all moments and all situations remain stationary and thus acquire the ontological order of the archetype."[13] In this cosmogonic vision, the historical moment does not simply imitate mythical time but becomes mythic by being repetitive. Whereas rites and rituals negate history so that the individual could immigrate to the mythic beginning of the world, the eternal return transforms history itself into a mythical timelessness. This was not only a form of negation of history, but also a way to change the essence of history. History was not only forgotten or inhibited but also completely reconstructed as one eternal epoch.

As I will argue in chapter 3, despite some similarities with this notion of repetition, Rosenzweig's model of Jewish cyclical time is essentially different from the Eliadean archaism.

The Afterlife of the Archaic Eternal Return in Christianity and Judaism

The idea of eternal return entered the classical Greek world in diverse forms and traditions. In Greek philosophy, the eternal return was adopted by Heraclitus, Protagoras, but most prominently by the Stoics.[14] In Greek historiography, the idea had notable echoes in second-century BC historian Polybius but also in Herodotus (fourth century BC) and Thucydides (fifth century BC). In Polybius, however, it is given a slightly different meaning. The eternal return underpins his theory of the rise and decline of civilizations *in* history. This insight had its roots in archaic society. In many instances in the archaic world, the eternal cycle of creation and destruction was portrayed as an apocalyptic drama. History did not simply return to itself; it also performed a cycle of rise and decline (usually of thousands of years), starting in a Golden Age and ending in cataclysmic catastrophe. This formulation of the eternal return helped archaic society tolerate what Eliade terms "the terror of history": the archaic world usually positioned itself at the end of world cycles, and this helped explain away present evils as the direct result of a specific historical position. This particular notion of eternal return gained currency with Greek historians. By learning the past, they were able to uncover the grand cycle of creation and destruction of the world and to identify where exactly in that cycle Greek society was presently located. This vision also made historians into fortune-tellers of sorts: for Polybius, claims Karl Löwith in his *Meaning and History* (1949), "it was 'an easy matter' to foretell the future 'by inference from the past.'"[15]

In early Christianity, however, the idea of the eternal return turned into an abhorrence. The eternal return—an idea of "false and deceiving philosophers"—was famously discussed by Augustine in the twelfth book of his monumental *The City of God*. The archaic idea of eternal return, he rules, negates the basic teachings of the Christian dogma, especially the Christian foundational precept that the death of Christ for the sins of the world was unique: "For, Christ died once for our sins, and 'having risen from the dead, dies now no more, death shall no longer have dominion over him.'"[16] Cyclical time was an impossible vision, as it suggested the death of Christ happened in the past and would recur endless times in the future. The same applied to the Christian idea of redemption. The Christian dogma clearly states that at the end of history the Christians "shall *ever* be with the Lord."[17] However, under the assumption of cyclical time, it had to assume that Christ had already come back to the world and saved humanity, and that this salvation was dissolved by the next cycle of time.

Faced with this impasse, Christianity changed the form of time and rejected cyclicality for linearity: history was the medium that connected the first resurrection of Christ with the second resurrection. In other words, history was given a providential sense as it progressed from the Fall to redemption. Paradoxically, the Christian sense of linearity was itself made possible only through an idea of repetition—of the return of Christ—albeit a one-time event of return that is very different from the previous, "eternal" one. Thus, from an endless repetition of isolated units of time, history, under Christianity, became a single period. The eternal return was replaced by a series of singular consecutive events—the creation, the fall of humanity, the Crucifixion, the resurrection and the second resurrection to come—that would never happen again. If archaic society strove to reach mythic reality, Christianity emphasized the importance of historical events which disclosed God's grace. History now had a goal, and this made history fundamentally important.[18]

A common assumption is that the same logic of linear history applies to Judaism, the first religion, as Eliade reminds us, to inaugurate the preeminent importance of historical time.[19] The turn from myth to history is evident already in the prevalence of theophany in the Torah. In the story of the Exodus out of Egypt, the often-cited example in this context, the Torah emphasizes time and again that it was God who saved the Jews from Pharaoh. Not his angels and not his servants. This fact became the identificatory principle of God as He presented Himself to the Jewish people: "I am the Lord thy God, which have brought thee out of the land of Egypt, out of the house of bondage."[20] History, in Judaism, was the realm of divine acts and was therefore important in itself. The importance of historical time and the turn from cyclical time to linear history is also evident in the many prophetic pronunciations in the Torah that connect the historical actions of the Jewish people and the future of the Jewish nation.[21]

Still, the attempt to propose a duality of Greek *kairos* and biblical (Jewish and Christian) *chronos* as exclusive and distinct has met with wide criticism in recent decades. As some noted, indications of cyclical structures of time were prevalent in Luke and in early Christian theologians such as Clement of Alexandria and Marcus Minucius Felix and later in Albertus Magnus and Roger Bacon.[22] Vico and Machiavelli were key proponents of cyclical time in the Christian world in the early modern period,[23] a model that found new life in twentieth-century historiography in Arnold Toynbee's voluminous *A Study of History* (1934–61) and Oswald Spengler's *The Decline of the West* (first volume published in 1918). Recent works on Jewish antiquity offer similar conclusions. Paul Ricœur in "Biblical Time," for example, claims that narrative and linearity "constitute only the visible framework" of the Torah, pointing to both literary and historical nonlinear structures.[24] The theory of cyclical history proposed by the Galician Jewish scholar Nachman Krochmal—a nineteenth-century application of Hegelian philosophy of history to Jewish scholarship—professes that modern Jewish philosophy harbored notions of cyclicality as well.[25]

And yet the idea of cyclical time found its most prominent manifestation in Judaism in several works in medieval Kabbalah on what is known as the Doctrine of *Shemittot*.[26] This doctrine appeared in the pre-Zoharic writings of Kabbalists from the Gerona circle and was popularized by the twelfth-century Jewish sage Abraham ibn Ezra, his contemporary, Abraham bar Hiyya, but mostly by the author of the thirteenth-century book *Sefer ha-Temunah*. In the Doctrine of *Shemittot*, which, according to Gershom Scholem, slipped into astrological writings in Kabbalah through Indian and Arabic sources,[27] the cosmos is believed to inhabit cycles of creation and destruction dominated by the lower seven *Sefirot*. *Sefirah*, briefly stated, is a mode or an attribute through which God's infinity is manifested in existence in concrete and finite form. In most versions of the doctrine, one cycle of the cosmos is seven thousand years long (this period represents one cosmic week, as a thousand years are like one day of God); each cycle is governed by a different *Sefirah* whose specific divine nature informs the reality of the cycle. To give an example, cycles regulated by *Tiferet* (Beauty) express symmetry and balance, while those regulated by *Gevura* (Severity) express strength and judgment. It is believed that this *Sefirah* rules the current cycle of the cosmos, enforcing a reality organized by rules, commandments, and prohibitions, as prescribed in the Torah.[28]

Under the rule of *Yesod*, which in the weekly cycles rules Sabbath and therefore commonly represents a rest and a break, the cosmos is empty, and Being is resting and healing (much like the healthful interlude of nature in the seventh year of the seven-year agriculture cycles of *Shmitta*). This rest is framed, in several explanations, as the return of the powers of creation, after a complete cycle of 49,000 years, to their full potential in God. Some further assume that a new cycle will resume after the return of all to the *Ein-Sof*, while others warn against speculating about the form of existence beyond that point. "The cosmic jubilee of 50,000 years," tells Scholem, "is therefore the most comprehensive cosmic unit; in it the power of the Creator takes full effect in the sequence of the seven fundamental units of *shemittoth*, which together constitute the *yobhel*, the cosmic jubilee."[29] In this line of speculation, the cosmic cycles of destruction and creation deeply challenge any relations between humanity and redemption, as in archaic society. Redemption is set to appear at the end of each cycle, or at the end of the full 49,000-year cycle: "the Messiah himself no longer plays a visible role; interest is completely focused on the cosmic processes."[30]

The Doctrine of *Shemittot* had gained some traction in Kabbalah by the thirteenth century. Rabbi Moshe ben Nahman even claimed that the doctrine represented "a great secret from the secrets of the Torah" (*sod gadol be-sodot ha-Torah*).[31] The doctrine, however, met with strong opposition in the sixteenth century, as Rabbi Moshe Cordovero and then Rabbi Isaac Luria openly rejected the notion of cosmic cyclicality. It surfaced later but only in a few works by Sabbatians.

In recent years, Elliot Wolfson and Moshe Idel returned to the place of cyclicality and repetition in Jewish mysticism. Their work rejects the common notion of Jewish linear temporality propagated by Eliade. Rather than pointing to a dichotomy between Judaism and the Greek world, a vision that certainly over-essentializes both worldviews, they offer a reading of Jewish history open to the possibility that Judaism maintains different concepts of time, some of which are structured, importantly for the present argument, by cyclicality and repetition. Their work proves that the models of repetition in modern Jewish thought addressed in this work have a long history in Kabbalah. Idel, to start, argues that cyclical temporal consciousness was much more prevalent in medieval Kabbalah than in the Doctrine of *Shemittot*. Alongside the large cosmic cycles of *Shmitta*, he identifies smaller cycles of time in Kabbalah. These cycles, which Idel terms "microchronic," are structured on Jewish rituals and their relations to divine cycles. Cycles or rhythms of divine "time" were important to Kabbalists in the Middle Ages, partly because they were often taken to represent the "proper" moments for "an ideal way of life,"[32] such that "the ordered way of life, as regulated by Halakha, has been combined—or perhaps recombined—with astral rhythms."[33]

Elliot Wolfson goes even further in bringing the basic intuitions of Kabbalah on time and repetition into conversation with modern notions of repetition. In several works, Wolfson offers a hermeneutical exegesis of the "nexus of time, truth and death" in Kabbalah,[34] which shatters the simple differentiation of linear and cyclical temporality.

Unlike Idel, who allocates either cyclicality or linearity to different aspects in the life of the believer, to different periods in Jewish history, or to different theories of time in Jewish history, Wolfson suggests a new form of temporality. In some works in Kabbalah, he claims, time incorporates both cyclicality and linearity in "a dual deportment... as an extending line that rotates like a sphere or as a rotating sphere that extends like a line,"[35] which he terms "linear circularity, or circular linearity."[36] Importantly, Wolfson identifies in the Kabbalistic tradition, temporal structures which are strikingly similar—despite obvious differences between Jewish scholarship of the Middle Ages and nineteenth- and twentieth-century philosophy—to the "Nietzschean perspective presented by Deleuze."[37] In "Retroactive Not Yet," Wolfson even argues, after a summary of the concept of repetition in Deleuze, Heidegger, and Derrida, that the Deleuzian model of repetition "could well serve as a succinct summary of... the Kabbalistic conception of time."[38] My argument about the role of repetition (in its modern register) has an important affinity with Wolfson's argument about the concept of time in Kabbalah, especially the logic of difference that dictates the interweaving of past, present, and future in linear circularity.[39]

This brings us to modern philosophy, which, starting with Kierkegaard and Nietzsche, and later Heidegger and Deleuze, radically challenged the meaning and function of repetition in antiquity. For these philosophers, despite their obvious dissimilarities, repetition signals difference and dynamism rather than identity and sameness. The following section details this radical notion of repetition, as it provides a theoretical framework for my investigation of theories of history and repetition in the early twentieth-century German Jewish world.

Repetition and Modern Philosophy

Shortly after the idea of the eternal return appeared to Nietzsche near the Surlej boulder, his excitement turned into cautious anticipation. The challenges of a philosophical project shadowed the revelation he had experienced. In a letter to his friend the author Heinrich Köselitz (Nietzsche used the pseudonym Peter Gast), a week after the incident, the philosopher reports equal measures of buoyancy and restraint:

"On my horizon, thoughts have arisen unlike any I have ever seen before. I will not speak of them and will retain my unshakable tranquility. I will presumably have to stay alive for a few more years!"[40] Yet it took Nietzsche a bit less time than he anticipated. Already in the following year, Nietzsche referenced the eternal return at the end of book IV of *The Gay Science* (1882), in a section entitled "The Heaviest Weight." The eternal return made another appearance three years later in *Thus Spoke Zarathustra* (1885). In it, he offers the most developed version of his theory. The eternal return is similarly prominent in his unpublished *Nachlass, The Will to Power* (1901). Together with Kierkegaard's *Repetition*, these works inaugurated a philosophical tradition of repetition in modernity. To quote Giorgio Agamben:

> What is repetition? There are four great thinkers of repetition in modernity: Kierkegaard, Nietzsche, Heidegger, and Gilles Deleuze. All four have shown us that repetition is not the return of the identical; it is not the same as such that returns. The force and the grace of repetition, the novelty it brings us, is the return as the possibility of what was. Repetition restores the possibility of what was, renders it possible anew; it's almost a paradox. To repeat something is to make it possible anew.[41]

The following section outlines the basic principles of the idea of repetition in modernity. It focuses on two major trajectories to which the Jewish thinkers respond: The "repetition-as-difference" trajectory of Nietzsche and Deleuze, and the "repetition-as-recollection forward" of Kierkegaard and Heidegger.

Nietzsche: The Modernization of the Eternal Return

Nietzsche's philosophy of eternal return is in the foreground of Karl Löwith's influential *Nietzsche's Philosophy of the Eternal Recurrence of the Same* (1935). Löwith's book was the first major work (alongside Heidegger's Nietzsche lectures of 1936–1937 and Karl Jaspers's 1936 *Nietzsche*) to assign Nietzsche—considered by early twentieth-century scholarship to be a literary theorist—his rightful place in the philosophical world. And while there are many different interpretations of the Nietzschean eternal return, I refer in the following mostly to Löwith's, as his book informed much of the reception of Nietzsche's idea of repetition in his time.[42] Benjamin, I should note, was deeply influenced by Löwith's work in the later part of his *Passagenwerk* compilation.

In Löwith's reading, Nietzsche's theory of eternal return echoes the principles of repetition prevalent in archaic society. This link, he claims, is most evident in *The Will to Power*, where Nietzsche offers a theory of eternal return that is embedded in nineteenth-century thermodynamics but nonetheless echoes the cosmological explanation of the eternal return in archaic society. "If the world may be thought of as a certain definite quantity of force and as a certain definite number of centers of force," he argues, "it follows that, in the great dice game of existence, it must pass through a calculable number of combinations." In infinite time, continues Nietzsche, "every possible combination would at some time or another be realized." Therefore, "a circular movement of absolutely identical series is demonstrated: the world as a circular movement that has already repeated itself infinitely often and plays its game *in infinitum*."[43] The cosmos, claims Nietzsche, must return again and again, as there is a limited amount of force but endless time. Consequently, every organization of that force must return to infinity.

Nietzsche's cosmological argument has been almost unanimously contested by his readership.[44] Still, this argument, in Löwith's understanding, was important for Nietzsche's conceptual framework exactly because it brought the challenge of Nietzsche's nihilism to a climax. This is due to one crucial difference between Nietzsche's version of the eternal return and the archaic perception of cyclicality. In the Nietzschean version, the eternal return does not give meaning to history but expresses the meaninglessness of human existence. It reinforces the nihilism that resulted from Nietzsche's famous "God is Dead" proclamation. While Nietzsche's attack on religion emptied the world of divine meaning and truth, his theory of eternal return amplified the stakes of his claims: if existence was empty of meaning, would we ever want to experience it again? Nietzsche invokes this existential challenge in *The Gay Science*:

> What if some day or night a demon were to steal into your loneliest loneliness and say to you: "This life as you now live it and have lived it you will have to live once again and innumerable times again; and there will be nothing new in it, but every pain and every joy and every

thought and sigh and everything unspeakably small or great in your life must return to you, all in the same succession and sequence— even this spider and this moonlight between the trees, and even this moment and I myself. The eternal hourglass of existence is turned over again and again, and you with it, speck of dust!" Would you not throw yourself down and gnash your teeth and curse the demon who spoke thus? Or have you once experienced a tremendous moment when you would have answered him: "You are a god, and never have I heard anything more divine."[45]

Initially, Nietzsche portrays in this citation the abysmal, non-slavific implications of the eternal return of the same. Would we ever choose, truly choose the return of each and every moment of our entire life, the return of this moment? Would we ever be able to continue to will our lives with this thought hovering? Wouldn't that experience be a dreadful, painful testimony of the meaninglessness and emptiness of human lives?

Nietzsche's famous citation from *The Gay Science* explains why the eternal return was Zarathustra's "most abysmal thought!"[46] However, it also pictures the *potential* of the eternal return since, for Nietzsche, the individual's active willing of the eternal return, horrific and shocking as it is, offers an opportunity for self-affirmation. In the existential reading of this drama, a reading shared by Löwith, the idea of eternal return forces the individual to recognize the ultimate importance of every moment in his or her life and to affirm each one in full. The eternal return is an abyss; yet this abyss has transformational power. The dark image of the world under the rule of eternal return produces pessimism for the majority of humankind, but for the man and woman of the future, the eternal return highlights the infinite significance even of the most inconsequential events. In Nietzsche words, "All too small the greatest one! That was my surfeit of humans! And eternal recurrence of even the smallest!—That was my surfeit of all existence!"[47] Indeed, by the time *Thus Spoke Zarathustra* (1885) appeared, only a few years after *The Gay Science*, the eternal return had thus become the core of Nietzsche's philosophical enterprise, and Zarathustra was declared to be *"the teacher of the eternal recurrence."*[48]

Nietzsche's *amor fati* (love of fate)—a constitutive component of his philosophy of the eternal return—expresses further the implications of his version of the eternal return. In several places in Nietzsche's work, Zarathustra asks his followers to freely love their destiny, to love the moment, every moment, and to accept and affirm even those elements in their existence that were essentially and ultimately beyond their control. "My formula for human greatness is *amor fati*," writes Nietzsche in *Ecce Homo*, "not wanting anything to be different, not forwards, not backwards, not for all eternity. Not just enduring what is necessary, still less concealing it—all idealism is hypocrisy in the face of what is necessary—but loving it . . ."[49] This Nietzschean love of fate, however, is not a form of fatalism or resignation ("Russian fatalism," in Nietzsche's terms[50]). Nietzsche is very careful to differentiate between the life-affirming, value-creating noble who wills the eternal return, and the base, life-negating, reactive fatalist (embodied by Christianity) who falters when faced with the challenge of the eternal return. The love of fate is an active affirmation of the moment, not a submission to destiny and history.

Yet it is in this last point that Nietzsche markedly departs from the Greek philosophy of the eternal return. In the Greek tradition, the individual was destined to a certain fate, but had no favored position regarding that fate.[51] The Stoics believed that the eternal return was a movement of creation and destruction expressing the logic of Being. They had a complacent attitude toward this cosmogonic fact: they lived peacefully in the eternal return as it demanded nothing from them. In point of fact, the passing of the seasons and the changing of the moon were sources of comfort. There was nothing horrific in this reality of eternal return, nothing "terrible" as Nietzsche exclaims.[52]

Nietzsche's eternal return, however, injects a different, *modern* vision. Facing the gruesome nature of the eternal return, the individual, Nietzsche insists, is asked to *will* the eternal return. He or she must elect for the eternal return, which represents the greatest challenge but also the greatest reward.[53] This deviation from archaic repetition significantly informs the modern model, wherein the eternal return is seen as a *problem*, a test threatening the modern way of life.[54] In Benjamin's formulation, we will see later in the book, the eternal return would *empty* the world of meaning. It would inject destiny and stagnation into a world that wished to believe in its free will. In the early twentieth century, consequently, the eternal return was something that humanity must transcend, a challenge to be faced so that redemption, or revolution, would be ever possible.

A second change that Nietzsche brought to the archaic notion of the eternal return resonated with modern German Jewish theories of repetition. For Nietzsche, as I have already noted, the eternal return was not simply a fact of existence, but a reality that demands a response. This understanding changed the logic of the present in the modern reception of the eternal return. The Greeks did not privilege the present. The cycle of time was a fact that had nothing to do with a certain point in time. The present was as random as any other moment. For Nietzsche, however, the present was imperative, as it signaled the possibility of overcoming nihilism. It was an "ecstatic" moment, a crucial juncture, that afforded the complete transformation of the self.[55] The present ruptured the movement from the past to the future. It pierced the perfect cyclical motion of time and was a crucial point from within which a new reality could be built. Benjamin made this insight the corner stone of his model of repetition.[56]

Deleuze on Repetition and Difference

Nietzsche's theory of eternal return was the beginning and end of the archaic notion of repetition in modernity. In traditional interpretations (like Löwith's) the eternal return was a return of the same. The world repeated itself exactly as it was. The sameness which this repetition mirrored was the core of the horror the ancient model was supposed to evoke in Nietzsche's readers. Nietzsche's eternal return, however, was understood in starkly opposing terms in a series of works from the 1960s in French contemporary philosophy. I refer here to Deleuze's *Nietzsche et la philosophie* (1962), Pierre Klossowski's *Nietzsche et le Cercle Vicieux* (1969), Maurice Blanchot's *L'Entretien infini* (1969), and Derrida's *Otobiographies* (1976).[57] These thinkers shared a radical formulation of repetition and, subsequently, a different understanding of the eternal return in Nietzsche. Deleuze's work is the focus of the following. I then turn to Kierkegaard and Heidegger, who provide different examples of the tradition of repetition in modern philosophy.

Deleuze's philosophy of difference and repetition (*différence* and *répétition*) signals a high point of twentieth-century continental philosophy's attack on the basic paradigm of identity and representation of traditional philosophy.[58] In Deleuze's version of this criticism (I focus in the following on his earlier work), one of philosophy's greatest misunderstandings began in the Platonic admiration of representational thinking, which, according to Deleuze, reduced the multiplicity of the world to a logical schema. The ongoing philosophical need to represent phenomena vis-à-vis abstract notions, Deleuze claims, disregarded the heterogeneity of existence. In his words, "Representation fails to capture the affirmed world of difference.... It mediates everything, but mobilizes and moves nothing. Movement, for its part, implies a plurality of centers, a superposition of perspectives, a tangle of points of view, a coexistence of moments which essentially distort representation."[59] Deleuze's project breaks with this supposed philosophical fallacy, something he identifies in modernity in Hegel's phenomenology.[60] His project focuses instead on differences—rather than identities—as constitutive of reality. Deleuze develops his theory of ontological difference in a 1956 essay on Bergson,[61] and his 1969 *The Logic of Sense* focuses on the ethical and linguistic implication of his notion of difference. But his groundbreaking work is *Difference and Repetition* (1968), as it presents Deleuze's difference as a key concept in his ontology of radical immanence.

One way to understand Deleuze's notion of difference is to see how it is deeply connected to his revolutionary insight about repetition, as the opening lines of *Difference and Repetition* declare: "Repetition is not generality. Repetition and generality must be distinguished in several ways. Every formula which implies their confusion is regrettable: for example, when we say that two things are as alike as two drops of water.... Repetition and resemblance are different in kind—extremely so."[62]

We tend to think of repetition as something identical that repeats in experience, like the coffee in front of me right now that I get every morning from the same coffee shop. This notion of repetition is based on the identity between different instances—an identity that forms the basis for general laws in traditional philosophy. The problem, for Deleuze, is that this identity is also used to reject differences and inhibit singularity. We learn, to give a famous Hegelian example, to identify the color red by recognizing the differences between colors, but after arriving at the law, or at the color red in this example, the identity subsumes the differences, which are now understood to be historical, tentative, and eventually immaterial (according to the representational model of repetition, or Platonic repetition in Deleuze's terms). Here, the concept represents the event and all its future repetitions. Deleuze's repetition works differently. It is built not on identity, but on difference. This repetition is not the result of mimesis or similarities but of a more fundamental process that produces differences in and through repetition. To make this distinction, Deleuze identifies two radically different kinds of repetition: the repetition of the same and his "dynamic" repetition, or what I term "repetition-as-difference":

> The first repetition is repetition of the Same, explained by the identity of the concept or representation; the second includes difference, and includes itself in the alterity of the Idea, in the heterogeneity of an "a-presentation." One is negative, occurring by default in the concept; the other affirmative, occurring by excess in the Idea. One is conjectural, the other categorical. One is static, the other dynamic. One is repetition in the effect, the other in the cause. One is extensive, the other intensive. One is ordinary, the other distinctive and singular. . . . One involves equality, commensurability and symmetry; the other is grounded in inequality, incommensurability and dissymmetry. One is material, the other spiritual, even in nature and in the earth. . . . One is a "bare" repetition, the other a covered repetition, which forms itself in covering itself, in masking and disguising itself.[63]

Repetition can never be based on identity because we never actually find identity in reality. No two things or acts are absolutely the same. To go back to my example, my coffee today is different from the one I had yesterday. It may look the same, but this is only from a perspective that reflects "external," "static," and "abstract" effects. In truth, when we consider the "interior" of the coffee (think of the movement of the fluids, to give a vulgar example), we should recognize the "fullness" of the object, its "dynamic" nature. Again, the solution to these differences in philosophy usually amounts to trying to abstract from different incidents an essence, as that which is identical and repeats. But Deleuze invites us to stay with the differences and refuse the generalizations. His repetition highlights and pronounces these differences. It illustrates the peculiar and specific nature of the object, and rejects the logic of identity and analogy.

An important precursor of the emerging trend of New Materialism, Deleuze insists that differences constitute the possibility of repetition. True repetition, he explains in *The Logic of Sense*, is not a form of exchange or a sign of identity. Instead, it "addresses something singular, unchangeable, and different, without 'identity.' Rather than exchanging the similar and identifying the Same, it authenticates the difference."[64] To repeat, claims Deleuze, is not to identify sameness, but to allow new experience, to begin again, to evolve and to find out more, to experiment and to create. Repetition is positive and affirmative: to repeat is to emphasize dynamism over similarities, to recognize change over stability. In repetition, multiplicity is observable; the different qualities and intensities of objects are revealed; the deep mechanism of "pure movement"[65] is explained.

These basic philosophical insights inform Deleuze's reading of Nietzsche.[66] According to Deleuze, the traditional interpretation of the eternal return in Nietzsche that emphasizes sameness and identity perverts the ontological framework of Nietzsche's will to power paradigm, since if the same is that which returns, then the same has to constitute existence or being in Nietzsche.[67] The eternal return, therefore, has to be different; it could not be a process reflecting sameness. It is rather an act of *selection*: "The genius of the eternal return lies not in memory but in waste, in active forgetting. All that is negative and all that denies, all those average affirmations which bear the negative and all those pale and unwelcome 'Yeses' which come from 'Nos,' *everything which cannot pass the test of the eternal return*—all these must be denied."[68] The eternal return is crucial to Nietzsche's philosophy, not because it presents the same reality and functions as an existential test, but because it is a process with which one recognizes, identifies, and then selects differences in reality. "Only affirmation comes back, only what can be affirmed comes back, only Joy returns," writes Deleuze.[69] To give a first approximation of what this means in historical terms, Deleuze's vision of the eternal return suggests that if history is already determined, and reality is completely organized or set, then the return to the same moment should be seen as producing freshness or newness. Time is born again in each return, rescued from past determination. A return thus understood is an experience that rejects the world as it is, clearing away sameness and identity. In short, the eternal return is not a form of radical willing of *all* of one's reality, which Deleuze, in sharp disagreement with Löwith, believes to manifest an inferior slave-like mentality, but a process of careful choice.[70] In an allusion to Nietzsche's Spirit of Gravity, the eternal return thus reminds Deleuze of a "wheel, endowed with a violent centrifugal movement," which expels and make existence lighter.[71]

Deleuze's theory of repetition and his reading of Nietzsche's eternal return illustrates the "disruptive" essence of repetition, which became the cornerstone of modern Jewish theories of repetition. You will recall that repetition already had such a quality in archaic society. Repetition, notes Eliade, interrupted the flow of time. It ruptured the temporal orientation of archaic society and transported archaic man and woman into eternity. This basic feature returned in modern philosophy. For all modern philosophers of repetition, their differences notwithstanding, repetition is powerful because it generates a difference that is indeterminate. Repetition never simply follows previous instances but always produces a change, a movement, a break, which, by definition, transcends the pattern of previous cycles. *There is no mediation in repetition*: the next cycle of repetition always presents something unexpected, something irreducible to its own history. For Deleuze's Nietzsche, this break or shift allows us to actively reject sameness. And for Deleuze, the disruptive essence of repetition is key to his negation of the philosophy of identity, as he notes in *Pure Immanence* (1995): "Thus we must not make of the eternal return a *return of the same.... It is not the same that comes back*, since the coming back is the original form of the same, which is said only of the diverse, the multiple, becoming. The same doesn't come back; only coming back is the same in what becomes."[72]

The Deleuzian principle of difference sheds light on the function of repetition in Freud and Kafka. Yet, for Freud, repetition was an event in the *social and political sphere*. If for Deleuze and his Nietzsche, repetition was mostly relegated to the experience of the individual (in line with postmodern interest in what Fredric Jameson labels "aesthetic singularity"[73]), Jewish thinkers of repetition recognized the intersubjective significance of repetition and applied it in diverse ways to their theories. This shift turned modern repetition into a messianic model, while offering revolutionary insight into the communal nature of repetition, laying the groundwork for modern debates on community.

Kierkegaard's *Gjentagelse*

Kierkegaard, as I already noted, was the first in modern philosophy to rethink the meaning of repetition. Accordingly, his discussion of repetition (*Gjentagelse*, lit., "taking again") focuses first on the difference between (modern) repetition and (ancient) recollection, as two basic formulations of relations to the past in the history of Western philosophy. Recollection alludes to the Greek theory of knowledge (most notably in Plato's *Meno*), in which knowledge is acquired through the memory of eternal truths. In recollection, the world is static and unchanging, and the truth is in the past. This definition reminds us of Eliade's description of archaic eternal return. This definition reminds us of Eliade's description of archaic eternal return. Kierkegaard's particular understanding of repetition, conversely, expresses different relations with the past that are essential to Kierkegaard's worldview: "When you say that life is a repetition, you say: the existence, that has been, now becomes."[74]

Prescient of Heidegger's formulation almost a century later, for Kierkegaard, repetition essentially presents an opportunity to rearticulate the past from the position of the present; one through which the past reveals other possibilities for the present.[75] Repetition is not a return to the same, as in the ancients' recollection, but an experience or a recognition of something *new*. If in recollection, the world is a given and the present is identical to the past, in the Kierkegaardian version of "repetition-as-*recollection forward*," a reliving of the past changes the present. The past reappears but is different in its reappearing.

There are several dimensions to the experience of repetition in Kierkegaard's book.[76] First, repetition is an aesthetic experience. Kierkegaard explores this in the second half of *Repetition*, where he narrates an exchange of letters between Constantin Constantius, Kierkegaard's pseudonym in the book, and a "young man," who has just ended a romantic relationship. This exchange allows Kierkegaard to illustrate the different meanings of modern repetition, or, as Kierkegaard puts it, to initiate the young man—and the reader—into the world of repetition, that is, into the dynamic, changing nature of self and reality that repetition reveals. For the young man, dynamic repetition produces a heightened poetical experience of his previous love affair. In this reliving of the past in the present, the young man is able to experience his previous relationship in diverse forms. Repetition grants him an "equivocal" experience: because of repetition he is not only melancholic about past events, but also "happy, unhappy, comic, tragic."[77] Repetition, in other words, produces a change in the existential mode of the young man and brings about "an exponential power of consciousness (raising consciousness to the second power)."[78]

For Kierkegaard, then, repetition allows improved, clearer insight, like that of "a person who has acquired a sophisticated understanding of the world,"[79] by expressing the differences in what that person considers monotonous reality. This insight about repetition is foundational for Kierkegaard's philosophy, as for him, "modern philosophy teaches that life itself is a repetition."[80] This insight also inaugurated, together with Nietzsche's theory of the eternal return, the modern philosophical tradition of repetition. However, an important dimension of Kierkegaard's model allows us to differentiate his formulation from other modern formulations. Unlike Deleuze, Nietzsche, and even Heidegger, Kierkegaard offers more than a philosophical investigation. His work adds a religious dimension to the theory of repetition—one that "heretics cannot understand."[81] Of the young man, Constantin writes: "If he had had a more devoutly religious background, he would not have become a poet. Then everything would have received a religious meaning."[82]

Poetic insight is not all that repetition offers; repetition is of primary importance in that it serves as a "transition" to the religious experience.[83] Repetition is not only, not even primarily, a worldly phenomenon or a change in aesthetic consciousness; it is first and foremost a "transcendent, religious movement."[84] In Kierkegaard's book, in other words, repetition presents a road map to a deeper, meaningful relationship between the believer and God. This is exemplified in the story of Job,[85] who Kierkegaard characterizes as the paradigmatic hero of repetition (recall that Job first lost everything and then received everything back).[86] In Kierkegaard's interpretation of the biblical drama, the significance of Job's experience relates to his position on his loss: "The secret in the story of Job, the vital force, the core, the idea is: that Job, despite everything, is in the right."[87] While conventional readings explain the story of Job as affirming divine transcendence— when God finally answers Job, it is to condemn Job for questioning His actions—Kierkegaard emphasizes Job's self-reliance. Unlike his friends, Job had faith in God and loved God, notwithstanding his previous losses. Job never doubted himself: he knew that he was right, was undeterred by his friends' attempt to persuade him otherwise, and had an unbounded confidence in God that was never shattered by his miseries. Put in different terms, those around Job succumbed to history, that is, to external pressures and worldly disturbances. Job, on the other hand, had a clear and deep understanding of his world.[88] "The life of a poet begins in a struggle with all of existence,"[89] notes Kierkegaard; the believer, however, gains an "iron-like consistency" that absolves him from the power of history.[90] Job's experience, according to Kierkegaard, granted him an independent conception of the world. Job was thrown into a reality over which he had no control. But he did not let this reality define him; he was not entirely consumed by his misery. He knew he was right, and he pressed forward calmly and self-assuredly despite his misfortune.

In Kierkegaard's version of the biblical story, Job's peculiar repetitive experience produced the conditions for his conviction. Job was able to form an independent understanding of his cruel reality because he did not experience that reality as a predetermined succession of events or conceive his present as causally generated by the past. Simply put, Job did not connect his present misery to his past actions. Rather, in the ongoing, repetitive reliving of his catastrophe, Job's present retained his past. Still, in this retrieval of his past (to put it in Heideggerian terms), the past was experienced in disconnection from what directly preceded it; the present seemed to arrive from outside history. Repetition constituted the conditions for Job's *singular* experience: the present duplicated the past, not in relation to Job's history but as an intervention in history from the outside. Job's experience, in other words, was not enslaved to history: Job was able to create a different meaning for the present by re-experiencing his past in a new, different way, that is, as retained in the present but also disconnected from it. This retentive-but-disconnected quality of repetition constitutes the possibility of freedom in Kierkegaard's philosophy. In repetition, he argues, one acquires a personal, independent meaning in the midst of time; or, otherwise put, in repetition, one is free from history to create his or her life.[91] In John Caputo's *Radical Hermeneutics* (1987), repetition is therefore the "centerpiece"[92] of Kierkegaard's existential theory of the self: "Repetition is the power of the individual to forge his personality out of the chaos of events, in the midst of flux, the power to create an identity in the face of incessant 'dispersal' of the self, of the dissipating effects of the flux."[93]

Kierkegaard's insistence on the power of repetition to subvert historical determinations informed Heidegger's notion of repetition. In Kierkegaard's *Gjentagelse*, as in Heidegger's *Wiederholung*, the return of the past in the present negates the power of history on the individual. Despite Heidegger's lack of recognition of this link, Kierkegaard's emphasis on the forward movement of repetition, his recognition of the role of repetition in the constitution of meaning and identity, and the formulation of repetition as self-relations—all in the context of his concept of anxiety—prefigured Heidegger's early philosophy.[94]

Heidegger: Repetition as Retrieval

Heidegger discusses repetition, or *Wiederholung*, in chapter 5 on Temporality and Historicity in the second division of his *Being and Time*.[95] His model of repetition is developed there in the context of his analysis of Dasein's historicity. In this section, Heidegger explains the transition of Dasein from being thrown into the world of the "they" to becoming the authentic Being-in-the-world. This transition, we will shortly see, depends, at least in part, on a rearticulation of the relations between Dasein's past and present, i.e., on repetition.

Briefly stated, for Heidegger, the reality of being among the "they," as the inauthentic mode of being, is one in which "Being has been taken away by the Others."[96] In this mode, Dasein understands itself as if it was a worldly thing; drifting, in Heidegger's words, "back and forth between 'worldly' possibilities which it has not seized upon."[97] The world seems to be not its own; its future is already decided. When Heidegger puts this condition in temporal terms, he notes that in this inauthentic mode, Dasein is, in essence, determined by its past. The present of Dasein is the direct and unavoidable result of the past, and the future, in the same vein, is the outcome of the present. In Heidegger's rationale, the past defines the present of Dasein in the same way as outside forces define the world of Dasein. In this kind of experience, history itself is conceived as composed of a set of consecutive and necessary events, and the Now (*das Jetzt*) is simply an instance of empty transition from the past (as the no-longer-now) to the future (as the not-yet-now).[98]

To negate such a mechanistic understanding of self and world, Heidegger suggests different relations to the past and thereby to the future. These relations are first explained in connection with the act of bringing one back to one's ownmost self: "The authentic coming-towards-itself of anticipatory resoluteness is at the same time a coming-back to one's ownmost Self... In anticipating, Dasein brings itself again forth into its ownmost potentiality-for-Being. If Being-as-having-been is authentic, we call it 'repetition' [*Wiederholung*]."[99] In a moment of awareness, of resoluteness, which Heidegger terms a "moment of vision" (*Augenblick*), Dasein returns to its "ownmost Self" by *reappropriating* its personal past.[100] The return to the past opens up new possibilities in the present (which Heidegger terms "potentiality-for-Being") because in this "moment of vision," the past is perceived differently. The past is no longer an event that determines the present in a mechanistic series of events, but is seen as a pool of latent opportunities that Dasein, in the present, can return to and retrieve. In other words, Dasein's ability to reshape its life is grounded on a recollection of the past, in which the past is opened up to more than one absolute road.[101]

The "coming-back to one's ownmost Self" is dependent, according to Heidegger, on Dasein's possibility of narrating itself a different history, and therefore a different future, from that which he has been given by others (to put it in Arendtian key). This history is reclaimed by a different understanding of the present, which is possible, Heidegger claims, only if we recognize the present as a *repetition* of the past.

The resoluteness which comes back to itself and hands itself down, then becomes the repetition [*Wiederholung*] of a possibility of existence that has come down to us. Repeating is handing down explicitly [*die ausdrückliche Überlieferung*]—that is to say, going back into the possibilities of the Dasein that has-been-there... Repetition makes a *reciprocative rejoinder* to the possibility of that existence which has-been-there. But when such a response is made to this possibility in a resolution, it is made in *a moment of vision* [*Augenblick*]; and *as such* it is at the same time a *disavowal* of that which in the "today," is working itself out as the "past." Repetition does not abandon itself to that which is past, nor does it aim at progress. In the moment of vision authentic existence is indifferent to both these alternatives.[102]

The repetition Heidegger has in mind is not the repetition of the same. Repetition is not an imitation or a copy of the past in the present but a *reciprocative rejoinder* (*erwidert*) to the past. The present never repeats the past as it was, but only in and through a difference, which, in Heidegger's—somewhat Kierkegaardian—version of repetition, constitutes a dialectics of new and old: in repetition, Dasein reclaims the past but in reclaiming it, Dasein also reassigns it new meaning.[103] As Derrida notes, repetition is thus "merely a passage from the implicit to the explicit that a movement of our freedom would make possible and continuous, and so on."[104] This duality of repetition signals the duality of Dasein's temporal orientation: Dasein looks backward in order to look forward. The future is always open, and Dasein experiences this undefined openness by returning to the past and retrieving new, previously unrecognized potentialities.[105]

Heidegger's *Wiederholung*, however, in contradistinction to Kierkegaard's *Gjentagelse*, indicates not the recurance of one singular moment, but an ongoing circular movement that defines Dasein's way of being. John Caputo emphasizes this constant movement between Dasein's past and future in *Radical Hermeneutics*. In his reading, "Dasein's own Being 'circulates' between its 'futurity' [*Zukünftigkeit*] and its 'having been' [*Gewesenheit*]. The Being of Dasein is constantly projected ahead, never in a free-floating and absolute way, but always toward possibilities into which it has all along being inserted."[106] Repetition, in other words, constitutes a structure of kinesis that actualizes Dasein's structure of futurity. The potential to move forward is grounded on an endless circular movement of being in which Dasein retrieves from the past a latent potential for the future. In chapter 6, I return to Heidegger's model of *Wiederholung* to investigate Benjamin's "repetition of opposites." There, Dasein's retrieval of new possibilities in the past will explain the dynamism of Benjamin's articulation of the now-time.

The next chapters detail how modern German Jewish thinkers drew from this vibrant tradition of repetition to rethink the messianic in Judaism. But their turn to the past was not in the form of simple repetition: rather, Kierkegaard, Benjamin, Kafka, and Freud intervened in the modern tradition. They reappropriated the principle of modern repetition and the essential dimensions of the modern project, thereby producing a wealth of new insights on dynamic repetition in modernity.

CHAPTER 2

Tradition and Repetition in German Jewish Modernity

In a section on childhood dreams in *The Interpretation of Dreams* (1900), Sigmund Freud documents a series of dreams about Rome; over the years, these dreams, featuring the center of Christendom, came to represent his tensional relations with his Jewish heritage, as well as his fascination with Christianity. In one of these childhood dreams, which he remembered many years later, Freud is standing on a hill looking on Rome "half-shrouded in mist."[1] Moses is not mentioned in this dream, yet Freud seems to be well aware of its meaning: "There was more in the content [of the dream] than I feel prepared to detail; but the theme of 'the promised land seen from afar' was obvious in it."[2] In Freud's dream, Rome is revealed from afar and is beyond reach, just as the Land of Israel was beyond the reach of Moses. Still, in a fascinating move, young Freud changed the script of the biblical drama in a manner that reflects the complicated reality of many of his generation in the German Jewish world. In the dream, the holy land was reconfigured as Rome, and, more importantly, Moses's longing for Judaism was translated into Freud's unconscious wish to be accepted by Rome, the capital of the Christian world.[3]

The dream of young Sigmund of Rome, as he stands high on the hill, far from the Christian city below, mirrored the challenges of Freud and his generation in their struggle to find a place for themselves on and between the borders of the German Jewish community and the Western secular world. Freud, like Benjamin, Kafka, and Rosenzweig and many members of the young German Jewish community, aspired to join German society; many, however, never succeeded. Still, their attempts to move away from Jewish traditional ways of life, even if unsuccessful, endangered the Jewish community from which they came. The rejection of Jewish costumes and traditions disrupted the Jewish communal experience and brought about a "sickness"[4] of the Jewish tradition, as Benjamin termed it. This "sickness," on which the following focuses, motivated a series of attempts by the Jewish communities in Europe to find, indeed to reinvent, new forms of Jewish communal life.

In what comes, I follow Michael Brenner, who claims in *The Renaissance of Jewish Culture in Weimar Germany* (1998) that German-speaking Jews, facing processes of secularization and a loss of social and individual identity, "selected certain aspects of the rich Jewish heritage and integrated them into modern European culture, as expressed in the realms of scholarship, art, and literary fiction. The result was the formation of a new tradition that had enduring influence on Jewish existence in the modern world."[5] What is interesting to me about this historical moment is that the recreation of Jewish life, which had much to do with modern political, social, and economic discourses, did not represent a break with the past. Instead, faced with the challenges of modernity, the German Jewish community turned to its past as a source for Jewish renewal. Confronted by an experience of discontinuity with a Jewish past and a withdrawal from Jewish practice and everyday content of Jewish life, Jewish thinkers tried to reconstruct a continuity with the Jewish past, by retrieving or rediscovering earlier Jewish practices and figures. The past was not neglected or repressed but *repeated*, resulting in what I call—despite the seeming contradiction in terms—a new Jewish tradition. This search for a "new," modern Jewish tradition, which informed much of the historical moment of Benjamin, Freud, Rosenzweig, and Kafka, brought to the surface of the Jewish cultural imagination various ideals and notions of repetition that are the focus of this work. These Jewish models of repetition or reclamation were fertile soil for Jewish theories of "dynamic repetition."

In this chapter, I give a historical introduction to the different ways heterogeneous models of return and repetition proliferated in the early twentieth-century German Jewish world, thereby setting the historical context for the theoretical interest in repetition in that period. Rosenzweig's search for new models of Jewish education and the fascination with East European Jewry serve as one example of the wide circulation of ideas of return and repetition in the German Jewish world in that formative period. Zionism marks another, somewhat unexpected, example of the prevalence of ideas of repetition. I point here to the Zionists' idealization of the Jewish nationality of two thousand years before and its fundamental role in the construction of several tenets of Zionist ideology. The imaginary return in Zionism to the Jewish past, which grounded the factual return of Jews to the Land of Israel in the early twentieth century, offered a vivid illustration of the "messianic" powers of repetition—one that informed German Jewish imagination.

I begin the chapter with a short discussion of the crisis of tradition in Jewish modernity. Here, I briefly examine the impact of the crisis of tradition on the life and work of the figures prominent in the following chapters—Rosenzweig, Benjamin, Kafka, and Freud. I then turn to a concise historical survey of the disparate models of return and repetition in the modern search for a new Jewish tradition, as experienced in new models of German Jewish education, the idealization of Eastern European Jews, and Zionism.

The Crisis of Tradition:
The Post-Assimilatory Generation

In the vast literature on the German Jewish modern world, the break in the continuity of tradition in Jewish modernity is often connected to the response of Jews in the second half of the nineteenth century to a series of decrees granting full civil rights to the Jews in Germany in the early days of the Bismarck era.[6] This long-awaited transformation in the Jewish political position resonated with major portions of the middle- and upper-class German Jewry, who adhered to the ideals of progress and *Bildung* of the German *Aufklärung* and were therefore happy to join German secular society, hoping to gain economic, social, and political advantages.[7] Processes of secularization that dominated the Jewish world in the long nineteenth century added to the danger of the dissolution of the Jewish way of life. The *Wissenschaft des Judentums* movement contributed as well to the enthusiasm of the Jewish bourgeoisie: the insistence of the movement's leading figures, Jewish historians like Heinrich Graetz and Leopold Zunz, on defining Judaism as a *Volk*, rather than as a religion, provided a new foundation for Jewish secular identity that facilitated the participation of Jews in German public and economic life.

Yet as in many other examples of the acculturation of minorities, the struggle for acceptance required Jews to abrogate their Jewish cultural and religious markers. They had to abandon their Jewish identity to become citizens of the European community. This demand was openly made by Count Clermont Tonnerre at the French Revolutionary Assembly (the first to grant political rights to the Jewish community), when he called out: "For the Jews, everything; for the Jewish nation, nothing." The Jews were accepted into the public sphere, but as German, French, and Austrians, never as Jews. Steven Aschheim notes this conundrum in *Brothers and Strangers* (1982): "Assimilation was not merely the conscious attempt to blend into new social and cultural environments but was also purposeful, even programmatic, *dissociation* from traditional Jewish culture and national moorings. . . . In this tortured process, marked by constant pressure to prove their fitness for equal rights, German Jews provided assimilation with its most systematic ideological articulation."[8]

Kafka's "Letter to the Father"

The crisis of tradition in German Jewish modernity was experienced firsthand by Benjamin, Rosenzweig, Freud, and Kafka. Their personal histories represent the many, diverse, and at times conflicting challenges faced by the post-assimilatory generation.[9] For them as for others, these struggles flared up within the nuclear family structure. The relationship of Gershom Scholem, the preeminent scholar of Jewish mysticism and Benjamin's closest friend, with his father, Arthur, is a perfect example of this generational tension. Scholem's father was a German patriot, family patriarch, proud citizen, and successful businessman, who rejected his Jewish past for a comfortable bourgeois life in Berlin. In his autobiography, *From Berlin to Jerusalem* (1977), Scholem describes many incidents in the long history of his family in Germany in which his father openly defied his Jewish heritage. Every Shabbat evening, Scholem remembers, after the *Kiddush* prayer, which was still chanted but only "half understood," the father lighted his cigar with the Shabbat candle. "Since the prohibition to smoke on the Shabbat was one of the most widely known Jewish regulation," he explains, "there was deliberate mockery in this act."[10] On Yom Kippur, still widely observed by the Jews, Arthur Scholem went to work as every other day and had "no thought of fasting."[11] Yet, and here we see how the experience of German Jews is truly complicated, Scholem's father remained an ethnic Jew: this German patriot disapproved of his son's Werner's marriage to a non-Jewish proletarian, and, as Gershom writes, he never saw a non-Jew in his home. Scholem's espousal of Zionism at a relatively young age (he started studying Hebrew by himself at the age of fourteen, joined the Zionist group *Jung Juda* in 1914, and immigrated to Palestine in 1923) is a common response of those in his generation to their parents' loss of Jewish identity.

Benjamin had a similar experience in his childhood years. His mother had some sympathy for Reform Judaism and his father was more inclined to orthodoxy, but his upbringing had very little engagement with Judaism. As Howard Eiland and Michael Jennings document in their biography of Benjamin, the family celebrated "Christmas in high style, and there were Easter egg hunts for the children."[12] Years later, in "Berlin Chronicle" (1932), Benjamin documented an incident that illuminates how marginal Judaism was to the family. On the eve of the Jewish New Year, Benjamin was supposed to take a friend to the synagogue, but he lost his way. "To make my way independently to the synagogue," remarks Benjamin, "was out of the question, since I had no idea where it was. This bewilderment, forgetfulness, and embarrassment were doubtless chiefly due to my dislike of the impending service, in its familial no less than its divine aspect."[13]

Rosenzweig presents a different experience of the same reality. The only child in an acculturated family from Kassel, he dedicated the first portion of his life to the study of German philosophy, especially Hegel and Schelling. In July 1913, while still working on Hegel's Philosophy of Right and surrounded by several close friends and family members who converted to Christianity, Rosenzweig suffered a spiritual crisis that led to a near-conversion experience. His eventual return to Judaism during the Yom Kippur ceremony after long weeks of internal conflict is now an archetypal story of the renewal of Jewish spirit in modernity. In the next decade of his life, Rosenzweig initiated several projects, including a translations enterprise and the founding of the *Freies Jüdische Lehrhaus* in Frankfurt, that illustrate his understanding of the necessary response to this personal and communal crisis.

It is, however, Kafka who embodies the archetypal example of the young Jewish generation.[14] In his now canonical "Letter to the Father," which he wrote at the age of thirty-six but the father never received, Kafka expresses the liminal position of his generation, alienated from the tradition their parents abandoned. For Kafka, the rupture of the previous generation from Jewish tradition abetted the fall of the younger generation, who on the one hand were forced to join secular society like their parents, but on the other hand were asked to perpetuate, in some way, their alliances with the tradition their parents left behind. Kafka's memorable words voice this existential impasse. In his letter, he remembers how he suffered from guilt as a young boy, "for not going to the synagogue often enough, for not fasting, and so on."[15] Yet when he grew up, this guilt was replaced with anger, as Kafka "could not [have understood] how, with the insignificant scrap of Judaism [his father] possessed, [he] could reproach [Franz Kafka] for not making an effort . . . to cling to a similar, insignificant scrap. It was indeed, so far as [Franz Kafka] could see, a mere nothing, a joke—not even a joke."[16] Later in life, Kafka realized that his father's distance from Jewish tradition was not as complete as the father presented. He writes: "You really had brought some traces of Judaism with you from the ghetto-like village community."[17] However, these traces of Judaism were not enough for young Kafka. They may have provided the father with the basic principles of Judaism, which he remembered from his own childhood and was able to live by. But they failed to grant the son the comprehensive worldview he needed: "Even in this there was still Judaism enough, but it was too little to be handed on to the child; it all dribbled away while you were passing it on."[18] The son did not have memories from his father's childhood house to enliven the shadows of Judaism his father imparted. He was cut off from the tradition that flickered in his father's memory, despite his father's disavowal of it.

Sigmund and Jacob Freud: On Freud and Judaism

Freud's relations to Judaism should be understood along similar lines. Like Benjamin and Kafka, his ambivalence to his Jewish heritage is a truism—the "Godless Jew" is an all-time favorite citation in this context.[19] Admittedly, his numerous disclaimers about the division between his science and Judaism and his rejection of the religious worldview led many to mark on his animosity to his heritage. However, as recent contributions demonstrate, Freud was much more ambivalent about his Judaism than his fight to cleanse his science let on.[20]

Freud was immersed in the Jewish tradition from which he was so careful to distance his work and knew and cared much more about Judaism than he was willing to publicly admit. His close relationship with the B'nai B'rith movement and the Yivo Institute indicated his deep conviction that Judaism offered a "source of energy that cannot be found anywhere else."[21] Freud supposedly presented an ideal image of the assimilated Jew. Yet he was surrounded by Jewish friends and relatives, and the close group of visionaries who joined him in the early days of psychoanalysis was almost exclusively Jewish. Freud usually expressed his association with Judaism in private communications and wrote about Jewish culture and history only indirectly—his 1901 *The Psychopathology of Everyday Life* was basically psychological research on jokes of East European Jewry, and *Moses and Monotheism*, his masterpiece on the beginnings of Jewish people, had to wait until his final years. And yet, in a preface to the Hebrew translation of *Totem and Taboo* in 1934, he allowed himself to reveal his inner inclinations to his readers. His impassioned language expresses the basic conflict of that generation of Jewish intellectuals:

> No reader of [the Hebrew version of] this book will find it easy to put himself in the emotional position of an author who is ignorant of the language of holy writ, who is completely estranged from the religion of his fathers—as well as from every other religion—and who cannot take a share in nationalist ideals, but who has yet never repudiated his people, who feels that he is in his essential nature a Jew and who has no desire to alter that nature. If the question were put to him: "Since you have abandoned all these common characteristics of your countrymen, what is there left to you that is Jewish?" he would reply: "A very great deal, and probably its very essence."[22]

This emotional complexity partly reflects Freud's relationship with his father.[23] Freud was born into a family that made the first steps away from traditional Judaism. The mother came from an Orthodox family and spoke mostly Yiddish at home; the father was an assimilated Jew who struggled all his life to be accepted into German-speaking secular society. He left his father's (Sigmund's grandfather) Orthodox house in Galicia and immigrated to Moravia where he began a long process of assimilation. A few years after Sigmund was born, the family moved again to settle in Vienna, mostly for economic reasons. However, despite his attempts to assimilate, Jacob Freud kept the clothes and mannerisms of Jews from East Europe, a fact that greatly embarrassed Freud during his childhood years. This is evident in a memory from the age of ten or twelve, which Freud documented in *The Interpretation of Dreams*. In one of their walks, Freud remembers, his father spoke of an incident aimed to prove to young Sigmund how much better things were than they had been in his father's youth. The story was about antisemitic harassment at the time of Sigmund's birth. Jacob was walking in the street when a passerby knocked off his cap and shouted: "Jew! Get off the pavement!" However, that was not the worst part in Sigmund's memory. The father's response to this attack was even more humiliating for young Freud. When Sigmund asked his father what he had done, the latter quietly said: "I went into the roadway and picked up my cap." Years later, Freud admits, "this struck me as unheroic conduct on the part of the big, strong man who was holding the little boy by the hand."[24] Freud's reaction reflects much of his frustration with his parent. Freud was especially offended by his father's timid reaction: The father showed weakness and submissiveness that Freud deeply despised. Sigmund was also ashamed of the fact that his father was so easily recognized as a Jew. The story was written more than thirty years after Freud first heard it from his father, but he still remembered that his father had "a new fur cap on his head." The father, young Freud felt, was an uneducated Jew from Eastern Europe, unfit to engage with the modernized world. His clothes revealed his Jewish identity, which he—so clumsily—fought to deny.

The inability of the father to integrate himself and his family into Austrian society mirrored the challenges confronting young Sigmund. Since even if Jacob behaved like a fish out of water in Vienna, he was still connected to the Jewish tradition in a way that Sigmund, exactly like Kafka, could never be.[25] Freud, put bluntly, had no fallback plan. Like many in his generation, he was exiled from the Jewish tradition, and had to find a new home, since, unlike his father, he did not have memories from his grandfather's house in Galicia that could ground his

Jewish identity. And like Kafka, Freud was drawn to the Jewish reality he was asked to reject. In his father's house, the Bible had an important place in family life. Jacob Freud wrote all the important dates of family events in it. He also gave it to his son on his thirty-fifth birthday, as a gift that symbolized the forming of Sigmund's new family. However, this reality was not enough to constitute a Jewish world for Freud.

It is possible to interpret Freud's life work as a response to these contradictory demands. Disconnected from the past, Freud created his science of psychoanalysis as a new and alternative tradition, for himself, for his Jewish friends and family, and, in the end, for the gentile society in which he lived. In thinking of psychoanalysis in these terms, it may come as no surprise that in Freud's new science, which so many tried to isolate from Judaism, the Jewish past was very much alive. This is perhaps most obvious in the psychoanalytic description of the child's relations with his parents during the formative stage of the Oedipus complex, exactly where the crisis of Jewish tradition was most urgent to Freud. The ambivalence to the father felt by Kafka and many others of Freud's generation became, in Freud's imagination, one of the foundational principles of human development. According to Freud, it is not only the Jews who suffer from ambivalent relations with their fathers. We all do. Freud, living in an environment in which the fathers failed to provide meaningful and coherent worldviews, devised a theory of the mind that emphasized the important role of the father in transmitting social norms and values. He grappled with the crisis of his generation by claiming it was eternal and universal. Little wonder, then, that Kafka was one of the first to uncover these Jewish origins of psychoanalysis, exactly where he and Freud found a true alliance: "Psychoanalysis lays stress on the father-complex and many find the concept intellectually fruitful.... Most young Jews who began to write German wanted to leave Jewishness behind them, and their fathers approved of this, but vaguely (this vagueness was what was so outrageous to them). But with their posterior legs they were still glued to their father's Jewishness and with waving anterior legs they found no new ground. The ensuing despair became their inspiration."[26]

In what comes, I will discuss how the Jewish community responded to the crisis of tradition that so evidently impressed Benjamin, Freud, Rosenzweig, and Kafka. Here, certain patterns of repetition and return came to inform the imagination of the early twentieth-century Jewish world—the patterns prominent in the theories of history and messianism of the four thinkers.

Returns and Repetitions in the Jewish Cultural Imagination

One way to think the intricacies of the modern German Jewish world is to consider the resemblance of Jewish modernity to the Italian Renaissance. I refer to the political crisis that triggered the Renaissance period; one that had interesting reverberations with the crisis of Jewish tradition.[27] The medieval crisis flared around the year 1400 when the consolidation of the Italian city-states disturbed centuries-long sociological and political traditions, and powerful cities such as Venice and Florence replaced the medieval system of alliances. The attempts to establish the power of these large city-states naturally faced strong opposition from the outside—mostly from the Papal State at Rome and the Holy Roman Empire—yet inner tensions threatened them as well. The city-state suffered, among other things, from a crisis of identity: the people from in and around the city had to be convinced to be loyal to the new political order. Centuries of political tradition that centered on the Pope or the King had to be replaced with a new civic discourse and a new form of patriotism centering on the city, its patrons, and the republican constitution. The solution to this political challenge was found in part in discourses and images drawn from the past. The leaders of the Renaissance evoked a return to Rome in whose image they fashioned a new identity for the city-state. This return promoted, in Michelet's classic words, a kind of a "rediscovery of the world and of man" and bolstered a surge of scholarship in ancient Greek and Roman art, literature, theology, philosophy, and even jurisprudence, later known as Renaissance Humanism.

The return to the past by Renaissance men and women of letters bears a certain affinity with the response of the Jewish community to the crisis of tradition in modernity. Like their Italian counterparts of five hundred years before, the twentieth-century German-speaking Jewish community, facing the eradication of communal strata, devised its modern identity by a move best defined as a return to its cultural, social, and religious past. Albeit in a necessarily mythologized form, the Jews shared the Renaissance battle cry of *"ad fontes!"* (Back to the sources!) While some denied their Jewish heritage, many in the Jewish community attempted to refind and even reinvent this tradition. They refashioned a new foundation for the Jewish community by attempting to repeat a mythologized past in the present. This enterprise generated a growing fascination in things Jewish, which Martin Buber enthusiastically described in 1901 as a new "Jewish renaissance."[28] And as in the Italian Renaissance, the process of creating a new tradition produced a prosperity of Jewish art, literature, music, education, and scholarship matched only by the Golden Ages of Jewish culture in the Iberian Peninsula in the tenth to twelfth centuries.

The Jewish renaissance was, however, vastly different from Orthodox dependency on traditional ways of life. The German Jewish world did not simply copy or imitate the past. Hasidism was much too radical for the liberal Jews in Berlin or Munich, who hoped for a new Jewish tradition that could be integrated into modern reality. The German Jews wanted to reshape their present according to a version of an "authentic" past that was, in turn, deeply indebted to modern secular imagination. Renaissance means "rebirth," and this Jewish "repetition" of the past was not a simple return to origins, but also an invention. In a project that had several correlates with Reform Judaism, the Jewish community retrieved or reclaimed from the past various principles, concepts, ideas, and images, as much it borrowed from German society. The Italian Renaissance returned to a mythologized version of Rome to invent modernity; the Jewish renaissance reclaimed a mythologized version of Judaism to invent Jewish modernity.[29] It is my suggestion that this enterprise animated a lively discourse about reclamation, repetition, and return in the German Jewish community, setting the historical context for the theories of history and models of messianic thought of Benjamin, Rosenzweig, Freud, and Kafka.

German Jewish Imagination and the Search for Jewish Origins

We find a prime example of the Jewish fascination with their past in David Myers's *Resisting History* (2003). Myers shows how the search for traces of the Jewish past led to the study of history and took shape in the establishment—mostly after 1871—of numerous institutions and organizations dedicated to Jewish history. Myers mentions the proliferation of such associations as the *Historische Commission für Geschichte der Juden in Deutschland* (1885), the *Gessellschaft zur Förderung der Wissenschaft des Judentums* (1902) and the *Gesamtarchiv der deutschen Juden* (1905), as well as the establishment by 1900 of 131 Jewish societies for the study of Jewish history and literature (the *Vereine für Jüdische Geschichte und Literatur*). These societies, he notes, "provided an outlet for a Jewish public—young and old, women and men—increasingly hungry for knowledge about a rapidly vanishing Jewish past. Through such institutions, historicization seemed to enhance, not diminish, the communal commitments of German Jews."[30] The allure of history spread to many areas of German Jewish culture: architecture, painting, and literature increasingly "bore the imprint of history," and popular Jewish journals, like the *Allgemeine Zeitung des Judentums* dedicated a "surprisingly" large portion of their pages to material of a historical nature.[31]

Another important example of the growing importance of the past is the revival of Jewish scholarship in early twentieth century. Franz Rosenzweig was one of the most celebrated proponents of this revival. He, in fact, enrolled in 1914 in the Berlin *Hochschule für die Wissenschaft des Judentums*, where he formed a lifelong friendship with Hermann Cohen. A few years later, in 1920, Rosenzweig founded the *Freies Jüdische Lehrhaus* in Frankfurt, upon the invitation of the local Jewish community leaders. In what came to represent the kind of repetition the Jewish renaissance symbolized, the *Lehrhaus* borrowed from the then-prevalent German format of adult education (the *Volksvorlesung*) but also echoed traditional models of Jewish education.[32] The classes, for example, replicated the educational ideals of medieval Beit Midrash—they were small and demanded the active participation of the students, unlike the great lecture halls of the modern universities in Germany. Non-Jewish themes were introduced, but the curriculum was based on an extensive study of the Torah and the Talmud, with special emphasis on the Hebrew language.

In Rosenzweig's vision, the need for a new form of the study of Judaism was deeply connected to the crisis of tradition. In a series of pamphlets, he claimed that his new educational project was "to recreate that emotional tie between the institutions of public worship and the individual, that is, the very tie which he has lost."[33] This task was accomplished by a conscious return of the past, one that, as Rosenzweig strongly emphasized, was done from the position of the present. "The book around which we once gathered stands forlorn in this world, and even for those who regard it as a beloved duty to return to it at regular intervals, such a return is nothing but a turning away from life, a turning one's back to life," he declares. Rosenzweig envisioned a "new" learning, saying, "It is a learning in reverse order. A learning that no longer starts from the Torah and leads into life, but the other way around: from life . . . back to the Torah. That is the sign of the time."[34] The new study of the Torah was not to be built on a fundamentalist turn to the past. Rather, the learning had to be reversed. The Torah had to be studied from "the sign of the time."[35]

The Jewish fascination with the past took a surprising form in the enchantment of German Jewry with Jews from Eastern Europe. The history of the relations of German Jews with East European Jewry is famously complicated and often bitter. However, in the period we are dealing with, the East European Jew, often mocked and despised, presented an almost unexpected alternative for those fighting against the assimilatory tendencies in the German Jewish community. Previously denigrated for being left outside the modernization enjoyed by German Jews, in the early twentieth century, the East European Jew became an exciting model of bona fide Jewish life. While German Jews faced religious and cultural disintegration due to processes of secularization and assimilation, the East European Jew embodied a reality "where Jewish peoplehood had been preserved, [and] Jewish traditions [were] still alive."[36]

Buber's reverence of Hasidism and Rosenzweig's admiration of the Jewish East European authentic culture—on which he wrote excitedly to his mother in 1918 from a training center in Rembertow near Warsaw—are famous examples of a movement that quickly transcended the religious sphere and informed much of the cultural production in the German Jewish community of the period. Arnold Zweig's report of East European Jews from his service in the German army in *Das ostjüdische Antlitz* (1919), Alfred Döblin's travel book to

Poland *Reise in Polen* (1925), and Isaac Brauer's popular *Ein Kampf um Gott* (1920) and *Falk Nefts Heimkehr* (1923) are other important examples of the new ways German Jewish authors engaged with East European Jews. To this list, we can certainly add many of Kafka's novels and parables and works by prominent representatives of East European literature, such as Hayim Nahman Bialik or Shmuel Yosef Agnon, who spent some of their formative years in the vibrant Berlin community of Yiddish speakers from Eastern Europe. The same applied to the musical Jewish world: the East European style had an increasing influence on Jewish liturgical music in Germany, as composers such as the musical director of the Munich Jewish community, Heinrich Schalit, and others "used both oriental and East European models in their search for authenticity."[37] Yiddish theater, which usually attracted mostly immigrants from Eastern Europe and was performed in small halls, also met with growing enthusiasm from young German Jewish intellectuals in the first half of the twentieth century. This shift in taste explains some of the success of the 1926 European tour of the then Russian Jewish theater Habima.[38]

Note that in all realms of the Jewish cultural world, the interest in Eastern European Jewry had a mytho-historical dimension.[39] The Jews from Galicia and Lithuania offered an imaginary Jewish "authentic" life of past generations. In contrast to German Jews who lived "in history" and therefore evolved according to the times, East European Jews managed to stay "out of time." In German Jewish eyes, the East European Jews kept a way of life they imagined to resemble their lost origins. They signaled an alternative to the historical life of the Jews in Germany and thereby provided an imaginary bridge with the past, which permitted German Jews to conceive a new beginning for themselves.

Admittedly, the admiration of the Eastern European Jewry had some ramifications. The Eastern European Jews were admired but were also regarded as essentially benighted. Hermann Cohen's essay "The Polish Jew," published in Buber's *Der Jude*, offers an example of this double-edged sword. The essay, written following Cohen's lecture tour in Eastern Europe and Russia, declares Cohen's admiration of the "inexhaustible energy"[40] of Polish Jews and of the spiritual energy which "has its source in the literary treasures of the Jewish religion."[41] In contrast to the young Zionists' skepticism, ignorance, and alienation, he argues, the Polish Jews offered a vision of vital Jewish life: "the more familiar a Jewish generation becomes with these millennially ancient and eternally youthful treasures ... the more alive and the more universally appealing its religious strength will be, along with an ethical and aesthetic self-esteem for its own right to live and for the historical future of the religion of the one God."[42] Yet for Cohen, the Polish Jews were still principally a "problem."[43] While the German Jews, the "free Jews,"[44] as Cohen emphasizes, achieved a unity between religion and *culture*, the Polish Jews were ignorant and superstitious. They were an important resource against assimilation, no doubt, but they still needed to be modernized and civilized. Cohen, therefore, called for an establishment of seminaries for the Science of Judaism to introduce Polish Jews to "a true life of religiosity for a cultured man."[45]

Whether naïve or apprehensive, the twentieth-century attempt to form new Jewish tradition was based on the dialectics of new and old, reminiscent of the logic of modern repetition. The Jewish tradition was built on modern discourses, but it also involved a return to an imaginary past.[46] This return was aimed at constituting a Jewish community, different from both German secular society and Orthodox Judaism. The Jewish community did this by joining modern and old: the modern component of the new Jewish tradition promised a *new* tradition; the Jewish past made this tradition into a *Jewish* tradition. In other words, the German Jews used the resources of the past to imagine a different, *Jewish* present and future. Thinking historically, if the chain of historical events brought about a modern non-Jewish reality, the Jews returned to the past to overturn this fact. The attempt to repeat the past, even a mythologized past, in the present allowed the Jewish community to create a different path for itself. Importantly, the reclamation of the Jewish past allowed German Jews to intervene in their own history: in repeating what they took to be a Jewish past, the Jewish community negated the flow of history that brought about the destruction of the Jewish tradition. This repetition or reclamation of a Jewish past produced a new moment in history. If history effected a decline in the Jewish way of life, the repetition of the past in the present upended this decline and afforded the Jewish community a new direction. In that sense, repetition was a powerful force: it negated the recent history of Jewish assimilation and subverted the devastating consequences of "historical progress." This insight about the effects of repetition, I suggest, finds interesting reverberation in the work on history of Benjamin, Rosenzweig, Freud, and Kafka.

Zionism and the Return to Jewish Antiquity

The early twentieth-century scheme of return to a mythologized past found a surprising form in Zionism, which in itself offered a different solution to the crisis of tradition and Jewish assimilation. The history of the Zionist movement is far too complicated to enumerate in a few lines, especially as Zionism harbored a cluster of social ideals and political utopias. Zionism is often understood as paradigmatic for several nineteenth-century ideologies—from socialism to settler colonialism—yet in what follows, I briefly touch on the place of Jewish antiquity in some strands of the Zionist ideology.[47] I do so to show how Zionism was informed by the same mytho-historical structure I have just identified in other realms of German Jewish life. In Zionism, we will see, a reply to the crisis of tradition was based on a return to the past, one which constitutes a new future.

From its early stages, several major Zionist thinkers conceived Zionism mostly in terms of Jewish emancipation. In one of the founding documents of Zionism, "Auto-Emancipation" (*Selbstemanzipation*), from 1882, for example, Leon Pinsker, the founder of the Hibat Tsiyon movement, emphasizes the importance of Jewish self-rule.[48] The accepted narrative is that disappointed with their incessant failure to assimilate into the liberal European community and faced with growing antisemitism, Jewish activists like Pinsker recognized the need to reorganize the Jews national existence in the diaspora. In Pinsker's words, "This is the kernel of the problem, as we see it: the Jews comprise a distinctive element among the nations under which they dwell, and as such can neither assimilate nor be readily digested by any nation."[49] However, rather than seeking the civil emancipation of the Jews in Europe to allow them to participate in social, political, and economic life as *individuals*, Pinsker and later Hertzel (after witnessing firsthand the Dreyfus Affair and its disastrous aftermath) were devoted to the ideal of the auto-emancipation of the Jews as a *nation*. The solution for the Jewish predicament was not in Europe for the Jews as European citizens, but elsewhere, for the Jews as an independent collective.

Such a radical change in the Jewish national consciousness, that is, the transformation of the Jewish diaspora to a sovereign nation, required, besides material resources, political ingenuity, and social organization, a new Jewish myth. Some, like Moses Hess, one of the leaders of Labor Zionism, and Yitzhak Tabenkin, a key figure in the Kibbutz Movement, focused on the present economic and social condition, and, building on the works of Marx and Engel, imagined a socialist revolution spearheaded by the Jews in Palestine. Others turned to the Jewish past to find such a myth. For them, the transformation of the Jewish consciousness in the diaspora depended on a rehabilitation of ancient Judaism as a shared point of origin for the Jewish people in the present. This ideological stance shaped the place of history in parts of the Zionist worldview.[50]

Prima facie, the Jewish past was problematic for Zionism, as Zionists aimed to create a New Jew, free of the faults of the diaspora. And yet Zionism, which had much in common with the Romantic fascination with the past of many national movements across Europe, gave the past a special place in its core ideological principles. Zionism drew a direct line between the present condition of the Jews in Europe and the Jewish nationality of two thousand years before. As the Proclamation of Independence of the State of Israel notes in its opening lines: "The Land of Israel was the birthplace of the Jewish people. Here their spiritual, religious and political identity was shaped. . . . After being forcibly exiled from their land, the people kept faith with it throughout their Dispersion and never ceased to pray and hope for their return to it and for the restoration in it of their political freedom." Here, as in many other works, the Jewish present, to put it in the terms of the present volume, was seen as a repetition of or return to Jewish antiquity.

This narrative demanded some strands of Zionist historiography make a clear-cut separation between two historical periods—antiquity and diaspora. The diaspora was portrayed in distinctly dark colors and was usually represented as a long period of collective suffering and enslavement (Jews in the diaspora were characterized as weak, anxious, fearful, submissive, the men oftentimes depicted as feminine). Jewish antiquity, meanwhile, was pictured as the Golden Age of Jewish competency, self-assurance, and effectiveness. The long period from the second temple to the explosion was glorified, while all that happened since the Jewish expulsion was suspicious and contemptible and had to be negated.[51] This crude oversimplification of Jewish antiquity and *Galuth* overlooked major cultural, religious, and social achievements in two thousand years of vital Jewish life. Nevertheless, this myth of the Jewish past was extremely effective in producing a different history, that is, a *new tradition* for the Zionist movement.

Zionism celebrated Jewish antiquity as the true foundation of the present. Most famously, Max Nordau, Herzl's partner in the Zionist movement, in a speech on Muscular Judaism (*Muskeljudentum*) at the Second Zionist Congress held in 1898 in Basel, called for a corporeal and spiritual renewal of the Jews by way of remembering and copying glorified figures such as Bar Kokhba. Zionist historiographers like Joseph Klausner, who worked on the Second Temple period, or Yehezkel Kaufmann, who studied the biblical period, followed suit and chronicled stories about ancient Jewish heroes.[52] Others, like the poet Uri Tzvi Greenberg, believed themselves to be the direct descendants of the kingdoms of David and Salomon, with the effect that for some the present battle for the Jewish nation repeated similar battles in antiquity, as in the cry of the Hashomer Jewish organization in Palestine (from Yaakov Cohen's poem, *Habiryonim*): "In fire and blood did Judea fall; in blood and fire Judea shall rise." Even Ahad Ha'am, who rejected Herzl's political Zionism, turned to the Jewish prophets in the Torah in his search for a new foundation for his vision of cultural Zionism in the present.

In its structure, then, the Zionist interest in Jewish antiquity resembled the fascination of the German Jewish world with its imaginary past. Similar to the movement of repetition that informed Rosenzweig's *Lehrhaus* and the German captivation with the image of the Eastern European Jew, Zionism founded a new tradition by reconnecting to the past. The Zionist turn to the past had, however, a very different purpose. For Zionism, any and all forms of Jewish life in the diaspora presented a negation of the proper trajectory of Jewish history. The Zionist reconstruction of the past was to create the conditions for a radical transformation in Jewish history that would end the unnatural condition of diaspora. For the German Jews, to remind the Jews in Galicia lived on the shores of history. This was the reason they were so admired as an alternative to the conundrum of modern Jewish experience. The Zionist break from the historical continuum was comparatively much more severe: while the German Jewish repetition of a mythologized past meant to change the course of the *recent* history of assimilation to create a new tradition for Jews *in* Europe, the Zionist repetition was designed to *completely* end all of the *Galuth*. Furthermore, the Zionist imaginary return to Jewish antiquity was to create the conditions for a factual return: the return to Jewish nationality was ultimately to lead to a return to the Jewish historical homeland in the Land of Israel. No wonder, then, that in Zionist literature, this change in Jewish life was often described in messianic terms.[53] The Zionist return to the past was to change that which many believed to be a reality that only God could have advanced. This conceptual structure highlighted the messianic implications of repetition: for Zionism, the repetition of the past in the present created the conditions for secular redemption. This convention had a web of connections with the model of repetition of German Jewish thinkers, like Benjamin, for whom as well repetition had the power to introduce messianic session into history.

There is, however, an important difference between the "repetition" of Zionism and the four thinkers, especially in their understandings of the messianic vocation. Unlike Rosenzweig, Freud, Kafka, and Benjamin, the Zionists rejected the *Galuth* for what they perceived as the "correct" historical existence. Their messianism disconnected the Jewish people from their alienated present and injected them back *into* history. In Benjamin, Freud, Kafka, and Rosenzweig, we will see, repetition ruptured linear time to produce difference and alterity. For Zionism, the repetition of the past in the present intended to do exactly the opposite: it was to erase Jewish alterity and produce the conditions for the return of the Jewish people to their supposed proper, and thus linear, progressive history. In other words, the Zionist repetition of the past in the present *broke* a certain historical continuum of diaspora but did not *reject* continuous history altogether. This repetition transformed Jewish history to universal history: it changed the course of Jewish history of alienation and *Galuth* so that the Jews could join the history of the world.

In the next chapters, I will examine how modern Jewish thinkers and authors implemented such diverse images of repetition into their theories. From the intellectual and cultural imagination of their time, they borrowed a set of intuitions that guided them as they struggled to find solutions to the problem of linear history in modern Jewish reality. Their solutions—from a Jewish context—start an important conversation on repetition in nineteenth- and twentieth-century philosophy.

II · Repetition and Its Others

CHAPTER 3

"Die weltliche Unlebendigkeit"
Eternity and Repetition in Rosenzweig

Franz Rosenzweig is probably best known for his *Leipziger Nacht-gespräch* (Leipzig night-talk), in which he went through a near conversion experience. A young, assimilated Jew of moderate origins, Rosenzweig engaged during the night of July 7, 1913, in a long conversation on Jewish experience and faith with his close friends Eugen Rosenstock and Rudolf Ehrenberg that led to a spiritual crisis. This experience fittingly mirrored the "crisis of tradition" of the German Jewish world, as discussed in the second chapter. Rosenzweig's response to this experience and his eventual return to Judaism, often seen as the quintessential story of the "discovery of Judaism" in modernity,[1] will be the focus of this chapter.

The stakes of Rosenzweig's famous return to Judaism are still debated. Yet it is fair to argue that the July night and the months that followed encouraged Rosenzweig to formulate a new understanding of Judaism. Most importantly, his personal crisis prompted him to seriously reconsider the significance of Judaism to his life, but also, and more generally, it prompted him to reconsider the importance of Judaism to humanity in modernity.[2] In the words of Paul Mendes-Flohr, Rosenzweig maintained that "if Jewish religious life is to be true to its pristine calling, it must have a bearing on the most ultimate questions of human existence."[3] Rosenzweig's response to this challenge partly materialized in *The Star of Redemption*. In this monumental work, which began in a series of letters he sent to his mother during the First World War, the Jewish people were assigned a special role in world redemption, alongside Christianity. Specifically, they were given the task of anticipating redemption in the present. This role

entailed a unique form of Jewish temporal existence: the Jewish relation to redemption demanded that they *reject historical life for eternal
life*, as Rosenzweig explains in a letter to Hans Ehrenberg (his cousin)
on May 9, 1918:

> I am not arguing for a reality for Judaism that is identical to another
> outside reality. I straightforwardly admit the worldly unliveliness of
> Judaism [*Die weltliche Unlebendigkeit*].... Judaism has life only when
> it is with God. Only when the world is *also* with God will Judaism be
> granted worldly life. This is, however, again only at the other side of
> history.[4]

In this chapter, I aim to unpack Rosenzweig's enigmatic notion
of Judaism's "worldly unliveliness," with its profound suggestion of
a uniquely Jewish temporality. It is my suggestion that the Jewish
"unliveliness" is best understood through a careful analysis of Rosenzweig's model of repetition (*Wiederholung*). Repetition is discussed in
the third part of *The Star of Redemption*, where Rosenzweig explains
his idea of redemption in the "midst of time."[5] There, Rosenzweig
proposes that the Jewish people cultivated an awareness of the cyclical repetition of the week and the year that produces an exceptional
relation to time: a set of liturgical practices that make manifest the
cyclical repetition of time form the conditions for Jewish eternal life.
As Rosenzweig explains it, through repetition, "man frees himself
from the perishability of the moment."[6]

On the face of it, the fact that the repetition of the Jewish weekly
and yearly festivals produces Jewish eternal life, suspiciously hints
of Rosenzweig's debt to archaic notions of the eternal return. In
short, repetition produces eternity, and this supposedly echoes the
production of atemporal divine reality in archaic society. I argue,
however, that Rosenzweig had a different vision of repetition, and
consequently a different formulation of eternity. In Rosenzweig's
book, the experience of repetition reconnects the Jewish people
to this world, and makes them conscious of the *dynamic nature*
of the world as *life*. That is, even if the Jewish experience of repetition anticipates a condition of eternity and redemption—as in
archaic societies—this eternity was not experienced as a freezing
of time, which the archaic model of repetition appears to produce.
Rather, repetition affirmed the worldly, productive, and life-filled

character of time, similarly to the function of repetition in modern formulations.

Most readings of Rosenzweig fail to grasp the dialectical character of this relationship to time. Stéphane Mosès and Emil Fackenheim are exemplars of this one-sided reading. To counter this misunderstanding, the chapter offers a reinterpretation of Rosenzweig's theory of time, considering how it recapitulates the theme of a dynamic repetition that, as observed in earlier chapters, informs modern philosophy. The chapter focuses specifically on the theory of repetition and eternity of Søren Kierkegaard. Rosenzweig, who worked in the "neighborhood of the Kierkegaard revival,"[7] shared with him an understanding of the place of repetition in the construction of these dialectical relations. The investigation of Kierkegaard is particularly fitting because of Kierkegaard's commitment to a religious worldview. Analogously to Rosenzweig (and unlike others in the tradition of repetition in modern philosophy), Kierkegaard's repetition constituted a fundamental component of the world of the believer. As I will show, several central concepts from Kierkegaard's basic insights in *Repetition* illuminate the fundamental role of Rosenzweig's repetition in the relation of the Jewish people to time, history, and, ultimately, redemption. For Rosenzweig, I argue, the repetition of the week and the year grounded the anticipation of redemption, changed the relationship to history, and informed the temporal existence of the Jewish people.[8]

To be clear, I am not claiming that Rosenzweig had a Kierkegaardian theory of repetition in mind. The theological differences between the Jewish philosopher and Kierkegaard's Christian worldview are inherent and essential. Nonetheless, Kierkegaard's differentiation of recollection from repetition, and his fascination with the figure of Job, who resisted history and maintained his freedom in the midst of time, are key aspects of his theory of repetition, which can help us understand Rosenzweig's theory of repetition in *The Star of Redemption*.

In putting Kierkegaard and Rosenzweig together, the chapter also points to a significant difference between them, one that marks a fundamental disparity between modern Jewish theories of repetition and modern philosophy. Kierkegaard's emphasis on repetition involved an experience providing *individual* redemption, while Rosenzweig's model of repetition in the Jewish context depended on liturgical *communal* practices, which constituted the anticipation of redemption of the *entire* Jewish community. This difference has structural and conceptual implications for Rosenzweig's theory of repetition. It also highlights the unique contribution of Jewish theories of repetition to the modern tradition of repetition in philosophy. Taking Rosenzweig as a case study, his model of social practice of repetition breaks new ground in suggesting a new understanding of the communal nature of repetition and thereby of community as such.

Repetition in *The Star of Redemption*

Rosenzweig's description of the Jewish people as the people "at the goal [*am Ziel*]"[9] is developed in the third part of *The Star of Redemption*. In the section titled "The Configuration, or, the Eternal Supra-World," Rosenzweig offers an analysis of Judaism and Christianity as two opposing ideals of communal lives and temporal modalities. Both are essential to world redemption. Rosenzweig first defines the difference between Judaism and Christianity in material terms. The Jewish people, he claims, formed a special community that flourished thanks to their exceptional relation to land, language, and law. In Rosenzweig's judgment, the Jews were essentially travelers:[10] while all other nations adhered to earthly endeavors of wars, power, and productiveness, the Jewish people never had a home and were never rooted in a land. The same applied to the Jewish alienation from historically evolving language and state law. All other peoples had their own languages, each subject to changes according to worldly conditions (note: language indicates "that which is most alive of the people, indeed its life itself").[11] In contrast, the Jews had an "eternal" language, that is, biblical Hebrew. They were outside the worldly languages of other nations, always foreign, never fluent or familiar with the intricacy of mundane life and essentially prevented "from ever living entirely at one with the times."[12]

Echoing several works on the Jewish diasporic experience— most importantly that of Hermann Cohen, his friend and teacher— Rosenzweig believed the Jews' exile or homelessness expressed a significant truth about their existence: exile informed their relationship to redemption.[13] To put it briefly, for Rosenzweig world redemption was only possible in and through God's dual covenant with Jews and Christians. The Christians worked in history for world salvation: their world was one of holy wars, in which Christian expansionism served to unite humanity under God and prepare the way for world redemption. The Jews were given a different path. Their estrangement from mundane reality had a special purpose, that is, to lay the foundations for the anticipation of a reality of redemption in the present: "its peoplehood is already at that place to which the peoples of the world only aspire. Its world is at the goal."[14] The Christians mastered their world and changed their reality in the course of human history to achieve eternity in an unforeseen future. The Jewish people, on the other hand, were tasked with introducing redemption into the present and thereby negating this world. They were "already beyond the opposition which shapes the actual moving power in the life of the peoples."[15] This task grounded the role of the Jewish people in world redemption. The Jews served as a model for the Christian world: they anticipated *in the present* the point that the Christian world would reach *at the end of time*. For Rosenzweig, as for Hermann Cohen, the Jews assumed the role of the great educators of humanity—they showed all other nations the path to redemption.[16]

Rosenzweig's analysis of the Jewish condition frequently underlined its uncanny nature. Putting aside wealth, power, and success, the Jewish people were uprooted, dislocated, and alienated from the histories of nations and their commonplace reality: "by living the eternal peace, [the Jewish people] stand outside of a warlike temporality,"[17] he writes. Their world was "a world where one no longer feels at home, a disquieting world."[18] At certain points in *The Star of Redemption*, the description of the Jewish reality is so radical that it resonates with Paul's messianic vocation. Rosenzweig describes the Jews as so committed to redemption and eternity to the effect that some day-to-day activities became meaningless: "[The Jewish people] must renounce full, active participation in their life with its daily solutions that resolve all contradictions. It is not permitted to acknowledge the solution of contradictions in the today, because through this it would become unfaithful to the hope for the ultimate solution of contradictions."[19] More important to the main argument, in thinking of this alienation in temporal terms, Rosenzweig seems to suggest that the role of the Jewish people in world redemption transported them into an *atemporal eternity*. In several places in *The Star of Redemption*, the Jewish negation of the world comes across as suggesting a negation of time itself, for, as Rosenzweig notes, the Jews were "without time."[20] Elsewhere, he remarks that "temporal life is denied to this people for the sake of eternal life."[21]

In what follows, I aim to investigate and ultimately refine this theoretical position. In my reading of Rosenzweig's model of Jewish temporality, the Jewish negation of linear history certainly had a temporal dimension—it shifted the temporal orientation of the Jewish people. This shift is based on their experience of cyclical repetitive temporality. In contradistinction to archaic society, however, repetition does not project the Jewish people outside the world. Rather, the Jewish cyclicality—seemingly paradoxically—produced an experience of eternity which reconnects the Jewish people with time. That is, thanks to their unique form of repetition, the Jewish eternity is not outside time, but rather *in time*. Repetition is not a way to disengage from profane reality, as in Eliade's notion of archaic repetition, but to reconnect with reality. To quote Robert Gibbs in "Messianic Epistemology: Thesis XV": "Rosenzweig develops an account of eternity that requires eternity not to be a flight from time, but an insertion of eternality into temporality. Our lived time must itself become changed, and become in that sense messianic."[22]

The first clue to Rosenzweig's notion of eternity and redemption is found in his description of the Jewish people as the eternal people. This notion was heavily laden with meaning for Rosenzweig; however, for the purposes of this chapter, let us take note of his terminology in the section in which he discusses the differences between Judaism and Christianity.[23] The participation of the other nations in history implied for Rosenzweig their transiency. For example, other nations trust the land to give them a sense of permanence, but their land is often conquered by other nations, and they subsequently "perish" with the land.[24] Their language also changes with time and is thus not "less perishable."[25]

Contrastingly, the Jewish people are the "eternal people": for them, "the homeland never becomes its own in that sense; it is not permitted to sleep at home."[26] Because they are without home, disconnected from history, the Jewish people have been able to resist the flow of history. Their alienation has guaranteed their eternity by keeping them away from transiency. They have had no land or state law or worldly language, nothing external to rely on, and this has forced them to rely only on themselves, to take root only in themselves.[27] In other words, the Jewish people, according to Rosenzweig in this passage, are eternal in a very specific sense. The eternity of the eternal people does not denote an extratemporal reality, but a *different relation to history*: they are eternal because their temporal existence is organized in a way that safeguards them from the power of history.

In what follows, we will see that Rosenzweig's notion of cyclical time offers an explanation of the eternal life of the Jewish people that reflects this insight, by emphasizing a different relation to time, rather than an abolition of time.

Rosenzweig's *nunc stans*

In *The Start of Redemption*, Rosenzweig arrives to the idea of repetition in his discussion of the Jewish people's anticipation of redemption in the present—a notion which posed a significant philosophical and phenomenological challenge. If redemption is essentially only in the future, how could humanity attain a meaningful relation to redemption in the present? If the eschatological dimension of historical progression is, in effect, irrelevant to the present, how can the Jewish people "make eternity into the very nearest thing, into the today"?[28] Rosenzweig's solution to the challenge of the duality of the present and redemption, time and eternity is given first in terms that echo the theological concept of *nunc stans* (lit., "standing now"):

> Such an anticipation of the future in the moment would have to be a true turning of eternity into a today. What would such a today be like? Above all, it could not perish; for even if we know nothing else about eternity, this is certain: that it is im-perishable [*Un-vergängliche*] .... An imperishable today [*Ein unvergängliches Heute*]—but has it not, like all moments, flown away with the speed of an arrow? ... There is only one way out: the moment we are seeking must, since it has flown away, begin again already at the same moment; in the sinking away it must already begin again; its perishing must be at the same time a beginning again.[29]

Rosenzweig's definition of eternity here is based on an unconventional formulation of the *nunc stans*, a term long debated in the history of philosophy. The *nunc stans* has its origins, in part, in the Parmenidean theory of changeless reality and was developed in Neoplatonism to imply an everlasting now (*nunc aeternitatis*). It was later adopted by early Christian thought as a model for divine eternity. For Rosenzweig, however, the *nunc stans* had a very different meaning. In fact, in my reading, Rosenzweig's theory of time offers an important critique of the Christian theological concept of *nunc stans*. As I see it, Rosenzweig rejects the Christian understanding of the *nunc stans* as a moment outside time and replaces it with a notion of intensive experience of the now.

The entry point to Rosenzweig's version of *nunc stans* is his insight that the *nunc stans* is that which is imperishable. Eternity is not an atemporal condition, or time outside history, a collapse of time or a sacred time, as often characterized in the Christian tradition, but a reality of permanence with important reverberations for a specifically Jewish form of imperishability. Eternity is a moment that "could not perish," like a rock in the middle of the river of history, one that never moves despite the power of the stream. But what could make time itself imperishable? If eternity is not a moment outside time, how can time become eternity and yet remain time?

Here the theme of repetition comes to the fore. Rosenzweig's argument is that the everlasting moment offers eternity only as a moment that repeats itself. The *nunc stans* is not a different category of temporality, as assumed in previous theological works, but a particular form of worldly time: the result of a specific mechanism in the flow of time. Time becomes "eternal" because the same moment repeats again and again: "In the daily-weekly-yearly repetition of the cycles of prayers of worship, faith makes the moment into the 'hour' and time ready to receive eternity; and eternity, by finding a reception in time, itself becomes—like time."[30]

Eternity, Repetition, and Narrative Form

Rosenzweig diverges from traditional formulations of *nunc stans* when he recognizes that the *nunc stans*, despite its name, was, in fact, never merely a moment.[31] A moment, he claims, is an empty temporal unit and therefore too short to offer any meaning. If the *nunc stans* is to be effective, if it is to be *collectively* experienced, it must offer more than an empty moment. This claim is crucial for understanding Rosenzweig's model of repetition. Rosenzweig insists that the *nunc stans* must be more than a moment, because he thinks of eternity as a communal experience. The *nunc stans* is supposed to produce a change in the temporal condition of an entire community. It therefore cannot be a simple, contentless moment. It must be a unit of time with a meaning, one that constitutes an experience an entire community can recognize. Thus, for Rosenzweig, repetition is based on a different temporal scale than that of the moment. The basic unit of eternity is longer—at least an hour. The hour has enough volume that we can identify: it is a human institution whose cycle produces content. However, even if the hour is the basic unit of repetition, from a phenomenological point of view, it still does not offer a substantial (liturgical) content that will manifest an experience of eternity at the social level. Accordingly, Rosenzweig recognizes two other temporal units that embody this difference: the week and the year.

The operations of narrative are key for understanding this model of repetition. In Rosenzweig's judgment, repetition is meaningful only if it represents a beginning-to-end cycle: "With beginning, middle and end, it can become what the mere sequence of single ever new moments can never become: a circle that flows back in itself."[32] Simply put, the demand for temporal content materialized in Rosenzweig's model of repetition as a demand for narrative. Temporal repetition, Rosenzweig asserts, is not a result of relations between meaningless units of time. Cutting time into smaller pieces is not enough to create an experience of repetition. The year and week do not form a repetition just because there is a random point at which we begin to count the moments again. For Rosenzweig, time becomes cyclical when it plays out a narrative that we can recognize and experience.[33] A single moment displays only an ongoing beginning and thus never a meaningful content, but the hour, the week, and the year provide a full circle of time: they encapsulate a story. In ancient civilization, cyclical time reflected a similar logic: the year repeated itself because it portrayed the cyclical transition of the seasons—it was not enough to decide that the beginning of the year was scheduled at Tishrei or Pesach. The year was experienced as a meaningful unit when it told a story with a beginning, a middle, and an end. Only as such was it a temporal unit that repeats.[34]

In short, the content of repetition differentiates between true repetition and linear time. Time is cyclical when time presents a narrative. Otherwise, all we have are marks on a calendar that mean nothing and tell us nothing.

Repetition and Liturgy: The Week

The differentiation between repetition (of full cycles) and a series of transitions of fleeting moments was quickly translated in Rosenzweig's thought into religious terms. The basic theoretical insight was expanded by a liturgical rationale to express the application of his theory of repetition to the social level. The beginning-to-end narrative was rearticulated in the synagogue as a cycle of creation, revelation, and redemption, which the Jewish congregation could identify and experience. The year or the week had to tell a specific cosmogonic story: repetition was a true cycle only if it represented a series of events that started in a celebration of creation and ended in the commemoration of redemption. This repetition reiterated the geometrical meta-structure of Rosenzweig's project—the week and the year were true repetitions under the condition that they provided the symbolic movement of Rosenzweig's *Star*.

Markedly, the cycles of the Jewish week and the Jewish year met this basic requirement. For Rosenzweig, the Jewish week takes the shape of a cycle: it celebrates a transition from creation to redemption—the six days of the week stand for creation, and Shabbat is a symbol of redemption. The week is time for labor, and Shabbat ends this cycle as a universal day of rest. "Even servant and maid must rest," he insists.[35] In the same way, the cycle of the Jewish year expresses creation, revelation, and redemption in the three pilgrimage festivals: Pesach, Shavuot, and Sukkot.

Christian temporality, however, works differently. Rosenzweig notes that the difference between the Christian and Jewish weeks was initiated by the Church Fathers, who, in order to break away from

Judaism, moved the Christian holy day from Shabbat to Sunday.[36] This, however, changed the form of the Christian week, which now ended in the beginning of a new week, rather than in the end of the cycle of the same week. Thus, while the Jewish week exhibits a narrative of creation to redemption, the Christian week signifies only "always a beginning."[37] The church transformed the Christian cycle into a *fleeting moment*: the difference in content changed the essence of Christian time. If the Jewish Shabbat is "the holiday of redemption... for it celebrates the divine rest of the seventh day," the Christian Sunday is a symbol of creation: "Under the allegory of the beginning of the world, it chiefly celebrates the beginning of the week. The Christian is eternal beginner; the completing is not his affair—all is well that begins well."[38] Rosenzweig's assertion that "the Christian is [an] eternal beginner" has, in this case, more than symbolic meaning. The difference in calendars has deep ontological implications: for Rosenzweig, Christian time is a transition of beginnings, while Jewish time is one of repetition.

To clarify, the Christian week is certainly not meaningless or unimportant according to Rosenzweig. In fact, the opposite is true. "Sunday," he declares, "with its power radiating its blessing over the daily work of the week, is the authentic image of this ever freshly, ever youthfully, ever newly shining power of Christianity upon the world."[39] The Christian week symbolizes a beginning, which perfectly complements the linear, progressive task of Christianity in world redemption. The Christian world does not have a perverted version of repetition; rather, the linear temporality of Christianity is perfectly aligned with Rosenzweig's vision of Christianity. While the Jewish people have repetition so that they can negate history and experience eternity, the Christian world has linear temporality so its people can effectively work *in* history for world redemption. The different ways Judaism and Christianity structure their week expresses their different roles in world redemption.

"An Infinite Life": Ontology and Redemption

Rosenzweig's distinctive integration of the theory of time and repetition with liturgical practices is an important example of his ongoing attempt to reconnect philosophy and theology in what he calls "New Thinking." In the context of his model of repetition, Rosenzweig's work shows how liturgy impacts the temporal experience of an entire community. Specifically, liturgy structures the Jewish and Christian calendars and thereby their temporal consciousness.

Granted, the yearly cycle of festivals of creation-revelation-redemption presents the Jewish community first and foremost with an immediate religious experience. Passover, to give an example, is a holiday of creation, because it celebrates the "creation of a people into a people."[40] It materializes in vivo a specific religious content. Similarly, "the Day of Atonement, [placed] the eternal Redemption into the midst of time."[41] In *Franz Rosenzweig and the Systematic Task of Philosophy* (2009), Benjamin Pollock offers a similar interpretation of the function of Jewish holidays. Pollock builds on Rosenzweig's assertion that liturgy is "the burning mirror [*Brennspiegel*] that collects the sunbeams of eternity in the tiny cycle of the year,"[42] to claim that, for Rosenzweig, the different festivals allow Judaism and Christianity to get closer to a reality of redemption by presenting them with a vision of the unity of God-World-humanity within time. The liturgical form "is the only way in which we can come to see the unity of the All that will be in the redemptive future."[43] My argument about the function of cyclical time, however, is on a different register. I argue that for Rosenzweig, the liturgical content of the cycle of the year has an immediate effect on the *temporal* condition of the believer. Passover is crucial, not only because of its religious content, but also because of its function in cyclical temporality. Passover changes the form of Jewish temporality because it is the beginning of a yearly narrative that produces cyclical experience. It is telling, in this context, that for Rosenzweig two different holidays symbolize redemption: besides Yom Kippur, the true holiday of redemption, Sukkot is also a celebration of redemption, but *only within the framework of cyclical temporality*.[44] Redemption is not only experienced directly (during Yom Kippur), but also as a yearly festival that changes the form of the Jewish time (vis-à-vis Sukkot). In short, apart from the immediate religious importance, yearly festivals are critical for cyclical temporality: the cycles of the week and the year must have a specific content (beginning-to-end narrative) to be considered repetitive models of time, and that content is delivered in the social realm through liturgical practices (creation-revelation-redemption). This liturgical content certainly has an important religious function, but it also has a crucial impact on the temporal experience of the Jewish people.

Repetition and Liturgy: The Year

The intricate place Rosenzweig assigned to liturgy in his theory of repetition has caused some confusion, especially when considered alongside his ambiguous notion of *nunc stans* and his focus on cyclical temporality. Consider Stéphane Mosès, who, in his *System and Revelation* (1982), links Rosenzweig's repetition with Mircea Eliade's work on the "cyclic return of primordial events" in archaic societies.[45] In Mosès's reading, the repetition of the year delivers eternity, much as the archaic return of the same produces eternity. Subsequently, for Mosès, Rosenzweig's repetition promises eternity to both Judaism and Christianity.[46] The Jewish and Christian cycles of the year are identical in function (the production of eternity) but different in liturgical content. Both the Jews and the Christians experience repetition, but in different ways. The Jews celebrate creation and redemption and so can anticipate redemption in the future, while the Christians have a liturgy that memorializes only creation and thus commits to a return to the beginning of time. In short, for Mosès, repetition elevates all to eternity—only to a different eternity.

This position, however, misconstrues Rosenzweig's theory of repetition. For Rosenzweig, I argued, the content of time affects the form of time: the liturgical medium grounds the possibility of repetition at the level of the community. There is no repetition if time does not encapsulate a beginning-to-end narrative materialized and shared in a specific liturgical celebration of creation and redemption. The discussion of the Christian year in *The Star of Redemption* clarifies this point. According to Rosenzweig, the Christian year, like the Christian week, is not cyclical. In Christianity, "a special holiday of Redemption is missing."[47] The cycle of the year, just like the cycle of the week, has no end—the year, like the week, signifies only a beginning: "Redemption itself... has no place in the ecclesiastical year."[48] For that reason, the Christian cycle of the year is not a repetition in the way the Jewish year is. Liturgy, to go back to Mosès's claim, is not an addition to the experience of repetition. Rather, liturgy has an essential part in producing the communal experience: without the right liturgical content, there is no room for a communal experience of repetition and, consequently, no room for eternity.

In a short passage on worldly holidays, Rosenzweig expands on this difference between the Jewish and the Christian years. On the one hand, the Jewish year, Rosenzweig claims, has rarely changed in history. It has added only three "historical" holidays (Tisha B'Av, Purim, and Hanukkah), which over the years have become fixed in the Jewish calendar. The church, on the other hand, has added content from diverse sources that has changed the form of the Christian year. It has accumulated holidays and celebrations as part of its mission of world unification under God. "Where it is drawn up according to the national frontiers, it arranges, annually or for the great events of the life of the people, days of penitence and prayer."[49] This openness to the world changed the structure of Christian time: the Christians inserted the "temporal and worldly into the eternal circle that yet already for a long time no longer remains a circle through place and time in these festivals of the eternal path of Redemption that vary with time and place, but opens into a spiral."[50] The year was loaded with events and festivals to the degree that it is transfigured into a *spiral*. In contrast, the Jewish people have retained a closed cycle of the year; they have added few changes to their year, all from their own history, keeping the cyclical structure of beginning-to-end (creation to redemption) narrative intact. In other words, the Jewish people were able to experience cyclical time because their year is closed and stable, and their narrative is coherent, while the church has added diverse holidays from diverse sources, causing the Christian year to lose its cyclical form. Here again, Christian time echoes the relationship of Christianity to history: their calendar is global—that is, it notes holidays and events from diverse worldly contexts—thereby reflecting their role in world redemptions. Rather than a comprehensible cycle, Christian time is an open spiral signaling forward movement on the Eternal Way.

Rosenzweig's Ontology and the Archaic Eternal Return

The attempt to connect Rosenzweig to archaic models of repetition is problematic for a second and more pertinent reason: the archaic return of the same, which Mosès invokes, entailed static reality and timelessness, and these are incompatible with Rosenzweig's ontological framework. Indeed, the conflation of Rosenzweig's theory of repetition with the archaic return of the same proved fertile for those who criticized Rosenzweig for his supposedly stagnant vision of eternity and Jewish life. Emil Fackenheim, for example, blamed Rosenzweig for "raising [Judaism] above all history" in a manner that "sacralized Jewish history or made Jewish existence ahistorical."[51] I, however, argue that the Jewish people have no sacred time that could lie outside history. Their eternity is an intensive experience of time in the present.

As I noted in chapter 1, in *The Myth of the Eternal Return*, Mircea Eliade, the Romanian historian of religion, famously offers an analysis of sacred time and its relations to the eternal return. In archaic society, Eliade claims, the meaning of objects and events was transcendent. A thing or an act gained its essence or its place in reality only by repeating an eternal archetype. This explains the function of myths: they presented divine models or prototypes, which archaic man and woman could copy to make their world meaningful. In temporal terms, sacred reality was believed to symbolize a timelessness outside history that Eliade terms "mythical time," or *in illo tempore* (in that time). The archaic world strove to experience this eternity during diverse rituals and rites. Participation in such rituals, however, did more than connect the archaic world to sacred meaning. It also changed the temporal condition of archaic society: the individual who copied the divine model was delivered to sacred timelessness. The actualization of the myth in archaic society therefore transformed the archaic world: it abolished history and transported the individual to the beginning of the world where "revelation took place."[52] In this context, the repetition of the year was critical to the return to the act of creation, to the "beginning," as it were. The beginning of the year signaled "cyclical regeneration of time":[53] the archaic festival of the beginning of the year was an opportunity to reject the past, to forget last year, and thus to experience timelessness. Archaic cyclical time produced an atemporal experience: it constructed "an absolute beginning" and restored "the initial instant, the plentitude of the present that contains no trace of history."[54]

I contend that nothing could be more different from Rosenzweig's vision of repetition. In fact, in his wartime notes from 1916–17 collected under the title "Paralipomena," Rosenzweig had already termed this archaic model of eternity-as-atemporality a "pagan" model. "Eternity [*Ewigkeit*], from a naturalistic point of view," he writes, "is beyond all relation to time; it is neither longer than the longest nor the shorter than the shortest. In this sense, antiquity [pagan, *die heidnische*] developed the concept of the eternal. Therefore, it has no concept of history."[55] The rejection of pagan eternity is further explained in Rosenzweig's discussion of modern metaphysics in *The Star of Redemption*.

Rosenzweig's basic metaphysical position is developed in the first part of *The Star of Redemption* within his theory of metalogic. Herein, Rosenzweig, a student of German idealism, offers a sweeping criticism of Hegel's philosophy. For present purposes, we should note his critique of Hegel's disinterest in factual, contingent existence—a critique that bears an important resemblance to Deleuze's critique of Hegel in *Difference and Repetition*, which I mentioned earlier in the book. In Hegel's ontology, Rosenzweig argues, logic takes the place of the multitude of phenomena, abstraction replaces concrete actuality, and individual objects are lost in general concepts. In *The Star of Redemption*, Rosenzweig therefore famously rejects the Hegelian dictum to unite "rationality" and "actuality." Instead, his work follows Schellingian metaphysics and underscores the importance of factual reality and the ever-changing, spontaneous nature of existence.[56] This line of criticism implies a rejection of Eliade's interpretation of archaic ontology and its emphasis on changelessness and timelessness. Instead, Rosenzweig's metaphysics espouses a vision of the world as "becoming."[57] "There is still something else in [the world]," he declares, "something always new, pressing, imposing. Its womb is insatiable in conceiving, it is inexhaustible in giving birth."[58] Unlike the archaic wish to subsume the world within atemporal divine stasis, for Rosenzweig, the world presents a "living, ever renewed flow of the phenomenon";[59] it indicates an open-ended infinite productivity: "for the being of the world is not an infinite essence at rest. The inexhaustible plenitude of visions in the world, without cease newly generated and newly received, the 'being full-of-figure' of the world—this is exactly the opposite of an essence unceasingly at rest."[60]

The definition of the world as becoming is applied even when Rosenzweig considers redemption as a metaphysical category in the second part of *The Star of Redemption*. Put simply, for Rosenzweig, redemption grants the world an essence (*Wesen*). Redemption changes the world from a random combination of individual and separate phenomena to a concrete *unified* world, which he terms a living entity (*das Lebendige*). Pure becoming is a negative definition of the world that prevails in the present and indicates mere factual and temporal existence [*Dasein*]. In redemption, however, such formlessness transforms into a form of life. "We are seeking an infinite life [*ein unendliches Leben*], and we are finding one that is finite . . . The world must become fully alive . . . Existence must be alive through and through [*Das Dasein muß an allen seinen Punkten lebendig sein*]. That it is not yet so means simply, once again, that the world is not yet finished."[61]

Rosenzweig's recourse to the category of life marks his alliance with Dilthey's *Lebensphilosophie*.[62] And like Dilthey and Schelling before him, Rosenzweig utilizes the metaphor of life to imagine a dynamic wholeness of the world. Importantly, the category of life indicates a core of enduring presence: the world as a living entity is granted a self-determined essence that can "withstand the inherent weakness of existence as creature."[63] However, contrary to Western philosophical traditions "from Parmenides to Hegel," as Rosenzweig puts it, and in opposition to archaic ontology, this essence does not compel the world toward never-changing, static reality. Redemption does not change the spontaneous productiveness of the world; rather, it reformulates it within a nuanced vision of the world as life.[64]

Consequently, Rosenzweig's use of the term *nunc stans* is different from its original meaning in archaic thought. He does not intend eternity to be a static reality outside time as in the archaic eternal return. His world is a world of life, of constant and everlasting productivity. Rosenzweig's model of repetition, I argue, acknowledges those basic characteristics of the world. If in redemption the world

transforms to a vibrant and dynamic unified whole, the Jewish anticipation of redemption echoes and replicates such vision. In what follows, I explain how Kierkegaard's theory of repetition as expressed
in his book *Repetition*, despite theological and conceptual differences,
shares Rosenzweig's antagonism to the archaic return of the same and
expresses the dynamic nature of the world as becoming. I build on this
semblance to discuss Rosenzweig's vision of repetition.

Kierkegaard and Rosenzweig on Repetition

Søren Kierkegaard's *Repetition* was written under the pseudonym
Constantin Constantius and published in conjunction with his *Fear
and Trembling* in 1843. Writing the book, Kierkegaard was partly motivated by his recently broken engagement with Regine Olsen. His book
expresses an overt wish to negotiate the meaning of a return to, or
repetition of, a lost object of affection. This book, however, offers
more than a biographical backstory. It presents, rather, mind-boggling
series of existential, psychological, aesthetic, and religious arguments
about repetition. The multidimensionality of repetition in Kierkegaard's thought is also eloquently echoed in the book's unconventional
structure. The first half introduces Kierkegaard's philosophical argument, and the second poetically presents his notion of repetition in
epistolary form. In what follows, I focus on the insight into the logic
of history and eternity that Kierkegaardian repetition gives (mostly
vis-à-vis his interpretation of Job). This insight sheds light on Rosenzweig's theory of repetition in *The Star of Redemption*.

Kierkegaard's *Logic of Repetition*

Initially, repetition is understood in Kierkegaard's book in aesthetic terms: repetition produces a heightened poetical experience,
which allows the "young man," with whom Constantin Constantius
exchanges several letters in *Repetition*, to re-experience his previous
love affair in diverse forms. In repeating the past from the position of
the present, the young man is able to relive the past as alternatively
happy, comic, and unhappy. Repetition, in this sense, generates "an
exponential power of consciousness."[65] However, for Kierkegaard,

the true force of repetition is its religious and existential dimensions. Much like Rosenzweig's model, in Kierkegaard's model, "eternity was the true repetition."[66] The story of Job helps Kierkegaard unravel how repetition offers a road map to a deeper, meaningful relationship with God. Kierkegaard is interested especially in Job's understanding of his own predicament and his refusal to accept the blame for his loss. While his friends found him responsible for his misfortunes, Job always insisted he was "in the right."[67] Job, unlike his friends, refused to perceive his present condition as a direct continuation of the past. The past did not cause his present in a predetermined succession of events. Rather, through repetition—Kierkegaard emphasizes that Job gained everything back the second time—Job's present was created *anew*, as if from outside history. Job was thrown into a reality over which he had no control. But he did not let this reality define him: he was able to create a different meaning for the present by re-experiencing his past in a new and different way. This insight also points to the possibility of freedom: in repetition, Kierkegaard argues, the individual is free from historical determination in that he or she is able to create personal, independent meaning of his or her reality.

Such a freedom from historical determination and the relations with God mark important aspects of the transcendence produced by Kierkegaard's model of repetition. Still, in Kierkegaard's book, repetition is also portrayed as intensifying the experience of the present. Job, Kierkegaard maintains, experienced repetition as a thunderstorm: "When everything has ground to a halt, when thought ceases and speech is silenced, when explanation retreats in despair—then a thunderstorm is necessary."[68] The gathering clouds and swirling winds portray the emotional condition of Job, who lost everything, but they also mark the intensification of the now. Unlike his friends, who suffered a monotonous experience, repetition heightened Job's relation with actuality.[69] In *The Concept of Dread* (1844), the intensification of the now, of an individual's relations with reality, is deeply connected to Kierkegaard's notion of the individual subjective passion constituting the world of the believer. The religious experience of faith is possible because, in Kierkegaard's model, repetition's movement of transcendence rejects historical logic and provides an opportunity to experience the "passion of the absurd."[70]

In Kierkegaard, thus, repetition presents a duality of presence and alienation. Job's experience of unjustified catastrophe first produced an alienation from history—normally experienced as an intrinsically connected flow of sequential events—but, at the same time, it intensified his experience of the present. In that respect, Job's "repetition-as-recollection forward" refused the logic of linear history but not the logic of time. What Kierkegaard characterizes as Job's repetition entails a rejection of the control of history but also a heightened experience of the now. Job's repetition tore the veil of history and, by so doing, generated a better connection with factual existence: the world was closer, but the individual was immune to its power. Rosenzweig, we will now see, attributes a similar function to repetition in the social sphere: he postulates a theory of temporality in which the Jewish people resisted history and, yet, at the same time, experienced the true essence of time and transitoriness.

Rethinking Repetition: Rosenzweig and the Form of Time

The comparison with Kierkegaard's *Repetition* sheds light on the mechanism of Rosenzweig's theory of repetition. Clearly, Kierkegaard was committed to a Christian theological framework, worlds apart from Rosenzweig's Jewish philosophy, and his focus on individual revelation significantly diverged from Rosenzweig's emphasis on the communal medium of repetition. Nevertheless, Kierkegaard's theory of repetition spells out the formative place of repetition in Rosenzweig's ontological framework. This shared vision of repetition is most evident in Rosenzweig's description of Shabbat:

> Every Sabbath is by and large like every other, but the change of the scriptural portion distinguishes each from the other, and in this that differentiates them makes it evident that they are not a last link but only the single links of a higher order, of the year; for only in the year does that which differentiates the single links again close into a whole. The Sabbath grants existence to the year. This existence must be created anew every week. . . . Only in the expiring sequence of Sabbaths is the year made round into a wreath. Precisely the regularity in the sequence of Sabbaths, just this fact that, up to the weekly portion, one

Sabbath is essentially like the other, makes them into the foundation stones of the year; the year in spiritual guise is first and foremost created through them.[71]

There is much to unpack in this section. First, note that for Rosenzweig, the return of Shabbat is *not* a return of the same. The basic narrative of the week is always the same: the six days of the week end in redemption. Nevertheless, the portions of the Bible change from one Shabbat to the next, so redemption is told differently. Each Shabbat ends the week differently, and this, according to Rosenzweig, expresses the essence of the Jewish year. The experience of the year is built on differences. *Time* is built on *differences*. The repetition of Shabbat reflects sameness but also the inherent differences of and within time. And these differences between one Shabbat and the next reveal the essence of temporality. Contrary to the archaic notions of the return of the same, Shabbat is critical to the experience of time exactly because it exhibits difference, change, and dynamism.

Rosenzweig took up this issue again in his translation of the poems and hymns of the medieval Jewish philosopher and poet Jehuda Halevi. The poems constitute a body of liturgical works recited in synagogues throughout the Jewish year. In the last section of the *Nachwort* to his book, Rosenzweig discusses the relations between the poems in a way that is reminiscent of his vision of time in the *Star of Redemption*:

> The flow of the words known to all and of old has to be, interrupted by them, dammed up into the lakes that bring into view unaccustomed shorelines. In the recurrence they are the variable, but because in their variation they are bound nevertheless to recurrence, they are necessarily forced into a certain similarity... Repetitions were not experienced as such, or, as far as they are experienced, it is entirely in order. For this recurrence in the year is after all the essence of the festival, as, in the final analysis, repetition is altogether the great and only form man has for expressing what is entirely true for him.[72]

I will discuss Rosenzweig's Halevi translations in detail in the next chapter. At present, simply note that, as in Rosenzweig's description of Shabbat, Halevi's poems have patterns of similarity and difference. On one hand, they repeat each other: they deliver the same basic liturgical experience. On the other hand, they are different from each other, as are the holidays in the Jewish year. This relation of sameness and difference is the experience the poems are intended to deliver to the reader. The poems make concrete the intricate dialectics of sameness and difference manifested by the Jewish week. Specifically, the differences express the dynamic nature of time and provide an experience of the cyclical repetition of the week: the differences do not deform the relations between the holidays; rather, they manifest the dynamism and fluidity of Jewish temporality. These features, these alterations, have helped the Jewish community articulate the essence of the world as becoming. In more general terms, repetition allows for a life in the midst of time: the Jewish people recognize eternity not by freezing time, but by emphasizing the differences within time.

The similarity between Rosenzweig and Kierkegaard, however, does not end with their understanding of repetition as an experience built on differences rather than similarities. In view of Kierkegaard's model of repetition, we can also see how eternity is not a static moment outside of time for Rosenzweig. Repetition, for Rosenzweig, does not signal an atemporal reality, but an intensification of *this* reality. In line with Kierkegaard's repetition, which focuses the believer on factual existence, for Rosenzweig, Jewish eternal life does not represent timelessness but is a powerful confirmation of world and time. And as in Kierkegaard's account of freedom, in Rosenzweig's account, the Jewish people are indeed outside the homogeneous time of the rest of the nations—but not outside of time.[73] Rosenzweig notes: "The temporal needs the support of the eternal. But of course: not until life has become entirely temporal, or, put differently, time has an entirely living, an entirely real river flowing through the vast space above the crags of the moment; no sooner can eternity fall upon time. Life, and all life, must be entirely temporal, entirely living before it can become eternal life."[74] For Rosenzweig, in this passage, worldly time is the location of eternity. Eternity exists purely within the fullness of time, the living essence of time. The Jewish people are close to God not by escaping time, but by experiencing time, as living and dynamic, *with* God. Their redemption is not dependent on the abolition of time, but on an intensive experience of time, or, in other words, on the recognition of time. Rosenzweig's vision of redemption, in which the Jewish people experience their "own time," has deep metaphysical importance in addition to its theological implications: the Jewish people are privileged to see reality as it truly is, in its becoming; that is, what Rosenzweig calls repetition provides the Jewish people with an understanding of the world as already redeemed.[75]

What is more, with Kierkegaard, we can see how repetition becomes a principle of individuality of the Jewish people. For Kierkegaard, remember, repetition allows the individual to reconfigure the present, to free him or her from the determination of historical progress, to envision a different future. With repetition, the individual is able to refashion the self, and, like Job, to differentiate herself from those surrounding her. Importantly, this logic applies to the Jewish people: they too are able to reject historical progress and create a different reality with repetition. The Jewish people rejected Christian imperialism because they were able to constitute different temporal cyclical modus: their repetitive cycles tore them from the rest of the world and provided unique, individual-yet-collective experience. This also explains Rosenzweig's idea of the anticipation of redemption, one of the most debated topics among Rosenzweig's readership. As noted, Rosenzweig strongly believed that the Jewish people anticipate redemption in the present. At times, he even seems to argue that the Jewish people *experience* redemption in the present. How, I asked earlier in the chapter, is this possible? What is the meaning of such anticipation of redemption? Kierkegaard's notion of "repetition-as-recollection forward" may serve as one possible explanation. In Kierkegaard, the possibility of a different present opens up different possibilities for the future. The Jewish people, I suggest, experience a similar phenomenon on a larger scale: their cyclical temporality does more than structure their present reality. It also allows them to produce a different vision of the future. That is, because the Jewish people have constructed a unique collective reality, they are able to anticipate their distinct vision of world redemption. Rosenzweig notes this when he explains the logic of the cycle of the year: "in the cycle of its year the future is the motive power; the circular movement does not give birth as it were by push but by tug; the present elapses, not because the past shoves it forward, but because the future drags it along."[76]

Thinking again of Rosenzweig's discussion of the Jews as the eternal people, we see repetition is fundamental to his description of their eternity. As noted previously, the Jews are eternal because they have a different relationship to history than other nations. They were exiled from land, worldly law, and a historically evolving language, and therefore distanced themselves from the influence of history. However, their eternity, or imperishability in Rosenzweig's terms, is not static. This negation of history was dependent on their experience of repetition. The cycles of the week and the year provide an experience of continuity and permanence, indeed an experience of eternity that is different from the experience of other nations. Still—and this is the crucial point—this eternity is experienced as dynamic and changing. Jewish temporality is constituted by what we might call, seemingly paradoxically, dynamic sameness: repetition produces a non-historical eternity, which is, in itself, dynamic and changing.[77]

This "dynamic" eternity explains Rosenzweig's notion of the "worldly unliveliness" (*Die weltliche Unlebendigkeit*) of Judaism. In his letter to Ehrenberg, at which I glanced earlier, Rosenzweig notes, "Judaism has life only when it is with God. Only when the world is *also* with God will Judaism be granted worldly life." One reading of this (for example, the readings of Mosès and Fackenheim) is that the Jewish people, unlike the Christian world, were not part of history, that they negated the worldly life of other nations. I suggest, however, that Rosenzweig's definition of Jewish unliveliness offers more than a mere negation of reality. In my reading, the Jewish worldly unliveliness, in fact, secured the Jewish people's relation to the living essence of the world. Compared to other peoples, the Jews were distanced from reality and alienated from history. However, as in Kierkegaard's reading of Job, this distance conditioned a different kind of existence, through which the Jewish people could have a true understanding of the world as life. By being outside the rule of history, they could have a clearer vision of time. The worldly essence of other nations hid from those nations the dynamic and ever-changing form of reality. Their worldly life enslaved them to the flow of history, while the worldly unliveliness of the Jewish people dialectically tore them away from the world but also granted them a deeper relation to time.

Cyclical Time and the Christian Path to Eternity

Rosenzweig's description of the Christian path to eternity manifests the fundamental differences between Judaism and Christianity as just discussed. Rosenzweig analyzes this difference in a section of *The Star of Redemption* entitled "Messianic Politics." Here, he details how other nations, who do not have access to the cyclical repetition of the Jewish calendar, still generate an experience of eternity: "A cycle, the cycle of the year, guarantees its eternity to the eternal people. The peoples of the world are in themselves without a cycle, their life rolls downstream in a wide river. If eternity should come to them from the State, the river must be stemmed, dammed up into a lake."[78] Repetition is the guarantor of eternity of the Jewish people. The other peoples of the world, however, are "without a cycle." As a result, they must relate differently to time. Thus, in a passage echoing the growing suspicion of state laws found in other radical Jewish thinkers, Rosenzweig argues that the Christians stopped time with "violence,"[79] like a dam on the river of time.

It is with laws, Rosenzweig claims, as artificial and coercive instruments, that the state inflicts on history a façade of eternity. While reality is ever-changing, state laws freeze reality: "Now something is suddenly there that persists," he writes.[80] To stop time, the state cuts history into isolated and homogeneous periods, or, in Rosenzweig's terms, into "epochs."[81] Each epoch is dominated by a different set of laws or political institutions, which stop the flow of time to a standstill, breaking the ongoing movement of time and reality into small fractions of sameness, each masquerading as eternity. And this, claims Rosenzweig, goes directly against the essence of existence as movement: "The law of change prohibits something that persists from changing as it prohibits something from preserving itself in the change. Life can be either only rest or only movement. And, since time cannot be denied, movement triumphs. Into the wave of the same river you do not go the second time."[82] The state has, apparently, only limited power. State laws stop time only for short periods; as the state and its laws are transient institutions by themselves, their stability is only momentary. Epochs are just a short stop in the flow of time. In the end, the stream of time floods the dam, and new laws take the place of the old ones. A new epoch arrives.[83] Put simply, the state is unsuccessful: it produces only "hours of eternity," while Jewish repetition places "untroubled and intact ring upon ring round the trunk of its eternal life."[84]

The answer to the state's challenge of historical transiency was given by the Christian dogma. Like the rest of the world, Christianity, "the supra-national power,"[85] also seeks eternity vis-à-vis the epoch. However, unlike the political epoch, the Christian is eternal: it started with the Coming of Christ and will end with the Second Coming of Christ. If the state extracts epochs as temporary series of isolated periods, as series of pools in the river of time, the Christian church changed that movement into one big epoch, one endless lake, in which the believer is always in the middle point, in an endless present between the First Coming and the Second Coming of Christ. "In between stands a single hour, a single day, the Christian world time in which everything is middle, everything equally as light as day."[86] While the Jewish people negate transiency through repetition, the Christian world encounters eternity by thinking of the present as an ongoing experience of "between time and time."[87] The eternal moment does not repeat in Christian temporality but is prolonged to capture the whole of history. Eternity is not based on the rhythm of repetition, but on the extension of the logic of the moment to history itself.

Thus, as in the case of politics, the Christian epoch interrupts the natural flow of time. In Christianity, "time acquires weight . . . it possesses materiality; it is like a thing."[88] If the Jewish people have introduced eternity to the midst of time via repetition in a way that recognizes the true essence of temporality, Christianity has forced time to a full stop: "Time does not bounce off Christianity like off the Jewish people, but fleeting time is captured and must now serve as an imprisoned slave."[89] The Jewish people have formed a community with a time of its own, on the shores of the flow of history. Christianity has conquered time completely, becoming "master over time."[90] Once more, the role of Judaism and Christianity in world redemption informs their respective experiences of time. The Jews negate the linear trajectory of history by extracting a cyclical eternity by living "next to history," while the Christian world creates eternity by ruling history; the Jewish people acknowledge the dynamism of the world, while Christians repress and inhibit this dynamism; the eternity of the Jewish people anticipates a different reality of redemption in the present, while the Christians work for redemption in the end of time.[91]

Repetition and Community

One significant difference between Rosenzweig's and Kierkegaard's theories of repetition, however, merits further discussion. While Rosenzweig in *The Star of Redemption* defines repetition as a communal practice, Kierkegaard was "reluctant to forsake the realm of the individual,"[92] claiming that "in the individual, then, repetition appears as a task of freedom."[93] I would like to focus on the philosophical implications of this point of disagreement to suggest a possible contribution of Rosenzweig's work on repetition to the philosophical tradition of repetition.

At the outset, it is noteworthy that Kierkegaard did refer to the application of repetition to the social realm, a point clarified in his unpublished reply to Johan Heiberg—an influential historian and Hegelian—who, in *The Astronomical Year* (1844), misattributes Kierkegaardian repetition to the natural celestial cycles. Heiberg's misunderstanding is not surprising. While Kierkegaard's main criticism is directed at the Greek notion of recollection, his true interlocutor in *Repetition* is Hegel, whose system of Spirit suggests a philosophical theory of mediation that, like Kierkegaard's, aims to replace the static ontology of Platonic philosophy.[94] In his reply to Heiberg, Kierkegaard takes the opportunity not only to clarify the divide between his model of repetition and the model of history proper to Hegel's Spirit but also to give reasons for his insistence on applying his notion of repetition "only for the contemplating [individual] spirit."[95] His point is based on the issue of immanence and history. The Hegelian Spirit, Kierkegaard argues, designates an immanent movement of (collective) progress in history: it follows a set of necessary stages that end in the absolute Spirit. Kierkegaard's repetition, however, negates such a logic of immanence. Most importantly, Kierkegaardian repetition manifests freedom from history and inserts difference into logical determinations. In Kierkegaard's words, "Modern philosophy makes no movement. In general, it merely makes a commotion. To the extent

that it makes a movement, it is always within the sphere of immanence. Repetition, on the other hand, is *transcendence*."[96] Nations or
peoples (*Volk*), he argues, are in the realm of spirit and thus obey the
Hegelian logic of immanence. The individual, however, is able to transcend historical necessity via repetition. Repetition must be an act of
the individual, partly because it delivers the individual from history:
"In the sphere of freedom, the word 'mediation' has again done dam-
age, because, coming from logic, it helped to make the transcendence
of movement illusory. In order to prevent this error or this dubious
compromise between the logical and freedom, I have thought that
'repetition' could be used in the sphere of freedom."[97] This repetition-
derived freedom, Kierkegaard further argues, grants the individual a
revelatory insight into history and reality, something those enclosed
within the Hegelian Spirit are unable to attain.

Remarkably, Rosenzweig confirms Kierkegaard's formula of history, determination, and mediation but still finds a third way. In *The
Star of Redemption*, there is one people, the Jewish people, who, parallel
to Kierkegaard's description of the individual, evade the fate of all
peoples and enter the realm of eternity in the midst of history. Unlike
all other nations, these people specifically use repetition to negate
history. The Jewish people, and not only the individual, are in danger
of "losing [themselves] in events, fate,"[98] yet like the Kierkegaardian
believer, they find a solution in the cycles of time and experience repetition, like Job, in the form of alienation from the world. The peoples of
the world conform to the Hegelian Spirit by envisioning only a past of
eternal truths and by working within history to bring about universal
redemption. The Jewish people are different: they have the ability to
gain access to the redemptive reality within time through the cycle of
the year. The subversion of history is viable for the Jews as a people,
not only as individuals.

This difference between Kierkegaard's individual repetition and
Rosenzweig's communal repetition had important structural ramifications. In Kierkegaard's model, repetition produces unexpected
difference and is therefore a wondrous, extraordinary experience.
Kierkegaard makes note of this early in *Repetition* in his description
of a trip Constantin Constantius makes to Berlin in a premeditated
attempt to have the same experience he had the previous year. Con-

stantin Constantius, however, fails.[99] The trip is too calculated, too much like a scientific experiment, to be a model for Kierkegaardian repetition. Constantin intentionally goes to the same places and attends the same show, but he does not experience repetition. The conscious reproduction of the same reality amounts to a perversion: It produces repetition under a general form, not as a meaningful experience. Repetition is supposed to subvert historical progress, to create the conditions for individual meaning, to constitute a different future; therefore, there is an unexpected difference, an undefined newness, that Constantin's experiment is inherently unable to repeat. "So repetition is possible. But when? No human language can say," Constantin admits.[100] As is typical of Kierkegaard, the pseudonym is more than a name; as his name implies, Constantin Constantius finds only constancy, never repetition.

Rosenzweig's repetition has a different mechanism. For Rosenzweig, repetition grounded the experience of a whole community for many generations. It had to be, consequently, an organized, systematized, and methodical enterprise if it was to influence the Jewish people. The repetition of the Jewish people showed the whole community *identifiable* differences in time. Because of the shift to the realm of community, these differences had to be constructed in a definite rather than accidental way. Kierkegaard's repetition is a single and unique experience with no specific content; it creates newness that is never predefined. For Rosenzweig, cyclical time is based on a specific content. The Jewish people needed a specific narrative to identify repetition. The yearly festivals presented a collective story through which they created their own time. The newness in Rosenzweig's theory of repetition is not unexpected but explicitly generated: the differences between different Shabbats are grounded on the different portions of scripture and must be crucial, observable differences to create an experience valuable to the whole Jewish community. Kierkegaard could not have accepted such a program for his repetition. His repetition is assigned to the individual. It is not something the individual could systematically preconceive, and not an experience he or she could share with anyone else. In Kierkegaard's repetition, the experiments of Constantin Constantius and the young man fail because they struggle to invent that which must be spontaneously created. The Jewish people do not have the luxury of failing: repetition structures their communal way of life.

This difference between Rosenzweig and Kierkegaard reflects their respective theories of the intersubjective realm. Compared to Kierkegaard's famous emphasize on individual, singular, irreducible experience,[101] Rosenzweig insists on the primal importance of community in organizing, and indeed defining, the world of the believer. As Leora Batnitzky notes in *Idolatry and Representation* (2000), "*The Star of Redemption*'s structure may be best characterized as a kind of hermeneutical argument that privileges the epistemological status of communal frameworks over and against individual experience and logic."[102] Repetition, in Rosenzweig's version, has to be a communal experience if it is to have such a dramatic effect on the individual: to anticipate redemption, to live in the midst of time, the individual must engage in communal practices. To change her way of being, the individual must undergo a shift in temporal infrastructure, which, in Rosenzweig's philosophy, is based on a communal framework. Put otherwise, for Rosenzweig, and in contradistinction to Kierkegaard, private repetition can only portray similarities and differences, and these have little impact. The shift in temporal modus must be mitigated by communal reality: only the form of the Jewish calendar can enforce a relation to eternity and a recognition in the dynamic nature of time.[103]

In the next chapter, we will see how the need to produce Jewish experience of cyclical time implicated Rosenzweig's literary strategies in his book of translation of the poems and hymns of Jehuda Halevi. The book allowed Rosenzweig to put into effect his model of Jewish cyclical time: he inserted a temporal condition of repetition to his translations, thus endowing his book with a messianic function.

CHAPTER 4

Repetition and Alterity
Rosenzweig's Translations of Jehuda Halevi

In a speech celebrating the completion of the Buber-Rosenzweig Bible in 1961, the first drafts of which were composed in 1925, Gershom Scholem praised the utopian vision of the authors. The Buber-Rosenzweig Bible famously garnered equal parts commendation and condemnation, and Scholem's praise was not without its own irony:

> And I am not able to close without saying a word about the historical context of your work, which must remain a question and a very concerned question . . . There was a utopian element in your endeavor. For the language into which you translated was not that of the everyday speech nor that of German literature of the 1920s. You aimed at a German which, drawing sustenance from earlier tendencies, was present potentially in the language, and it was this utopianism which made your translation so very exciting and stimulating.[1]

The Buber-Rosenzweig translation, Scholem argued, aimed to create a new language that transcended the German of their time. This new language was utopian because it presented a "very exciting and stimulating" potential for collaboration between or coexistence of Germans and Jews. History, however, proved Buber and Rosenzweig wrong. Therefore, Scholem added, "I cannot refrain from asking: For whom is this translation now intended and whom will it influence? Seen historically, it is no longer a *Gastgeschenk* [but rather] a tombstone of a relationship that was extinguished in unspeakable horror."[2]

This chapter returns to the utopian function of translation in Rosenzweig's work, which is, I argue, much more multifarious and nuanced than what Scholem reservedly assigned to the Bible translation project. Concretely, my aim is to show how the utopian function of translation is embedded in Rosenzweig's concept of repetition and its constitutive place in Jewish temporal consciousness. This vision is more clearly laid out in Rosenzweig's perhaps lesser-known project: the translation of the poems and hymns of the medieval Jewish philosopher and poet Jehuda Halevi. This project occupied most of Rosenzweig's scholarly work after the completion of *The Star of Redemption*.

To make this argument, my plan is to investigate how Rosenzweig's translations of Jehuda Halevi produce two different kinds of alterity, each serving as a different model for ideal Jewish life in modernity. The first kind of alterity in Rosenzweig's Halevi translations is based on linguistic structures. It emerges in Rosenzweig's insistence on the foreignization of the German language with Hebrew (*das Deutsche umzufremden*).[3] Compared with previous translations that Germanized or Christianized Hebrew—most famously, Moses Mendelssohn's 1783 Bible translation—Rosenzweig is loyal to the contours of Halevi's Jewish Spanish language. Instead of subordinating the Hebrew to German, his translations preserve crucial Hebrew elements, creating a realm of Jewish/Hebrew otherness within the German language. Against Scholem's criticism of the Bible translation project, I argue that this linguistic alterity provides a model for sustainable Jewish-German relations: it affords an imaginary autonomous safe place for the Jewish people in the German language, out of which a healthy relationship between Jews and Germans could develop.

The second kind of alterity is based on temporal structures. My argument builds here on Rosenzweig's messianic politics in *The Star of Redemption*. Particularly important is his conception of the Jewish cyclical repetition of the year, which I have already discussed in the previous chapter in detail. For his translations book, Rosenzweig selected poems and hymns of Halevi with an important place in structuring the Jewish liturgical calendar—they were recited on different events of the week and the year. According to Rosenzweig, these poems, besides their religious and literary value, were supposed to manifest an experience of Jewish cyclical time. The poems not only helped the believer communicate with God or celebrate a Jewish festival; they also actualized the Jewish calendar: they materialized a temporal matrix of cyclical repetition that, in Rosenzweig's understanding, had messianic implications. This chapter investigates a series of literary maneuvers Rosenzweig develops to manifest the experience of repetition to his readers. I am especially interested in the structure of the Halevi book, most of all, the place and function of Rosenzweig's commentaries on Halevi's poems, which reflect and generate, in my understanding, the Jewish temporal index.

Rosenzweig's translations thus establish two distinct levels of Jewish alterity: the first secures the foreignness of Jews as a condition for their conversation with German society, and the second produces a unique temporal code of repetition. One evokes alterity for the purposes of communication with the neighbor; the other produces alterity as a condition for Jewish anticipation of redemption. This duality of present time and eternity, of life in conversation with German society but also in disconnection from history, highlights the paradox of German Jewish life in modernity.

Translation and Alterity in Rosenzweig

Rosenzweig's Jehuda Halevi book was part of a larger translation enterprise to which he dedicated most of his time in the last few years of his life, after completing *The Star of Redemption*. In the spring of 1920, still working on his philosophical masterpiece, even during his honeymoon, Rosenzweig worked on translating the traditional Grace After Meals (*Birkat Ha-Mazon*) prayer. The translation was published as a short booklet in the series *Jüdische Bücherei* by the Berlin publisher Gurlitt.[4] A year later, Rosenzweig translated another selection of prayers from the Friday Night Service. This collection was not published in his lifetime. He dedicated the next year to translating Jehuda Halevi's poems.[5] By this time, Rosenzweig was struggling with amyotrophic lateral sclerosis, an illness that considerably limited his productivity and would ultimately prove fatal at the end of 1929. His next and famous cooperation with Buber in the translation of the Bible resulted in part from the process of producing the Halevi book. Rosenzweig asked Buber for advice on numerous occasions during his work on the translations and dedicated the book to him as a token of his appreciation. Thanks to this semi-collaboration, Buber insisted, upon receiving an invitation to write a new translation of the Bible from Lambert Schneider, that Rosenzweig's participation was crucial and was quick to enlist him in the project.[6]

Translation and Revelation

Rosenzweig's book of translations of Jehuda Halevi was a natural conclusion of his philosophical work in *The Star of Redemption*. In this earlier work, Rosenzweig famously suggests a tripartite ontological structure. In contrast to Hegel's ideal of unity of Being, Rosenzweig identifies three kinds of beings—Man and Woman, God, and World. These beings, he further argues, are initially distinct: separated and independent. In his short essay, "The New Thinking," written to explain *The Star of Redemption*, he writes: "None [of God, humanity, and world] can be reduced to the other, but instead the reverse, that each can be reduced back to itself. Each is itself 'essence,' each is itself substance—with the entire metaphysical weight of the expression."[7] The separateness of these beings has, however, existential consequences: in their reclusion, they become empty being or Nothing (in Rosenzweig's terms).[8]

The radical isolation of humanity, world, and God posed a theoretical problem and existential crisis, which Rosenzweig struggled to solve. Drawing from nineteenth- and twentieth-century dialogical theology, he emphasized the importance of a meaningful dialogue between God, humanity, and world, which, in his philosophical vision, had the power to generate a radical change in their primordial way-of-being. Focusing, for example, on the relations between man and woman with God, this dialogue is defined as a loving relationship and is conceptualized as revelation; that is, the dialogue is aimed to restore the individual's "hidden" self—secluded in its own existence—to its full potential. Revelation, he writes, "can be nothing other than the self-negation of a merely mute essence by a word uttered out loud, the opening up of something locked, of a silently reposing permanence by the movement of a blink of the eye."[9] Revelation awakens the unique I-hood through the love of God and promotes a revolution in the human mode of being. It comprises a series of movements or conversions in the life of the believer: from "self-negation" to world "affirmation,"[10] from isolation to relation, from silence to love, from nothingness to fullness, and from reason to faith (this movement, to note, has corresponding implications in God).

Redemption followed this logic, yielding a second movement of reconnection. In redemption, man, woman, and world are united under God, with redemption defined as "the reciprocal belonging and the meeting of the three 'real' elements of the All, God world man."[11] Here, the loving relationship between the individual and God informs the loving relationship between the individual and the social and natural environments.[12] For present purposes, I emphasize that both the first transition from isolation to personal connection with God and the second, from isolation to the "loving community" under God, are grounded on love and relationship. Moreover, revelation and later redemption are based on speech—first on the dialogue of man and woman with God, and then on man and woman with their neighbors. A third movement of the relations between God and world, which Rosenzweig understands under the concept of creation, is beyond the scope of this work.

Rosenzweig's *The Star of Redemption*, in brief, provides an onto-existential analysis of existence and offers a conceptual solution: the problem is isolation and separateness, self-negation and solitude; the solution is a meaningful and loving relationship between God and the individual. However, as Rosenzweig was quick to realize, the coveted conversation of the individual with God—which was to save him or her from a hollowed existence—was an empty ideal for the large majority of the German Jewish world, who lived in an assimilated society. Rosenzweig founded the Frankfurt Jewish *Lehrhaus* in 1920 as a first attempt to solve this problem. The adult Jewish education center was to instruct the Jewish community, which since its emancipation had withdrawn slowly but steadily from Jewish life, in the basic principles of Jewish traditions, practices, and knowledge. It would provide the German Jewish community a structure within which a conversation with God was once again possible. His project of translation offered a second, literary solution: the translations, he thought, would provide the German-speaking Jewish community with a new medium through which to communicate with God. The translations offered the words of God in German, the only language German Jews understood. Rosenzweig's early short translations of a selection of prayers were a first attempt at this. The translation of Halevi's hymns and poems illustrated his growing commitment to this project, and it culminated in his collaboration with Buber in the translation of the Bible, the ultimate medium for God's words to humanity.

Jehuda Halevi was, in this context, an ideal candidate for Rosenzweig's enterprise of the renewal of Jewish life. One of the most important philosophers and poets of the Golden Age of Jewish culture in Spain, Halevi struggled in his philosophical book, *Kuzari*, with neo-Platonic notions of divinity. He rejected rational conceptions of religion and offered instead the ideas of revealed religion and personal God. In contrast to Maimonides' worldview, God was neither distant nor transcendent for Halevi, but accessible and present, and his extensive body of liturgical poems and hymns put this philosophical vision into practice. Halevi's poems express his wish for a loving intimacy with God and emphasize the foundational importance of religious experiences. The following lines, taken from his poem "Prayer," exhibit this vision: "Oh God You, when I extend my Prayer to you / hear my voice, my cry, oh God / . . . Oh God You, only You does all my thinking desire / and my soul speaks: my part, oh You God."[13]

Rosenzweig's Model of Translation as Foreignization

Yet strangely, even if the main purpose of Rosenzweig's book of translations was to promote better communication with God through Halevi's text, his translations were, in fact, not transparent—as his readers soon discovered—and made for challenging reading and comprehension. The book did not offer an easy introduction to Halevi's world, as his audience may have hoped. Still, this challenge was not accidental, as Rosenzweig explains in the opening lines of book's *Nachwort*: "Jehuda Halevi was a great Jewish poet in the Hebrew language . . . So it was not my aim to make the reader believe that Jehuda Halevi composed in German, nor that he composed Christian church songs, nor that he is a poet of today, even if only a *Familienblatt* poet of today—all this as far as I can see the aims of my predecessors in translation."[14] The Halevi book was written against the common tendency of some modern translators to make the original more understandable, more readable, and at times more coherent, than in the first language.

Halevi was a Jewish poet, not Christian; he lived in medieval Spain, not modern Germany; and he wrote *shirei qodesh* (devotional poems), not church songs. Rosenzweig's translation sought to emphasize these differences, departing from previous attempts to erase or mediate them.[15]

This editorial decision resulted directly from Rosenzweig's theory of translation. To explain, for Rosenzweig translations are not aimed to "dress the masterpieces of the past and of foreign lands in 'modern garb.'"[16] Rather, a translation needs to change something within the target language: German should not absorb the language of Halevi; instead, Halevi's words should be accorded a distinct place within it. The translation is "not to Germanize what is foreign, but rather to make foreign what is German."[17] Rosenzweig, in short, aimed to modify the German language with his translation. His text structured an alien terrain within German: "The translator makes himself the mouthpiece of the foreign voice, which he makes audible over the gulf of space or time. If the foreign voice has something to say, then the language must afterwards appear different from before."[18] In Halevi's case, this alienation had historical, theological, and cultural dimensions: the translations of Halevi, in Rosenzweig's plan, would add medieval Jewish and Arabic contours to modern Western culture. The practical implications of this plan were substantial. Rosenzweig presented a literal translation of Halevi in a manner that brings to mind the radical literalness of Hölderlin's famous Sophocles translations. Rosenzweig also insisted on maintaining the rhyme-form and meter of the Hebrew Spanish dialect. For him, the Hebrew metrics presented a form of "unnaturalness,"[19] and thus introduced into German "a really marked foreignness," which he strove to maintain.[20]

Besides their literary implications, Rosenzweig's translations had an important political function. The translations produced the necessary conditions for a kind of utopian political *alterity*. To understand this alterity, we need to see it in the context of predominant formulations in Rosenzweig's time of translation as an *act of integration*. I aam referring to a model prevalent among many translators of Hebrew to German, most notably the translations of the Bible by Moses Mendelssohn (1783) and Leopold Zunz (1838), who believed that translations formed a bridge not only between different languages, but also between different peoples and nations. In that tradition, translations afforded an interlinguistic conversation that promoted "a spiritual embrace—attempted or consummated—between the Jewish and German peoples," as defined in Naomi Seidman's *Faithful Renderings* (2006).[21] However, as Rosenzweig well knew, in practice, this model consistently encouraged translators to Germanize the Hebrew language. In effect, Jewish acculturation forced the suppression of Hebrew: these translators domesticated their Hebrew and silenced any signs of Jewish linguistic differences to facilitate the assimilation of Jews into German society.

Rosenzweig structured his translations differently. As noted earlier in the book, in *The Star of Redemption*, Rosenzweig rejected Jewish assimilation.[22] He insisted that the Jewish people formed a special order of human existence with a special role in world redemption. The Jews were to create a community anticipating redemption in the now. Rosenzweig's theory of translation echoed these principles. His translation was not an act of submission but one of infiltration: translation was to alter the target language. Rosenzweig's book enforced Jewish alterity on the new language: it demarcated within the German language an otherness that was never to be controlled. An alterity appropriate for the Jewish people. In that sense, Rosenzweig's translations resembled, according to Mara Benjamin's *Rosenzweig's Bible* (2009), "a form of 'cultural resistance' in which the sharp edges of the biblical or poetical original in Hebrew are not softened or smoothened but emphasized and celebrated."[23] Rosenzweig was not aiming at naïve multiculturalism. His goal was not to erase Hebrew, but to secure the place of Hebrew in German, of Judaism in Germany.

Rosenzweig's insistence on Jewish alterity was, however, different from the ideals of separatism prevalent in the interwar period and after the Second World War. Scholem, perhaps the greatest popularizer of such ideas, articulated this vision of German Jewish disintegration in his address to the World Jewish Congress in 1966, entitled "Jews and Germans." Briefly stated, Scholem stood for the argument that Jews, despite political declarations of emancipation, had never truly been allowed to join German society *qua* Jews, and even when they did try to assimilate or Germanize themselves and join German society as Germans, their "enthusiasm for self-sacrifice" was not rewarded but understood as "conspiratorial": "for it was precisely the desire on the side of the Jews to be absorbed by the Germans that hatred understood as a destructive maneuver against the life of the German people."[24] Faced with this impossible conundrum, Scholem felt that only the separation of Jews from Germans and from Germany would enable a different form of relationship. Echoing Max Brod's "distant love," Scholem suggested that an actual distance from Germany would allow the Jews to maintain their independent identity and, consequently, would provide the context for a different, more favorable connection with the Germans. The Zionist insistence on a national home for the Jews in Palestine provided such a geographical and existential gulf, across which he hoped that an honest conversation between equals would be possible again.

Rosenzweig's vision was, however, more nuanced. While Rosenzweig, like Scholem, constantly fought against the submission of Hebrew to German, and of Judaism to Christianity, he was suspicious of nationalistic political ideals. He rejected Jewish assimilation, but he also rejected Jewish segregation and acknowledged the value of Jewish life in exile. This stance informed his theory of translation. Rosenzweig's translations constructed edifices of Hebrew within German. In contrast to previous attempts at symbiosis between Jews and Germans, Rosenzweig insisted on constituting a realm of otherness *within* German. However, this otherness was not to politically disconnect the Jews from Germans, but to provide a metaphor for their relationship. In other words, in constructing an independent realm of Hebrew in German, Rosenzweig envisaged an equal standing for the Jewish people in Germany. His translations opened up a realm for the original within the new language that serves as an allegory for healthy and respectable communication. Translation granted the minor language a secure realm of alterity from which a conversation of counterparts was possible. It offered a realm in which Jews could be both Jews and Germans.

Recalling Scholem's derisive reaction to the Bible project as a gift to the Germans, we can see Rosenzweig's translation as a gift for the Jews who struggled to have both a Jewish identity *and* German humanistic culture.[25] Within the German language, Rosenzweig resurrected a literary domain for Jews that granted them an imagined realm from which to negotiate their "dual destiny: to live simultaneously within and beyond culture, within and beyond time."[26] Zionism produced geographic separation, but with Rosenzweig's translation, the Jewish people were able to stay in Germany while also keeping their foreignness, their identity. And it was the linguistic difference of translation that grounded the possibility of this unique conversation with their neighbors.

Rosenzweig and Benjamin on Translation and Revelation

In insisting on Hebrew forms in his translation to German language, Rosenzweig constructed a linguistic dimension of independence. This alienation paradoxically appeared to instantiate a hope for Jewish *conversation* with German, rather than an *absorption* of Jewishness into Germanness or a separation of Jews from Germany. As the following discussion makes clear, this linguistic alienation had more than political implications: it had a potential for *revelation*, one that Rosenzweig assumed all languages had.

Rosenzweig's unequivocal insistence on the alienation of Hebrew within the German translation was grounded in a theory of translation that resonated with Walter Benjamin's famous theory of language, as expressed in "The Task of the Translator" in 1923, a year after the publication of Rosenzweig's work on Halevi. The resemblance is apparent in Rosenzweig's invocation of pure language:

> Pure language—There is only one language . . . Upon this essential oneness of all language and upon the dependent commandment, namely that of universal human mutual understanding, is based the possibility as well as the task of translating, its Can, May and Shall. One can translate because in every language is contained the possibility of every other language; . . . and one should translate so that the day of that harmony [*Eintracht*] of languages, which can grow only in each individual language, not in the empty space "between" them, may come.[27]

Rosenzweig believed translation was possible because of the existence of an *Ursprache*. Separate languages, he argued, originated in a primary language, or pure language—a language that represented, for Rosenzweig, perfect communication: "universal human mutual understanding." Translation expressed this "kinship" between languages, to use one of Benjamin's famous terms:[28] it reconnected, much like in Benjamin's theory of translation, one language to another and afforded a glimpse at the original unity of all language in their Adamic origin (I follow here the common "metaphysical" interpretation of Benjamin essay). Specific languages might be inherently lacking, but the recombination of languages in translations offered, in Rosenzweig's words, the "renewal of a language through a foreign one."[29]

The alienation of the source language within the target language of German is crucial here since, as in Benjamin's theory, pure language is accessible only through the *intervention* of one language in the other. The differences between languages, which proper translations should express rather than mitigate, afford in this sense a revelatory insight of the (pure) language behind both languages. The task of the translator for both Benjamin and Rosenzweig was consequently to self-alienate the target language through the source language: the translator "must expand and deepen [his or her] language by means of the foreign language," as Benjamin writes.[30] The translator was to "release" language by incorporating another language within it.[31] An attempt to reconcile linguistic differences, to bring languages thoroughly together, was evidently counterproductive, as it was bound to erase this revelatory realm.[32]

There was, however, a fundamental disagreement between Benjamin and Rosenzweig on this point, and this forecloses any attempt to assign a Benjaminian theory of language and translation to Rosenzweig. While both Benjamin and Rosenzweig believed language was revelatory and translation allowed for that revelation, they significantly diverged in their understanding of the function of language in revelation. For Benjamin, language was revelatory in its ability to provide access to the spiritual essence (*geistige Wesen*) of the world, as I will discuss in more detail later in the book. In an earlier work on language, "On Language as Such and on the Language of Man" (1916), Benjamin proposes that revelation is concerned with the expression and the knowledge of this essence.[33] The story of the fall from the Garden of Eden expressed for Benjamin how the diversification of languages reflects our inability to truly express that essence: profane language provides only partial understanding and is inherently incapable of capturing essences like pure language. Translation was to reconstitute the possibility of expressing and knowing this lost spiritual essence. For Rosenzweig, on the other hand, "every word [was] a spoken word."[34] Language was essentially a channel for *conversation*. The Adamic language was unique, not as a way to relate to the world, but as a perfect medium for a dialogue.[35]

This difference between Benjamin's and Rosenzweig's theory of language is manifested perhaps most clearly in their understanding of profane language. For Benjamin, pure language was a vehicle for the spiritual essence of the world. The story of the Fall demonstrated how language changed its function and became a vehicle of communication. Language lost sight of truth and became a system of signs, replacing the immediacy of truth with mediated abstractions, thereby demoting the Adamic name to "the empty word," and language to "the abyss of prattle."[36] Rosenzweig, however, believed language was always meant to be spoken. For him, language after the Fall did not change in function, only in efficacy: it lost its universality and coherence. In short, for Benjamin, communication constituted the perversion of language in its profane form, whereas for Rosenzweig, it embodied the ultimate function of language per se.

Translation and Cyclical Time

Rosenzweig's theory of language and practice of translation assigned, as we have seen, a crucial function to alterity. The foreignization of the target language had a political function and a revelatory implication, and the preservation of alterity complicated common understandings of translation as a medium of integration. This foreignization is also significant for my arguments on the importance of a specifically Jewish form of repetition. To explain this, I turn to an entirely different kind of alterity in translation, one that concerns the liturgical function of the Halevi book. My argument is that Rosenzweig's translation constituted a second level of foreignization, one based on the introduction of a unique temporal index of dynamic repetition.

Liturgy and Halevi's Poems: The Jewish Calendar

To clarify the significance of temporality and alterity in Rosenzweig's translation, I first consider his published notes to Halevi's poems.

These short commentaries (some only a few lines) explain the poems, discuss their theological, philosophical, and historical contexts, and occasionally introduce the reader to the intricacies of the work of translation. In "The New Thinking," Rosenzweig emphasizes that the notes are, however, more than just simple explanations, as they provide "instructive examples of the practical application of the new thinking."[37] Even so, Rosenzweig was initially unsure about adding them to his book, saying to Buber in December 1922: "To translate ten lines is time better-served compared to writing long 'about' them. The public, naturally, wants the 'about' and disregards the most wonderful food (or worst, gobbles it down heedlessly), when the menu is not under his nose."[38] Rosenzweig was concerned that his commentaries would take the place of the poems. The public would find it easy to read his work "about" the poems and ignore the poems themselves. In the end, however, Rosenzweig decided to keep his commentaries. In fact, they came to define the text much more than might have been expected. Located at the end of the book, the notes established a new form of reading thanks to the liturgical function of Halevi's poems in the synagogue: "[These] poems originally of course are not intended for reading, but, as in all ages where poetry, or a part of the poetry, was a popular event, for performing.... The purpose is in this case a performance by the cantor and the singing along of the congregation at set points of the liturgical year."[39] Rosenzweig dedicates a long passage at the end of *Nachwort* to explain his editorial strategy in choosing the poems for his book. The list of Halevi's poems in Rosenzweig's time was considerably longer,[40] and after some consideration, Rosenzweig decided to select the poems for his book according to their *liturgical* function.[41] Halevi's poems were "composed for a certain circle of men and [were] received by them."[42] They were recited in the synagogues at important events and festivals, and his book would express this reality to the reader. To give an example, some poems represented the Shabbat; others were recited every day, and some only on certain holidays. The first poem, "Praised Be He" (*yehe shime'cha*), for another example, was an "introduction to the Kaddish prayer," and "Return" (*shiva*), was recited on the Day of Atonement.[43]

In this, I argue, the poems reproduced a temporal reality crucial to Rosenzweig's model of eternity within historical time in *The Star of*

Redemption: the cyclical repetition of the Jewish year. In Rosenzweig's philosophy, as noted in the previous chapter, the Jewish exilic reality was not accidental but fundamental to Jewish life—it allowed the Jewish people to anticipate redemption in the now. Cycles of repetition constituted this unique Jewish temporal orientation, and these cycles were manifested in the Jewish liturgical practices of the year. Halevi's poems, I suggest, exhibited, expressed, and instantiated this repetition. They concretized repetition for the German Jewish community. This is evident in a section from the *Nachwort* mentioned in the previous chapter: "the different poems indeed were then divided by a full, really a full year full of events of the life of the synagogue.... For this recurrence in the year is after all the essence of the festival. As in the final analysis repetition is altogether the great and only form which man has for expressing what is entirely true for him."[44] As a body of liturgical works recited in synagogues throughout the year, the poems comprised a cycle of one year. They prescribed the "full year" as the temporal presence of the "recurrence of the year," which, as I have argued, was fundamentally important to Jewish redemption.

This function of Halevi's poems posed a conceptual and aesthetic problem, one that brings us back to Rosenzweig's notes. The poems had temporal significance—originally, they were supposed to imitate the experience of Jewish year. However, this temporal peculiarity was dangerously obscured by the linear form of Rosenzweig's book. The linearity of the literary object went against the circular temporality that Halevi's poems were meant to exhibit. By writing the poems in a book, one after the other, Rosenzweig could have dangerously perverted their temporal function: instead of representing separate events of the Jewish year, and thereby manifesting the experience of the cyclical repetition of the year, the poems were at risk of reflecting a monotonous linearity. Rosenzweig therefore had to devise a particular mode of writing to safeguard the relations of the poems to Jewish temporality. In essence, he had to prevent the reader from acting like a reader: if the everyday readers read poems linearly one after the other, Rosenzweig had to design a method that would allow them to experience the poems as *events in cyclical time.*

Rosenzweig's Notes: The Production of Repetition

Rosenzweig accomplished the transformation of the poems to events in cyclical time with his notes. In Rosenzweig's book, the notes are more than just commentaries: they form a series of dams and breaks within the book that force the reader to stop before moving to the next poem. Rosenzweig constructed these dams in the book by insisting that the notes and the poems must form a unified whole, as he explains to Buber in a letter from January 1924: "The coherence of the poems and the notes, however, will be rendered impressive in a much stronger way. Namely, the table of contents in the front, that catches the reader's eye through its symmetry, will include for every poem two numbers: one in Roman type and one in italics, the first leads to the poem itself, the second to the note."[45] The notes were not placed immediately after the poem but in the end of the book. And since the reader must read the poem *together* with the relevant note, as Rosenzweig insists, this forced the reader to turn away from the poem and jump to the note at the end of the book before reading the next poem. This movement is not simply mechanical. The notes are in German, while the poems are written in Rosenzweig's exceptional German-Hebrew phrasing. The poems are artistic and lyrical, but the notes are academic. In reading the poem and the note together, the reader is therefore asked to transition back and forth between the world of Halevi and that of Rosenzweig, from medieval Spain to Germany, from poetry to philosophical scholarship, and from the beginning to the end of the book.

This reading produced an effect that supposedly mirrors the experience of the Jewish year that the poems originally performed. As Rosenzweig comments, "But the main purpose [of the notes] is the other: to induce the reader to take each poem as a thing for itself, just as the poet has composed it as *a thing for itself and just as the singer and the hearer, in the place for which it is meant, sang and heard it, sings and hears it, will sing and hear it.*"[46] On one level, Rosenzweig declares that the notes are meant to transform the consumer into a reader—a way to encourage a meaningful relationship between the reader and each and every poem. In Rosenzweig's terms, the notes motivate readers "to consume the poems not like cherries but like peaches."[47] I argue, however, that these breaks and dams between the poems serve a second, *temporal* purpose. Indeed, the notes separate the poems. They essentially establish each poem's *distinctness* and individuality. Yet this separation is not simply to allow the reader to focus on the content of the specific poem. Rather, the book is structured in such a way to help the reader re-experience the liturgical function of the poems. In transforming the series of poems into individual literary entities, the notes transfigure the poems into *events in time* and effectuate the experience of reading the poems in the synagogue throughout the Jewish year. The divisions reproduce Jewish repetitive temporality in an artificial form: the reader can experience the poems as singular units, and he or she can therefore go back to the specific time and place for which each poem was designed, to the time when each poem was "sung and heard." Rosenzweig contends with his readers reading like readers: the insertion of the notes and the interruptions of the text dislocate the reader from the present and reconnect him or her to the Jewish calendar. The notes introduce the reader to the originally intended temporal and spatial index of the poems: they reconnect the reader to the "original time" and actualize the experience of the cycle of the year, and, in that, according to Rosenzweig's philosophy, they have *messianic implications*.

The structure of the book provides another and perhaps a more concrete experience of dynamic repetition, in that, according to Rosenzweig, the poems resemble each other. In the *Nachwort*, he notes, "It is not the case that just whole parts of a poem are repeated . . . but what is repeated are rather thoughts and images. Not merely in the individual poem, but precisely whole poems appear in many ways as variations of set types."[48] The poems, claims Rosenzweig, rehearse the same religious content in different ways. Rosenzweig admits that these repetitions may be "aesthetically less delightful,"[49] but they serve an important role: they deliver an actual experience of repetition central to the Jewish experience of time. The reading of Rosenzweig's book is intended to be cyclical: the reader is meant to read one poem, go to the end of the book to read the relevant note, then return to the middle of the book to read another poem, which partly repeated the previous poems, and then go back to the end. This cyclical movement of reading the same "basic" poem over and over again realizes in practice Jewish cyclical temporality: by reading the poems with breaks in the middle, and not one immediately after the other, the reader is able to experience how the poems repeat each other. Thus, instead of featuring a movement *from one to the other*, the notes make the poems into individual units that *repeat each other*.[50]

The same cyclical motion informs the general structure of the book, as Rosenzweig notes in a 1924 letter to Buber: "Regarding the sequence—I conceive [*empfinde*] the organization of the book differently. That is, not going from the front to the back, but rather from the covers [*den Deckeln*] to the middle."[51] Rosenzweig wrote a book that rejects linear form: "I definitely don't want the snotty [*schnodderig*] afterword as the end of the book," he remarks, "but rather to have the last note as the end. The afterword works only if it is all chained up back and front as it is now."[52] The book was not to start with an introduction, nor to end with an afterword, but rather to start with the poems, to end with the notes, and to have the afterword as a bridge between them. This structure replaced linearity with circularity. The reader was expected to read the book "from the covers to the middle": each dyad of poem-and-note brings him or her closer to the middle of the book in a cyclical motion, thus echoing the Jewish repetition that places "untroubled and intact ring upon ring round the trunk of its eternal life."[53]

Sadly, this critical function of repetition is missing in the third and last edition of Rosenzweig's Halevi book. In the first and second editions, published during Rosenzweig's life, the notes were at the end of the book, as was his *Nachwort*. The editors of the third edition of the book (published in Rosenzweig's *Gesammelte Schriften*), however, initiated a few crucial changes: they inserted the notes in the body, each after its respective poem, and they moved the *Nachwort* to the beginning. Both changes were made to simplify the reading of the book; as Raphael Rosenzweig explains in his introduction to the text, it was done with "the intention to facilitate the engagement of the reader with the material and the translation style."[54] However, this well-intentioned change had the effect of distorting the cyclical temporality, and thereby the messianic function of the book, which Rosenzweig insisted on and the first editions accordingly generated. While the notes were still an important part of the book, their effectiveness in generating a different temporality was diminished, since the reader was no longer asked to change his or her focus from the poems to the end of the book, from one page to a different page, from one temporal modus to another.[55]

Messianism and Translation:
Rosenzweig and the Production of Alterity

Rosenzweig's Halevi book presents a series of cycles and repetitions. First, the poems deliver an experience of festivals and other events in the synagogue, and, consequently, of the cyclical repetition of the year. Second, by repeating each other, the poems present "small" cycles of repetition. Third, the book is structured in a cyclical form, moving "from the covers to the middle." These repetitions have a special function, when considered in the context of Rosenzweig's theory of Jewish temporality: they concretize the Jewish liturgical year and as a consequence reproduce the conditions necessary for the Jewish anticipation of redemption.

Thinking on the implications of Rosenzweig's translation in terms of alterity, I argue that the book thus creates a second layer of alterity. In his translation of Halevi, Rosenzweig foreignizes German not only through the interpolation of Jewish meter and rhyme, but also, and perhaps most radically, through the introduction of *Jewish temporality*. The book inserts a temporal code of repetition into German linear time: it reproduces within a German context a specific kind of a temporal modus that encapsulates Jewish time. Consequently, in contrast to the conventional view of the function of translation (i.e., to bring two cultures together), his work on Halevi encourages the separation of the Jews in both literary and temporal terms.

In Rosenzweig's corpus of philosophical works and translations, the Jehuda Halevi book provided him with a unique messianic opportunity. While his philosophical work analyzed Jewish temporal modus, his translation of Halevi made it available to the Jewish community of his time. Rosenzweig's translation provided more than an opportunity to renew Jewish life: it allowed the Jewish assimilated community an opportunity to experience a different temporal existence that Rosenzweig believed was unique to them. Through his book, even those Jews who never attended synagogues in Germany were able to experience the festivals of the year and thus to participate, even in a small measure, in the Jewish cycle of the year.

Rosenzweig believed that "every translation is a messianic act, which brings redemption nearer," and this directly affected his work on Halevi. Compared to Benjamin, for whom the revelatory potential of translation was its ability to offer fleeting glimpses of the divine unity of the Adamic language, Rosenzweig had a much more radical vision in mind. While approving the notion that translation from one language to another provides an image of revelatory language, he nevertheless designed his translation of Halevi's poems to do more. His book re-grounded the Jewish temporal alienation from history. His translation was meant to not only show something inherently beyond humanity's reach, but also to effectively intervene in Jewish life in modernity. The translation of Halevi marked a moment of alterity within the German tradition. It had more than the potential for sparks of revelation: the Halevi translation was intended to advance Jewish eternity *in factum*.

Intermezzo
Abrahamic Variations in Kafka and Kierkegaard

One evening after his second visit to the courthouse, Josef K, the protagonist of Kafka's monumental *The Trial* (*Der Process*), accidently stumbles into a scene that profoundly upsets him. On his way from his office to the main staircase of his office building, he hears groans coming from a closed junk-storage room (*Rumpelkammer*). As he opens the door, K finds a room with a low ceiling, lit by a candle on a shelf. The floor is covered with old printed forms and ink-bottles. Inside he sees three men bending down because of the low ceiling. Two of them, whom he later recognizes as Franz and Willem, the guards who arrested him a few days earlier, are about to be given a thrashing, apparently because of K's complaints to the examining magistrate about their behavior that day, or so they tell him. A third, unknown person stands next to them with a cane in his hand. K immediately tries to intercede and help his former offenders: "'No,' said K, staring at them, 'I didn't complain, I just said what had happened in my apartment. And your behavior wasn't exactly irreproachable either.'"[1] This explanation leads to a long series of questions and justifications, confessions and exculpations that do not prevent the beating of Officer Franz. In the end, K even facilitates the beating, by throwing Franz, who tries to hang onto him, onto the floor and sending away the office messengers who come running after hearing Franz's screams.

The next day, the events of the previous night keep haunting K: he "could not get the guards out of his mind. He couldn't concentrate on his work, and to get it all done he had to stay a little longer in the office than the previous evening."[2] On his way home that night, K sees a sight that disturbs him even more than the one of the previous evening. Walking in the same corridor, K opens the door of the junk-storage room "as if out of habit." However, instead of the darkness he expects to see, he discovers the exact same scene he saw the day before: "Everything was unchanged, was just as it had been when he had opened the door the previous evening: the printed forms and ink-bottles immediately behind the door, the thrasher with his cane, the guards, still fully dressed, the candle on the shelf."[3] This time, however, K's response is different: as the guards begin to moan, he does not intervene but immediately closes the door and escapes to the messengers' office. After a few moments in the safety of their company, K finally gets his courage up and goes home, "weary and his mind a blank."[4]

Many have asked about the nature of K's experience of repetition. Why does Kafka's K have to witness the same experience of beating, and why do these scenes need to be exactly the same? Is it to illustrate the timelessness of the law, as no time seems to have passed between the first and second occurrences, or is it to concretize the endless repetitive nature of the procedures of the law? Or maybe something else, inherent in repetition itself, captures Kafka's imagination. Indeed, it is worth recalling that Kafka's oeuvre is dotted with various incidences and kinds of repetition. A structure of repetition, to give an example, forms the piecemeal construction of the Chinese wall in Kafka's famous parable; repetition informs his *The Metamorphosis* (*Die Verwandlung*), as each of its three acts depicts Gregor Samsa's repetitive failed attempts to reach out to and reconnect with his estranged family; repetition appears in Kafka's many doppelgängers: for example, the three boarders in *The Metamorphosis*, the doorkeepers in "Before the Law," and the assistants in *The Castle* (*Das Schloß*); it defines the relations between different stories by Kafka—"Before the Law" famously reiterates and duplicates *The Trial*—as well as the relations between Kafka's parables and the biblical narrative; finally, the repetition of words, signs, and voices is also pervasive.

This long series of repetitions has not escaped Kafka's readers, who for the most part interpret his repetition metaphorically as a sign of being stuck or trapped, or as a sign of an uncanny form of modern alienation. One common interpretation is that Kafka's protagonists are consumed by repetitions insofar as their world is meaningless and beyond repair, and attempts to change it are inconsequential and nonsensical. Because of that, they seem to be repeating the same experience rather than evolving or changing. This is in line with the traditional interpretations of Nietzsche's eternal return.[5] In other readings of Kafka, repetition is connected to traumatic experience, as Stanley Corngold argues in *The Commentator's Despair* (1973): "The form of Kafka's fiction is circular; his stories are marked by a repetition of a trauma."[6]

My claim is that repetition is much more than a metaphor for being stuck or for modern trauma. Rather, Kafka's stories constitute a laboratory for the research of repetition: he uses repetition to disturb common notions and abstract generalities. For Kafka, repetitions are not aimed at making an idea clearer, nor do they simply accentuate a message or reaffirm a belief. Repetition, instead, ruptures and distracts identity, continuity, and sameness. In what follows, I elucidate these preliminary claims about the place of repetition in Kafka by investigating a repetitive series of stories about Abraham and the story of the *Akedah*, which he wrote in a June 1921 letter to his friend Robert Klopstock, whom he met the previous year when they were both treated for tuberculosis. This letter, written largely in response to Kierkegaard's *Fear and Trembling*, offers an example of how repetition is used to produce differences, destructing and rupturing homogenous reality and identity, and how it eventually relates to gestures of messianism in Kafka.

Kafka, in his retelling of one of Judaism's foundational stories, rejects the Christian reading of Kierkegaard, while at the same time implementing a different, messianic vision of history. He subverts Kierkegaard's vision of Abraham's singular experience by suggesting several alternative descriptions of the biblical story of the *Akedah*. These descriptions form a repetitive structure in Kafka's letter, which disturbs Kierkegaard's reading of the biblical story: the repetition of the stories produces difference and multiplicity in the figure of Abraham, whereas Kierkegaard insists on Abraham's unicity. Importantly, in this literary maneuver, Kafka is grappling with the two main trajectories of repetition in modern philosophy: he utilizes a model of repetition which echoes Deleuze's "repetition-as-difference" to counteract Kierkegaard's vision of Abraham—a hero of "repetition-as-recollection forward" next to Job.

"A Next-Door Neighbor": Kafka on Kierkegaard

Kafka first took an interest in Kierkegaard in the summer of 1913, after getting hold of *Buch des Richters*, a selection of Kierkegaard's auto-biographical notes that was translated into German in 1905.[7] The book documented Kierkegaard's existential grapplings and his failed engagement with Regina Olsen, which, in Kafka's eyes, resonated with his own conflicts in his engagement with Felice Bauer. For both Kafka and Kierkegaard, marriage was an ideal and in large part a remedy for their despair and melancholy, but also a reality that was impossible because of their artistic vocation. Kafka notes this affinity enthusiastically in a diary entry on the day he got Kierkegaard's book: "As I suspected, [Kierkegaard's] case, despite essential differences, is very similar to mine, at least he is on the same side of the world. He bears me out like a friend."[8] Inspired by Kierkegaard, Kafka decided to draft a letter to his fiancée's father "which, if I have the strength, I will send off tomorrow."[9] The letter was written in an apologetic tone and gave numerous reasons why marriage was impossible for him, foreseeing his future doubts about his object of love.

Four years later, between fall 1917 and spring 1918, Kierkegaard recaptured Kafka's interest. After being diagnosed with tuberculosis in August 1917, and following his second and final break with Bauer, Kafka spent several months at his sister's house in Zürau, where he was able to continue reading Kierkegaard. We find most of Kafka's references to Kierkegaard from that period in his letters and in several paragraphs in the fourth notebook of *The Blue Octavo Notebooks* (*Oktavhefte*), a series of eight notebooks which Kafka wrote at the time alongside his diaries. The *Octavo Notebooks* chronicle Kafka's philosophical and theological interests and fittingly include his ruminations about Kierkegaard.

Kafka was especially attracted to the figure of Abraham in Kierkeg-aard's *Fear and Trembling*, which, by portraying the existential crisis of Abraham in the days and hours before the Binding of Isaac, addresses the problems then preoccupying him.[10] In particular, Kafka, who hesi-tated to make the final decision to end his relationship with Bauer, was deeply impressed by Kierkegaard's depiction of Abraham's courage and determination.[11] However, unlike Kafka's earlier enthusiasm, the second period of interest featured a more nuanced understanding of the philosopher and increasing criticism of him and his portrayal of Abraham. In January 1918, while Kafka still reports to Brod that he is "reading passionately" *Either-Or* (written, he notes in admiration, "with the sharpest of pens") he also carefully remarks on the book's "hatefulness" which drives one to "despair" to a degree that "even the healthiest lungs feel short of breath."[12] The language is harsher and the disappointment is even more apparent in Kafka's remarks on *Fear and Trembling* in another letter to Brod two months later: "[Kierkegaard] doesn't see the ordinary man . . . and paints the monstrous Abraham in the clouds."[13] In the same letter, Kafka announces that his "'physical'" identification with Kierkegaard has "evaporated. It's as if a next-door neighbor had turned into a distant star, in respect both to my admiration and to a certain cooling of my sympathy."[14]

The disillusionment with Kierkegaard culminated a few years later in a 1921 letter on Abraham to Robert Klopstock, to whom he had given a copy of *Fear and Trembling*. In this letter, Kafka counters Kierkegaard's Abraham with his own version of biblical story of the *Akedah*, one that, as Theodor Adorno aptly notes, clarifies how "Kafka used motifs from Kierkegaard's *Fear and Trembling* not as heir but as critic."[15] I cite Kafka's letter at length:

> I can imagine another Abraham, who, to be sure, would not make it all the way to patriarch, not even to old-clothes dealer [*Altkleiderhändler*]— who would be as ready to carry out the order for the sacrifice as a waiter would be ready to carry out his orders, but who would still never manage to perform the sacrifice because he cannot get away from home, he is indispensable, the farm needs him, there is always something that must be attended to, the house isn't finished. But until the house is finished, until he has this security behind him, he cannot get away. . . .
>
> Next day: Have been meditating a good deal about this Abraham, but these are old stories, no longer worth discussing; especially not the real Abraham; . . . It was different with the above-mentioned Abrahams: they stand on their building sites and suddenly are supposed to go to Mount Moriah. Possibly they do not even have a son and are called upon to sacrifice him. These are impossibilities [*Unmöglichkeiten*] and Sarah is right to laugh. All we can do is suspect that these

men are deliberately not finishing their houses, and—to name a very great example—are hiding their faces in magical trilogies [*Magischen Trilogien*] so as not to have to lift their eyes and see the mountain that stands in the distance.

But another Abraham. One who certainly wants to carry out the sacrifice properly and in general correctly senses what the whole thing is about but cannot imagine that he is the one meant, the repulsive old man [*widerliche alte Mann*], and his dirty boy. He does not lack the true faith [*wahre Glaube*], for he has this faith; he wants to sacrifice in the proper manner, if he could only believe he was the one meant. He is afraid that he will, to be sure, ride out as Abraham and his son, but on the way will turn into Don Quixote.... It is as if the best student were solemnly to receive a prize at the end of the year and in the expectant silence, the worst student, because he has misheard, comes forward from his dirty back bench and the whole class falls apart.[16]

When we read Kafka's version of the biblical story, we cannot avoid the impression that Kierkegaard's Abraham was a fanatic "murderer, and by antiphrasis, a Cain."[17] *Fear and Trembling* is often read as eulogy to Abraham's faith, resoluteness, and bravery. The book famously praises the difficulties involved in the suspension of the ethical and acclaims Abraham's infinite resignation. Kafka, however, rejects Kierkegaard's "monstrous" Abraham. His letter points to the essence of the story as he judges it, that is, that Abraham was *willing to kill*, not sacrifice (as Kierkegaard insists), his son. Unlike Kierkegaard's Abraham, who heeds God's command, Kafka's Abrahams delay their response. Abraham is not a knight of faith, but an ordinary man, a waiter, an ugly old man, or the worst student, who, in contradistinction to Abraham's submission, has too many duties back home, or is too ugly and dirty to believe that God could have called upon him. The irony of Kafka's Abraham is vital to understand this tale, especially when contrasted to Kierkegaard's solemn narration. So is his humor.[18]

In his essay "Abraham, The Other" (2003), Derrida notes the tactics of postponement and deferral used by Kafka's Abrahams. Rather than being an epitome of compliance and resignation, in Derrida's reading, Kafka's Abraham sets an example of a radical refusal to enter a discussion, to communicate, or to participate: "one must know (and this is the first Abrahamic teaching, prior to any other) that if everything begins for us with the response, if everything begins with the 'yes' implied in all responses, then any response, even the most modest, the most mundane, of responses, remains an acquiescence given to some self-presentation."[19] In short, in waiting and ultimately refusing even to answer, Kafka's Abrahams suspend divine law and thereby offer a glimpse at a different, radical relations to the political, which "Before the Law" and many other stories and parables by Kafka supposedly explore.[20] In what follows, I would like to consider an interrelated issue concerning Kafka's Abrahams. What interests me in Kafka's letter is the fact that Kafka decides to write *three* different versions of the Abrahamic tale to Klopstock.

Kafka's letter on Abraham presents a myriad of repetitions. His letter, in a way, repeats Kierkegaard's book, at least in recounting Kierkegaard's version of the story and reframing it; both Kafka's and Kierkegaard's Abrahams represent "repetitions" of a sort of the biblical story of the patriarch. In Kierkegaard's book, the story of Abraham also repeats several times: Kierkegaard narrates four different stories in the exordium to *Fear and Trembling*.[21] So, why does Kafka use repetitions? Is it only to nod to, or maybe even mock, Kierkegaard's own repetitive series of Abrahams?

Abraham's Doubles: Deferral, Refusal, and Self-Determination

Let me begin with Kafka's decision to write three and not two versions of the Abrahamic story—the "prompt waiter," the "other Abrahams," and the "ugly old man." My suggestion is that in writing more than two versions of the biblical plot, Kafka opened his letter to the possibility of a series of many more such stories. If there were only two Abrahams, the letter could be understood as presenting two concrete possibilities; an either-or logic. Abraham could be this or that. Kafka, however, recounts three different plots. With three variations, rather than two, it is clear that Kafka is organizing his stories according to a repetitive structure. The trio of stories can be seen as merely the first in a longer series of stories; three suggests "and possibly more" in a way that two does not. In other words, in opening up his letter to more than a dualism of yes and no, this or that, here or there, Kafka hints that his Abrahams participate *in potentia* in infinite multiplicity.

Earlier in this book, I argued that in modern Jewish thought, repetition produces different effects on several levels. I noted two major trajectories of repetition in modern philosophy: the "repetition-as-recollection forward" of Kierkegaard and Heidegger, which Rosenzweig echoes in *The Star of Redemption*, and the "repetition-as-difference" of Nietzsche and Deleuze. For the latter, repetition undermines a sense of homogenous reality; it produces differences, shifts, and breaks and distracts the course of predetermined causal relations. Repetition generates newness and uncovers previously unforeseen conceptual and historical relations, hidden by mundane reality. Kafka's repetitions in his letter to Klopstock echo these patterns. Kafka, I argue, applies to his poetics a logic of repetition and difference that recalls the logic of Nietzsche and Deleuze and is also found in several parts of Benjamin's oeuvre and Freud's ruminations on repetition in *Moses and Monotheism*. More concretely, the repetitive structure of the Abrahamic tale reveals variations, differences, or moments of heterogeneity in the figure of the Jewish patriarch; these variations and differences serve as a second layer of the refusal of a divine command.

The repetition of the figure of Abraham in Kafka's letter disrupts a sense of the biblical hero as consistent and unitary. If Kierkegaard's Abraham is a person focused on a clear ethical and religious dilemma, Kafka's repetitive variations of the biblical story multiply and unsettle the coherent figure of Abraham. The variations dissolve the integrity of Abraham: in suggesting different, multiple stories, Kafka suggests that there is no cohesive figure of Abraham, only discrete incidents, separate parts, and different histories that can never be reconciled. Kafka's variety of repetitions breaks down the figure of Abraham into different biographies and diverging accounts. His Abrahams refuse God's call differently, and, in that, they represent different versions of the same plot. These differences are constitutive of Kafka's letter. Owing to the disparate repetitions, for example, the motivation of Abraham's actions is unclear: while the first Abraham is "indispensable" and has to stay and to tend to his "household," the third Abraham is eager "to perform the sacrifice altogether" but just cannot believe "he was the one meant." The range of variations also denies the basic outline of the story: in the second story there are many Abrahams, and they don't even have a son, a fact that makes the interaction with God seem ridiculous: "These are impossibilities, and Sarah was right to laugh." Thus, if Kafka's Abraham letter is an example of the most radical form of refusal possible, as Derrida claims, Kafka's repetitive variations present a second layer to the refusal: in repeating the figure of Abraham, Kafka rejects the notion of an integrated, self-identical Abraham. Kafka's Abraham refuses God not only because he does not answer, but also because the repetition of the story goes against the notion of a unitary figure *able* to answer in a cohesive, organized voice. This second kind of refusal directly relates to Kierkegaard's Abrahamic ideal.

As noted, Kierkegaard wrote several versions of the biblical story: four were documented in the exordium and many others in his diaries.[22] The four in the book basically follow the original biblical narrative; each story introduces a different variation and emphasizes a different aspect of Kierkegaard's understanding. To give an example, in the first story, Kierkegaard focuses on the scene at the mountain, where Abraham violently throws Isaac to the ground, his gaze one of "sheer terror," crying that this whole thing is entirely according to his "desire."[23] In the second story, Abraham acts differently: he is silent, even traumatized by the experience on the mountain; and in the third, Abraham rides alone to the mountain after the *Akedah* to ask for God's forgiveness, for "he had been willing to sacrifice Isaac."[24]

These repetitions of the story of the *Akedah* have attracted the attention of Kierkegaard's readership.[25] Most agree that the different narratives of Abraham depict examples of "faithless Abrahams."[26] In line with Kierkegaard's religious existentialism, *Fear and Trembling* does not provide a simple, specific, and concrete formula for the kind of faith and infinite resignation Kierkegaard has in mind, and Abraham embodies but a long and detailed excursion into the complicated and paradoxical condition of spiritual life. Kierkegaard accomplishes this in a series of stories of Abraham, whose outcome is not faith but rather a *failure* to achieve the faith Kierkegaard valorizes. Rather than describing faith conceptually or directly, Kierkegaard resorts to a series of examples that provide clear insight into what faith is *not* and by that portray an "outline" of true faith.[27] As Edward Mooney notes in *Knights of Faith and Resignation* (1991), "by considering skewed variations, [Kierkegaard] circles from the *outside*, as it were, isolating the narrative-symbolic space within which an effective interpretation will fall."[28] Kierkegaard, by means of repetition, zeroes in on the spiritual experience of Abraham. This is a form of attunement:[29] the repetition of the story of Abraham is supposed to create a harmonious vision of Abraham's faith through a series of examples of different Abrahams, none as "great" as the biblical patriarch.[30]

In *Fear and Trembling*, the repetition of the story of Abraham helps us understand the experience of Abraham because Kierkegaard's stories are all different "examples"[31] of the same plot. Together they chart his vision of Abraham, one that he is unable to explain or exhibit directly. Kafka, in contrast, turns to repetition to *dismantle* the unitary representation of Abraham. His variations on Abraham do not produce harmony. His letter does not provide better insight into Abraham but emphasizes the differences between his fabulated Abrahams. Put otherwise, Kierkegaard's variations produce an imaginary space for understanding Abraham, while Kafka's variations preclude such an understanding. The recipient of the letter, Klopstock, is not able to understand who Abraham is, nor can he identify with or admire his dedication. The letter produces confusion, perhaps disorients its reader(s).

To briefly summarize the argument, in *Fear and Trembling*, Kierkegaard celebrates Abraham's resoluteness and decisiveness. His book emphasizes the fact that Abraham answered God and left his home without hesitation and not expecting reward. Compared to the rest of humanity—in a state of "despair," and suffering from the "emptiness hid beneath everything" and "an eternal oblivion," Abraham is a "hero,"[32] "the greatest of all,"[33] who "*did not doubt*."[34] Resoluteness and lack of doubt are the centerpieces of Kierkegaard's eulogy to Abraham: "Cheerfully, freely, confidently, loudly he answered: Here I am . . . He hurried as if to a celebration, and early in the morning he was at the appointed place on Mount Moriah."[35] Kafka, I argued, openly transgresses against this understanding of Abraham, first in suggesting a series of Abrahams who delay their response to God's call. In contrast to the happy willingness of Kierkegaard's Abraham, Kafka's Abrahams engage in anything but God's mission, and, in that, they present a radical form of refusal, as Derrida notes. The repetitive variations of Kafka's Abrahams complement this logic of refusal, by inducing distraction and ambiguity into the figure of Abraham. Furthermore, in this particular enactment of repetition, Kafka also subverts the logic of self-control and determination that Abraham symbolizes. If Kierkegaard's Abraham is self-possessed and acts without doubt, Kafka utilizes his series of Abrahams to doubt the figure of Abraham, to rupture the conviction suggested by Abraham. Rather than one man determined to accomplish his mission, Abraham becomes many different figures in Kafka's variations. These figures experience different and sometimes opposing realities; they act differently and from different motivations, thus questioning the directedness and resolve of Kierkegaard's Abrahamic ideal. In the next section, I address another aspect of Kafka's letter—the messianic implications of his repetitive narration.

Gestures of Messianism:
Abraham and the "Uniformity of this World"

For Kierkegaard, who published *Fear and Trembling* on the same day as *Repetition*, Abraham is, like Job, a hero of repetition on a theological/ Christian register. Abraham experiences repetition in his relationship with God—he "got a son a second time."[36] This is the core of the Abrahamic absurd: Abraham is resigned in terms of the immediate loss of his son but has complete and unshaken faith that he will have his son back. As in the story of Job, repetition structures his relations with God. Kafka, who read *Repetition* when his "similarity" with Kierkegaard had "evaporated,"[37] applies the philosophical principles of modern repetition to the story, albeit in a way that turns it on its head. Notably, despite his focus on Kierkegaard's Abraham, Kafka utilizes a principle of repetition closer to that of Nietzsche and Deleuze. Unlike Kierkegaard, Kafka is not thinking of repetition in terms of rearticulating the present by reappropriating the past. Rather, by using repetition closer to the "repetition-as-difference" trajectory, he aims to distract the uniformity and unicity of Abraham and, by so doing, to resurrect the story of the *Akedah* from the Christian interpretation of Kierkegaard.

In the previous pages, I noted the destructive function of Abraham's repetition—suggesting that Kafka's letter breaks down the uniform figure of Abraham, thereby subverting Kierkegaard's Abrahamic ideal of decidedness and self-control. Let us now consider the positive, constructive aspect of the letter. In Kierkegaard's *Fear and Trembling*, Abraham represents a singularity that cannot be comprehended by or reduced to logical or ethical concepts or frameworks of thought. Abraham's singular experience is completely out of context. It is absolutely and categorically unique. "Abraham *cannot* speak," Kierkegaard declares again and again in *Fear and Trembling*.[38] Kierkegaard's models of repetition reflect this logic of singularity. As in Job's story, in which repetition presents a form of freedom from historical necessity, repetition in the Abrahamic tale creates a sphere that buffers Abraham from reality and through which Abraham is able to "forge his personality."[39] The purpose of Kierkegaard's retelling of Abraham's story in *Fear and Trembling* is to mark this irreducible singularity. His stories circle around it, marking the limit between Abraham's unique experience and human shared reality, as if forming a ring around Abraham.

Kafka's repetitive variations on Abraham produce a multiplicity that undermines this singularity. His variations open Abraham up to differences rather than closing him. If Kierkegaard takes the context out of Abraham's story, Kafka reinserts it. Repetition, in Kafka, is enacted in a series of stories that do not illuminate Abraham's singular experience but provide endless possible *different* plots for Abraham's story. Rather than simply disrupting the figure of Abraham, the Kafkan variations expand Kierkegaard's story of Abraham; they make space for different possible meanings; they contextualize and animate Abraham. In repetition, Abraham "speaks": the towering, unimaginable story of Abraham, which the Bible tells and Kierkegaard's book amplifies, breaks down into a series of small, almost inconsequential stories that bring Abraham back to human reality. Put more generally, Kafka's repetition participates in the modern project of repetition of Nietzsche and Deleuze precisely because of Kafka's rejection of the ideal. Kafka's Abraham reintroduces the concrete, the material, in place of Kierkegaard's abstractions. In telling this story again and again, Kafka is able to transform Abraham's unreal figure to many concrete, worldly, and lively individuals. As in the work of Nietzsche and Deleuze, his repetitive stories generate clarity and actuality: Abraham is a waiter and he must work; he is a student conscious of his limitations; he is a builder who must build his house. All these stories take place in a simple, "ethical" reality in Kierkegaard's terms, one the recipient of the letter can and should comprehend.

This unraveling of Kierkegaard's Abraham in Kafka's letter suggests a messianic vision. To explain this vision, I remind readers of the common notion that, in the monotheistic tradition, Abraham symbolizes the point of origin, the beginning of Jewish history (in contrast, Freud's *Moses and Monotheism*, as I discuss in chapter 7, sees in Moses the true and only patriarch of the Jewish people). My argument is that in thinking differently about the figure of Abraham, Kafka suggests a way to think differently about Jewish history and, in fact, about history in general. That is, if we are used to thinking of history as predetermined and homogeneous, as singular as Abraham's experience, Kafka's letter, in conjuring different, other Abrahams, sets an example of how we can recognize in a single moment of history different histories that suggest different versions of Judaism or even humanity. This is not a rearticulation of the past from the position of the present, as in Kierkegaard's model of "repetition-as-recollection forward," but an opening up of the present moment itself to different possible meanings. The present of Abraham, in Kafka's reading of the biblical story, is open to new, unforeseen interpretations; it is fundamentally multidimensional. The same, I argue, may apply to history.

Taking my cue from Kafka's Abraham, I suggest a triple movement in the figure of Abraham: in the Torah, Abraham represents the foundation of Jewish history; in *Fear and Trembling*, Abraham represents ontological singularity, a unitary figure of resolute faith. Kafka's Abrahams takes both into account, but in reverse form. In contextualizing the figure of Abraham, Kafka puts forward a reading that could be seen as inserting multiplicity back to Abraham, that is, back to history. The variations on Abraham provide a model for recognizing in the unity of the historical moment threads of differences and other possibilities. This brings to minds Kafka's diary entries about Kierkegaard's Abraham in *The Octavo Notebooks*:

Abraham falls victim to the following illusion: he cannot stand the uniformity of this world. Now the world is known, however, to be uncommonly various, which can be verified at any time by taking a handful of world and looking at it closely. Thus this complaint at the uniformity of the world is really a complaint at not having been mixed profoundly enough with the diversity of the world.[40]

Abraham, Kafka claims, could not "stand the uniformity of this world." In Kafka's letter, however, every different moment in history has the potential for a different history, just as Abraham's binding of Isaac, a seemingly singular moment in history, can be subject to wildly dissimilar variations. The messianic in Kafka's letter lies exactly here, in seeing the historical moment as already encompassing concrete, material, different histories. The opening of Abraham's story to different histories suggests a mode of existence not captured by historical necessities. It marks a messianic impulse that takes shape in the perception of differences in history rather than uniformity and semblance.

In the last chapters, we saw how Rosenzweig in *The Star of Redemption* and later in his book of translation of hymns and poems by Jehuda Halevi applied liturgical practices to change the temporal orientation of the Jewish people. For Rosenzweig, the cyclical reading of different portions of the Torah in Shabbat meant to produce a different experience of time, an anticipation of redemption in the now. Kafka suggested a similar function to the literary form: his different, repetitive interpretation of Abraham's story allows us to imagine a different Abraham and therefore a different history. In the following chapters on Benjamin and Freud, we will see how a similar messianic impulse informs their understanding of time and history.

III · The Breaking of History

CHAPTER 5

To Know No History
Benjamin's Eternal Return

In December 1914, when he was seventeen, Gershom Scholem had a discussion with his friend Erwine Briese on the Bible and Jewish pride, which he was careful to document in his diary. We are uncertain about the specific content of the discussion, but we can assume that it had to do with an attack by Briese, the closest of Scholem's non-Jewish schoolmates at the time, on the value of the Bible.[1] "Why do people laugh their heads off when they read the Bible?"[2] Scholem angrily wrote later that day, possibly frustrated by his friend's mockery. Scholem was especially upset with the fact that many around him believed the Bible was "silly and perverse," mostly because, he assumed, they read it in search of "dogma," rather than "for its own sake." This bias led to a misunderstanding of the biblical stories, which were, Scholem strongly believed, the "mightiest kinds of myths . . . No other nation can easily match this wonderfully complete world-myth that we've created." The book of Genesis was a good example:

> What does the book of Genesis teach us? It reveals the greatest discovery a human can make, which is the divinity of daily life. This is the reason why it's not at all stupid to deny humans the ability to come up with such myths. These tales recount not monumental things but completely normal everyday life with a few festive interruptions . . . That is what's so fabulous about them. They present common life as being truly divine and ideal. Beauty is uncovered amid endless repetition.[3]

In great measure, this chapter is about this "divinity of daily life" that Scholem found in biblical stories and its perversion in modernity. Like Wordsworth and Schlegel, Scholem, still very young, found inspiration in daily, mundane life that repeated in simple cycles of day and night, winter and summer, sowing and harvesting, life and death. This is, I might add, in line with the archaic admiration of cycles of nature. However, in contrast to Scholem's appreciation of the Bible's "endless repetition," many in modernity, starting with Hegel and Nietzsche, highlighted the malefic implications of this vision. For them, the eternal return of life in mythic reality signaled not graceful existence but regimented reality ruled by fate and destiny. In their understanding, the salvation that ancient civilization found in mythic repetitive experience and which Scholem detected in the Bible presented, in fact, hellish reality.

Walter Benjamin, I will argue in the pages to follow, was torn between these two perspectives. On the one hand, for Benjamin, myth harbored images of the past that supported the constitution of possibilities of a different reality and therefore had redemptive qualities. On the other hand, he was also extremely concerned with the experience of archaic eternal return in modernity, which, he believed, tormented modern consciousness.[4] This chapter uncovers this tension in Benjamin, discussing his work on repetition in his monumental Arcades Project (hereafter *Passagenwerk*), where he took it upon himself to identify and then analyze the detrimental effects of repetition on modern experience.

Benjamin's *Passagenwerk* focuses on Paris in the nineteenth century as the epicenter of the drama of modernity. The project took its name from the Paris Passages built in the early nineteenth century and representing the point of origin of modern consumerism. For this unfinished work, Benjamin collected numerous citations, quotations, artifacts, poems, and other literary and historical materials, gathering most of the materials from Berlin's Staatsbibliotek and Paris's Bibliothèque Nationale. The data were stored in thirty-six files, or convolutes, usually without any additional commentary or explanation of the data's arrangement.[5] Benjamin initially intended to write an article about these passages—most of which were already closed to the public or demolished in his time—with his close friend, German author and translator Franz Hessel, with whom he had very recently completed a translation of three volumes of Proust's *À la recherche du temps perdu*. This article never took shape, but his work on the passages continued. In fact, Benjamin soon had greater aspirations than producing an article. His intention in this project, now with the working title of

"Paris, Capital of the Nineteenth Century," was to create a "literary montage"[6] of the emergence of urban capitalism. While never published in Benjamin's time (although Benjamin did extract some of the materials for smaller publications), this work displays perhaps in the most extravagant way possible Benjamin's ongoing attempt to weld together different perspectives and schools of thought: the work of the so-called "Frankfurt School" and its influential projection of non-orthodox, non-dogmatic strains of leftist/Marxian theory, analysis, aesthetics, and activism; the cultural-anthropological meanings of mystical bodies of thought of Jewish messianism; the literary, aesthetic, and cultural intuitions of German Romanticism; and the deeper implications of Surrealism.[7]

Benjamin takes on the issue of repetition in convolute D of *Passagenwerk*, entitled by the editors "Boredom, Eternal Return"; here, he documents what he perceives to be the return of the archaic eternal return in modernity. The first half of the convolute presents Benjamin's growing fascination with the modern experience of boredom. Boredom is one theme in a series of interrelated terms, including memory, experience, collective unconscious, dreams, newness, and tradition, that Benjamin carefully studied to uncover the widespread impact of the eternal return on modern society. In the subsequent pages, I will place special emphasis on Benjamin's reading of Baudelaire's work, as it was formative of Benjamin's attempt to explain the intricate ways the eternal return deforms modern experience. In the second half of the convolute, Benjamin documents how the widespread experience of the eternal return in modernity informed the intellectual *Weltanschauung* of nineteenth-century thought. He focuses on the works of Friedrich Nietzsche and French socialist revolutionary Louis-Auguste Blanqui. Both thinkers gave Benjamin a conceptual framework to theorize the relations of the eternal return to modern reality.[8] They offered a theory that, in contrast to the favorable estimation of the eternal return in antiquity, presented the horrific reality of bourgeois life. Unlike Baudelaire, who endeavored to find a way out of the modern eternal return, Blanqui and Nietzsche presented the eternal return as a truth defining human life in general. The fact that radical revolutionary visionaries—and not reactionary thinkers—recognized repetition as a natural, undeniable reality, demonstrated the pervasive, resistant, and durable aspects of the idea of eternal return in modernity to Benjamin.

What is interesting in the *Passagenwerk* period is that Benjamin assumed the modern reality of eternal return could be overcome if we could identify a specific structure of dynamic repetition, which I term, in the next chapter, "repetition of opposites." That is, for Benjamin, repetition of the same was the problem of modernity, but repetition of opposites played an important part in thinking of a solution to this problem. Convolute D, in this regard, presented a formidable opportunity: the work on the eternal return allowed Benjamin to fine-tune his own "repetition of opposites." His interest in experiences of repetition in modern big-city life, as well as his fascination with Nietzsche's and Blanqui's ideas of eternal return, served as an intellectual resource for his experiments with his own vision of dynamic repetition. Especially, his excursions into modern repetition of the same highlighted the potential violent force of repetition. By studying the eternal return, Benjamin learned how repetition dislocates the masses from the historical continuum, ruptures their experience, and breaks their connections with reality.

Benjamin's work on the eternal return and tradition, we will also see, adds an important insight to our understanding of the responses to the problem of tradition in the German Jewish world in the beginning of the twentieth century. In chapter 2, I suggested that this problem encouraged the proliferation of notions of return and repetition in modern Jewish consciousness: the response to the shattering of tradition inspired historical, national, and religious images and ideals of return and repetition. And yet, remarkedly, with Benjamin, the theme of eradication of tradition was conceptualized in terms of the return of the same. In other words, repetition represented the *problem* of the crisis of tradition in its universal form, not (only) the *solution*.

To investigate Benjamin's theory of repetition, I treat Benjamin's works in non-chronological order. I focus on the horrific description of modernity as a period of eternal return developed by Benjamin in the 1930s in the *Passagenwerk*. I start with Benjamin's investigations into the repetition of the same vis-à-vis his work on tradition, experience, and collective dreaming, partly by way of his interpretation of Baudelaire, and I then discuss Nietzsche and Blanqui. In that, this chapter presents the *problem* of the eternal return, I detail Benjamin's *solution* to the eternal return—his own model of repetition of opposites—in the next chapter. To that end, the next chapter starts with Benjamin's earlier work on the baroque drama, *The Origins of German Mourning Play* (submitted to the University of Frankfurt in 1925 and published in 1928), and his works on language from the 1910s, where he lays the theoretical foundations for his vision of repetition of opposites. I then return to Benjamin's *Passagenwerk*, where this vision attains its messianic implications.

Benjamin's Excursion into Modern Eternal Return

In the early stages of *Passagenwerk*, Benjamin used the idea of a sleeping or dreaming collective (*Das träumende Kollektiv*) to explain the captivating spell of capitalism on modern society. Dreams had excited Benjamin's imagination already in the 1920s as he made a series of short explorations of the nature of sleepwalking and daydreaming.[9] This interest evolved in the 1930s to become an important theoretical structure in *Passagenwerk*.[10] Benjamin's work on dreams was inspired by Bergson and the Surrealist movement, in addition to the Marxist notion of mass consciousness.[11] It also had important reverberations with Carl Jung's work on the collective unconscious and Freud's theory of dreams. Benjamin's intellectual curiosity in Freud followed that of others in the Institute for Social Research, like Fromm, and Marcuse, who took advantage of the close physical affinity of the Institute with the Frankfurt chapter of the psychoanalytic society (they were located in the same building) to apply Freud's theory to their understanding of modern social and political reality. Freud was one of several other thinkers, like Weber and Nietzsche, who offered new perspectives on modern capitalist reality, which seemed immune to traditional Marxist theory and practice.[12]

Dreaming of the New

Benjamin's approach to the dreaming collective suggested a new set of metaphors and images with which to think of the stagnation forced on modern society by the capitalist system. Echoing Marx's criticism, the dream expresses Benjamin's conviction that society appears to be in a state of sleep, and this began with the establishment of capitalism. The dream highlighted dormancy and inactivity and offered a model to determine the effects of capitalism in terms of processes that work on the unconscious level of the social organization. The dream also provided a theoretical framework to envisage a possible solution to this dire situation. Specifically, it allowed Benjamin to conceptualize the possibility that hidden images of a different, redemptive reality still inhabited modern culture as dream wishes of the dreaming collective. Fittingly, Benjamin also imagined the change in modern conditions as an awakening from a dream. This notion of awakening, missing from the Surrealist manifestos from which Benjamin extensively borrowed,[13] is emphasized in one of the most celebrated inserts of convolute D, where Benjamin first announces the theoretical focus of his project: "The new, dialectical method of doing history presents itself as the art of experiencing the present as waking world, a world to which that dream we name the past refers in truth. To pass through and carry out what has been in remembering the dream! Therefore: remembering and awaking are most intimately related. Awakening is namely the dialectical, Copernican turn of remembrance."[14]

In *Passagenwerk*, Benjamin intended to find clues for collective dream images in the abundance of historical data he collected. His goal was to interpret those images, which, he was convinced, had the potential to point to a different reality.[15] The idea of a dream, which illustrated the predominance of social inactivity and submissiveness in the capitalist system, also inspired Benjamin to examine the role of memory, forgetfulness, consciousness, and apathy in modern experience. He dedicated the first half of convolute D of *Passagenwerk* to the analysis of this conceptual structure, focusing on boredom, one of the important tropes of his early work.[16] And it is in this context that Benjamin evokes the image of the eternal return: "The dreaming collective knows no history. Events pass before it as always identical and always new [*immer Nämliches und immer Neuestes*]. The sensation of the newest and most modern is, in fact, just as much a dream formation of events as 'the eternal return of the same' [*die ewige Wiederkehr alles Gleichen*]."[17]

As far as I can tell, the term *eternal return* appeared first in Benjamin's oeuvre in "Goethe's Elective Affinities" (1924–25) and has been understood there primarily in the context of a discussion on the place of fate and destiny in Goethe's work.[18] Benjamin addressed the idea of eternal return shortly thereafter in *Trauerspiel*, in his discussion of the "drama of fate."[19] In both places, the eternal return is figured in line with the traditional Nietzschean paradigm—that is, the eternal return is understood as an expression of a reality of fate and destiny which humanity is unable to change and whose logic is always inherently beyond reach.[20] In convolute D, however, Benjamin emphasizes the emotional and psychological toll of the eternal return. The eternal return echoes the experience of boredom: it is, as we will shortly see, an experience of ongoing sameness and emptiness that generates a form of hell, to put it in Benjamin's theological terms.[21]

The problem with the eternal return, however, was not only its wide effect on modernity. Rather, it was Benjamin's seemingly incongruent estimation that modern society, under the spell of capitalism, was unable to recognize this hell. In *Passagenwerk*, Benjamin calls attention to the imperceptibility of the eternal return, which he describes as constitutive of the experience of modernity but at the same time also hidden from view. If for Nietzsche the eternal return was a challenge, for Benjamin it was almost a mystery. It governed modernity, but in a concealed way, like a dream that the dreamer does not recognize having had. The reason for the failure of recognition was that modern reality seemed to be very different from the always-the-same that marked the Nietzschean model of eternal return (in its traditional interpretation). In fact, modern society perceived itself to be antithetical to mythic reality and hence eternal return. Paris in the nineteenth century epitomized the Golden Age of progress: new technologies, new ways of communication and transportation, fashion and consumer goods, proved the dynamic, progressive nature of modernity. The new captured the imagination of the masses. Innovations signaled development, improvement, and hope. And yet Benjamin persistently argued that this stream of innovations—'newness" [*nouveauté*] is his term—strangely only *strengthened* the always-the-same. "Monotony feeds on the new [*La monotonie se nourrit de neuf*]," he quotes Jean Vaudal in *Le Tableau noir*.[22] In another entry in *Passagenwerk*, he elaborates:

Modernity, the time of hell. The punishments of hell are always the newest thing going in this domain. What is at issue is not that "the same thing happens over and over" (much less is it a question here of eternal return) but rather that the face of the world, the colossal head, precisely in what is newest never alters—that this "newest" remains, in every respect, the same. This constitutes the eternality of hell and the sadist's delight in innovation [*Neuerungslust*]. To determine the totality of traits which define this "modernity" is to represent hell.[23]

Benjamin's understanding of the always-the-same echoed the logic of György Lukács's *History and Class Consciousness* (1923). In a capitalist system, he claims with Lukács, as the value of human life decreases and commodity is fetishized, capital (as a qualitatively identical "substance") is the only thing that circulates. This devalues the human environment to such a degree that it transforms into a reality of always-the-same: the individual is unable to recognize in herself or in her environment any points of significance, since every meaningful thing or experience is quantified in terms of capital. All is the same because all is subsumed under the same token, and, as a consequence, an experience of sameness that endlessly repeats defines human reality.[24]

The new does not end this sameness but contrarily exacerbates it. Exactly that which modern society idolizes is an expression of its biggest curse because the new commodity—be it a new brand of shoes or a new set of golf clubs—is *not* important thanks to its intrinsic value. It is alluring only because it presents an *image* of newness, promising meaningful improvement or change. Benjamin, echoing Marx's critique of commodity fetishism, claimed that the accumulation of such new objects has nothing to do with their function or purpose, and everything to do with the excitement and false hopes they produce. The new, therefore, does not change the structure of capitalism—it only reinforces it. In Benjamin words, newness is "a quality independent of the use value of the commodity. It is the origin of the semblance that belongs inalienably to images produced by the collective unconscious . . . This semblance of the new is reflected, like one mirror in another, in the semblance of the ever recurrent."[25] The appearance is of newness but the essence is of always the same. To borrow from Freud, for Benjamin, the new expresses a secret, deep wish of modernity for a difference, for meaning and value. In modernity, however, this wish for the new transgresses against the wisher. The wish does not deliver something new—only a façade of newness, in that the new does not fulfill the wish but consolidates the conditions that prolong the dream.[26]

Still, for Benjamin, the investigation of the supposedly new exposed the underlying eternal return of modernity. The new expresses nothing, and yet, in its empty cyclical track, it brings to light the order of the eternal return. It is an empty sign, whose rhythm reveals a sequence of repetition of the same emptiness, resembling an analog clock that hauntingly strikes the same hour again and again. The rhythm of the new on the cultural stage expressed the rhythm of the eternal return, which was, to put it poetically—following Benjamin—the rhythm of hell. In the following sections, I will explain how Benjamin strove to identify more concretely this rhythm of repetition. For now, however, let me stay with the theoretical implications of Benjamin's exploration of the modern eternal return of the same.

Primal History and Utopia

In the early stages of *Passagenwerk*, the idea of the collective unconscious was more than a conceptual framework to investigate the mal-effects of the eternal return. The collective unconscious also provided Benjamin with a framework to think of the solutions to this experience, since the collective unconscious is, Benjamin argues, a reservoir that keeps images of the past intact. The past promised a solution to present calamities, which the dream left untouched. The historian is to analyze this dream so that these images of the past will become available again in the present. Benjamin termed this primordial past "primal history" (*Urgeschichte*). In the German tradition, *Urgeschichte* usually designates archaic knowledge or memory that predates documented history.[27] The traces of myth in the term had reverberations, as we will soon see, in Benjamin's primal history.

The notions of primal history and collective unconscious were, however, placed under suspicion in Benjamin's intellectual milieu, as they were widespread in the vocabulary of reactionary thinkers such as Carl Jung and Ludwig Klages. For Jung, for example, the collective unconscious denoted certain universal human attributes that return in different historical periods and thus proved the unchanging essence of human nature and civilization. Archaic structures were similarly attractive to neoromantic thinkers, who endeavored to reconstitute the Golden Age of the *Volk*. Benjamin was well aware of the atavistic implications of such ideas. In a 1937 letter to Scholem, he is careful to distance himself from Jung in this exact sense: "It is my desire to safeguard certain foundations of 'Paris Arcades' methodologically by waging an onslaught on the doctrines of Jung, especially those concerning archaic images and the collective unconscious."[28] Adorno was acutely aware of this problem as well. In his critical response to the first exposé of the *Passagenwerk* of 1935, which Benjamin wrote to introduce his project to the Institute of Social Research, he rejected Benjamin's notions of primal history and the collective unconscious: "You construe the relationship of the oldest to the newest, which of course was already central to the first draft, as one of utopian reference to the 'classless society.' Thus the archaic becomes a complementary addition instead of itself being the 'newest'—and is thus dedialecticized."[29] According to Adorno, the image of primal history was disconnected from the sufferings in the present and therefore lacked critical power and value. As we will see in the next chapter, Benjamin's model of "repetition of opposites" directly addressed this line of criticism.

Many readings of Benjamin followed Adorno's criticism and downplayed the place of primal history in *Passagenwerk*. And yet in the very early stages of the project, primal history served as a critical concept with which Benjamin was able to reframe the widespread presence of the eternal return in modern society beyond the limits of traditional Marxist theory. More importantly, the idea of primal history gave Benjamin an opportunity to consider possible alternatives to present calamities. Benjamin expressed this vision in the opening lines of an early version of the first exposé of 1935 in the following way: "The utopian images which accompany the emergence of the new always, at the same time, reach back to the primal past. In the dream in which each epoch entertains images of its successor, the latter appears wedded to elements of primal history."[30] In Benjamin's vision, primal history had a utopian potential: it provided rich and diverse models and examples from which human society at different points of history was able to radically change its present. These images were kept in the collective unconscious "in a thousand configurations of life, from buildings to fashions."[31] Benjamin, who was deeply influenced by Saint-Simon and Fourier, focused on one such image. He believed that the archaic model provided the ultimate redemptive image of a "classless society." His work on Paris in the nineteenth century intended to uncover and expose the archaic content buried deep in the modern technological nightmare and redeem it, that is, to make it available again in the present. Primal history, in short, had to be relevant to the present. Benjamin's project was to dissolve it into history: to make the critical power of "a not-yet-conscious knowledge" available again.[32]

Yet a perversion in this role of primal history in modernity brought about the horrors of the eternal return. In principle, primal history promised a potential for change. The collective unconscious harbored images of redemption that the historian was supposed to make available in the present. Utopia was accessible through the images of the past. However, in modernity, archaic knowledge functioned in a quite different fashion. A certain, single aspect of ancient structures became all consuming. The collective dreaming was overcome by one aspect of antiquity—that of the eternal return. In effect, the dominance of the archaic eternal return in modern consciousness repressed the diversity of archaic knowledge and hindered its radical power. This was the double-edged sword Benjamin faced in *Passagenwerk*. The dreaming collective was unable to activate the potential that primal history usually nurtured because the collective unconscious was possessed by a single element of archaic structure—the eternal return. The potential for a plurality in primal history was quashed by a specific aspect of primal history. How did this perversion in modernity come to be? What made it so prevalent, and why did the eternal return alone dominate the presence of the archaic in modernity?

The End of Tradition:
Transmissibility and the Eternal Return

Part of the answer to these questions lies in Benjamin's discussion of tradition. The idea of tradition, which, as I noted in chapter 2, troubled the German Jewish community in the early twentieth century, was foundational to Benjamin's theoretical work on human experience in the 1930s.[33] Briefly stated, Benjamin believed tradition was a "thoroughly alive and extremely changeable" intersubjective medium that grounded the possibility of meaningful human experience. I will give more details later, but at this moment it is important that Benjamin argues that a crisis in modern experience, which emerged in and through the experience of the eternal return, should be understood in terms of a "sickening,"[34] or "shattering of tradition [*einer Erschütterung der Tradition*]."[35] That is, a "sickening" of tradition perverted modern experience, and this transpired in an experience of the eternal return.

Benjamin worked on the subtle yet alarming impact of the eradication of tradition in several works from this period. In the "Storyteller," a somewhat nostalgic piece from 1936 on the premodern art of storytelling, he investigates the eradication of tradition by studying the cultural function of the storyteller. In this short essay on the Russian novelist Nikolai Leskov, Benjamin describes how storytellers in the past introduced their audience to significant life experiences. Their stories expressed a wisdom passed from village to village and from generation to generation, thus presenting visions deep from within "life's fullness,"[36] a truth that mattered and was related to personal and social realities, a truth that was transferable and translatable, dynamic and changing. This "living tradition," Benjamin argues, was crucial for preserving *communal meaningful experience*; closing this cultural niche was a "symptom" of the eradication of tradition by capitalism and, subsequently, of the decay of modern experience.[37]

For the purposes of this chapter, what is significant is that the social function of the storyteller sets an important model for the relations between tradition and primal history in Benjamin. Specifically, I want to highlight Benjamin's claim that in modernity, as the tradition of storytellers has vanished, so too has wisdom or experience become unavailable. "It is," bemoans Benjamin, "as if a capability that seemed inalienable to us, the securest among our possessions, has been taken from us: the ability to share experiences."[38] The eradication of tradition, embodied in the sad history of the storyteller, resulted, I argue, in the dominance of the archaic form of eternal return in modernity.

In *Passagenwerk*, tradition provides access to primal history. The storyteller was an agent of voices and ideas from primordial time. Here we might think of storytellers who revived tales of an ancient past and made the prehistoric concrete and attainable. The stories reminded people of other ways of life, of different orders of the world. The storyteller molded the "once upon a time" into a concrete story that society was able to use in the present. He or she kept the images of the past alive. Benjamin quotes from Nikolai Leskov, whose work is at the center of his "Storyteller" essay, to make this point: "[The story transports the reader to] that old time when the stones in the womb of the earth and the planets at celestial heights were still concerned with the fate of men—unlike today."[39]

Tradition was the vehicle that transported the content of the past into the present. Archaic knowledge was relevant in the present because it was translated and revived in and through tradition. Tradition was not simply a verbatim repetition of the past; it was dynamic and changing, always open to differences and ruptures and therefore allowed different formulations of such structures in the present.[40] Tradition, in its flexible reuptake of the past, guaranteed the dynamism required by primal history. However, as this dynamic sort of tradition discontinued, the road connecting prehistory to the present was blocked as well. And as dynamic tradition became unavailable, the primal history it had transported into the present became unavailable as well. At this stage, modernity was left only with the structure of life in antiquity that kept haunting it from the past.[41] Put simply, the collapse of tradition created the conditions for the perverted uptake of primal history in modernity. Without tradition—being now in crisis, the *contents* of primal history could not have crossed the gap between the present and the past. The *structure* of antiquity, however, still prevailed. Primal history continued to inform the present, but now had no specific content. Only the structure of antiquity as eternal return remained.

Modernity suffered from the eternal return not only as an effect of the semblance which capitalism enforced, but also as the only remnant of primal history to survive the destruction of tradition. In a Freudian key, we could say that like a repressed wish haunting the conscious mind of the individual, the repressed content in the collective unconscious kept punishing modern society. The power of the repressed grew stronger when the repressed was unable to be expressed. Primal history became less available in terms of its contents, but, at the same time, in the dominance of the structure of archaic eternal return, the structure of the life in the ancient world became much more powerful. Benjamin gives clues to this when he notes: "In the idea of eternal recurrence, the historicism of the nineteenth century capsizes. As a result, every tradition, even the most recent, becomes the legacy of something that has already run its course in the immemorial night of the ages. Tradition henceforth assumes the character of a phantasmagoria in which primal history enters the scene in ultramodern get-up."[42] When tradition collapsed, it assumed the character of phantasmagoria and primal history "entered the scene" in perverse form, that is, in the form of archaic eternal return, with none of the content of the archaic past that would offer alternative visions for society. Primal history was still working, still powerful, in the persistent structure of eternal return, but since nothing communicated its archaic content to the present, it became horrific and dangerous. The eternal return was the result of this great suppression: it was the core of life in primal history that prevailed even when, indeed because, tradition failed.

The persistence of the archaic structure of eternal return of the same was crucial for Benjamin's project because it mirrored the horrific semblance that capitalism inflicted on modernity, the seeming newness that, in fact, was nothing new at all. There was, however, a second, more pertinent reason for Benjamin's insistence on the investigation of primal history and the eternal return. I suggest that Benjamin focused on the eternal return not only because of its mal-effects on modern consciousness, but also, and perhaps even more importantly, because the eternal return itself was the actual *form* of primal history.[43] The archaic structure of eternal return was the last point from which to access images of redemption that had become impossible because of the shattering of tradition. The eternal return was the "product of primal history's decomposition." It was a product of decomposition, but it was also the sole remnant of the primal history that contained liberatory images. Could this remnant still harbor redemptive value?

Baudelaire and Modern Experience

Benjamin's work on the dreaming collective informed the first exposé of *Passagenwerk* in 1935. Benjamin wrote this short essay to introduce his project to the Institute of Social Research. He sent it to Adorno, who, in his response letter from August 2, 1935, was especially concerned, as I just noted, that Benjamin's vision of the collective unconscious was inherently *"undialectical."* Partly in response to Adorno's criticism, over the next few years, Benjamin searched for a different conceptual framework for his work on the eternal return and the ever-the-same. He found his solution in Baudelaire, especially his famous *Les Fleurs du mal*, which I discuss here, and in Blanqui and Nietzsche, on which the next section focuses.

Experience and Psychic Fragmentation

One of Benjamin's challenges in the late 1930s was to investigate how his theoretical insight on the eternal return translated into *everyday life*—how mythic reality changed modern experience, or, put into Benjamin's terminology, how the material conditions of capitalism produced an overwhelming experience of the eternal return of the same. Benjamin tackled the problem of modern experience in a series of works from the period, including "One-Way Street," "Experience and Poverty," and "On Some Motifs in Baudelaire," on which I focus here. "On Some Motifs in Baudelaire," published in January 1940, the same year as Benjamin's death, was composed of an abundance of materials that Benjamin extracted from *Passagenwerk* with the intention of publishing a book on Baudelaire.[44] In this essay, Benjamin explained the direct impact of the end of tradition on the experience of the individual in the context of Baudelaire's work on big-city crowds and factory workers.

Benjamin's argument in "On Some Motifs in Baudelaire" begins with a distinction between *Erfahrung*, usually translated as "experience" and denoting the individual's capacity to comprehend, remember, and communicate his or her experiences in a cohesive fashion, and *Erlebnis*, a term denoting isolated or singular "lively" experiences and memories.[45] The focus on *Erfahrung* and *Erlebnis* reiterated Benjamin's long interest in experience, starting with his 1918 essay "On the Program of the Coming Philosophy." While in his earlier work, Benjamin was critical of Kant's theory of experience, he now directed his attention to the growing admiration of *Erlebnis* in *Lebensphilosophie*. Benjamin focused on Dilthey's *Das Erlebnis und Dichtung* (1914), where the term *Erlebnis* suggests pre-reflective, immediate, and therefore rich and meaningful experiences, which Dilthey believed to be superior to the reflective, rational, and mediated experiences of neo-Kantian philosophy. Benjamin concurred with Dilthey's criticism of the rationalization of experience in the Kantian tradition, but at the same time he was critical of Dilthey's *Erlebnis*, which he found to instigate a dangerous fragmentation of inner life. At stake here is Benjamin's understanding that *Erlebnis* did not prescribe unmediated meaningful experience, but rather the degradation of experience to a stream of disconnected and unorganized memories that the individual was unable to tie together to form a unified, meaningful whole. A shift Benjamin identified in modern experience from *Erfahrung* to *Erlebnis* made understanding these fractured experiences increasingly prevalent. These shattered experiences, I go on to explain, precipitated the modern experience of the eternal return.

Freud's theory of memory and the unconscious effects of trauma in *Beyond the Pleasure Principle* (1920) proved crucial to Benjamin's criticism of *Erlebnis*. Benjamin was interested in Freud's theory of consciousness and memory, especially with Freud's suggestion to see in consciousness a defense mechanism against trauma. Stated briefly, for Freud, events that registered at the unconscious level have lasting effects on the individual. (These memories, Benjamin clarifies in "On Some Motifs in Baudelaire" in a Proustian note, become a component of *mémoire involontaire*.) In contrast, when events register *only* in consciousness, they usually do not leave any memory traces behind. Benjamin quotes Freud: "Becoming conscious and leaving behind a memory trace are incompatible processes within one and the same system."[46] The registration of experience in consciousness has to do with the level of excitation of the stimuli. Low levels of stimulation are allowed to register in the mind while high levels of stimulation are relegated only by consciousness, which protects the psyche from overstimulation. Benjamin applied this principle to his understanding of modern experience, arguing that "perhaps the special achievement of shock defense is the way it assigns an incident a precise point in time in consciousness, at the cost of the integrity of the incident's contents."[47]

In Benjamin's application of Freud's theory, consciousness defends the psyche from stimuli by dividing experience into small "hourly" incidences isolated from the rest of experience. The purpose of the division of the mental material is to protect the mind from overflowing excitation, that is, from traumas: the memory is fragmented, and the trauma is therefore less harmful. However, in avoiding trauma, the individual suffers a fractured experience. The mind is saved from the horrific influence of the trauma, but this comes at a very high price: the fragmentation of human experience. Thinking of Dilthey's *Erlebnis*, Freud's theory suggested that *Erlebnis* is not a superior form of experience but a perversion of one: these isolated experiences result from trauma and dangerously fragment the human mind. *Erlebnis* is not a solution to Kant's reflective, rational experience; rather, it portrays a failure to achieve meaningful experience in modernity.

Erlebnis and Repetition

Benjamin believed this kind of psychic fragmentation was typical of modernity. Baudelaire's poetry was decisive to his thinking, as it depicts an overwhelming, indeed traumatic, experience of life in the modern metropolis. "Fear, revulsion, and horror were the emotions which the big city crowd aroused in those who first observed it,"[48] Benjamin writes in his book on Baudelaire. The engulfing presence of the modern city, described by Baudelaire in his poems—as by others in the early twentieth-century discourse of the city, such as Georg Simmel, Emile Durkheim, and Oswald Spengler—generated endless distractions and interruptions, which produced, in turn, an experience of shock [*Chockerfahrung*], a trauma in Freudian vocabulary, that, as Freud showed, ruptured experience.[49] The individual in the city crowds, claims Benjamin, is not simply swallowed by the masses but is broken down under the influence of the city. His or her life is disassembled into a series of interruptions and disruptions.[50] But how are these interruptions turned into an experience of repetition?

In Freud's *Beyond the Pleasure Principle*, the traumatic fracture of *Erlebnis* produces a compulsion to repeat (*Wiederholungszwang*)—a repetitive return to the trauma that signals an attempt to come to terms with the trauma. (We will return to this in chapter 7.) And indeed, for Benjamin as well, the fragmentation of experience results in repetition, albeit for different reasons. In his words, in *Erlebnis*, because we are unable to reflect and comprehend, "there would be nothing but the sudden start, occasionally pleasant but usually distasteful, which, according to Freud, confirms the failure of the shock defense."[51] For Benjamin, and we should note how his logic is similar to Rosenzweig's argument about the *nunc stans* in chapter 3, experience in modernity turned into a series of isolated beginnings. Because *Erlebnis* degrades human lives to an endless series of disconnected multiplicity, these memories are experienced, in effect, as a series of "sudden starts": different experiences are meaningless and isolated, and, as such, they seem to reflect a new beginning, one that we cannot connect to other experiences or memories, and therefore one that must remain only a beginning. This fragmentation engenders inner chaos, which, because of its meaninglessness and emptiness, reflects an experience of the eternal return. Thus, much like the experience of newness at the level of the society, the individual suffers from a series of events that he or she is unable to process and therefore experiences as repetitive.

In short, for Benjamin, at its core, the problem of experience in modernity is one of repetition: the degradation of *Erfahrung* to *Erlebnis* reduces life to isolated memories, resulting in an eternal return of interruptions. Corresponding to the dreaming collective that "knows no history," this experience of repetition entails *temporal disorientation*: "The man who loses his capacity for experiencing feels as though he has been dropped from the calendar. The big-city dweller knows this feeling on Sundays ... [Human beings] are like the poor souls that wander restlessly but have no history."[52] The shattering of connected experience affects the historical index of the masses: the internal rupture of inner life bolsters a rupture from history and dislocates the person from the historical continuum: if the dreaming collective knows no history because everything in capitalist society seems to be the same, the individual suffers from a rupture from history because all the shattered experiences in the chaos of "sudden starts" are experienced as identical. There is no continuity, no past, and no future in such experiences—only repetitive disturbances that cannot be tied into meaningful, long, and cohesive unity.

Capitalism and "Sudden Starts":
Repetition and the Worker at the Machine

The degradation of experience in modernity had important correlations with technological and economic developments. In essence, the same effect of repetition Benjamin previously identified among city crowds applied to the experience of factory workers: "The shock experience [*Chockerlebnis*] which the passer-by has in the crowd," he writes, "corresponds to the isolated 'experiences' of the worker at his machine."[53] Here, the Marxist criticism of the monotonous and repetitive experience of the workers on the assembly lines in factories across Europe proved fertile: "The hand movement of the worker at the machine has no connection with the preceding gesture for the very reason that it is its exact repetition. Since each operation at the machine is just as screened off from the preceding operation as a *coup* in a game of chance is from the one that preceded it, the drudgery of the laborer is, in its own way, a counterpart to the drudgery of the gambler. Both types of work are equally devoid of substance."[54] The capitalist mode of production, Benjamin deducts, causes an experience of eternal return of the same. It degrades the lives of the workers into a series of repetitive, disconnected actions in a way that reflects the effect of shock experiences on the masses and in modern consumerism.[55] To be clear, Benjamin's vision of technology was much more nuanced than the regressive view expressed in these lines. He was certainly aware of and discussed the revolutionary potential of technology and technical representations.[56] However, in his work on the assembly line, technology demonstrated the prevalence of the archaic eternal return in modernity. The changes in modern industry proved to him that the eternal return was affecting more than the masses in the big cities or the social and economic order of modern consumerism. They provided the context for Benjamin's understanding that the return of the same is topical to modernity.

Importantly, for Benjamin, both experiences of repetition—that of the city crowds and that of the factory worker—were inherently connected to the problem of the discontinuation of the traditional way of life in modernity. Benjamin notes that when he discusses the degradation of *Erfahrung* to *Erlebnis*: "Experience is indeed a matter of tradition, in collective existence as well as private life. It is less the product of facts firmly anchored in memory than of a convergence in memory of accumulated and frequently unconscious data."[57] To explain, in Benjamin's judgment, tradition structures the form in which the past is remembered and related to the present. As an "historical determination of memory,"[58] tradition constitutes a net of meaningful conscious and unconscious connections that instruct the accumulation and appropriation of memories, and thus helps the individual maintain a unified vision of herself and her world, even in a world of ongoing excitation. However, with the destruction of such tradition, the ability to unify experience collapses, and the individual becomes susceptible to outside infringements. The end of tradition speeds the end of cohesive experience and, in that way, stimulates modern temporal disorientation and life in a turmoil of eternal return of the same. The same dynamic applies in the modern factories, when workers, torn from their traditional practices and age-old conventions, are forced to serve a function in an environment in which the repetitive action of the machine defines their lives: "The unskilled worker is the one most deeply degraded by machine training. His work has been sealed off from experience; practice counts for nothing in the factory."[59]

The structure of Benjamin's argument in both instances recalls his work on primal history. Tradition functions on a different register here, yet in all of Benjamin's investigations of the eternal return, a discontinuation of tradition in modernity—whether the traditions of the storytellers or those of the factory workers—lacerated dynamic historic connections and thereby reduced the content of the experience in modernity. This emptying of experience materialized in an experience of repetition which dissociated one from history. Benjamin's work on Baudelaire verified his basic intuitions: the problem of the discontinuation of tradition created the conditions for the growing control of the eternal return of the same over modernity.

There was, however, a lesson to be learned. Benjamin's excursions into modern experience also led him again and again to the same important conclusion. His work illustrated the *violent potential* of repetition. In the factories and the big-city streets, repetition fractured the experience of the individual. It disintegrated unified experience into a series of disconnected memories. Furthermore, Benjamin's reading of Baudelaire proved to him that repetition could rupture human relations to history. In modernity, Benjamin learned, history is experienced as a series of "sudden starts," which interrupt the flow of homogenous, linear time. In Benjamin's hands, we will shortly see, repetition has a similar power to interrupt history, but in this case it creates the conditions for a messianic cessation of happening.

Blanqui and Nietzsche:
The Modern Formulation of the Eternal Return

Baudelaire's work on the masses gave Benjamin an opportunity to develop an intimate understanding of the horrors of the modern uptake of the archaic eternal return. It uncovered the nightmare of the eternal return stamped onto the experience of the masses and factory workers. Alongside these more traditional "Frankfurt School" investigations, Benjamin's post-1935 work focused on the philosophical and theoretical implications of the modern experience of the eternal return. Benjamin dedicated much of the second half of convolute D to this inquiry, specifically to a pseudoscientific book on cosmology, *L'éternité par les Astres*, which he came across by accident in the winter of 1937 while browsing in the French Bibliothèque Nationale. This work by Louis Auguste Blanqui, the famous nineteenth-century French plotter and revolutionary, was, as Benjamin told Horkheimer a few weeks later, "a rare find, that will decisively influence my work."[60] The book dealt with the theme of the eternal return in ways that reverberated with Nietzsche's philosophy and Baudelaire's poetry, supporting Benjamin's assumption that the idea was "something 'in the air' at the time."[61] The shift in Benjamin's conceptual framework is evident in his second exposé from 1939. Benjamin wrote the exposé at Horkheimer's request, hoping it would get the attention of Frank Altschul, a New York banker. His dream theory was "strikingly absent"[62] from this short piece, which now focused in large part around Blanqui. Benjamin continued to work on his dream theory mostly through his work on Baudelaire.

Blanqui, the Martyr

L'éternité par les Astres was the last thing Blanqui wrote during his imprisonment at Fort du Taureau after one of his failed attempts at insurrection, this time on the eve of the Paris Commune revolt of 1871. In this "odd little causerie,"[63] Blanqui developed a theory of eternal return based on a simple and elegant intellectual experiment in materialist philosophy. In principle, Blanqui's idea was based on a fundamental discrepancy he believed to have found between infinite matter and the finite number of configurations of matter. On the one hand, Blanqui asserted (erroneously according to modern science) that the cosmos is endless in time, space, and matter, but on the other hand, he noted that there are a limited number of ways simple particles can be configured and reconfigured. The universe is unlimited, whereas the number of combinations or types of things in the universe is finite. This insight caused Blanqui to rethink modern cosmology. He hypothesized that the cosmos must be populated by an endless number of solar systems, each of which expressed only one type or configuration of matter. Put in anthropological terms, Blanqui assumed infinite solar systems, each exhibiting one specific history. And since there was a limit to these histories, or configurations of matter, but infinite solar systems, Blanqui arrived at the conclusion (possibly following Epicurus and echoing Nietzsche's revelation of 1871 about the eternal return) that many, indeed infinite, solar systems must display the exact same reality: "in order to fill its expanse, nature must repeat to infinity each of its *original* combinations or *types*."[64] Human freedom does not change this celestial picture. Blanqui admitted that while nature has the same laws everywhere, human will can introduce differences in the same material conditions. There are other star constellations, he contended, where the French won at Waterloo. However, despite these changes, the infinity of matter triumphed: Blanqui insisted that our exact reality, in its most particular and minute historical manifestations, must exist in boundless repetitions of endless space and time.

Blanqui's ultimate dreadful conclusion about his own life in prison was no different, as Benjamin documents in *Passagenwerk*: "What I write at this moment in the cell of the Fort du Taureau, I have written and shall write throughout all eternity—at a table, with a pen, clothed as I am now, in circumstances like this."[65] This last revelation of Blanqui in his cell at Taureau, along with several others at the end of his small book, caught Benjamin's attention. A mediocre work in cosmology, *L'éternité par les Astres* intrigued Benjamin because of its *political* implications. For Blanqui, the human world was dominated by fate because everything that happens and will happen, must have already happened in other worlds. "Chances or your choice—it makes no difference," Benjamin's Blanqui declares, "for you will not escape your destiny."[66]

Benjamin learned of Blanqui's life mostly from Gustav Geffroy's *L'Enfermé* (1897). In his biography of the French revolutionary hero, Geffroy emphasizes the radical isolation of Blanqui at Fort du Taureau, an army post where he was treated as a prisoner of war.[67] In Geffroy's view, *L'éternité par les Astres* expressed Blanqui's wish to escape from his cell. The book documents the fantasy that there is, somewhere in the stars, a different world where Blanqui could finally be successful and the revolution would prevail. For Benjamin, however, the book expressed Blanqui's *helplessness*, indeed his last failure, as Benjamin reported to Horkheimer: "the cosmic vision of the world which Blanqui lays out . . . is an infernal vision. . . . What is so unsettling is that the presentation is entirely lacking in irony. It is an unconditional surrender."[68]

Benjamin saw Blanqui as a revolutionary spirit who in the end, after many decades of attempts of revolutions, succumbed to modernity. In his solitary imprisonment, his cell "dark and damp," and suffering from the "worst conditions,"[69] Blanqui surrendered. "This resignation without hope," Benjamin writes in the second exposé, was "the last word of the great revolutionary."[70] Blanqui was a prisoner not only because of his captivity but also because his intellectual imagination gave in to the façade of the eternal return of the same. "The terrible indictment he pronounces against society takes the form of an unqualified submission to its results,"[71] Benjamin writes in the exposé of 1939. Blanqui's failure was profound because it admitted to the very thing he fought against all his life. His last work confirmed that no revolution was to truly change history: his new cosmological perspective made human action insignificant.

To be sure, Benjamin's reading of Blanqui's book is not the only possible interpretation. His argument that this work presented an "unconditional surrender" is certainly a matter of contention.[72] In Geffroy's *L'Enfermé*, which Benjamin read, much of the last chapter of the biography is dedicated to Blanqui's political activities during the latter part of imprisonment at Clairvaux and after his release in mid-1879. In the last years of his life, Blanqui attended many public rallies and political events, wrote articles in several newspapers, and seemed to have returned to full activity until a stroke of apoplexy ended his life in 1881. Benjamin, however, emphasized a *surrender*.[73] In his understanding, Blanqui must have surrendered; he must have relinquished all hope, to write about the eternal return. There was no hope in the eternal return, only suffering.

Yet if Blanqui inspired Benjamin, it was not because of his hope but because of his political and revolutionary violence. As I explain in the next chapter, Benjamin applied this violence to his formulation of "repetition of opposites." More than denoting simple resignation, Blanqui's theory of the eternal return epitomized a reorganization of his revolutionary spirit. Benjamin's Blanqui was a modern Samson, who realized he had lost his last battle. However, in his surrender, in this final effort, he punished the society he struggled all his life to change. A true rebel, his surrender was still impressively spirited: he "yielded to bourgeois society," Benjamin writes, "but he's brought to his knees with such force that the throne begins to totter."[74] Blanqui's book replanted in modernity the most horrific idea of the eternal return of the same. The French author intuitively grasped the "warm gray fabric" that covered modern life and wrote his book to reflect it back to society. Much like Baudelaire's attempt to incite shock effect on his readers, Blanqui's book stamped modernity with the *horrors* of repetition. "In Blanqui the idea of eternal return itself takes the form of an obsessional idea," writes Benjamin elsewhere.[75] Blanqui's eternal return *punished* modern society: it mirrored the "true" essence of the world, inflating its implications, as Benjamin notes in the introduction to the 1939 exposé. Blanqui, he writes, "in his last piece of writing, [reveals] the terrifying features of this phantasmagoria. Humanity figures there as damned . . . Blanqui's cosmic speculation conveys this lesson: that humanity will be prey to a mythic anguish so long as phantasmagoria occupies a place in it."[76]

Blanqui showed Benjamin that in the mirroring process of the eternal return, something breaks. Instead of continuation, there is an interruption, or at least a slight one. The violence of Blanqui was, however, ineffective, punishing his readers rather than changing their political and social circumstances. In the end, Blanqui was a martyr, who, surrounded by walls, took vengeance on modernity, proving to Benjamin that the eternal return only confirmed phantasmagoric reality. True difference, Benjamin now knew, must be produced in a different way.

Nietzsche's Heroism

Somewhat modest in its volume, certainly in comparison to the pages dedicated to Blanqui, Nietzsche's philosophy offered a second layer to Benjamin's philosophical excursions into the eternal return of the same.

Benjamin's curiosity about Nietzsche's philosophy was piqued decades before he found Blanqui. As early as 1912, he discussed Nietzsche's *Zarathustra* with his friend Ludwig Strauß.[77] He never produced anything dedicated specifically to Nietzsche, but the philosopher stimulated Benjamin's thought throughout his career.[78] In *Passagenwerk*, Nietzsche's work on eternal return, one of the philosopher's key concepts, is documented immediately after that of Blanqui. Benjamin learned of Nietzsche's eternal return mostly from Löwith's *Nietzsche's Philosophy of the Eternal Recurrence of the Same*. He copied several paragraphs directly from Löwith's book and several others from Nietzsche's *The Will to Power*. And to a great extent, Benjamin accepted Löwith's reading of Nietzsche, on which I elaborated earlier in the book. A quarter of a century before the Nietzsche revival in French continental philosophy, Benjamin conceived of Nietzsche's eternal return along more traditional lines. For Benjamin, Nietzsche's eternal return presented a modern rearticulation of the archaic eternal return of same. In his understanding, the Nietzschean doctrine suggested an endless repetition of the same reality, which removed all meaning from existence. The following note, which Benjamin found in one of Nietzsche's unpublished papers, clarifies this logic: "On eternal recurrence: 'The great thought as a *Medusa head*: all features of the world become motionless, a frozen death throe.'"[79]

Like Blanqui, Nietzsche illuminated for Benjamin first and foremost the widespread impact of the eternal return at the superstructure level of human society. However, unlike Blanqui's vision, Nietzsche's theory of the eternal return was important also to Benjamin's theory of time. The philosopher's insistence on the dramatic importance of the present, of each and every moment, informed Benjamin's famous notion of the now-time.[80] The now, as I detailed in chapter I, presented an urgent opportunity for radical self-transformation for Nietzsche, who saw in each and every moment an indispensable prospect of change, the prospect of a decision that would rupture the mechanical transition of events. In a series of unpublished fragments entitled "Noon and Eternity" from 1881, in which the figure of Zarathustra appears for the first time in Nietzsche, this moment of decision, of clear and precise vision of one's own reality, a moment of self-metamorphosis, is signified by noon as a moment of standstill.[81] This quality of the now in Nietzsche resembles Heidegger's "moment of vision" and resonates with Benjamin's famous "dialectics at a standstill." I will return to this matrix of meanings in the next chapter.

Still, as in his work on Blanqui, Benjamin took the opportunity to learn from the misconceptions of his predecessor. In Nietzsche, as in Blanqui, history sadly became, Rolf Tiedemann notes, a "mythical *nunc stans* which extends itself into the present."[82] There was, nonetheless, an important difference between Nietzsche and Blanqui that we need to emphasize. Nietzsche did not falter like Blanqui, but fought to affirm life. His philosophy promoted a heroic struggle with destiny. This was mostly because Nietzsche aimed to transcend the horrors of the eternal return, while Blanqui's book only corroborated them. In Nietzsche's philosophy, the recognition of oneself in one's destiny, in the eternal return of the same, is the first step in the heroic ascension to the *Übermensch*. His theory of eternal return offers hope to the man of the future. Blanqui, in stark contrast, was helpless. His theory echoes the horror that Benjamin noticed in Paris of the previous century. In *Central Park*, a series of aphorisms Benjamin wrote in the second part of 1938 (it includes several citations from the *Passagenwerk*), Benjamin focuses on this fact:

> Show with maximum force how the idea of eternal recurrence emerged at about the same time in the worlds of Baudelaire, Blanqui, and Nietzsche. In Baudelaire, the accent is on the new, which is wrested with heroic effort from the "ever-selfsame [*Immerwiedergleichen*]"; in Nietzsche, it is on the "ever-selfsame" which the human being faces with heroic composure. Blanqui is far closer to Nietzsche than to Baudelaire; but in his work, resignation predominates. In Nietzsche, this experience is projected onto a cosmological plane, in his thesis that nothing new will occur.[83]

Benjamin admired Nietzsche's heroism in his struggle to transgress modern boredom. He did so, however, with a touch of irony.[84] For Benjamin, the eternal return was a *tentative* problem, an archaic structure that took over modernity; one that emerged out of the suffering inflicted by capitalism on modern consciousness. The eternal return was essentially and ultimately something that modernity brought on itself, and that he struggled to fight against, to reject, to replace, and, most assuredly, never to accept. Benjamin wanted modern society to awaken from that dream, not to continue to dream, even if this dream was about a heroic struggle. Nietzsche was poles apart. In Nietzsche, Benjamin tells us, "the accent lies on eternal recurrence." His eternal return was a fundamental *truth* that constituted one of the main articles of his philosophy. Benjamin, in contrast, strove to move beyond the reality that made the archaic eternal return possible. He did not want to affirm the eternal return but to uncover its deepest mechanism.

The Nietzschean ideal of self-affirmation disorientated modern consciousness: Nietzsche promised an opportunity for the few, and, in that, he planted the idea of eternal return as an undeniable truth in the hearts of the many. In offering hope, he was more dangerous than Blanqui (oh, the irony). Meanwhile, Benjamin searched for a radical solution for *all*. He moved away from the individual to the social sphere and from the metaphysical to the messianic. If Blanqui terrified modernity with his image of destiny, and Nietzsche armed some of his readers against it, Benjamin strove to end it. He uprooted the eternal return of the same with his own version of repetition. Inspired by Nietzsche's heroism and Blanqui's violence, Benjamin devised a theory of dynamic repetition that harnessed the power of the eternal return to rupture human experience. His repetition signaled the dynamism, change, and difference inhibited by capitalism. He used the power of repetition to create the conditions for a radical change at the collective level, something both Blanqui and Nietzsche deemed impossible.

CHAPTER 6

Revelatory Discovery
On Benjamin's "Repetition of Opposites"

In *The Story of a Friendship* (1975), in an anecdote about what Scholem believed to be a "contiguity"[1] of Benjamin's work with "Hebrew Texts,"[2] Scholem recalls a couple of conversations with Max Rychner and Theodor Adorno about Benjamin's *The Origins of German Mourning Play* (*Ursprung des deutschen Trauerspiels*, hereafter *Trauerspiel*). In the conversations, which took place almost two decades after the completion of the book, Scholem was told of Rychner's and Adorno's meetings with Benjamin, during which Benjamin declared that "only someone familiar with Kabbalah could understand the introduction to [my] book on tragic drama." This was "very strange,"[3] Scholem ironically notes, since both Rychner and Adorno had met Benjamin around 1930, after Benjamin's supposed turn to historical materialism, thereby proving Benjamin's lifelong affiliation with Jewish thought and tradition. Scholem, however, does not hide his frustration as he immediately recounts that Benjamin never mentioned this significant affiliation to him. This is especially odd because he was Benjamin's closest friend, and he and Benjamin had long conversations on theories of language in Jewish mysticism, one of Scholem's own lifelong subjects of interest in his work on Kabbalah. So why didn't Benjamin reveal such an important interpretation of his own work to his friend? Did he intend to hint this implicitly, Scholem wonders, when he wrote the dedication in Scholem's copy "To Gerhard Scholem, donated to the *ultima Thule* of his Kabbalistic library"? Was it that obvious, he continues, that it "required no explanation—which is true to a certain content—or was he indulging in a game of hide-and-seek with me"? Scholem's last comment clearly shows his resentment. "Did he succumb to the temptation to indulge in some showing off, or did he wish to shroud the reproach of incomprehensibility that this introduction must have suggested to him, like few other pages of his writing, by referring to something even more incomprehensible (which is how Kabbalah must have seemed to these men)? I don't know."[4]

My intention in the next pages is to follow Benjamin's advice to his friends. I focus on the *Trauerspiel*'s much-discussed Epistemo-Critical Prologue to investigate the place of Jewish mystical traditions in Benjamin's vision of repetition and, consequently, of history and redemption. As I will show, in the prologue Benjamin uses principles he identifies in Jewish mystical traditions to propose meaningful historical repetitive structures, which ground his messianic vision of the 1930s.

In the last chapter, I addressed the detrimental effect of the eternal return on modern experience as developed in the 1930s in the *Passagenwerk*. The next pages discuss Benjamin's *solution* to this experience, by way of his own formulation of what I term "repetition of opposites." In order to introduce Benjamin's model of repetition, I first focus on the works preceding the *Passagenwerk*—his 1928 book on the baroque drama, where he lays the theoretical foundations for his vision of repetition of opposites, and his works on language from the 1910s where he discusses mystical theories of language. The chapter then returns to Benjamin's *Passagenwerk*, specifically to his development of the political and messianic implications of his model of repetition.

I begin the chapter with a lengthy discussion of Benjamin's articulation of repetition in *Trauerspiel*. Recent decades have seen a surge of philosophical work on Benjamin; Howard Caygill, Peter Fenves, Eli Friedlander, and Andrew Benjamin are important examples of the effort to understand Benjamin in the context of modern philosophical traditions.[5] In what comes, I share their basic motivation and put Benjamin in conversation with the modern interest in repetition in philosophy.[6] In that vein, I note similarities between Deleuze's nominalism and Benjamin's nominalism in *Trauerspiel*. In the last part of this chapter, in which I address Benjamin's messianic vision, I elaborate on the correspondence between his vision of repetition and the "repetition-as-recollection forward" trajectory of Kierkegaard and Heidegger. However, to clarify, it is not my intention to claim that

Benjamin conceived his model of repetition with either Nietzsche or Heidegger in mind. As Pierre Missac rightly points out about Benjamin's deployment of repetition in *Passagenwerk*, Benjamin "scarcely notices, or at least does not mention, the analogies between the dialectical image and Kierkegaardian repetition."[7] And yet, he continues, there are "resemblances in the mechanism, the instruments, and the aims" between Benjamin's repetition and the modern formulations of repetition. I argue that the convergence between what I call Benjamin's "repetition of opposites" and modern theories of repetition helps elucidate Benjamin's understanding of history. I am interested in Benjamin's intervention in the modern understanding of repetition, especially the changes he introduced to the structure and function of repetition, which allowed him to consider its messianic implication.

In the second part of the chapter, I turn to Benjamin's early work on language and revelation, which markedly borrowed from Jewish mystical traditions. Benjamin turned to mystical structures of meaning in response to what he perceives as the poverty of meaning in modernity. In an anticipation of his later work in *Passagenwerk*, he believed that it was possible to arrive at revelation and truth by way of an investigation of simple, mundane objects and artifacts as long as we put them together in meaningful structures. Focusing on Benjamin's 1916 essay "On Language as Such and on the Language of Man" (*Über Sprache überhaupt und über die Sprache des Menschen*), I will argue that in borrowing from a mystical understanding of language, Benjamin's model of repetition offers an intervention in modern philosophical discourses. Specifically, Benjamin's insights about the relations between repetition and the Adamic act of naming complicates the basic dichotomies of sameness and difference, singularity and historical connections that inform modern philosophy.

The last section of the chapter returns to Benjamin's approach to history in *Passagenwerk* to argue that it can be understood as the culmination of his cogitations of history and repetition in *Trauerspiel*. Earlier, I noted the problem of the dominance in modernity of the archaic model of the eternal return. The eternal return was one of the models with which Benjamin analyzed the hellish reality of the always-the-same, which resulted, at least in part, as I have argued, from the eradication of tradition in modernity. The eternal return of the same expressed a reality devoid of meaning; because reality was empty and nonsensical, it eternally returned. In *Passagenwerk*, Benjamin struggles to find a solution to this reality from many interrelated perspectives. His work on Proust's involuntary memories and on the *flâneur*, his representation of collective unconscious, his notion of aura, and his earlier model of translation are all prominent examples of his incessant attempts to locate instances of difference and a possibility of change in the modern overflow of sameness and meaninglessness. Benjamin's theory of repetition of opposites had a foundational role in this enterprise. Most importantly, his model of repetition of opposites was refashioned so that it could present rare images of "redeemed life." Thus, if in the 1920s, Benjamin's model of dynamic repetition provided, we will see, the groundwork for a revolution in art history and theory of truth and grounded the possibility of revelation, in *Passagenwerk*, repetition serves as a central motif of his messianic thought. This shift in the operation of repetition for Benjamin is significant. In the later part of his project, Benjamin is not interested in a personal knowledge of the relations between works of art, but in elaborating a structure of repetition that could change the course of history.[8]

To be sure, scholars of Benjamin have extensively researched his debt to theology and Judaism in his later work. His famous examples of the ink blotter and the hunchbacked dwarf, as well as his notion of messianism, have all been hotly debated and well explored. As Robert Gibbs notes in "Messianic Epistemology: Thesis XV," "There is likely no theme more-exposed and over-theorized in Benjamin's work than the messianic."[9] Still, my plan in the following is to examine the operations of *repetition* in Benjamin's messianic thought. Rather than constructing a meta-analysis of the messianic in Benjamin, my intention is to uncover the function of repetition of opposites in his vision of redemption. Indeed, what made Benjamin's work on repetition so important in that period was his ability to express a messianic vision in a basic formulation of "dynamic repetition" of difference—to use a model indebted to Nietzsche, Deleuze, Kierkegaard, and Heidegger. Specifically, Benjamin capitalized on the discontinuities and differences that modern philosophy of repetition emphasized to portray a messianic interruption of historical time. Put in more general terms,

Benjamin harnessed exactly those dynamic and reclamatory qualities that define repetition in modernity and differentiate it from archaic forms of the eternal return of the same, so as to combat the domination of the archaic eternal return in modernity. In other words, Benjamin turned repetition against itself: modern, dynamic repetition was the main armament in Benjamin's arsenal against the archaic eternal return which haunted modernity.

To examine the place of this dynamic repetition in his messianic vision in the 1930s, in the last section of the chapter, I focus on convolute N of *Passagenwerk*, which presents Benjamin's later theory of knowledge and history and documents the principles of his theory of "repetition of opposites." I also look at Benjamin's essay "On the Concept of History" (*Über den Begriff der Geschichte*). The latter, compiled from fifteen short aphorisms, was written in Paris between February and May 1940, after Benjamin's release from the internment camp for German émigrés at Nevers; he intended it to serve as a theoretical framework for his Baudelaire book. This short piece was Benjamin's last work on history, one that famously came to symbolize his last will and testament after his suicide a few months later in Portbou.

"Repetition of Opposites"

Benjamin's *Trauerspiel* was written between May 1924 and early 1925 with the intention of submitting it as an *Habilitationsschrift* to the University of Frankfurt am Main. Benjamin started to work on his ideas on the baroque shortly after the First World War, but he made more progress during a writing retreat in Capri, when chances for the acceptance of *Habilitation* still seemed favorable. The book manifests Benjamin's ongoing interest in the history of German art, a continuation of his doctoral thesis on art criticism in German Romanticism and his recent essay "Goethe's Elective Affinities." The prologue to the work, however, offers a theory of knowledge and representation deeply indebted to Benjamin's decade-long fascination with mystical theories of language and revelation. The focus in the prologue on such theories was motivated by the main argument of Benjamin's work.

In *Trauerspiel*, Benjamin is critical of the tendency of German neo-classicism to connect the seventeenth-century baroque mourning play (*Trauerspiel*) with classical Greek drama—an association that usually resulted in the derogation of the *Trauerspiel* in many works on the period. The modern genre was seen merely as "a caricature" of the glorious tragic drama, and "offensive or even barbaric to refine taste."[10] Benjamin's book offers the baroque mourning play an alternative lineage through which the merit of the genre is established. Specifically, Benjamin suggests *Trauerspiel* is an independent aesthetic genre whose history began in medieval mystery plays and whose future lay in modern expressionism. To clarify the categorical difference between classic tragedy and the mourning play, the prologue exposes the shortcomings of Benjamin's predecessors' principles of categorization. It offers a new theory of classification, indeed a new theory of knowledge and representation, one that substantiates Benjamin's revolutionary interpretation of the baroque drama. Thus, much like the introduction to his book of translations of Baudelaire's *Tableaux Parisiens* (1923), the Epistemo-Critical Prologue of *Trauerspiel* transcends the specific context of seventeenth-century Europe and suggests not only a theory of the baroque but also a theory of history and of truth.

The Specter of Nominalism

Benjamin arrives at the idea of repetition in the Epistemo-Critical Prologue with the same basic motivation that informs Deleuze's *Difference and Repetition*. Like Deleuze, Benjamin is critical of traditional theories of representation, but his work, unlike Deleuze's book, focuses on art.

Benjamin's main critique is that in classical theories of art, the "phenomena were subordinate to concepts": the value of individual works of art was deduced from the genre, and the art object was intelligible only to the degree that it resembled or mirrored the genre.[11] For that reason, and Benjamin moves here to make larger claims about traditional philosophy, the systemization of knowledge was built on the abstraction of the concept from all possible incidents. Philosophy, argues Benjamin, engaged with an "encyclopedic accumulation"[12] of facts. The concept had to be extracted from all its possible manifestations: the larger the sample, the more accurate and precise the concept. This theoretical attitude informing the work of several German theorists of art, misrepresented, according to Benjamin, the material world: "When facts are amassed in this way... the less obvious original qualities are soon obscured by the chaos of more immediately appealing modern ones."[13]

Benjamin's solution to the problem of representation in art is radical. The art scholar, he claims, must initiate an "investigation which does not, from the very outset, commit itself to the inclusion of everything which has ever been described as tragic or comic, but looks for that which is *exemplary* [*Exemplarischem*]."[14] The investigation should focus on "significant works,"[15] or "authentic [*echte*]"[16] works with "original qualities" that could generate deeper understanding; works which, in his words, "establish the genre or abolish it; and the perfect work [which] will do both."[17] This problem has practical implications in *Trauerspiel*. Benjamin is critical of previous scholars, for example, German theorist Johannes Volkelt, who misunderstood the *Trauerspiel* exactly because they inadvertently connected "multiplicity of sources, forms and spirit" to a "false appearance of a real unity of essence."[18] Instead, in his book, Benjamin applies a different methodological strategy, one that aligns with his philosophical convictions. He directs his attention to minor and under-researched writers and dramatists (such as Andreas Gryphius, Johann Christian Hallmann, Martin Opitz, and others) whose literary production presented "major"[19] unique contributions and therefore captured the true nature of the German baroque.

This criticism of traditional literary aesthetics confronts Benjamin with the problem of nominalism that Deleuze aimed to dissolve in his philosophy of difference. I follow here on Adorno, who remarks in his 1955 introduction to Benjamin's first collected papers that "in the preface to the *Trauerspiel* book [Benjamin] attempted a metaphysical rescue of nominalism."[20] In basic terms, if objects were indeed independent and had meaning that was not reduced to the concept, it was unclear what principle of representation applied to such objects.[21] Deleuze, I noted earlier in the book, completely rejected such a principle or a relation. For Deleuze, repetition was a "difference without concept."[22] Benjamin, however, insists on the validity and importance of such a principle. Like Deleuze decades later, Benjamin recognizes the inadequacy of the philosophical concept, but he does not give up on the attempt to find a different principle of representation elsewhere.

In a December 1923 letter to his close friend German theologian and writer Florens Rang, Benjamin details his solution: "It is a foregone conclusion for me that there is no such thing as art history... In terms of its essence, [art] is ahistorical. The attempt to place the work of art in the context of historical life does not open up perspectives that lead us to its *innermost core*."[23] We should be careful not to understand Benjamin's claim as a suggestion that art has no history, that is, that works of art have no relations to other works of art.[24] In stating that art is "ahistorical," Benjamin refers to his conviction that to avoid nominalism, we must find a different category of relations between works of art. The explanation of art has to be more than an explanation of its history or of the genre. The "history" of works of art—their relations to each other within a genre—has to be conceptualized "in a way that is *comprehensive* and *fundamental* at the same time."[25]

"An Eddy in the Stream of Becoming": *Ursprung* and History

The prologue was written with the purpose of presenting a solution to this challenge of "ahistorical" historical connection, one based on a reappropriation of two concepts long debated in the history of Western philosophy: the "idea" (*Idee*) and the "origin" (*Ursprung*). First, the idea. The idea is one of the most complicated concepts of Benjamin's early period. Benjamin credits Plato for the inauguration of the system of ideas in philosophy;[26] the idea also has important reverberations with Leibniz's monad and therefore can be misunderstood as taking part in the idealist tradition.[27] But as I will shortly explain, in the prologue, Benjamin takes certain intuitions and notions from Plato and Leibniz to suggest his own version of the idea, which has significant reverberations with Jewish mystical theories of language. At this stage, it is sufficient to note that in *Trauerspiel* the idea is defined as an *essence* and is the true object of "philosophical investigation."[28] Truth, in the context of Benjamin's theory of ideas, is the product of the investigation of essences and envisaged as the harmony between them.[29]

Important to Benjamin's materialism, unlike the concept, which reduces the phenomenal world to abstract notions, the idea is a representation of the phenomenal world that safeguards the value of the specific object. In one of the popular slogans of *Trauerspiel*, he notes that "ideas are to objects as constellations are to stars."[30] Yet how an idea could be different from a concept? In what way does the idea "respect" the individual value of objects in reality, and how do the relations between the idea and phenomenal world differ from the reduction of existence in conceptual thinking? The origin, or *Ursprung*, is one of the metaphors with which Benjamin explains the solution to this problem. Traditionally, the *Ursprung* resonates in German language with source, beginning, and origin. It was employed in various theoretical configurations by Goethe and Herder to describe the root cause of a phenomenon. The search for origins also informed several systems in the modern philosophy of such figures as Hermann Cohen, Nietzsche, Heidegger, and Foucault.[31] In Benjamin's *Trauerspiel*, the *Ursprung* is a metaphor for thinking concretely of the relations between the idea and the phenomenal world. More specifically, the *Ursprung* presents the historical actualization of the idea in a series of objects, or exemplars, in Benjamin's terms, whose investigation constitutes the possibility of knowing the idea:

> Origin (*Ursprung*), although an entirely historical category, has, nevertheless, nothing to do with genesis (*Entstehung*). The term origin is not intended to describe the process by which existent came into being, but rather to describe that which emerges from the process of becoming and disappearing. Origin is an eddy in the stream of becoming, and in its current it swallows the material involved in the process of genesis. That which is original is never reveled in the naked and manifested existence of the factual; its rhythm is apparent only to a dual insight (*Doppeleinsicht*). On the one hand it needs to be recognized as a process of restoration and reestablishment, but, on the other hand, and precisely because of this, as something imperfect and incomplete.[32]

There is much to unpack in this short paragraph, one of the most cited from the prologue. Let me begin by noting Benjamin's understanding of the historical presence of the *Ursprung*. Perhaps despite its name, the *Ursprung* is not an event at the beginning of history, or an abstract concept outside history, or a point of origination (*Entstehung*) before history. The *Ursprung* is not a beginning that predetermines a certain history. Rather, the *Ursprung* is nothing other than the material, concrete manifestations of the idea in history. Unlike traditional theories of presentation, in which the concept is alienated from history, the *Ursprung* is embedded in history. It is part of history, and it therefore indicates the corporeal actuality of the idea. In Benjamin's terms, therefore, the *Ursprung* is not a process in which "the existent came to being" but the emergence of a process of "becoming and disappearance."[33]

The corporeal actuality of the *Ursprung* prescribes a historical connection between objects that seemingly paradoxically kept their *absolute individuality*.[34] This is possible because the *Ursprung* presents a structure of "dynamic repetition." The *Ursprung*, Benjamin states, repeats in history, but this repetition is not a repetition of the same. To understand the historical existence of the *Ursprung*, its form of "ahistorical" historicity, we have to see it, according to Benjamin, in a double way. The *Ursprung* designates a kind of "imperfect reestablishment": on the one hand, the *Ursprung* returns in history through different objects or works of art. Each work presents a different side of the idea. But on the other hand, the *Ursprung* never offers anything identical in its returns, just as those objects (works of arts) are essentially different from each other. Each instance participates in the idea as an essence but in a different way. The works of art are both connected and separate, individual and part of a constellation.[35]

At first glance, then, Benjamin's model of repetition in *Trauerspiel* resembles that of modern philosophy, in that each repetition of the *Ursprung* offers something new and different. The *Ursprung* is reinvented in its repetitions. It never fully reiterates its previous expressions. It appears in history, but this appearance is always different and never identical to its other manifestations.

Benjamin's *Ursprung* and Goethe's *Urphänomen*

Earlier in the book, I noted that in the archaic model of repetition of the same, individual objects were meaningful by being in direct relations with eternal or mythical forms. This connection was *ahis-*

torical: it prescribed unmediated relations of the profane with the sacred. It also resembled the platonic theory of forms in which specific phenomena repeat the idea to become intelligible. I defined "archaic repetition" as this connection between individual things and their eternal archetypes. In archaic repetition, I noted, the historical connection between different repetitions of the archetypes in history was meaningless. Only the relations between the object and the sacred were relevant and valuable. Benjamin's notion of repetition is based on a different logic, which Benjamin explicates in his famous mother metaphor:

> Just as a mother is seen to begin to live in the fullness of her power only when the circle of her children, inspired by the feeling of her proximity, closes around her, so do ideas come to life only when extremes are assembled around them. Ideas—or, to use Goethe's term, ideals—are the Faustian "Mothers." They remain obscure so long as phenomena do not declare their fate to them and gather round them.[36]

The mother metaphor reflects a unique understanding of the historical determination of the *Ursprung*. According to Benjamin, the idea is not perceived through one specific artifact, or exemplar, but in a process that takes into account different manifestations of the *Ursprung*. Think of a constellation of stars for example. Its structure is almost indiscernible if we recognize only one star. However, this structure is attainable if we learn more about the rest of the stars in the constellations. To bring this back to his theory of *Ursprung*, Benjamin believed the idea is recognizable only through the examination of *actual* contributions of different objects or works of art; each repeats previous objects but is also different from them, much like patterns of similarities and repetition in family relations.[37]

The mother metaphor also explains why Benjamin's investigation was not focused on individual objects in isolation. The constellation is perceived only when the relations between objects are taken into account, for example, the spatial relations between the stars in the constellations. In Benjamin's words, "There takes place in every original phenomenon a determination of the form in which an idea will constantly confront the historical world, until it is revealed fulfilled, in the totality of its history. Origin is not, therefore, discovered by the examination of actual findings, but is related to their history and subsequent development."[38] The relations of the world with the idea are, therefore, not one-dimensional, that is, grounded on the connection of one object and the idea, but always multidimensional—it is dependent on the interrelations of several objects in reality. Benjamin's investigation, in other words, had to focus on the structure of repetition characterizing the *Ursprung*: the dynamics of sameness and change, the rhythms of difference and similarities between series of exemplary objects, and the structure of their repetition all mirror the structure of the idea.[39]

The insistence on the investigation of repetitive structures rather than isolated objects resulted from Benjamin's conviction that by juxtaposing different instances of repetition, hidden aspects of the idea were revealed. This insight prompts Benjamin to emphasize the differences between different repetitions of the *Ursprung*: "The idea is best explained as the representation of the *context* within which the *unique* and *extreme* stands alongside its counterpart."[40] It is not only the individual object, but also its relations with other objects, or, more concretely, the differences between these objects, that are so crucial for knowing the idea. Conceptual analysis levels these differences, or extremes, but Benjamin insists that the idea must preserve them, and philosophy must uncover them. Here I follow Eli Friedlander who, in *Walter Benjamin: A Philosophical Portrait* (2012), elaborates on the importance of these extreme differences, suggesting that Benjamin borrowed from Goethe's theory of *Urphänomen* (original phenomenon).

Goethe's *Urphänomen* was introduced in his first scientific publication, *The Metamorphosis of Plants*, written after his trip to Italy from 1786 to 1788. The *Urphänomen* designated the formative part of a natural organism or structure—the leaf is Goethe's eminent example—through which the whole structure, say that of the plant, was revealed in unmediated form.[41] One of the basic concepts of Goethe's theory of science, the *Urphänomen*, was foundational to his theory of morphology and his theory of colors. Benjamin comments on Goethe's *Urphänomen* in his doctoral work (in his last chapter on Goethe's aesthetic theory) and later in his essay on Goethe's Elective Affinities. He nonetheless downplays Goethe's contribution to his own formulation of the *Ursprung*, which he finally acknowledges only years later in *Passagenwerk*.[42]

In Goethe's science, the recognition of the *Urphänomen* is based on understanding the oppositional relations between different objects in nature. To explain, in Goethe's philosophy of nature, two forces produce the variety of natural objects: polarity (*Polarität*) and intensification. Intensification pushes nature toward growth, while polarity (the equivalent of the power of attraction and repulsion in magnetism) is responsible for multiplicity in nature. If nature is one organism, as Goethe, following basic romantic paradigm, believed, polarity explains the process by which infinite Being is "split" into diverse, finite, individual objects.[43] This logic informs Goethe's theory of the *Urphänomen*. Since polarity generated the multiplicity of finite beings, the *Urphänomen*, that is, the original form, is recognizable when objects are reorganized in the original polarized structure in which they were created, that is, when the polarization that split Being into beings is reversed. More precisely, Goethe declares: "Whatever appears in the world must divide if it is to appear at all. What has been divided seeks itself again, can return to itself and reunite.... The union may occur in a higher sense if what has been divided is first intensified; then in the union of the intensified halves it will produce a third thing, something new, higher, unexpected."[44] The epistemological process of knowing the *Urphänomen* took objects away from their natural arrangement and put them into a meaningful opposition. This opposition recreated the tensions producing the individual phenomenon in the first place, and it thereby allowed the recognition of the *Urphänomen* in the present. This notion of productive tension informed, claims Friedlander, Benjamin's theory of *Ursprung*.

While Benjamin discards the idealistic assumptions of Goethe's theory of nature and forces, he still implements Goethe's insights on the place of oppositionality and tension in the production of knowledge. As in Goethe's science, the historical investigation of the *Ursprung* reorders objects into a structure of opposing relations formative of the recognition of the idea. These oppositions between extremes produce tensions through which unrecognizable facts in the object became accessible. Friedlander writes: "Polarization is the creation of a tension when phenomena are held together as extremes. Facts as such are inert, but they can be polarized and span a field of meaningful tensions ... Polarization assumes that the presentation of what is valuable or significant depends on equally holding to all sides."[45] In Benjamin's model, the opposition between objects creates the necessary condition for a truth that is unavailable when objects are in isolation. However, the idea is not recognized by a mere comparison: objects must be put in *polar* tension to be meaningful.[46] Exemplary objects, the focus of Benjamin's investigation, are not like parts of a puzzle. Their comparison is not based on how they overlap, but on the differences between them through which hidden aspects can be known. Repetition is another name for this process: historical repetition—not of the same event or object but of "opposites"—creates the relations between the objects and the tensions which expose these hidden facts. It produces a series of interconnected oppositions, or in Benjamin's terms in *Passagenwerk* a "constellation *saturated with tensions*," that reveals the idea.[47] Philosophical history— the science of the origin—therefore "is the form which, in the remotest extremes and the apparent excesses of the process of development, reveals the configuration of the idea—*the sum total of all possible meaningful juxtapositions of such opposites*." The representation of an idea, Benjamin adds, "can under no circumstances be considered successful unless the whole range of possible extremes it contains has been virtually explored."[48]

Benjamin's model of repetition is what I call "repetition of opposites." The *Ursprung* repeatedly appears in history, each time revealing different, opposing faces, which, when juxtaposed with its previous and future repetitions, restores a revelatory insight unperceivable otherwise in profane reality.[49] *Trauerspiel*, appropriately, was inspired by this notion of repetition-driven knowledge. The book is composed of diverse and often opposing examples of baroque drama, which, when put together, juxtaposed to each other, create a meaningful presentation of the object of investigation. The same applies to Benjamin's earlier "Goethe's Elective Affinities," where Benjamin seeks to portray the nature of Goethe's drama by reflecting on its internal polarities.

Benjamin's discussion of the extreme is evocative of Deleuze's theory of repetition. It also, however, demonstrates the differences between the thinkers. For Deleuze, repetition is not a repetition of the same but one that produces difference. Repetition illustrates the uniqueness of the object, its particular qualities that the concept inhibits. And repetition does so by recognizing what Deleuze terms, not unlike Benjamin, the "extreme." In Deleuze's words, "Only the extreme forms return—those which, large or small, are deployed within the limit and extend to the limit of their power, transforming themselves and changing one into another. Only the extreme, the excessive, returns; that which passes into something else and becomes identical."[50] For Deleuze, the extreme expresses the univocity of phenomena, an excess that the concept is unable to recognize or to explain, and it therefore must repress. The extreme is the principle of repetition: it is the expression of the difference that returns.

Benjamin's notion of the extreme echoes Deleuze's insistence that repetition is never repetition of the same. For both thinkers, such repetition is meaningless and distracting. However, in Benjamin's Goethean notion of extreme, the emphasis is not only on the difference, but also on the hidden, fruitful collaboration that the extreme secretly promises. Benjamin would have agreed with Deleuze that repetition is a "difference without concept." However, for Benjamin, the idea, a higher form of knowledge, is revealed through repetition. When one object is positioned as the polar opposite of other extreme repetitions of the *Ursprung*, this structure provides an understanding. In other words, Benjamin's repetition is one of *opposition*, not simply of differences. The extreme is not a symbol solely of radical univocity but is revelatory of deeper relations uncovered by repetition. In the phenomenal world, Benjamin agrees with Deleuze, this repetition highlights differences. And yet these differences constitute meaning on a different level of being. The object is extreme because it holds a liminal position between sameness and radical difference: it is certainly different from previous repetitions of the *Ursprung* but it also offers insight into the constellation of an idea. Put shortly, in the work of both Deleuze and Benjamin, repetition is a principle of selection. However, the stakes of the act of selection are different: for Benjamin, selection produces a condition for apprehension of essences; in Deleuze, selection rejects an epistemological error. Yet the difference between the two does not end here. Benjamin's theory of extremes, we will see now, impacted his understanding of time and history.

Repetition, Tension, and Intensification

In *Trauerspiel*, Benjamin's understanding of history reflects German Romanticism. Much like Goethe and then Schelling, for Benjamin, in this work, time is not homogenous but pregnant with tensions. To explain this model of time, consider Benjamin's theorization of tensional constellation, as inspired in the 1930s by the Eiffel Tower, which fascinated Benjamin during his exile in Paris. In a passage cited in the Arcades Project, Benjamin is especially fixed on the relations between small, apparently immaterial parts that hold the entire structure together. His interest echoes his enchantment with the montage, a key methodological concept used in his later work to explain his notion of constellation: "On building the Eiffel Tower: 'Thus, the plastic shaping power abdicates here in favor of a colossal tension (*spannung*) of spiritual energy, which channels the inorganic material energy into the smallest, most efficient forms and conjoins these forms in the most effective manner.'"[51] Benjamin's constellation works in a manner similar to the core tension supporting the Eiffel Tower. Its many tensional connections create a structure through which the idea is perceivable. These tensional relations charge time with force. Benjamin suggests this understanding relatively early in his previously mentioned letter to Rang from 1923, where he complains about the shortcomings of previous theories of art history. "There remains an *intense* relationship among works of art," he notes.[52]

Benjamin's early theory of history is nothing like the stale and linear vision of history in the nineteenth-century German historicism of Ranke or Droysen. His history is not composed of an endless series of equally important historical facts but is crowded with nonlinear connections between events, works, and objects that infuse history with vibrancy. The difference between individual repetitions of *Ursprung* generates productive antagonism, not harmonious reality, as Benjamin further explains in the same letter: "For in interpretation, relationships among works of art appear that are timeless yet not without historical relevance. That is to say, the same forces that become explosively and extensively temporal in the world of revelation (and this is what history is) appear concentrated in the silent world (and this is the world of nature and of works of art)."[53] Benjamin's correspondence with Rang in the early 1920s illuminates the early stages of the composition of his book on the German baroque, when Benjamin struggled to merge German philosophy, Romantic aesthetics, and theology. I will discuss the place of revelation in Benjamin's theory shortly, but at present I want to focus on his vision of tension. The world of nature and art seems silent, he writes, but it is actually rife with "forces" with the potential to be "explosive."

In *Passagenwerk*, Benjamin elaborates on the tensional relations of the constellation in a different key: "The fore- and after-history of a historical phenomenon show up in the phenomenon itself on the strength of its dialectical presentation. What is more: every dialectically presented historical circumstance polarizes itself and becomes a force field [*Kraftfeld*] in which the confrontation [*Auseinandersetzung*] between its fore-history and after-history is played out."[54] In Benjamin's imagination, repetition *enlivens* homogenous time. The opposition between repetitions, that is, between different manifestations of *Ursprung*, changes the architectonics of time: it creates sites of tension and pressure in the vast, empty desert of reality. The historical relations between works of art are not just conceptual or theoretical: repetition injects dynamism and intensity into reality. These historical tension-relations ground the possibility of knowing the idea: repetition intensifies tension in historical time, and this tension creates a "force field" within which the "confrontation" between the past and future of the *Ursprung* is "played out." Tension and force, in other words, provide an opportunity to recognize truth. The intensification of time is crucial for revelation: it produces vibrant relations that surmount empty time and through which the idea is accessible.

The implications of the *Ursprung* to Benjamin's early model of history cannot be overstated. Benjamin's work on repetition suggests a new logic for history. Repetitions are the basic elements of history, the building blocks of the idea; in such transformative repetitions, significant, authentic phenomena appear on the surface of history. Homogenous time is filled with unbounded multiplicity. This disconnected reality is rather meaningless: objects with no historical dimension, that is, no repetitive relations to their past and their future, have no relations with the idea. They are "primitive 'facts,'"[55] in Benjamin's terminology. They appear only momentarily on the stage of history.

However, when put into repetitive relations, objects acquire value and meaning.[56] Furthermore, repetition functions as an accelerator of energy in history. As the *Ursprung* repeats in history, repetition generates more points of contact that charge history with oppositionality and intensity. The force field is more powerful with every repetition. Each cycle of repetition changes the fabric of historical time by charging force into empty time. Instead of a desert of sameness, repetition creates a topography saturated with tensions and forces.

In point of fact, repetition is a somewhat unexpected framework for thinking of history. Remember that in the previous chapter, I noted how an overflowing experience of eternal return resulted from the meaninglessness inflicted by modern capitalism on society. In Benjamin's understanding, reality was "ever-the-same," and this sameness was experienced in a form of an eternal return. And yet in *Trauerspiel*, written several years earlier, a different kind of historical repetition is the principle with which Benjamin resolves sameness. In this case, "repetition of opposites" produces meaningful relations between previously isolated objects, through which truth is possible. The emptiness that the eternal return exhibits is surmounted by a different form of repetition of the *Ursprung*. This insight later grounded Benjamin's messianic vision.

Lastly, thinking of the German Jewish intellectual world, Benjamin's model of repetition reflects some of the concerns of his time. As noted, in the beginning of the twentieth century, the German Jewish community suffered an experience of disconnection from Jewish tradition because tendencies of assimilation and secularization appeared to dismantle the German Jewish way of life. In response to this crisis, the German Jews found new inspiration by turning back to their imagined origins, through which they hoped to rebuild their present. This turn to Jewish origins produced a surge of interest in things Jewish in the *fin-de-siècle* Jewish world canonized by Buber as a "Jewish renaissance." Benjamin's *Ursprung* echoes the attempt to refashion the origins of the Jewish community. His notion of *Ursprung* provided a framework within which dynamic relations to an origin produced meaning in history, exactly when the German Jewish community was searching for models of communal meaning by returning to its own origins. Benjamin's work, however, also suggests a criticism of the

Jewish project. In the Jewish form of return, most evidently in the Zionist project, the past was glorified. The Jews struggled to insert their present practices and institutes into a relationship with this past, with the Jewish imagination reflecting this past. Yet Benjamin's formulation of origins holds no ahistorical truth that the Jewish community could reintegrate in the present. For Benjamin, the *Ursprung* illustrates a model of return that problematizes the autonomy of origins and questions the automatic attribution of superior truths to the past. Rather than a return to a beginning, in the German sense of *Wiederkehr*, the *Ursprung* is a series of repetitions (*Wiederholungs*) that rearticulate the idea again and again from different perspectives. The past, put differently, in Benjamin's reformulation of the notion of origin, has no real command over and beyond the now. The Jewish search for origins could be recast, instead, according to the *Trauerspiel's* theory of repetition: an "origin," as portrayed by Benjamin, constitutes a series of repetitions of different cultural realities; yet this series is not meaningless or valueless, as it harbors, according to Benjamin, rare images of great importance.

Repetition and the Mystical Construction of the Idea

Trauerspiel, basically like any other work by Benjamin, amalgamates various political, cultural, literary, religious, and philosophical traditions and worldviews that could have and probably did influence Benjamin at the time of composing different parts of his corpus. In what comes, I do not attempt to synthesize a unified theoretical position.[57] We already recognized the crucial place of Goethe and Leibniz in the construction of his model of *Ursprung*; I now turn to his debt to Jewish mystical theories of language, one he recognized in his conversations with Adorno and Rychner, as noted in the opening lines of this chapter. Benjamin, in fact, openly declares this contiguity in a short passage in the prologue. "The idea," he writes, "is something linguistic, it is that element of the symbolic in the essence of any word."[58] A few lines later, he adds: "Ultimately... this is not the attitude of Plato, but the attitude of Adam ... Ideas are displayed, without intention, in the act of [Adamic] naming, and they have to be renewed in philosophical contemplation."[59] My intention in the following is to build on the contiguity of Benjamin's notion of idea with Jewish mystical theories of language to suggest a solution to a problem left partly unanswered by the prologue. I refer here to the problem of recognition of repetition when that repetition is of extremes, differences, or opposites.

Dialectic of Difference and Similarity

In *Trauerspiel*, the historical repetitions of the *Ursprung* present a structure of repetition of opposites. Each manifestation of the *Ursprung* always confronts previous cycles. These works of art and exemplary objects are different, not similar. They are individual, singular expressions of the *Ursprung* rather than simple copies. And yet if these repetitions are so different, even opposing, how can we tie them together? What principle identifies a repetition when all the particular incidents of that repetition are so different? How can we find exemplary art, when the historical points of reference of that art are inherently dissimilar?

Of course, this problem has practical implications in *Trauerspiel*. The connection of such disparate repetitions is an urgent issue in Benjamin's work on the German baroque, a field of study whose multiplicity and diversity dismayed many previous scholars.[60] The stakes of this problem to modern philosophy of repetition are also far-reaching. Since, in modern philosophy, repetition is based on differences, we need to ask: what makes repetition more than a random movement? What is the principle of connection between dynamic repetitions? In Deleuze, for example, any attempt to find a concept tying repetitions together went against the basic thrust of his philosophy of difference. Kierkegaard also refused to assign to his repetition any positive content. The same applied to Heidegger and his endless hermeneutic circle of repetitions. Benjamin, I argue, changed this picture. His reflections on the relations between the Adamic name in his "On Language as Such" essay and on the idea (in *Trauerspiel*) explain how we can recognize repetitions in history. Specifically, I posit that such recognition is analogous to the Adamic act of naming, in which Adam invents the name of the thing as much as he discovers it in reality. This structure offers a model of recognition that upends the simple dichotomy of identity and non-identity, similarity and difference which informs later conceptions of repetition, for example, in Heidegger and Deleuze.

Preemptively, we might address this challenge with the obvious remark that for Benjamin, *Ursprung* represents the principle connecting all its historical manifestations; that is, the *Ursprung* is that which connects different repetitions. However, the content of the *Ursprung*, we recall, is built on the ways it actually reappears in history. This solution also immediately begets another question: how do we recognize the *Ursprung*, the "mother," to use Benjamin's analogy? What is the principle with which we can recognize that a particular object is part of the *Ursprung*'s repetitive structure? We find a first clue to Benjamin's response to this challenge in *Trauerspiel*:

> It does not, however, follow that every primitive "fact" should straightaway be considered a constitutive determinant. Indeed this is where the task of the investigator begins, for he cannot regard such a fact as certain until its innermost structure appears to be so essential as to reveal it as an origin. The authentic—the hallmark of origin in phenomena—is the object of discovery, a discovery which is connected in unique way with the process of recognition. And the act of discovery can reveal it in the most singular and eccentric of phenomena, in both the weakest and clumsiest experiments and in the overripe fruits of a period of decadence.[61]

For Benjamin, the discovery of an exemplary object is connected in "a unique way" to a process of recognition. Benjamin reiterates this formulation a few years later in an essay on Austrian Jewish writer Karl Kraus, writing that "this 'origin' is the subject of a discovery that has a curious element of recognition."[62] The German original is important here: discovery is *Entdeckung*, sometimes translated as detection, exposition, or finding, an act we could assign to scientific observation or experiment. This discovery, however, Benjamin claims, must be connected to an act of re-cognition, or *Wiedererkennen*, which literally means an act of "finding again," or "knowing again." To translate this sentence literally, for Benjamin, the discovery of the object is conditional on a process of re-finding the object in reality. The discovery of the object is, in fact, a re-discovery: the fact always, in some way, is already given.

This act of re-discovery or re-finding characterizes Benjamin's repetition. According to Benjamin, to recognize an exemplary object in reality, we have to *find it in a repetitive context*. This finding is not a linear process in which the object is first recognized and then put in the context of other repetitions of the *Ursprung*. Rather, the finding of the object is always already within a repetitive structure. Put otherwise, the finding of the exemplary object is a finding of a structure of repetition. We cannot find individual objects, but only a group of objects, which, at the moment of their recognition, are understood as part of the repetitive structure of the *Ursprung*. This moment of recognition of exemplary objects and their structure of repetition, Benjamin tells us in the 1930s, happens in a flash: "The dialectical image is an image that emerges suddenly, in a flash. What has been is to be held fast—as an image flashing up in the now of its recognizability."[63] The process of recognition is not a process but a flash of recognition which produces salvation, in Benjamin's terms. In this flash, different objects (remember—they must be "extreme") are recognized as participating in the repetitive structure through which the idea is revealed.

This structure of "finding as re-finding" has important reverberation in the Adamic act of naming. In the following section, I briefly detail the basic principles of Benjamin's theory of language. I then return to Benjamin's model of repetition to ascertain, with his theory of language in mind, its revelatory potential.

Language and Revelatory Discovery

Benjamin's 1916 essay on language was written in the midst of intense correspondence with Scholem on the nature of language and mathematics. At the time, Benjamin was concerned with modern (bourgeois) theories of language. Essentially, he is critical of their main doctrine, namely that "man is communicating factual subject matter to other men,"[64] and "the word has an accidental relation to its object, that it is a sign for things."[65] Instead, Benjamin proposes a mystical theory of language that understands language as the realm through which the true essence of the world can be expressed. In his words, "all nature, insofar as it communicates itself, communicates itself in language, and so finally in man. Hence, he is the lord of nature and can give names to things. Only through the linguistic being of things can he get beyond himself and attain knowledge of them—in the name."[66]

As in Jewish mystical understandings, Benjamin's main argument is that each being in the world has a spiritual quality, or spiritual essence (*geistiges Wesen*), which only human language is able to express. Language, accordingly, is not a random system of concepts and symbols, as many philosophers of language of Benjamin's time believed, but rather the "ultimate reality" that grants beings their place in creation. In his words, "There is no such thing as a content of language; as communication, language communicates a spiritual entity—something communicable *per se*."[67] The Torah is useful to Benjamin in this context, as it presupposes "language as an ultimate reality, perceptible only in its manifestation, inexplicable and mystical."[68] Benjamin is interested primarily in the second story of creation in Genesis 2, where language structures the role of Adam in God's world. "God did not create man from the word, and he did not name him. He did not wish to subject him to language, but in man God set language, which had served him as medium of creation, free.... Man is the knower in the same language in which God is the creator."[69] Adam, Benjamin claims, was given the role of completing God's creation through language. He was the "lord of nature" in his capacity to name, that is, in his capacity to express spiritual essences.[70] Before the Adamic act, things possessed an inferior form of language, which Benjamin terms "language of things" (*die Sprache der Dinge*). This language was "imperfect language."[71] Existence at this stage was correspondingly "imperfect" and things "dumb."[72] The Adamic language, Benjamin explains, introduced a qualitative difference: "In names culminate both the intensive totality of language, as the absolutely communicable mental entity, and the extensive totality of language, as the universally communicating (naming) entity.... *Man alone has a language that is complete both in its universality and in its intensiveness* [*Intensität*]."[73]

The act of naming also defines Benjamin's early understanding of revelation. Revelation is a perfect pronunciation of the deepest, most obscure parts of the object, the uncovering of all that is hidden, remote, and unspoken.[74] Revelation, however, became unavailable after the Fall: "The paradisiacal language of man must have been one of perfect knowledge, whereas later all knowledge is again infinitely differentiated in the multiplicity of language," he writes.[75] In a world of linguistic multiplicity, human languages capture only small fractions of existence. The hidden parts of the thing are inaccessible, and humanity can only know the surface of reality. For Benjamin, the exile from Paradise symbolizes an exile from truth. Rather than knowing the inner essence of the world, men and women have only "a knowledge from outside, the uncreated imitation of the creative word."[76] The story of the tower of Babel signals this catastrophe by illustrating how language became simply a means of communication, forsaking its core role in creation and knowledge. The story suggests that human language has replaced the immediacy of truth with mediated abstractions: the name has been demoted to "the empty word," and language to "the abyss of prattle."[77]

Benjamin addresses the problem of language again in his introduction to his book of translations of Baudelaire's *Tableaux Parisiens* (1923), later separately entitled "The Task of the Translator." The model of language and translation in this essay is still hotly debated by Benjamin's readership. For the purposes of the present argument, I will follow the "metaphysical" interpretation of the essay.[78] In this reading, *The Task of the Translator* shows how translations are first and foremost an attempt at reconciliation of languages after the Fall. In Benjamin's important definition, "translation thus ultimately serves the purpose of expressing the innermost relationship of languages to one another."[79] They produce a "harmony of all the various ways of meaning," from which *sparks of revelation* of the Adamic language (now famously termed "pure language") emerge, even in profane reality.[80]

Trauerspiel represents a second stage of Benjamin's continuous struggle to locate sparks of lost revelation in profane reality. While *The Task of Translation* focuses on the promise of revelation in a literary context, *Trauerspiel* turns to a theory of art and history. This is possible since, for Benjamin, the ideas are analogous to the Adamic names which his new historical philosophy aims to present. Benjamin writes, "In this renewal the primordial mode of apprehending words is restored. And so, in the course of its history, which has so often been an object of scorn, philosophy is—and rightly so—a struggle for the representation of a limited number of words which always remain the same—a struggle for the representation of ideas."[81] Put shortly, for Benjamin, the repetitive structure of the *Ursprung* in history presents the "renewal" of the Adamic language. The *Ursprung* is the historical, albeit partial, return of the Adamic revelation. In its repetition, it grants glimpses of the idea, which Benjamin defines in terms of his theory of names.

Building on Benjamin's suggestion to see in the idea an "element of the symbolic in the essence of any word," I argue that his reflection on the relations of Adam with reality (in his essay on language) explains how we can recognize repetitions in history. In both cases, recognition involves active interaction with reality, not mere receptivity. Adam invented the name of the thing as much as he received it from the world; in a similar fashion, the historian must create and find repetitions in equal measures.

"Immersion and Absorption": On Discovering Repetitions

Benjamin's theory of language is built on a special structure of recognition. In Benjamin's "On Language as Such" essay, the relations between language and reality are different from those in other theories of language in German philological tradition. The spiritual essence of the thing, he argues, is not first set and then later identified in language, nor is it dependent on our preconceived notions. Rather, a thing accepts its meaning in the process of naming. This act involves both reception and spontaneity: "This knowledge of the thing, however, is not spontaneous creation ... Rather, the name that man gives to language depends on how language is communicated to him. In name, the word of God has not remained creative; it has become in one part receptive, even if receptive to language."[82] The name is a product of Adam's "productive listening." Benjamin is once again critical of the bourgeois theory of language, according to which names are only random signs that language assigns to reality. At the same time, however, he denounces the common mystical understanding of language, in which names are "simply the essence of the thing" and, as such, were determined prior to the interaction of man and world. The name is not a complete invention from the side of the subject nor is it pregiven from the side of the object. The name is neither intuitively produced nor passively received in this act of revelatory discovery: it is rather a form of recognition that both invents *and* accepts the spiritual essence of the thing. To put this in philosophical terms, in his "On Language as Such" essay, Benjamin repudiates both naïve realism and idealism. Adam was not a passive observer of the world, nor was he the sole creator of the meaning of that world. Instead, he interacted with divine creation to find the name of the thing. He produced a truth as much as he was given a truth; he imagined as much as he answered to reality.[83]

Benjamin revisits these relations nearly a decade later in *Trauerspiel*. In this case, he is interested in the relations of the observer, or art historian, with reality in the context of his theory of history. His argument here echoes that of the model of recognition in his theory of language. In a much-quoted passage mentioning his earlier theory of language, Benjamin writes:

> The being of ideas simply cannot be conceived of as the object of vision, even intellectual vision. For even in its most paradoxical periphrasis, as *intellectus archetypus*, vision does not enter into the form of existence which is peculiar to truth, is peculiar to truth which is devoid of all intention, and certainly does not itself appear as intention . . . Truth is an intentionless state of being [*intentionsloses Sein*], made up of ideas. The proper approach to it is not therefore one of intention and knowledge, but rather a total immersion and absorption in it.[84]

Benjamin's famous "death of intention" principle has received much attention from his readers.[85] It is my contention that this principle reverberates with Adam's relations with reality. The idea, Benjamin claims, is a product of revelatory *immersion* in the world. Benjamin's investigation demands a certain mode of attentiveness or involvement in reality through which we can uncover the idea, or the essence of the object. Just like premeditated conceptual inquiries, distant and disinterested observations hinder this understanding. The instruction is to be intentionless. This formula reiterates Benjamin's earlier understanding of the relations of Adam with the world: one had to be absorbed in history, to be immersed in the period, to find exemplary works of art, just like Adam, who, immersed in nature, named the spiritual essence of the thing. The Adamic naming, in other words, set the principles of recognition of meaningful structures in history.

What is interesting in Benjamin's "death of intention" principle is its addition of a second layer of meaning to his claim that the discovery of an exemplary object depends on its re-finding in other instances. This formula, we noted, expressed the importance of repetitive structures to finding exemplary objects, as every act of recognition entails an act of re-cognition of the object from within a repetitive structure. My claim is that the demand to discover an object in reality as if it is re-discovered resonates with the Adamic act of naming. To uncover the *Ursprung*, we have to relate to reality with a double insight: our investigation has to both actively identify the authenticity of the object and passively receive it from reality. Discovery is connected with a finding: the object is "named" in a process in which the object revealed itself back. Adam is the model for Benjamin's recognition: he portrays a mode of attentiveness in which we both find and re-find the object in reality.

This act of revelatory discovery is deeply connected to Benjamin's theory of *repetition of opposites*. As already noted, for Benjamin, the discovery of one exemplary object was contingent on the recognition of it as part of a repetitive structure. For this reason, we may say that the investigation of repetitive structures both actively "names" the structure and gets it back from reality. Similar to the Adamic act of naming, we *find* repetitions as much as we *create* them. A structure of repetition is not simply discovered but forged in an act of recognition. A repetition is produced as much as it is identified. This duality points to the origins of invention in the Latin *inveniō*, which denotes the act of finding out or a discovery, as I indicated earlier in my discussion of *Entdecken*. We *craft* the *Ursprung* and identify repetitions thanks to our contact with history. These structures are not given simply from the side of the object or ideally constructed from the side of the subject; repetition is not realistic description or intuitive creation. Instead, repetition is both discovered and recognized in an act of immersion.

Benjamin's mystical theory of language thus offers an important insight into modern philosophy of repetition. For Benjamin, repetition is not grounded on conceptual identity, or on a principle of non-identity, or yet again on a hermeneutical cycle of ongoing creation. Rather, it is grounded on non-conceptual relations forged in a *mystic-like experience of immersion of the subject in reality*.

Notably, the foregoing analyses of the double act of naming/recognizing are useful to explicate Benjamin's understanding of redemption. Benjamin engages with this theme in his discussion of language as the spiritual essence of man.[86] For Benjamin, language is the spiritual essence that Adam activated in naming: "But because the mental being of man is language itself, he cannot communicate himself by it, but only in it. The quintessence of this intensive totality of language as the spiritual being of man is the name."[87] In the act of naming, that is, in the act of expressing *other* spiritual essences, Adam was *in* language and thereby communicated his own spiritual essence to God: "*In the name, the spiritual being of man communicates itself to God.*"[88] Language, in other words, communicated both world and Adam to God. It communicated the thing to God when Adam named the thing, and it communicated Adam to God when Adam was in language to name the thing. The act of naming communicated both the agent of naming and the recipient of the act of naming to God. To put Benjamin's insight into theological terms, in this instance, naming was not only an act of revelation, in which the deep and previously mute spiritual essence of the world was expressed, but also an act of redemption, in which the speaker and the thing found their place in God's creation.

Naming, however, was a task, or even a duty, that Adam was able to fulfill only in the Garden of Eden. After the Fall, when language transformed into a profane form of communication, this task was no longer available. Profane reality was, in that sense, a reality of double self-alienation: the thing lost its truth, but so did Adam and his children, who, unable to name the thing, lost their ability to express their own spiritual essence. The deep impact of Benjamin's theory of repetition in *Trauerspiel* lies in this understanding. Simply stated, his work channels the human divine task into history. In place of Adam's revelatory discovery of the name, humanity in the present can get a glimpse of the idea with historical repetition. As in Benjamin's theory of language, this task has redemptive implications: the repetitive structure of the *Ursprung* affords contact with the Adamic name, thereby allowing humanity to express its spiritual essence. Humanity does more than find truth in historical repetitions. In investigating the idea, humanity has the potential to recommunicate, even if partially, its spiritual essence to God. Repetition, in that sense, provides an opportunity for a moment in which the world re-finds its truth, or a glimpse of that truth, and no less important, a moment in which *humanity re-finds its own truth*.

Repetition and Redemption

Benjamin continued to develop his theory of the "repetition of opposites" in the 1930s, but there was a significant difference in his formulation of repetition. In the *Trauerspiel* period, his theory of aesthetics and knowledge offered a conceptual framework to understanding German baroque drama. His mystical and epistemological insights provided the groundwork for a revolution in art history. Indeed, Benjamin's monadological impetus in *Trauerspiel* gives us a glimpse of the entire structure of the world, and his previous theory of language highlights the revelatory function of the "repetition of opposites." Yet his early versions of revelation and redemption miss the urgency that colors his later work: they describe the world; they do not offer a way to change it. In *Passagenwerk*, however, Benjamin is concerned primarily with the *present (die Gegenwart)*. He redefines his vision of repetition from within a theory of historical materialism that investigates the conditions of radical change in history.[89] His vision of time and his theory of knowledge focus on the now as an opportunity for messianic intervention. "Every present day," Benjamin writes in *Passagenwerk*, "is determined by the images that are synchronic with it: each 'now' is the now of a particular recognizability. In it, truth is charged to the bursting point with time."[90]

In the 1930s, Benjamin was still working within the framework of his theory of ideas but the mystical insight that resulted in the investigation of the constellation now had messianic implications.

Benjamin's Copernican Revolution

The reorientation of Benjamin's theoretical focus had both conceptual and methodological implications. This is perhaps most prominently noted in an insert in *Passagenwerk* where Benjamin explains his Copernican revolution. I touched on this paragraph earlier in my discussion of Benjamin's theory of the dreaming collective. "The

Copernican revolution in historical perception is as follows. Formerly it was thought that a fixed point had been found in 'what has been' [*das Gewesene*]; and one saw the present engaged in tentatively concentrating the forces of knowledge on this ground. Now this relation is to be overturned, and what has been is to become the dialectical reversal—the flash of awakened consciousness [*erwachten Bewußtsein*]. *Politics attains primacy over history*."[91] Benjamin's recalling of the Kantian Copernican revolution in philosophy is intended to clarify a radical transformation in the relations between past and present. In previous theories of history, especially in historicism, the historical object preceded the present: the historical object was a fact that historical consciousness understood as foreign or independent. The historian conformed to the object as if it "has already been," much like the way perception conformed to objects in pre-Kantian philosophy. However, in line with Kant's revolution in philosophy, for Benjamin, historical consciousness takes part in the construction of historical objects (in Kant's epistemology, objects are not independent from the subject but are created in the interaction with human cognition). The past is not a matter of fact that the historian finds, but is created from the position of the present, in an act Benjamin coins elsewhere as "a tiger's leap to the past."[92]

The Copernican revolution changed the method of construction of the historical object. First, Benjamin's early theory of the *Ursprung* was not committed to a point in time. The history of the Ursprung had no special relations to the present. Second, in the *Ursprung*, the historian had no privileged position in the investigation: he or she examined objects or artifacts as if from the outside. The investigation, I noted earlier, required an immersion in reality, but this reality was, in principle, disassociated from the historian's present. In the 1930s, however, the recognition of the historical object started from a specific position in time. Most importantly, repetition happened in and through the present. That is, while in his *Trauerspiel*, the constellation was composed of multiple and different manifestations of the *Ursprung* that repeated in history, in his later work, Benjamin narrowed his interest to a constellation between a certain past and the present, focusing on a specific repetition between two points in time. In a renowned example of this structure in thesis XIV of "On the Concept of History," Benjamin writes: "History is the subject of a structure whose site is not homogeneous, empty time, but time filled by the presence of the now [*Jetztzeit*]. Thus, to Robespierre ancient Rome was a past charged with the time of the now which he blasted out of the continuum of history. The French Revolution viewed itself as Rome reincarnate."[93] Robespierre, in Benjamin's understanding, was not interested in history for its own sake. He rather focused on the present and on a crucial repetitive structure he identified between the present and the past in order to change his present. This was not the endless repetition of the *Ursprung* as described in *Trauerspiel*, nor was it a repetition that ended before Robespierre's time, but a specific repetition of Rome and Robespierre's present.

In the 1930s, thus, Benjamin followed the Nietzschean insight on the unprecedented importance of the now as a point of difference. His vocabulary admits that the historical object still has both fore- and after-history, and, in that sense, the investigation could prescribe more than one specific past. Yet now, "politics attained primacy over history." Benjamin is interested in the redemptive nature of the opposition between the present and a particular past. Rather than a long historical repetition of the *Ursprung*, his work aims to uncover a specific connection of the past and the present that creates an opportunity to change the present.

Benjamin and Heidegger

This rearticulation of repetition brings Benjamin close to Heidegger's notion of *Wiederholung and Being in Time*. Specifically, Benjamin's reconfiguration of the past as *continuously* posited from the position of the present closely resembles Heidegger's cyclical motion of repetition.[94] In both, a certain connection with or reappropriation of the past from the position of the present opens up new opportunities to understand the present differently and to thereby change the future. The resemblance between Heidegger's and Benjamin's repetition is significant, as it suggests a kind of dynamism lacking in Benjamin's early theory. In *Trauerspiel*, the polarization of the constellation results equally from all the participant repetitions of the *Ursprung* in history. And since, in most cases, the history under investigation has ended, the constellation is unchanging and eternal. In the 1930s, however, the emphasis on the present changes the tensional dynamics of the constellation. Now, *the present polarizes the historical object*.[95] This is the deep insight of Benjamin's Copernican revolution. Remember, polarization makes knowledge of the idea possible. It uncovers the silent parts of the *Ursprung* in history by creating a matrix of connections through which the idea is revealed in a flash. Now, this polarization depends on the present, or, more precisely, the present is the source of polarized relations. And because the present always changes, the constellation always changes with it. The present, in other words, changes the way the historical object is recombined into a constellation. In Benjamin's words, "The historical evidence polarizes into fore- and after-history always anew, never in the same way. And it does so at a distance from its own existence, in the present instant itself—like a line which, divided according to the Apollonian section [*apollinischen Schnitt*], experiences its partition from outside itself."[96]

To put this in terms of repetition, in the 1930s, Benjamin changes the core of repetition in history. This is no longer a repetition that simply occurs in history and is recognized by the historian, but a repetition that the present creates and then recreates again and again in different now-times. As Benjamin tells us: "The present *determines* where, in the object from the past, that object's fore-history and after-history diverge so as to circumscribe its nucleus."[97] If, for Goethe, the polarization is natural, that is, depends on the unhistorical interaction between natural objects, Benjamin, echoing Heidegger's *Wiederholung*, suggests it is not static but historical and ever-changing: every present produces a different principle of polarization and therefore grounds a different structure of constellation. For the materialist historian, he declares, "there can be no appearance of repetition [*Wiederholung*] in history, since precisely those moments in the course of history which matter most to him ... become moments of the present day and change their specific character according to the catastrophic or triumphant nature of that day."[98] While Benjamin's earlier work on repetition partly resonated with Deleuze, his focus on the present in the 1930s brought him closer to Heidegger. Like Heidegger, Benjamin, in his later theory of repetition, argued that in each and every present, a different past is retrieved, new latent possibilities are envisaged, and, as a consequence, different futures are conceived. The constellation is different in different now-times. Consequently, different truths are available at different points of time. Truth is neither eternal nor simply contingent. It changes, but only in relation to the present as "the nucleus of time."[99]

In political terms, in *Passagenwerk*, Benjamin offers a vision of history that focuses on the problems of the present. His new formulation of constellation produces different political solutions to different miseries in different present times. The structure of oppression in the early twentieth century was obviously different from the structure of oppression in the eighteenth century and therefore demanded a different response. "Each now," Benjamin emphasizes again and again, is a now of "a *particular* recognizability." Rather than a predetermined universal image of redemption, the concrete and ever-changing present defines the essence of the required historical change. The utopic future is not simply out there, disconnected from the sufferings of the present. Instead, Benjamin views the future in terms of repetition, in that the possibility of a future depends on the interaction of the past of oppressed generations with the present of suffering.

Benjamin was well aware of the proximity of some aspects of his work to Heidegger's phenomenology.[100] And still, throughout the 1920s and the 1930s, he distanced himself from the German philosopher. In the spring of 1930, for example, he reported to Scholem that he and Brecht "were planning to annihilate Heidegger here in the summer in the context of a very close-knit critical circle of readers led by Brecht and me."[101] Earlier that year, when he told Scholem of his intention to write a systematic introduction to *Passagenwerk*, he had also emphasized the difference: "This is where I will find Heidegger, and I expect sparks will fly from the shock of the confrontation between our two very different ways of looking at history."[102] Focusing on their respective models of repetition, I suggest another point of divergence, one highlighting the messianic quality of Benjamin's repetition.

In Heidegger's view, the ongoing circularity of *Wiederholung* informed Dasein's ontology of becoming. Heidegger was interested in repetition as constitutive of Dasein's structure of kinesis. Dasein's movement of retrieval highlighted a structure of futurity: in the continuous turn backward, Dasein was able to form a future that subverted the historical continuum. Benjamin configured the relations between the past and the present similarly in terms of their potential, but differently in terms of their actuality. In the 1930s, Benjamin was focused on the present as harboring the *potential* for a change. His description of history as "the subject of a construction whose site is . . . time filled full by now-time (*Jetztzeit*)"[103] is one of the most quoted phrases on this insight. The emphasis in the description of time filled full by now-time is on the potential for redemption in the now. This potential, however, is covered under piles of debris, to use Benjamin's Angel of History image, which Benjamin attempts to "clear away" by suggesting alternatives to the now with his model of repetition.

In Benjamin, thus, historical repetition does not constitute *actual* mobility as in Heidegger's theory of *Wiederholung*. If for Heidegger, "the *being* of Dasein is constantly projected ahead," as Caputo aptly argues, for Benjamin it was a *potential* that constantly presented itself in repetition. Repetition was a principle not of actual motility but of potential difference. This difference was to be materialized in a moment of universal transformation (of history). The emphasis of Heidegger was on terms such as locating, retrieving, acknowledging, and finding—each indicates continuity—but repetition in its Benjaminian key stood for arrest and interference. It put a stop to the horrors of history, a messianic cessation of happenings—but this was a disruption not perpetuity.

Here again, the difference between Benjamin's messianic vision and Heidegger's philosophical work partly resulted from a difference in their subject matter: Benjamin focused on collective reality, but Heidegger's phenomenology in *Being and Time* focused on the individual.[104] Similar to the difference between Rosenzweig's collective experience of repetition and Kierkegaard's individual repetition, the historical scale marks Benjamin's unique formulation of repetition: while for Heidegger, *Dasein* is ever-dynamic *in actu*, for Benjamin, history is not. Benjamin insisted on thinking of *repetition* as ever changing so that different constellations and thereby different solutions would continuously present themselves. However, this dynamism was only *in potentia*. Because Benjamin thought of repetition in eschatological terms, that is, repetition conditions the "end" of history, the actual manifestation of repetition in reality had to be a single occurrence. That is, while Dasein is capable of experiencing ongoing fluidity, history can have changed only once.

This also highlights an important difference between Rosenzweig's and Benjamin's versions of repetition: while in Benjamin's version, repetition produces different visions of redemption which change as the present changes, in Rosenzweig's, repetition produces the condition for anticipating only one version of redemption. Repetition freed the Jewish people, according to Rosenzweig, not by presenting multiple ends to history, but by presenting one goal, which the Jewish people were able to anticipate partly because of the cyclical nature of the Jewish calendar. Thus, the Jewish people, Rosenzweig claims, experienced cyclical time *in actu*, as in Heidegger's and Kierkegaard's models of repetition. It was not a question of discovering repetition or recognizing repetition; for Rosenzweig, repetition informed the actual temporal orientation of the Jews. In other words, for Benjamin, repetition produced different messianic visions, and each applied to a certain present, because it was repetition *in potentia*. In contrast, repetition in Rosenzweig constituted the Jewish temporal experience, and therefore produced one eternal vision of redemption, one inherently disconnected from the miseries of the present. Benjamin was thus positioned between Heidegger and Rosenzweig: unlike Heidegger, Benjamin saw repetition as producing multiplicity only *in potential*; unlike Rosenzweig, he saw repetition as producing multiple potential differences, not *one* vision of eternity.

"Beyond the Sphere of Thought!"
Redemption and Repetition

In the previous chapter, I noted how *Passagenwerk* draws attention to a modern reality of stuckness and impenetrability: due to processes of eradication of tradition, practices reflecting alternative modes of existence have been repressed and forgotten, and change was therefore beyond reach. Cultural objects seem to have had no redemptive qualities and were empty of meaning. Reality was dominated by an experience of eternal return that presented only a phantasmagoria of newness. Benjamin's repetition of opposites responds to this situation. Principally, repetition allows Benjamin to imagine a different reality than that which would seem to follow "naturally" from the course of history because, as in his earlier work on the baroque mourning play, the structure of dynamic repetition offers a way to think of "ahistorical" connections between past and present. Instead of connecting moments in their consecutive transition, one after the other, Benjamin's model of repetition as revelatory discovery ties events in absolute disregard to their position in time. The nonlinear connections made in revelatory discovery provide images unrecognized in and through linear history. Repetition, in that sense, delivers the present and the past from their causal determinations and upends linear temporality. As Benjamin comments, "In order for a part of the past to be touched by the present instant, there must be no continuity between them."[105]

Like in Kafka's letter on Abraham to Robert Klopstock, in *Passagenwerk*, repetition is a *principle of difference*. It allows Benjamin to conceive of history as composed of more than a "sequence of events like the beads of a rosary," by highlighting a connection with a past that might have been irrelevant for the present from positivistic historical perspective. To put this in Benjamin's terms of that period, repetition is a new and different form of remembrance. It allows a certain, forgotten past to be remembered and actualized in the present over and above the limits of a historical homogenous transition of events. Benjamin puts this principle of interruption in messianic terms in the opening lines of his "Theological-Political Fragment," which, according to Adorno, Benjamin composed in 1937:

> Only the Messiah himself completes all history, in the sense that he alone redeems, completes, creates its relation to the messianic. For this reason, nothing that is historical can relate itself, from its own ground, to anything messianic. Therefore, the Kingdom of God is not the telos of the historical dynamic; it cannot be established as a goal. From the standpoint of history, it is not the goal but the terminus (*Ende*).[106]

In Benjamin's model of repetition, the (messianic) difference does not follow historical logic. The end of history is not the telos of historical progression: it comes as if from outside. Repetition is a form of interruption; it intervenes in the flow of homogenous time. It cuts off the historical object from its immediate environment and puts it in a constellation where new, unforeseen opportunities present themselves. In other words, Benjamin's repetition of opposites is not only grounded on differences between present and past (echoing the difference between the manifestations of the *Ursprung*), but it also has the power to produce a difference in history. Benjamin mentions this again in his notes to thesis XV: "The destructive or critical element in historiography is in the explosion [*der Aufsprengung*] of historical continuity."[107]

Benjamin's insistence on difference in his model of "repetition of opposites" caused consternation among Benjamin's friends at the Institute for Social Research.[108] They worried that the difference which Benjamin aimed to locate in history was outside the historical process, and they saw the dialectical image as an anarchic ideal that was disconnected from and, indeed, disconcerted with the suffering of the working classes. Benjamin's "constellation" approach to materialist history was seen as repeating one of his basic misunderstandings— his suggestion of primal history as a critical concept in the first exposé. Jürgen Habermas reiterates this criticism in his now classical commentary "Walter Benjamin: Consciousness-Raising or Rescuing Critique" (1972), where he criticizes Benjamin's "domesticated historical materialism." Habermas aims at Benjamin's integration of historical materialism and Jewish messianism, which clearly has to "fail, because the materialist theory of social development cannot simply be fitted into the anarchical conception of the *Jetztzeiten* that intermittently break through fate as if from above."[109] To put Habermas's critique in terms of repetition, Benjamin's model of now-time initiated a potential for a difference that was so radical that it was supposedly completely divorced from history. It interrupted history and produced "anarchic" difference "as if from above," exactly in line, let us note, with the radical difference of Deleuze's theory of repetition and difference.

However, Benjamin's theory of repetition is more nuanced. As I have observed regarding its resemblance to Heidegger, in Benjamin's new formulation of repetition of opposites, the dialectical image is produced *in and through the present*. In the following insert from convolute N, Benjamin defends this version of dynamic repetition: "It's not that what is past casts its light on what is present, or what is present its light on what is past; rather, image is that wherein what has been comes together in a flash with the now to form a constellation. In other words, image is dialectics at a standstill. For while the relation of the present to the past is a purely temporal, continuous one, the relation of what-has-been to the now is dialectical: is not progression but image, suddenly emergent."[110] In Benjamin's formulation of repetition, the horrors of the now and their relations to past atrocities constitute the possibility of a radical change in the history of the oppressed. Indeed, the constellation produces difference, but this difference corresponds to the demands of the now. This is not a random difference, but one that is motivated by the suffering around Benjamin. His repetition allows him to combine anarchism with historical materialism: the motivation for the investigation is grounded in the present—for example, the principles of the polarization of the idea reflect the miseries of the working class—but the result of the investigation transcends historical evolution. In this repetition, while the idea comes as if from outside history, it is deeply embedded in history.

Benjamin, in other words, does not settle for mere differences. Explosions or interruptions mark the negative aspect of his program for radical change of history. Yet, "materialist historiography does not choose its objects arbitrarily," Benjamin states.[111] In the following passage from *Passagenwerk*, Benjamin makes this demand explicit: "[For] the destructive momentum in materialist historiography is to be conceived as the reaction to a constellation of dangers [*Gefahrenkonstellation*] . . . Such a presentation of history has as goal to pass, as Engels puts it, 'beyond the sphere of thought!'"[112] In the late 1930s, Benjamin focused on a certain kind of constellation. He was not interested in essences or in truth in general, nor with constellation of art forms. He investigated a specific constellation, "a constellation of danger," of the suffering of past oppressed generations and the catastrophe of the present. In this constellation, an idea, or a dialectical image in Benjamin's materialist language of the 1930s, that had been unperceivable in modernity was attainable again. Benjamin's constellation of dangers produced not a bare difference in history, but a *specific idea* from "beyond the sphere of thought." The image that modernity was so sorely lacking was possible now from within Benjamin's mystical theory of repetition.[113] If Deleuze emphasized differences, Benjamin, in line with Heidegger, utilized these differences to bring about an image of redemption. For him, the revelatory act of recognizing repetition could not only uncover truth; it could also end history.

In the early stages of writing *Passagenwerk*, Benjamin hoped to find in primal history a model for a "classless society." In thinking of the present through his theory of the dreaming collective, he expected to disclose redemptive wish images that the present repressed but were nonetheless still available in the depths of the collective unconscious. Proust was crucial to this project in suggesting a new form of remembrance through which these valuable images would be possible again.[114] In the late 1930s, Benjamin believed his version of dynamic repetition—repetition of opposites—could provide exactly those images. He overcame the emptiness of the present with a theory of history that located—in the same present—instances of different, redemptive reality. His repetitions of opposites constructed by way of a mystic-like act of recognition a specific constellation, a constellation of dangers, through which a previously hidden idea of "reconciled life" was finally within grasp.

Thinking of Benjamin's work on the eternal return, Benjamin fought one repetition by using another. His repetition of opposites was the solution to the modern eternal return. His late model of repetition interrupted the endless motion of the eternal return. It injected difference that destabilized modern monotony and provided images of a different future.

CHAPTER 7

Freud on Moses
The Return of the Repressed and the End of Essence

In the spring of 1927, at the age of seventy-one, Sigmund Freud had just finished a new essay on religion. An accomplished public figure, Freud was, however, worried about the demons his work might awaken. He was especially concerned about his decade-long close friendship with Oskar Pfister, a Lutheran minister and one of the leading figures of the Swiss Society of Psychoanalysis. A true Viennese in temperament and manners, Freud was quick to warn Pfister of the upheaval to come:

> In the next few weeks a pamphlet of mine will be appearing which has a great deal to do with you ... The subject matter as you will easily guess—is my completely negative attitude to religion, in any form and however attenuated, and, though there can be nothing new to you in this, I feared, and still fear, that such a public profession of my attitude will be painful to you. When you have read it you must let me know what measure of toleration and understanding you are able to preserve for the hopeless pagan.[1]

In a book about Jewish messianism, Freud, the "hopeless pagan," is certainly the odd one out. As Freud expected, his essay on religion, published a few weeks later under the title "The Future of an Illusion," enshrined him beside Nietzsche, Feuerbach, and Marx as one of the greatest critics of religion in modern times. The text offered a damning portrayal of the religious believer as a "helplessly paralyzed"[2] child, who, unable to face reality, regresses to illusionary salvation. These condemnations were not the first Freud unleashed on those "weak" believers. His newest critique only exacerbated a previous analogy he proposed in 1907 between religious practices and neurotic obsessive actions, and another he hinted at, in the famous Schreber case, of the religious believer and feminineness.

Yet, in the last few decades, Freud's head-on confrontation with religion has been revisited and reinterpreted as secular and post-secular research finds new inspiration and provocation in his psychoanalysis. A renewed interest in the interconnections of psychoanalysis, religion, and political theory has emerged, giving new currency to Freud's illuminating examination of the origins of the Jewish people in *Moses and Monotheism*.

Moses and Monotheism was written primarily as Freud's most comprehensive attempt to tackle antisemitism. Freud began working on the book in the summer of 1934, a short year after the Nazis took power in Germany and had added his life's work to the list of blacklisted books. His new book was to apply his psychoanalytic theory to this urgent problem of the growing hatred of the Jews across Europe, as he revealed to his close friend Jewish author Arnold Zweig. "The starting point of my work is familiar to you—it was the same as that of your *Bilanz*. Faced with the new persecutions, one asks oneself again how the Jews come to be what they are and why they have attracted this undying hatred. I soon discovered the formula: Moses created the Jews."[3]

Freud finished the book in his exile in London in 1939, following his escape from Nazi Germany's annexation of Austria. It was only there, far enough from the antisemitic danger that Austrian ethnologist Pater Schmidt and others in the Catholic Orthodoxy had posed to himself, his family, but also, and perhaps most worryingly, to psychoanalysis in Vienna, that Freud was able to complete his last big project. He was especially concerned that a work on the origins of Judaism in the midst of rise of antisemitism could risk "a ban on psychoanalysis in Vienna and the suspension of all our publications here."[4] Consequently, while the first two of the book's three essays were published in 1947 in *Imago*, the journal of the psychoanalytic society, the third and last essay was delayed and published only after Freud's arrival in London in the spring of 1938. All the while, Freud had to "remain silent," as he complained in an early letter on his new Moses project to his close friend and follower Lou Andreas-Salomé.[5]

A book about antisemitism, *Moses and Monotheism* was in large part the culmination of the Jewish renaissance of the early twentieth-century German Jewish world. Unlike Freud's earlier—somewhat random—attempts to find explanations for antisemitism in emotional and psychological domains,[6] Freud delved in his last work into a historical study of the *origins* of Judaism to uncover a new explanation of "the deeper motives for hatred of the Jews."[7] Rather than providing a psychological analysis of the antisemitic character, the book locates a hitherto unrecognized point of origins of the Jewish people that explained millennia of hate and harassment. To the German Jewish community, which, suffering from growing assimilation and secularization, incessantly searched for a modern Jewish tradition, Freud offered new, psychoanalytically proofed beginnings. The problem was that these new origins were attached to a highly speculative theory of the *Egyptian* origins of Moses. This hypothesis, as Freud knew perfectly well in the months prior to the publication of his work, had to have a devastating impact on his people. The book therefore opens with the following statement:

> To deprive a people of the man whom they take pride in as the greatest of their sons is not a thing to be gladly or carelessly undertaken, least of all by someone who is himself one of them. But we cannot allow any such reflection to induce us to put the truth aside in favor of what are supposed to be national interests; and, moreover, the clarification of a set of facts may be expected to bring us a gain in knowledge.[8]

Whether Freud's book about the origins of the Jewish people in the orient, exhibits, albeit in dramatic overtures, the fascination of German Jews with other, supposedly authentic forms of Jewish life in East European and Sephardic communities, is a speculation I will not venture to make at this point. One thing is certain, however. The responses to Freud's attempt to relocate Jewish origins in Egypt were, as Freud predicted, less than favorable. *Moses and Monotheism* was harshly criticized at the time of its publication and seemed likely to pass into oblivion.[9] It was dismissed as the anxious reaction of an old man to his impending death in exile. A book disrupted by repetitions, inaccuracies, apologies, and contradictions, far from the solid scientific work of previous years, Freud's last work was perceived as sad evidence of his complicated relations—weakened in his struggle with throat cancer—with his Jewish identity and heritage. Martin Buber's shared those sentiments in his *Moses* (1946), dedicating only a short and dismissive footnote to Freud's book from half a decade earlier: "That a scholar of so much importance in his own field as Sigmund Freud could permit himself to issue so unscientific a work, based on groundless hypotheses, as his *Moses and Monotheism*, is regrettable."[10]

Still, a generation later Freud and his Moses have been awarded a prominent place in the history of modern thought. The interest in the book was initiated partly by Haim Yosef Yerushalmi's *Freud's Moses* (1991). Yerushalmi's book, framed within a long-standing scholarly concern for Freud's relations with his Jewish identity, expanded on Freud's revolutionary theories of tradition, history, and religion in *Moses and Monotheism* and reintroduced the deep insights of Freud's last work to a new and wider audience. Shortly thereafter, such prominent figures as Jacques Derrida, Jan Assmann, Richard Bernstein, and Edward Said made valuable contributions to investigations of the meaning and place of *Moses and Monotheism*, proving the value of the book for discussions of history and tradition, religion, and Judaism, political theory and identity theory, ethics, racism, and antisemitism.[11]

In the vast corpus of Freud's published work, *Moses and Monotheism* stands out as one of his most comprehensive projects. An intellectual semi-autobiography—Freud's identification with Moses in this book as well in his earlier 1914 essay on Michelangelo's Moses sculpture is apparent—the book offered Freud a valuable opportunity to readdress the basic paradigms of his life's work.[12] As Regina Schwartz observes, the scope of *Moses and Monotheism* "was so sweeping . . . that it gathered up his past psychoanalytic work into it, recontextualizing psychoanalysis within the purview of this vast ancient myth."[13] Edward Said echoes this commonly accepted assessment in *Freud and the Non-European* (2004), in which he famously argues that *Moses and Monotheism* should be understood as a prime example of late Style (*Spätstil*). As a work representative of late style—and like others by figures such as Adorno, Mozart, or Shakespeare—the book offered the dying Freud a final opportunity to challenge his long-held convictions. "Everything about the treatise suggests not resolution and reconciliation . . . but, rather, more complexity,"[14] writes Said. The many unnecessary repetitions, inconsistencies, and duplications in *Moses and Monotheism* which the four prefaces to the book only fitfully reflect, were not signs of old age, as many of his contemporaries believed, but of Freud's honest attempt to rethink his work. In this last, most "personal work,"[15] Freud was finally willing "to let irreconcilable elements of the work remain as they are: episodic, fragmentary, unfinished (that is, unpolished)."[16]

Drawing on the unique place of *Moses and Monotheism* in Freud's oeuvre, in this chapter I explore the indirect yet significant gestures toward a reflection on messianism in his last, most important work on Judaism. To be sure, when writing *Moses and Monotheism*, Freud had no deliberately messianic vision. He was clearly and unequivocally against any kind of messianic hope of salvation. And yet this chapter highlights a revelatory impulse, what we might understand with Benjamin as a weak messianism, that lays beneath the surface of his work, in large measure against Freud's own wishes. This revelatory gesture is found, as I will demonstrate, in the repetitive structure of history that Freud identifies in this work.

I begin by showing how Freud restructures our understanding of history with his application of the thesis of the return of the repressed to the history of religion. In *Moses and Monotheism*, the history of Judaism and Christianity is governed by the return of the repressed. Repetition, we may say, is the very "structure," the "backbone," of Freud's account of history. These historical repetitions, and the underlying structure of repetition they reveal for Freud, disrupt the presumed linear temporality that is seen to govern history in modernity. To shortly explain, according to Freud, the linear course of history collapsed under the pressure of the murder of Moses; this breaking of history radically changed religious and social realities. A similar collapse occurred with the death of Christ: in this instance as well, human civilization was transformed by a return of a repressed murder. Freud, in this sense, proved in *Moses and Monotheism* the climactic power of repetition in history in a different field of human knowledge from that of Benjamin or Rosenzweig. For him, as for Benjamin and Rosenzweig, a cyclical repetition produced difference into the seemingly homogenous reality of a seemingly linear history.

In the second half of the chapter, I suggest that the return of the repressed does not end in Christianity. Freud ultimately presented history as an *endless* oscillation between two psychological positions—guilt and sensuality—as embodied in the social, religious, and historical spheres in Judaism and Christianity. However, unlike Rosenzweig and Benjamin, Freud was indecisive when thinking about the implications of the repetitive structure he identified in history. On the one hand, Freud is very clear in stating that the repetition of religious forms of social organization, specifically, the repetition of Judaism and Christianity, is endless: it produces no essential change in history, but rather closes off history from the possibility of change. In this sense, Freud's repetition resembles the archaic eternal return, and it therefore lacks any messianic qualities. On the other hand, Freud appears to suggest that the endless oscillation between guilt and sensuality still offers a peculiar sort of revelation. In a nutshell, I argue that the historical transition between Judaism and Christianity represents Freud's latent motivation to reformulate the basic opposition between reason and sensuality, an opposition that, of course, informs the psychoanalytic project and largely determines Western philosophy. Freud's reflections on history in *Moses and Monotheism* support a reading in which historical repetition controverts the antagonism between reason and sensuality and it therefore points to a non-essentialist model of knowledge. That is, the historical oscillation between reason and sensuality can be seen to relieve us of the obligation to a supposedly abstract and absolute truth.

Freud, it is clear, rejected any messianic vision, and yet *Moses and Monotheism* provides what we may call a "messianic therapy" in line with Deleuze's "repetition-as-difference." In Freud's description of history, repetition serves as a "wheel, endowed with a violent centrifugal movement": the recognition of a structure of repetition devalues, according to this interpretation, the authority and validity of reason and sexuality as sources of eternal truths, a devaluation which in turn extirpates humanity's deep desire for absolute knowledge. To follow Edward Said's claim about *Moses and Monotheism* as an example of *Spätstil*, we may argue that in his last great work, Freud is grappling with the meaning of repetition: is it a sign of stagnation, as archaic society believed, or is it a force that can change history, as Benjamin and Rosenzweig claimed? We find no definite answer in *Moses and Monotheism*, only a series of arguments and counterarguments, in effect, a series of repetitions.

Moses and the Return of the Repressed
Guilt and Rebelliousness in *Totem and Taboo*

Before venturing into Freud's last work, let us return to the beginning of Freud's work on religion and history in *Totem and Taboo* (1913). *Moses and Monotheism* will partly adopt the structure of history of *Totem and Taboo*. However, like all repetitions introduced in this book, this return will be marked by the changes it introduces.

Totem and Taboo was written when the metapsychological foundations of psychoanalysis were being consolidated. The book demonstrated Freud's attempt to apply his clinical insights to larger cultural realities. Specifically, the book is intended to identify, in Freud's words, a "trace of the origin" of religion and neurosis in "one particular source."[17] In order to do that, Freud focuses on the totemic system of ancient religions and their curious similarities to the Oedipus complex. Based on many "valuable points of agreement,"[18] Freud famously hypothesizes that the beginning of human history was highlighted by the same tension between father and son that structures the Oedipal period of the early life of the individual. Freud draws on Darwin's hypothesis of the primal hordes to speculate that humankind was initially organized in large groups controlled by an authoritarian primal father with tyrannical control of all material goods. Freud then speculates that the sons in this primal tribe, who suffered under the father's control, decided to kill him as the only solution to his cruel dominion. The rebellion of the sons against the father, the absolute monarch, however, ended with unexpected results. The sons were pleased with and proud of their new freedom. But they also felt guilt for their act: "They hated their father, who presented such a formidable obstacle to their craving for power and their sexual desires; but they loved and admired him too."[19]

In Freud's early version of history, the murder of the primal father created a powerful emotional tension. The fatherless tribe was torn between two contradictory emotions: guilt, for the sons had loved their father, and rebelliousness, for they had hated him and his laws and wanted to take his place and enjoy his power. As a first response to this tension, the sons, struggling to relieve the overwhelming emotional stress, replaced the murdered father with a totem animal. The primeval totem religion helped them remember the murder in a way that unburdened them of their guilt. During the totem meal, a core element of the totem system, the sons consumed the totem animal, once again killing "his" flesh but also commemorating the "criminal deed."[20] The first totem religion, however, was not effective enough. The guilt was not completely relieved; it was, in fact, "too great for *any contrivance* to be able to counteract it."[21] The emotional tension created by the murder had a lasting effect. It became a fundamental force of history. "Whatever attempt was made at solving the religious problem, whatever kind of reconciliation was effected between these *two opposing mental forces*, sooner or later broke down, under the combined influence, no doubt, of historical events, cultural changes and internal psychical modifications."[22]

The emotional tension of guilt and rebelliousness shaped human history as future religions were created on the basis of this tension— they were an elaborate attempt to relieve humankind of the emotional distress of the primal murder. At their core, paganism, Judaism, and Christianity are an attempt to expunge the guilt of the event that started history. Their efforts, however, are *never* completely successful, since the tension is never to be truly relieved. Other forms of religious organization are bound to appear, as nothing will stop the primal guilt.

Totem and Taboo is an inspiring collection of essays on the beginning of human civilization but is less convincing when dealing with the history that preceded the murderous act of the sons. The last part of the book has some insightful anecdotes about paganism and Christianity, but not more than that. *Moses and Monotheism* fills this gap.

Moses and the Invention of Monotheism

From the inception of psychoanalysis, Freud's theory of the mind was severely criticized for its ahistorical nature.[23] In the early days of the Frankfurt School, Freud's essentialism was regarded as a fundamental obstacle to a modern theory of history: the unconscious, the Oedipal complex, libido and aggressiveness, the content of the needs, the inner drama of the ego, the super ego, and the id were eternal forms, universal in nature.[24] And if Freud had a theory of history, the argument usually goes, it suggested a linear progression of history in Comtean style and form. The primal father forced history onto a predetermined course of evolution, from the primitive totem religion to paganism and monotheism, which ushered in the modern age of enlightened science. Interestingly, in this line of interpretation, Freud's theory of history is in fact only a theory of prehistory, or of origins, since in *Totem and Taboo* Freud consistently emphasizes the insurmountable importance of prehistory over any later historical event. *In Moses and Monotheism*, Freud returns to this theory of beginning, to find the origins of the Jewish people.[25] This return, I argue, also offers Freud an opportunity to rethink his ahistorical model of history.

Moses and Monotheism was inspired by a set of crucial—and already well-researched in Freud's time—affinities between Jewish monotheism and a brief monotheist episode in Egyptian history. Encouraged by these similarities, Freud theorizes that Moses was an Egyptian nobleman who, when faced with the downfall of the Egyptian religion, adopted Israelite slaves and instructed them in monotheism to save his Egyptian religion from extinction. This speculation, which we also find in Schiller and Heine, is, however, much more than a story about the repressed identity of Moses, as Freud further claims that the Israelites, who were used to pagan sensuality, found the demands of renunciation made by monotheism unbearable. Moses's religion was "a rigid monotheism on the grand scale,"[26] one that "may have been even harsher"[27] than the original monotheism in Egypt. It prohibited making an image of God, denounced the existence of a world after death, and condemned magic.[28] Moses even retained the Egyptian practice of circumcision. Building on his work on the first totem religion, Freud speculates that these restrictions could have ended only one way. The Israelites slaves could not have tolerated such a "highly spiritualized religion," and, echoing the first murder of the primal father, "the savage Semites took fate into their own hands and rid themselves of their tyrant."[29]

Freud arrived at the idea of the murder of Moses by way of Ernst Sellin's controversial *Mose und seine Bedeutung für die israelitisch-jüdische Religionsgeschichte* (1922), which, on the basis of a few short sentences in Hosea, claimed that the Jewish people murdered Moses in the desert. However, in *Moses and Monotheism* the murder of Moses is more than anecdotal. In Freud's interpretation of the biblical story, the murder of Moses was the founding moment of a new kind of religion. The first response of the Israelites to the murder, however, did not reveal much. Like the brothers in the primal tribe, they repented. Fatherless–Freud insisted that Moses coerced the Jews into monotheism like a father who educates his children[30]—the Israelite sons were left alone, wandering in the desert. Yet unlike the murderous primal sons, who were quick to institute the totem religion with which they hoped to negate their guilt, the Jewish people joined another religion of a second Moses who was a priest of the pagan god Yahweh in Kadesh. They found solace in this second Moses and his "volcano God, . . . an uncanny, bloodthirsty demon,"[31] who offered them a return to the unrestrictive sensuality that defined their lives in Egypt. Under the rule of the second Moses, they were finally able to forget (or repress) the murder.

The defection of the Jewish people to Moses from Kadesh was nevertheless only temporal. Freud insists that the repressed trauma of the killing had to find its way back to the surface. After a long period under the second Moses, the Jewish people, who tried to oppose the coercive nature of monotheism, returned to the laws of the first Moses. They were now "exalted"[32] and even proud to be Moses's chosen people. Their return to the first Moses engraved the principles of the Egyptian Moses's religion on the Jewish character: the spirituality, rationality, and self-control that Moses demanded would distinguish the Jewish people to the present day.

Religion and the "Compulsive Power" of the Return of the Repressed

To explain this unexpected return of the Jews to monotheism, Freud applied in *Moses and Monotheism* his theory of the return of the repressed to social reality. The theoretical paradigm of the return of the repressed was one of the "essential features of a neurosis,"[33] which Freud recognized in his 1896 pre-psychoanalytic papers, but developed more significantly later in *Beyond the Pleasure Principle*.[34] In this book, written against the background of the massive psychological trauma of the soldiers who returned from the battle fields of the First World War,

Freud offers an explanation of the persistent reappearance of neurotic symptoms, whose appearance contradicted the pleasure-seeking psychical mechanisms of Freud's original theory of the mind.[35] The fact that a compulsion to repeat traumatic events was prevalent in clinical settings and also in everyday life (regardless of neurosis), encouraged Freud to assume that "there really does exist in the mind a compulsion to repeat which overrides the pleasure principle."[36] His work on the compulsion to repeat fundamentally changed the basic theoretical framework of psychoanalysis. Importantly, it added a principle of repetition to Freud's understanding of the human psyche.

Freud's earlier theory of instincts suggests that the primary purpose of the mental apparatus is to free the mind of mental tension. When such tension decreases, Freud famously explains, this process produces an experience of pleasure, hence the pleasure principle. However, in 1920, Freud added to this basic assumption. His new theory of the mind was based on the speculation that the function of consciousness was to defend the mental apparatus from inner or outer stimulation (I noted this mechanism in my discussion of Benjamin's criticism of *Erfahrung* in chapter 5). The mental apparatus, claims Freud, needs only a small amount of stimulus to comprehend the external world. It therefore generally invests in the attempt to bind or hold unwanted excitation. However, at times the amount of excitation is too large to contain: "And how shall we expect the mind to react to this invasion? Cathectic energy is summoned from all sides to provide sufficiently high cathexes of energy in the environs of the breach."[37] In these extreme cases, the overstimulation results in an extensive breach in the psyche, that is, a trauma, and the mental apparatus is forced to *produce* "an additional stream of fresh inflowing energy"[38] to bind the excess of stimulation.

Despite his initial hypothesis, Freud thus discovers that the psychical apparatus sometimes *produces* tension, that is, unpleasure, to master outside excitations. In trauma, the mental apparatus suspends the pleasure principle to control the excitation and safeguard the integrity of the psychical system. This character of the mind has "the appearance of some 'daemonic' force"[39] as it condemns the individual, when this process is in effect, to unpleasure. Importantly, when patients repeated maladaptive behaviors in clinical settings—a behavior that led to an experience of unpleasure—this was not an indication of giving in to the disease but a way of coming to terms with a previous trauma. The repetition of trauma was an indication of the existence of a trauma *and* of an attempt to confront it.

This compulsion to repeat encouraged Freud to revise his theory of instincts and to speculate about a new set of instincts—death and life instincts. He departed from his earlier framework to claim that "all instincts tend towards the restoration of an earlier state of things."[40] This discovery also prompted him to declare that the psychic life, in general, is aiming to return to an earlier, inorganic state, and "'the aim of all life is death.'"[41] Of particular relevance to this book, in *Beyond the Pleasure Principle* Freud finds that the mental life of the individual, and perhaps all of nature, is *governed by repetition*. In his words, the compulsion to repeat is "a universal attribute of instincts and perhaps of organic life in general."[42] A derivative of mental activity, repetition from the 1920s and onward is the *Urphänomen*—to borrow from Goethe—of the mental apparatus.[43]

In *Moses and Monotheism*, Freud references the return of the repressed to explain the mechanism of collective trauma in history:

Early trauma—defence—latency—outbreak of neurotic illness—partial return of the repressed. Such is the formula which we have laid down for the development of a neurosis.... The reader is now invited to take the next step... of supposing that events occurred of a sexually aggressive nature, which left behind them permanent consequences but were for the most part fended off and forgotten, and which after a long latency came into effect and created phenomena similar to symptoms in their structure and purpose.[44]

In Freud's theory of Jewish history, the trauma of the murder of Moses, which seemed to have been forgotten under the role of the second Moses from Kadesh, returned, after a period of latency. The comfortable life under the second Moses only hid the ongoing effects of the murder. However, the overflow of guilt tormented the Jewish people and forced them to accept the very demands of Moses they had so desperately struggled to escape. In psychological terms, their new religion was an attempt to bind the powerful psychic excitation the murder created. Accordingly, the period of latency that followed the murder of Moses was not a period of salvation but one of unseen turmoil of psychic pain. As for the individual, the trauma did not need to be on the surface of the conscious life of the collective to survive. In fact, the trauma withstood time, had more psychic force, and became more powerful when it was repressed and supposedly forgotten.

Freud's principle of repetition informed much more than his understanding of the origins of the Jewish people, however. In a letter to Andreas-Salomé I have already mentioned he expresses the larger theoretical stakes of his new paradigm. "Religions," he writes, "owe their compulsive power to the return of the repressed; they are reawakened memories of very ancient, forgotten, highly emotional episodes of human history."[45] The return of the repressed—a concept that Freud does not mention in *Totem and Taboo*—now explains the enormous and lasting power of religions in general. Religions are so powerful because they manifest the return of the emotional distress of the murder of the primal father. Significantly, these collective traumas created the basic characteristics of the collective just as the return of trauma changes the individual. The Jews, to return to Freud's Moses story, were rational people because the return of the trauma inflicted on them reason and spirituality like the symptoms that traumas inflict on individuals.

In Haim Yosef Yerushalmi's reading of *Moses and Monotheism* in *Freud's Moses*, this new formulation of religion provided Freud a new and revolutionary model to rethink the problem of Jewish identity in secular modernity. *Moses and Monotheism* proposes a solution to the problem that haunted the German Jewish community in Freud's time. Freud, in continuation of the early twentieth-century "Jewish renaissance," turned to history to find the true, hidden origins of the Jewish people. And while this return to origins expressed Freud's complicated and ambivalent relations of Freud with his Jewish identity, as Freud does claim that Moses was Egyptian, it also demonstrated his alliance with Judaism. To the urgent question of German Jewish identity, Freud responded with a theory of religion that grounded religious identity on psychological traits. Specifically, the return of the murder gave the Jews spirituality and reason. These qualities were not dependent on the adherence to religious practices or heritage but were part of the psychological infrastructure that would define Jews forever. In that way, Yerushalmi claims, Freud gave the final touch to a new kind of "psychological Jews": "Alienated from classical Jewish texts, Psychological Jews tend to insist on inalienable Jewish traits. Intellectuality and independence of mind, the highest ethical and moral standards, concern for social justice, tenacity the face of persecutions—these are among the qualities they will claim, if called upon, as quintessential Jewish."[46]

Yerushalmi's Freud separated Judaism (as culture, society, and historic community) from Jewishness, an essence independent of Judaism. In Freud's book, Yerushalmi argues, Jews are Jews because they share a set of basic qualities imprinted on their fathers following the murder of Moses. Those who leave the Jewish community or never keep Kosher are as Jewish as orthodox Jews: they all enjoy, even if unwillingly, the same innate, distinctive psychical (Jewish) character.[47] Judaism as Jewishness, Freud promised, will survive after the end of Judaism: it is an interminable form of Jewish existence that transcends the more finite Judaism (to refer to the subtitle of Yerushalmi's book, "Judaism Terminable and Interminable").

Repetition of Reason and Sensuality
History as Endless Repetition of Trauma

The return of the Jewish people to the monotheism of the Egyptian Moses had far-reaching consequences that rippled throughout the ancient world. From a narrow perspective, the Jewish return to Moses's religion signaled the Jewish people's growing sense of guilt at the murder of their leader. Like the sons in the primal tribe, guilt informed their social experience. This guilt, however, spread to other peoples: "A growing sense of guilt," observes Freud, "had taken hold of Jewish people, or perhaps of the whole civilized world."[48] And this overpowering guilt had to erupt, again, somehow.

As Freud learned in *Totem and Taboo*, guilt will never stop. Accordingly, the formation of the new Jewish monotheism was not the end of the story of the murder of Moses. Indeed, this trauma gave rise to a second form of monotheism in Christianity. "Paul, a Roman Jew from Tarsus," he reminds, "seized upon this sense of guilt and traced it back correctly to its original source.... A son of God had allowed himself to be killed without guilt and had thus taken on himself the guilt of all men."[49] In *Moses and Monotheism*, the death of Christ represents an attempt to reengage with the guilt over the murder of Moses. The Christian brothers, in Freud's retelling of history, "exorcized humanity's sense of guilt," which had haunted the Jews and the nations around them. This act symbolizes a new hope: instead of succumbing to the guilt of the Jewish people, the Christian brothers took things into their own hands and sacrificed one of their own. This presented, claims Freud, a "religious novelty."[50]

In principle, we find here that a structure of repetition is *central* to Freud's theory of religion. In *Moses and Monotheism*, the return of the repressed is not restricted to the history of the *Volk*. The return of the repressed explains history *in general*. For Freud, the killing of Christ *repeats* the murder of Moses, which itself *repeats* the previous murder of the primal father: "Christ became [Moses's] substitute and successor...Then, too, there is a piece of historical truth in Christ's resurrection, for he was the resurrected Moses and behind him the returned primal father of the primitive horde, transfigured and, as the son, put in the place of the father."[51] History is the realm of the return of the repressed, in which, murder after murder, humanity re-experiences the trauma that started history. The murder of Moses is not an isolated event in world history, but one in a series of murders of fathers that started with the murder of the first father of the primal horde and continued with the killing of Moses and later of Christ. "No other portion of the history of religion has become so clear to us," insists Freud, "as the introduction of monotheism into Judaism and its continuation in Christianity."[52] The primal father, Moses, and Christ each participated in one universal return of the repressed that grapples with the guilt of the murder of the father again and again.

The death of Moses was not an accident: the primal father before, and Christ after, repeated the same traumatic beginning of history. As Freud's earlier theory of history in *Totem and Taboo* makes clear, the historical power of religion is *endless* in essence. The guilt is never to end. New religions were always to reappear. History guarantees that there will be other religions, new forms of civilization, that will reengage with the original trauma. Importantly, this model does not apply only to future generations. When Freud revisits his theory of the totemic drama in *Moses and Monotheism*, he admits a peculiar point. The totem was not a single and unique event. "The story was told in enormously condensed form," Freud apologizes, "as though it happened on a single occasion, while in fact it covered thousands of years and was repeated countless times during that long period." *Totem and Taboo*, apparently, is the story of the *murders of the fathers* that "occurred to all primitive men."[53] Freud's story is not about monotheism and its beginnings in a primal father, but about all religions and their relations to their own murder of their respective primal fathers. Moses and later Christ are just two repetitions of those murders. The drama of all those killings—it is now clear to Freud—presents an endless repetition on a grand scale.

Judaism and Christianity: Two *Ur*-Positions of Human Civilization

Thinking of the return of Judaism in Christianity, Freud recognizes a curious yet crucial paradox: the death of Christ helped humanity unburden itself of the overwhelming guilt over the Jews' murder of Moses, yet Christianity also signaled a *regression* to a primitive reality. His understanding of this regression leads him to draw a basic distinction between the narratives of *Moses and Monotheism* and *Totem and Taboo*:

> The Christian religion did not maintain the high level in things of the mind to which Judaism had soared. It was no longer strictly monotheistic, it took over numerous symbolic rituals from surrounding peoples, it reestablished the great mother-goddess and found room to introduce many of the divine figures of polytheism ... Above all, it did not, like the Aton religion and the Mosaic one ... exclude the entry of superstitious, magical and mystical elements, which were to prove *a severe inhibition upon the intellectual development* of the next two thousand years.[54]

Earlier I noted that in Freud's vision, the Jewish people are marked by reason. Christianity is not. It successfully managed the guilt of the murder of the father, yet as far as the intellect is concerned, Christianity signaled a *return* to an earlier, primitive reality. It improved the way humanity controls the psychic wound of the primal murder, but at the same time reinserted those elements that guilt had successfully repressed. The return of Judaism within Christianity thus appears to be a reversal of Judaism's earlier position. The Jewish people suffered from guilt but were able to expunge magic and superstition and thus effect intellectual progress; Christianity erased part of that guilt, but, in so doing, reinstated sensuality.

For Freud, the killing of Christ entails a dialectic of progress and regression. The progress was registered in terms of guilt; the regression represented a movement from intellect to sensuality. The killing of Moses, and later the killing of Christ, did not move history in a certain direction; it only repeated a basic dichotomy. Instead of a universal development in which history brings about better forms of social organization in intellectual capacity and guilt management, history in *Moses and Monotheism* conveys progress in one *or* the other. "The triumph of Christianity was a fresh victory"[55] only when guilt alone was considered. As far as intellect and rational thinking were concerned, this was, as Freud confesses, "a severe inhibition" for thousands of years.[56]

On the face of it, the transition from Judaism to Christianity might seem insufficient to suggest a general theory of history. However, Freud, as I already noted, believed that the same structure of repetition informed *all* future and past world religions. The return of the repressed was at the core of *all* religions in history. In *Moses and Monotheism*, history guarantees that all religions and all forms of civilization could only reenact a previous human reality. Since guilt compels the return of the repressed, it seems that in his description of the transition from Judaism to Christianity, Freud has found a universal yardstick to measure past and future religions. All religions attempt to engage with guilt; thus all religions must express one of the basic positions represented by Judaism and Christianity. The ongoing attempt to manage the guilt of the primal father offers two contradictory realities: Judaism embodies the suffering of repression and guilt, Christianity represents a decline into sensuality, and all new forms of religion can only reprise a single role within this antagonism.

In short, Christianity and Judaism symbolize two basic and antagonistic meta (*Ur*)-positions in history. They do not represent consecutive stages of progress, but different styles and separate expressions of inner tension. In *Moses and Monotheism*, history is *oscillating between these two opposing possibilities*. The "Jewish/rational trajectory" offers a renunciation of instincts, coupled with higher intellectual capabilities that psychologically cohabitate with immense psychological pain. In contrast, the "Christian/sensual trajectory" that atones for that guilt signals the regression to primitive civilization. Therein, *Moses and Monotheism* openly exhibits the blind commitment of Freud to the Judeo-Christian tradition. For Freud, the history of religion is destined to replay the Judeo-Christian drama for eternity: either guilt and reason, or instinctual sensuality; civilization and neurosis or primitive chaotic experience.

This model of history has implications for the representation of historical time itself. Rather than representing history as taking a linear course, history is composed of distinct periods. Much like the vision of history in Benjamin and Rosenzweig, Freud's vision in *Moses and Monotheism* suggests the force of repetition. Repetition in Freud's version *ruptures* history. The killings of fathers create episodes or different chunks of history that start with a killing and end with a killing. Instead of a concept of homogeneous time, history is disintegrated by repetition, composed of separate *histories*. In each such history, the murder of the father that initiates the period creates different, distinct social and religious organizations. Life within one of Freud's histories has a certain logic, which the next period forcibly alters.[57]

Oscillation and Repetition in History: On Ambiguity

In *Moses and Monotheism*, history is shaped by a return to a primal trauma, endlessly oscillating between religions of guilt and sensuality. This, however, seems to preclude any messianic vision. Briefly stated, in Freud's last work, there is no hope for an end of history. The dialectic movement of progression and regression denies an eschatological vision: the return of the repressed promises that history will not choose between reason and drive, but will repetitively reenact one or the other. In that, Freud's model of history conspicuously mirrors the logic of the archaic eternal return, since, for Freud, human history is captured within a cycle of eternal repetition, just like the cosmos in the archaic world. In fact, Freud's vision may be even more radical than the one described by Mircea Eliade: while in the archaic eternal return, the cosmos mirrored cycles of creation and destruction, in which the cosmos comes to an apex only to be destroyed, in Freud's vision of human history, there is no creation or destruction, no highs or lows, only endless repetition of sensuality and reason. Freud, in other words, seems to have brought the logic of the eternal return to its harshest conclusion: his eternal return condemns humanity to the same cycle of reason and sensuality, without any hope of salvation, without even a hope of brief elation. Humanity will never transcend the duality of guilt and sensual pleasure; the trauma will never be annulled. Redemption, as a radical breakout or collapse of that eternal repetition, is therefore, in a deep sense, only empty "wishful phantasy."[58] The Hegelian unification of truth and reality should likewise be seen as a hysteric reaction to the structural limits of history.

In more general terms, Freud asks the readers of *Moses and Monotheism* to seriously consider the possibility that repetition is *not* messianic but signals sameness and stagnation. In his model of repetition, history does not change, and all that we can identify in the present are social and religious structures that repeat again and again, much like the structure of civilizations in Oswald Spengler's *The Decline of the West*. A religion of reason replaces a religion of sensuality; each has advantages, but each comes at a psychological price. It almost seems that Freud is calling for a Nietzschean confirmation of this eternal return. Like Nietzsche, in traditional interpretations, Freud is brave enough, indeed honest enough, to present us with history as it really is, and asks us to love it, to accept it, maybe even to welcome our collective fate.

And yet, although redemption is merely religious superstition, the oscillating history in *Moses and Monotheism* allows instances of difference to appear. *Moses and Monotheism*, I already noted, is an "eccentric"[59] work that allows Freud's uncertainties and unsolved dilemmas to appear on its surface. The book is a "hazy picture of [Freud's] opinions,"[60] not only because of its autobiographical nature, but also because, as Edward Said clarifies, Freud opens it up to the distractions and ruptures that haunted him throughout his entire professional life.

I now turn to those distractions and differences to argue that the theory of the return of the repressed may yield the possibility of *Freudian revelation*, a quasi-messianic, or weak messianic, relief of the burden of a unitary truth. To begin, let us note that, for Freud, the return of the repressed is *never* a return of the *same*. The trauma that initiates neurosis/history is played out via associative lines that rehearse or imitate the beginning, but never absolutely copy it. The return is "a belated *effect* of the trauma,"[61] an effect, not cloning, that promises varied and changing metaphors. It is indeed a "*partial* return of the repressed."[62] This implies that the return of religious trauma, and I focus now on the collective level, like any other trauma, is *never* the return of the same. Instead, the trauma is always slightly different. This difference, let us further note, aligns with the difference that the modern philosophy of repetition has emphasized time and time again.

Considering the return of the repressed via countless future and past parricides, I argue that in *Moses and Monotheism*, history plays out *manifold* differences of either reason or sensuality that one secluded event is prevented from exhibiting. Replayed for eternity, history brings into reality a variety of new, intertwining possibilities. This repetition of killing after killing, era after era, questions the distinct notions of reason and sensuality which essentially show themselves to be fluid, even unstable. Rather than the same structure of reason or sensuality, the eternal repetition of the historical *Ur*-positions unravels deep inconsistencies and concrete, subtle, yet crucial changes between each period, in a way that erodes the sharp, abstract ideals encapsulated by the two Moses.

In theories of representation in the tradition of Plato, as I noted in my discussion of Benjamin, the contingent historical and social forms are obstacles to eternal truth. Rationalist philosophy always aims at abstract and eternal forms, disregarding, in a way, factual existence. The concept, in Benjamin's terms, rejects differences and homogenizes reality. In *Moses and Monotheism*, however, Freud is highly suspicious of "pious" abstract truths that rest "on an optimistic and idealistic premise."[63] For him, the communal trauma is never ahistorical or abstract. Trauma has to be recognized as part of the reality of the patient, embedded in the patient's contingent experience and his or her social and individual history. In the same way, the historical event cannot be dislodged from its specific material configuration. There is no place in Freud's vision for a construction of sensuality or intellectuality in abstraction from their concrete historical manifestation. Rather, sensuality and intellectuality need to be understood from within their concrete social organization. In the context of this work, these concrete manifestations question the abstract notions of sensuality and reason. In simple terms, because of Freud's insistence on factual experience, history, in his theory of the return of the repressed, shows many forms of sensuality and reason. Moreover, as the return of the repressed is never the same and is only a *partial return* of the repressed, the differences between many forms of the social organization of sensuality and reason will become apparent. That is, rather than revealing abstract notions of reason and sensuality, formulated by Western philosophy as completely independent and absolutely different, history, in Freud's vision, reveals a diversified field of sensuality and reason, with new forms of interaction appearing between them. The historical repetition will never end the opposition and allow either reason or sensuality to win over the other; yet it will continue to show the clear-cut, well-defined, and starkly negating *Ur-positions* as interconnected, even interdependent.

Furthermore, while every religion presents either reason or sensuality, at the same time, every religion also presents a specific organization of this guilt or sensuality that converses with "the other side." This conversation between sensuality and reason breaks down their separation and, in the long run of history, shows their affiliation. For Freud, remember, the return of the repressed is a historical event that responds to the inherent problems of a previous religion. The movement from Moses and Christ was a *reversal of the repressed*: the effect of the previous murder was negated in the next murder. The killing of Moses brought about guilt, and the killing of Christ negated that guilt by regression to the gratification of the instincts. This reversal presented an endless attempt to respond to, to heal, a prior disease. As Freud remarks: "this later illness may also be looked upon as an attempt of cure."[64] As one social organization is tested in history, the next position negates the first's basic components, only to be replaced once more by the previous schema, forming an endless chain of repression and expression, renunciation and enunciation. Each religion repeats the same structure and also negates it: Christianity returned to the trauma of the murder of Moses but was also an attempt at healing that trauma. The next killing would simply return to the guilt that was supposedly relieved.

If history as *eternal return* shows manifold possibilities that subvert the abstract notion of guilt and sensuality, history as the *eternal reversal* shows the interchangeability of those notions. This chain of the returns of the repressed not only blurs the coherency of reason and sensuality, but also illustrates the reversal of reason into sensuality, and of sensuality into reason. History is the reappearing of reason as sensuality, the revelation of sensuality as reason. The reversal of history is critical: it distracts the lines of opposition of the antagonistic primary positions of the primal father and shows a symmetry between guilt and sensuality. History is not aiming to move beyond those lines, but it nevertheless shows the dichotomy of guilt and pleasure as tragic—as an enigma, as something that "has no sense at all."[65]

Freud's Deleuzian formula of "repetition-as-difference" promises the instability of what we might see from a specific position within time as Platonic eternal forms. *Sub specie aeternitatis*, history is not a realm of eternal truth but a realm of *ambiguity*. The recurring return of history does not produce sameness but invents difference: one generation after another, civilization (re)encounters new forms of social organization of reason or sensuality that previous lives thought impossible. Killing after killing, humanity finds new forms of religion to mitigate the murder of the primal father in new and unforeseeable ways. These new religions uncover new and hitherto impossible points of contact between drive and reason, sensuality and guilt, and therefore erase the abstract separation between them. In this sense, Freud's model of history as repetition emerges as the overcoming of potentiality by actuality: it does not prescribe the gaining of truth but the devaluing of abstract truth and thus represents a unique epistemological dimension of revelation. Much like Deleuze's interpretation of Nietzsche, Freud offers the return of the repressed as a point of difference: his model of repetition is not a simple repetition but a repetition that always transgresses previous cycles. Repetition, in this Freudian sense, is a movement within the limits of history—never outside history—that undermines those same limits.

To be sure, the return of history is not an attempt at sublimation. Sublimation points too often in psychoanalytic literature to the superfluity of rationality and, in the context of this work, to the mechanism of cultural progress.[66] Instead, in my reading, history is a "compensation":[67] a transition of sensuality to reason and then of reason back to sensuality, in a movement that blurs their distinctive and individual essence. Contrary to Kant, who, in "Idea for a Universal History from a Cosmopolitan Point of View" (1784), unifies history by its purpose, Freud, one of his biggest admirers, identifies no ultimate destination. Humanity is not closer to a truth in history, but rather finds one of the fundamental truths of Western thought—the antagonism of reason and sensuality—to be essentially problematic. History, in other words, is the realm of the distraction of essences through repetition.

More dramatically, we could say that this deessentializing operation of repetition constitutes a weak messianic power, undermining the dichotomies that structure the discourses of truth in Western philosophy. For Freud, the killings of fathers were forms of attempted salvation. But as Moses and Christ indicate, the repeated coming of the Messiah is futile: it ends nothing, brings nothing, saves nothing. Still, Freud's *Moses and Monotheism* may guarantee a weak messianic revelation.[68] This revelation is not the recognition or the attainment of eternal truths but the recognition of the falsehood of abstract, independent truths, not a figuring out of a truth but a *healing of humanity from the seductive power of eternal truths*.

Indeed, here, Freud finds an unexpected affinity with Nietzsche. My reading follows Foucault's foundational essay "Nietzsche, Genealogy, History," in which Foucault recalls Nietzsche's use of the concept of origins (*Ursprung*) in his 1887 *On the Genealogy of Morals* (*Zur Genealogie der Moral: Eine Streitschrift*). In the preface, Nietzsche defines the motivation of his project in terms similar to those used by Freud: "Eventually my curiosity and suspicion were bound to fix on the question of what origin (*Ursprung*) our terms good and evil actually have."[69] And like Freud, Nietzsche's search for the origins of morality reveals the impossibility of such a point of origins. The investigation does not uncover a beginning that defines reality as if from outside but questions the coherency of current moral positions. In Foucault's words: "if the genealogist refuses to extend his faith in metaphysics, if he listens to history, he finds that there is 'something altogether different' behind things: not a timeless and essential secret, but the secret that they have no essence or that their essence was fabricated in a piecemeal fashion from alien forms."[70]

For both Nietzsche and Freud, the search for origins demonstrates the unattainability of "timeless, and essential secrets." There is no essence of morality as there is no essence of reason and sensuality. The point of origin does not provide a truth but exhausts a truth. Still, the search for such an insight is not futile: while we find no essence, we do find that the search for such essences is hopeless. This model of origin, strange to say, serves as a form of messianic deliverance from the demand of essence. Put in psychoanalytic terms, while the search does not provide a positive answer to the question of origins, it frees us from a fantasy or a wish for such knowledge. We are clearing misunderstandings, like a "wheel, endowed with a violent centrifugal movement," to use Deleuze's reading of Nietzsche.

Freud's Moses:
Difference and Weak Messianic Power

As so many have observed, in his last work, Freud returned to the principles of his life project. One such principle was the embeddedness of reason in libidinal motivations. This psychoanalytic tenet is exemplified in Freud's early claims in his 1911 "Two Formulations on the Two Principles of Mental Functioning" that the reality principle serves the pleasure principle. This was later translated into his famous slogan: "The ego is not master in its own house."[71] The same applied to his work on sublimation where Freud shows that reason is grounded on sensual gratification. In *Moses and Monotheism*, Freud returns to this principle by way of his exploration of the Jewish people, more specifically, the effect of the sensual gratification the Jewish people received through the proliferation of their newly acquired rational behavior: "All such advances in intellectuality," he argues, "have as their consequence that the individual's self-esteem is increased, that he is made proud—so that he feels superior to other people who have remained under the spell of sensuality."[72]

For Freud, and this is a principle that guided him from his early days, reason is, in one way or another, grounded in libidinal structure, or, put otherwise, sensuality is at the ground of rational thinking and behavior. *Moses and Monotheism* takes this basic insight to its extreme in offering a historical framework to rethink the categorical difference between reason and sensuality. Hitherto, Freud thought of reason as embedded in sensuality but was careful to assume that reason was separated from sensuality. The secondary rational processes were developed out of primary processes but were still different from the latter. In *Moses and Monotheism*, the Freudian scheme of history suggests that history, when correctly understood, undermines these categorical differences. The interchangeability of reason and sensuality in history erodes their strict and eternal separation, unmasking the categorical difference between them as abstraction. Reason has more than roots in sensuality: in *Moses and Monotheism*, reason and sensuality are *interconvertible*. In what follows, I examine how Freud's theory of the return of the repressed and its radical theoretical implications align with the models of repetition of Benjamin and Deleuze.

Freud and Benjamin: The Subversion of Origins

In the opening remarks to section K of the *Passagenwerk*, I noted earlier in the book, Walter Benjamin famously defines his Copernican revolution in historical perception as the "dialectical turn to remembrance."[73] Benjamin is alluding to Proust, but his focus on historiography as a "technique of awakening" and his fascination with processes of unconscious production of cultural and historical reality in a capitalist society can also be seen as reflecting his growing interest in Freud's psychoanalytic theory. This attraction was noted by Theodor Adorno, who worried that Benjamin was about to develop an "undialectical"[74] notion of the collective unconscious. Adorno's earlier response to Benjamin's project in June 1935 was different. "It would be a blasphemy to express any particular praise of the work," he wrote to Benjamin. "But I cannot resist the temptation here of singling out some of the things in which it affected me most profoundly." One of those "things" was Benjamin's notion of fetishism, which Adorno believed had important connections with Freud: "You find yourself here, perhaps without being aware of the fact, in the most profound agreement with Freud; there is certainly much to be thought about this connection. In any case you should definitely read anything you can find by Freud."[75]

Adorno was not the only one to make this connection. In recent years, several works have secured Freud's place in Benjamin's oeuvre.[76] Thematically, most commentators focus on Benjamin's growing interest with memory and remembrance and his earlier treatment of mourning and melancholy in *Trauerspiel* as a site of contact with Freud's work.[77] These readings provide the context for the popular estimation that, in some instances, Benjamin seems to be "picking up where Freud left off."[78] This argumentation, important as it is to Benjamin's readership, suggests Benjamin's recitation of a monologue on a dead past. Freud is a silent partner; his psychoanalytic project is finished, ready for Benjamin to "pick up where he left off." Yet these readings obscure the fact that Benjamin and Freud participated in the same historical moment. Freud and Benjamin—and Rosenzweig and Kafka a decade earlier—were troubled by the same set of questions on the nature of history at the same time. Adorno's letter to Benjamin on the latter's psychoanalytic inclinations was written when Freud was working on the first draft of *Moses and Monotheism*, and Freud's book was published in 1939 in London, exactly when Benjamin worked on the drafts of "On the Concept of History" in Paris. Therefore, in the following, I aim at a different conversation between Freud's and Benjamin's theories of history, with Freud an active participant in the conversation. I focus especially on their respective theories of origin and repetition. This is not to claim that there is a direct influence of Benjamin on Freud, but to read Freud's theory of history in dialogue with Benjamin's basic insights. If it turns out to be a "constellation," as Rainer Nägele described their relations, let them both enjoy it.[79]

Freud's theory of the return of the repressed unveils a basic tension between repetition and singularity. On the one hand, religions—like Judaism and Christianity—repeat the trauma that initiated history. On the other hand, this repetition leads, as we have just seen, to new forms of historical social and religious organizations. Put otherwise, the historical repetition, that is, the return of the repressed murder, initiates the invention of new forms of religion. The tension between return and invention indicates the impossibility of "pure" or "classical" repetition and serves as a form of revelation. Benjamin's notion of *Ursprung* highlights and repeats this theoretical position. In *Trauerspiel*, history is composed of exemplary objects that repeat each other to varying degrees. Their repetition produces a connection that in turn creates an opportunity to recognize essences and truths otherwise hidden. Like Freud's return of the repressed, Benjamin's repetition is *not* a return of the same: it is "imperfect and incomplete."[80] For Benjamin, as for Freud, repetition expresses a critical tension between repetition and imperfection, unity and singularity. "This dialectic," claims Benjamin, "showed singularity and repetition to be conditioned by one another in all essentials."[81]

Furthermore, and now I move to Benjamin's later theory of history, for both Freud and Benjamin, repetition has the capacity to change the course of history. In Freud's theory of the return of the repressed, the return of the trauma of the primal murder interrupted the flow of historical events and structured a new form of social and religious organization that was markedly different from the previous one. Christianity, to give Freud's example, broke down the history that the murder of Moses inaugurated, and structured a different vision of humanity—one defined by sensuality rather than guilt. This principle of difference aligns with Benjamin's repetition of opposition in the *Passagework*, in which a constellation of dangers grounds the possibility of a radical shift in the present. Freud, in other words, defined in psychological terms that which Benjamin's historical materialism hoped to achieve: he found in history a repetitive structure that radically transforms one social and religious organization to another. What is also interesting is that both Freud and Benjamin thought of this breaking of history in terms of tension or intensification. For Benjamin, the constellation produces a "force field" or tensional relations between past and future through which a vision of redeemed life is possible, and, for Freud, the breaking down of linear time is based on the eruption of the psychical tension of the return of the repressed. For Benjamin and Freud, repetition has the power to intervene in history because it harbors a tension that was qualitatively different from homogenous, linear time. They both formulate the historical dialectics of sameness and difference in terms of intensity: sameness is a condition of relaxation (or nirvana, in Freud's terminology) and difference is the product of intensification.

There is, however, one crucial difference between Freud's and Benjamin's theories of repetition that needs to be clarified. For Freud, repetition will never end. Cyclicality is an essential feature of history. Repetition is not to redeem humanity: the difference it produces never surmount the limits of the trauma that inaugurated history. In Benjamin, however, repetition has the power to bring an end or produce something new. Repetition is not an eternal cycle in history, like in Freud, but a structure with the potential to make a radical difference of eschatological proportions. It does so by producing an image of redeemed life. If in Freud, repetition is meant to free us from our misunderstandings or to devalue a certain truth or truths, in Benjamin, repetition is to evoke a flash of truth with the power to change the course of history.

The resemblance of Freud and Benjamin's model of repetition reflects also their notions of origins. To recall, in Benjamin's early theory of history, *Ursprung* is "an entirely historical category," which has "nothing to do with genesis [*Entstehung*]."[82] *Ursprung* is not a simple return to an original beginning but is grounded on material concrete manifestations. It is not an abstract, eternal truth revealed in history, nor is it a truth that commands history from outside. Rather, it is a dynamic repetition that continuously changes in time. My suggestion is that we should understand Freud's theory of the primal murder in similar terms. More precisely, Benjamin's formulation of *Ursprung* permits us to uncover the radical implications of Freud's theory of the return of the repressed. Before I make this argument, let me spend a moment on Freud's theory of truth in *Moses and Monotheism*.

The truth status of his revelations in *Moses and Monotheism* haunted Freud from the very early stages of the project. Freud, who, as I noted earlier, declared in a September 1934 letter to Arnold Zweig that his Moses book was a "historical novel," knew that this definition would cast doubt on the value of his findings. In the first draft of the introduction to the book, Freud tries to explain his choice of words: "The mixture of historical writing and fiction gives rise to different products, which under the common designation of 'historical novel' sometimes want to be appreciated as history, sometimes as novel." Some aim to reproduce people and events faithfully. Others "invent persons and even events in order to describe the special character of the period." Freud's work, however, follows yet another definition: he treated "each possibility in the text as a clue, and fill[ed] the gap between one fragment and another according to the law, so to speak, of the least resistance."[83]

The definition of the project as a historical novel complicated the status of Freud's findings in *Moses and Monotheism*, and in *Totem and Taboo*, for that matter. Was Freud's project a novel or a history? Did a murder indeed inaugurate Jewish history? To answer some of these questions, Freud dedicated the last part of the third book of *Moses and Monotheism* to the question of truth. There he differentiates between two kinds of truths: material and historical. The first, material truth is that which is "manifest and literal."[84] The second, historical truth is the kind of truth suggested by Freud's project. In difference from material truth, historical truth is constructed psychoanalytically from raw historical material. To give an example, in *Moses and Monotheism*, the material truth is that of the Bible, or that which the historical record preserves, and the historical truth is the murder that Freud uncovers.[85]

In focusing on historical truth in *Moses and Monotheism*, Freud therefore creates a clear hierarchy among these types of truth. As his book proves, he valued historical truth and devalued material truth. Modern historiography, which focuses on traditional historical material and would thus in his categorization belong to "material truth," is demoted, while psychoanalytical analysis takes its place. In Freud's eyes, for too long historiography had been concerned with the written record, that is, with the organized and controlled information that one generation wanted to report to the next. It neglected, in fact, repressed, the mischiefs, the evils, and the murders that his project aimed to uncover:

> What had been omitted or changed in the written record might very well have been preserved intact in tradition. Tradition was a supplement but at the same time a contradiction to historical writing. It was less subjected to the influence of distorting purposes and perhaps at some points quite exempt from them, and it might therefore be more truthful than the account that had been recorded in writing.... A tradition of such a kind might meet with various sorts of fate. What we should most expect would be that it would be crushed

by the written account, would be unable to stand up against it, would become more and more shadowy and would finally pass into oblivion.[86]

Put in Benjaminian terms, in *Moses and Monotheism*, Freud was interested in the lost tradition of Judaism, the ruptures and distortions that were lost in the cultural treasures of the Jewish past, and that Benjamin intended to re-represent in his collection of marginal artifacts of nineteenth-century Paris in *Passagenwerk*. In the 1937 essay "Constructions in Analysis," which Freud composed while working on *Moses and Monotheism*, Freud further explains this process: "[The work of construction] would consist in liberating the fragment of historical truth from its distortions and its attachments to the actual present day and in leading it back to the point in the past to which it belongs."[87] This procedure aligns with Benjamin's investigation: both rescued the historical fact from its historical context, which brought about distortions and misunderstandings, and connected this fact with a structure of origin.[88]

The privileging of psychoanalytic analysis over traditional historiography changed the status of Freud's claims about the origins of the Jewish people. In principle, despite Freud's insistence to the contrary, his theory of historical truth suggests we can set aside his claims about the *material reality* of the murder of Moses as we will never truly know their objective status. Remember that Freud constructed historical truth using the same procedure as he used to construct the past of neurotic patients. For Freud, the historical truth in collective reality was equivalent to the psychological truth in the individual. However, as Freud continuously insisted, we can never truly separate inner and outer reality in clinical analysis. We never know if the trauma is the result of outside reality or inner fantasy. This was Freud's greatest insight in *The Interpretation of Dreams*. While his previous pre-psychoanalytic theory determined that an actual seduction had to have happened in the history of the neurotic patient, after the famous 1897 turn, Freud realized that a fantasy of such a seduction is just as effective and significant.[89]

Freud's psychoanalytic notion of historical truth thus blurs the difference between invention and discovery in analysis. Trauma results from either internal impulses or external traumatic events and in most cases from some kind of interaction between inner and outer reality. The same ambiguous definition of reality applies to his theory of history.[90] In view of Freud's psychoanalytic model of historical truth, it is likewise unclear, even immaterial, whether the murder of Moses actually occurred. In psychoanalytic terms, the murder could have been only a fantasy of the people who suffered under Moses just as it could have been a "material" fact. In all likelihood, it was probably some kind of interaction of such fantasy and historical reality that produced the trauma that created the Jewish people. For Freud, the "truth status" or objective reality of the murder is insignificant. Just as in the clinical setting, the psychoanalytic investigation of history could not be concerned with the external realities of objective history. As Freud argues, "We should equate phantasy and reality and not bother to begin with whether the childhood experiences under examination are the one or the other."[91] Reality or fantasy-based, the psychological impact of the murder is just the same.

To be clear, I am not interested in delving into the long discussion in psychoanalytic literature about the truth value of Freud's psychoanalytic construction.[92] My point is different. I argue that by putting Freud next to Benjamin, we recognize the subversive power of Freud's work on the origins of Moses. In defining the origins of the Jewish people in terms of "historical" truth, understood by Freud as reconstructed and retrieved from the commonplaces of historical material, Freud offers a fascinating theory of origins that, like that of Benjamin, transgresses against the origins it aims to locate. Freud's investigation suggests that the importance of the murder of Moses is not derived from the reality of a historical occurrence, whatever the status of its reality, but instead, on its return in history. To put it another way, the eternal return is what gave the origin its meaning, and not the other way around.

Like Benjamin's *Ursprung*, Freud's origin is meaningful as long as it is grounded in historical events.[93] The origin is truly a construction, a myth, or an "as if" story: we cannot know if it really happened, but we do know that history, especially Jewish history, is comprehensible only when such an origin is hypothesized. This model of origin, in both Benjamin and Freud, reflects a departure from the common understanding of the concept origin in modern intellectual history.

For Benjamin and Freud, in different ways, an origin is not an entity outside history that determines a subsequent trajectory of history, as I suggested earlier in the chapter. Rather, it is a construction that is illuminated or rendered legible from the position of the present, and useful only as far as it explains the present.[94] As in Benjamin's *Ursprung*, the return of the repressed is the most important fact, perhaps even the only fact, that we can learn in Freud's investigation. The historical reality of the murder of Moses must be treated as it is—a historical novel.

Disguises and Masks: Deleuze and Freud on Repetition

Deleuze's work on repetition, which I discussed at length in chapter 1, highlights the radical conclusions of Freud's Moses book. Deleuze addresses Freud's return of the repressed in the introduction and the second chapter of his *Difference and Repetition*. Generally, this review, which focuses exclusively on Freud's *Beyond the Pleasure Principle*, has received little attention, certainly compared to his later commentary on Freud in *Anti-Oedipus*, the first-fruit of his celebrated collaboration with French psychiatrist Félix Guattari.[95]

In *Difference and Repetition*, Deleuze addresses Freud's theory of neurosis as an important example of the kind of repetition Deleuze has in mind, alongside Kierkegaard's and Nietzsche's models. Deleuze seems especially impressed with the fact that in *Beyond the Pleasure Principle* Freud made repetition into a constitutive feature of the mind. In his words, "the turning point of Freudianism appears in *Beyond the Pleasure Principle*: the death instinct is discovered, not in connection with the destructive tendencies, not in connection with aggressivity, but as a result of a direct consideration of repetition phenomena."[96] Still, later in the book, Deleuze expresses his reservations regarding Freud's articulation of repetition. He is concerned specifically with Freud's characterization of repetition in conservative terms, that is, as a movement "backward." In *Beyond the Pleasure Principle*, repetition still reflects the fact that the "aim of all life is death," and is conceived as a movement that aims to bring life back to a kind of "nirvana." Deleuze, following Bergson, takes a different tack, claiming repetition is a productive force that reflects the affirmative quality of life set against the tendency of material to fall back to an inorganic state.[97]

Notwithstanding Deleuze's criticism of repetition defined in terms of the death instinct and retrogression, I argue that repetition functions differently in *Moses and Monotheism* than in Deleuze's characterization of *Beyond the Pleasure Principle*. My claim here is based on a shift in Freud's analysis of religion in the 1930s. In the rationalist-positivist understanding of religion expressed in *The Future of an Illusion* in the 1920s, religion is seen as a collective neurosis that demands healing; similarly, the religious believer is portrayed as a "helplessly paralyzed" child, as indicated in the opening pages of this chapter. In *Moses and Monotheism*, however, religion is the moving force of human history. The primal trauma grounds social reality, even in the present, and its historical returns produce new forms of social organization. Religion is seen as affirmative and not merely as destructive or harmful; it is at the core of civilization.

What is significant in this formulation of religion in the 1930s is that this shift is informed by Freud's theory of repetition. The move from the individual to the social sphere allows Freud to conceptualize repetition differently, that is, not as regressive but as productive. The return of the repressed in the collective realm represents a movement that yields multiformity rather than mere regression to the original condition of trauma. The basic diversity of collective forms of life is grounded on the different ways different societies relate to a previous trauma. Repetition, in other words, is a force that "invents" different human communal ways-of-being—a force that advances human heterogeneity. It is noteworthy that the death drive is not mentioned in Freud's last book; in its absence, I would suggest, a theoretical space is opened wherein repetition can become a fruitful model for Freud to think human heterogeneity.

The same argument applies to Deleuze's estimation of Freud's model of repetition in the introduction. I refer here to the question of the philosophical status of difference in Freud's repetition. Recall, my main argument in the present chapter is that the movement of the return of the repressed can be understood in Freud to produce differences at the social and religious level. In recognizing these differences, Freud's *Moses and Monotheism* challenges (1) the validity of abstract notions of reason and sensuality and (2) their antagonism. And initially, Deleuze adheres to this basic interpretation of Freud's repetition. Ultimately, he writes, "it is a question of the relation, between repetition and disguises. Do the disguises found in the work of dreams or symptoms—condensation, displacement, dramatization—rediscover while attenuating a bare, brute repetition (repetition of the Same)?" Thinking of the famous case of Dora, he adds: "From the first theory of repression, Freud indicated another path: Dora elaborates her own role, and repeats her love for the father, only through other roles filled by others, which she herself adopts in relation to those others (K., Frau K., the governess...). The disguises and the variations, the masks or costumes, do not come 'over and above': they are, on the contrary, the internal genetic elements of repetition itself, its integral and constituent parts."[98]

Freud, Deleuze claims, indicated from the very early days of psychoanalysis that repetition of the symptom was never repetition of the same. Dora repeated her love to her father throughout her childhood in diverse forms. Each return to the trauma had a new shape that was not "over and beyond" the experience of Dora, but "an internal genetic element of repetition itself." The same applies, I should add, to Freud's history of civilization: the return of the repressed produced different social and religious forms of life. The problem was, claims Deleuze—in an argument that echoes his later work on Freud—that Freud was unable to accept the radical conclusions of his own work. Freud, according to Deleuze, "was unable to prevent himself [from] maintaining the model of brute repetition, at least as a tendency. We see this when he attributes fixation to the id: disguise is then understood from the perspective of a simple opposition of forces; disguised repetition is only the fruit of a secondary compromise between the opposed forces of the Ego and the Id."[99] Freud, to put it simply, mistakenly insisted on reducing the concrete manifestation of the trauma to an abstract representation of instinctual conflict and thereby vitiated the deep insights his work was meant to offer. He translated the concrete experience into abstract psychoanalytic principle and, in that move, he reduced those repetition-produced differences to tentative incidents of the trauma, reformulating, as a result, his repetition of differences as a bare repetition of the same.

Here again, the shift from the individual to the social sphere makes a difference. To be clear, it is not my intention to claim that Freud is as radical as Deleuze. Yet thinking of Freud with Deleuze (and Benjamin) in mind, we can see how Freud, in his last work, suggests a theory of human civilization that emphasizes "masks" and "disguises" in history. In *Moses and Monotheism*, religions, as "disguises," have a value that transcends their relation to the trauma. Granted, Judaism was an attempt to come to terms with a trauma, but it was also, at the same time, and here Freud's argument becomes advantageous to post-secular literature, a form of life, valuable in itself. In *Moses and Monotheism*, Freud admittedly intends to find a trauma through which the history of the Jewish people could be represented in one complete narrative. He thinks of the return of the repressed as one unified psychological phenomenon. However, Freud also acknowledges the value of religion, even if, and perhaps because, it originated in a trauma. Put in more general terms, with Deleuze, we see how Judaism and Christianity become more than neurosis in Freud's last work: they are "disguises" that reveal essentially different ways of life. And as in Deleuze, these historical "disguises" or difference, which Freud identifies, transgress against the same worldview that Deleuze's project targets: the eternal truths of reason and sensuality and their antagonism that inform Western culture to the present day.

"*credo quia absurdum*": Freud on Reason

Moses and Monotheism is a work on the return of the repressed that returns to the beginning of Freud's psychoanalytic project; a work in which Freud "appears to be seeking a dialogue with his early counterpart, with the aim of himself looking back once again at his own beginning as a psychoanalytic thinker."[100] It is a text about history that reveals the incoherence of historical eternal truth; a text about *Entstellung* (distortions) that reveals a distortion in history. "In many instances of textual distortion," Freud honestly reflects, "we may nevertheless count upon finding what has been suppressed and disavowed hidden away somewhere else, though changed and torn from its context. Only it will not always be easy to recognize it."[101] The book is a prime example of such a text.

Freud's theory of history in *Moses and Monotheism* curiously diverged from his theoretical and personal motivations of the 1930s. In those years, Freud's youthful enthusiasm was turning to sober conservatism. The role of psychoanalysis in the criticism of Victorian sexual morality gradually gave way to an overemphasis on the crucial role of social and mental repressive mechanisms in the defense against human sexual and aggressive behaviors. Working amid the escalating antisemitism across Europe, Freud introduced measures of mental defense against racist violence to his psychoanalytic theory.[102] His earlier focus on the drives now seemed irresponsible. It was time to concentrate on agents of regulation and control in the psyche. This "Ptolemaic" shift (in Jean Laplanche's words)[103] assigned a growing importance to the ego. It was recorded in the prioritizing of the ego in the structural model and entrenched in the second anxiety theory that implied "a concession to the ego that it can exert a very extensive influence over processes in the id."[104] Freud's *New Introductory Lectures* (1933) celebrated that change in one of his most consequential slogans: "*wo Es war, soll Ich werden.*"

Moses and Monotheism supposedly professes a similar conceptual commitment. In a book designed to answer why "the Jews have come to be what they are and why they have attracted this undying hatred,"[105] Freud's answer to the challenge of antisemitism is a subtle yet persistent attempt to reintegrate Jews into modern society. In *Moses and Monotheism*, Freud rewrites the Jewish people as the intermediary of ethical and intellectual excellence. Jewish renunciation of the instinct is suggested as a prefiguration of the European enlightenment; Judaism symbolized reason and self-control, thereby becoming an iconic image for modern culture. In Freud's new history, the Jewish people should have been warmly accepted to German secular society. In line with Herman Cohen's and Franz Rosenzweig's thesis on the Jews as the great educators of humanity, Freud's Jewish people were "a privileged minority, which was superior because of intellectual powers, [and] exalted ethical standards," and destined to reeducate humanity to adult and rational behavior.[106] In this last book, Freud's political agenda—his version of the previous century's *Wissenschaft des Judentums*—and his Ptolemaic tendencies consolidate his insistence on the victory of the Mosaic religion. Psychoanalysis as the science of ego and reason, and Judaism as the modern emissary of logic and self-control, seem to be in perfect harmony.

Yet in defiance of the need to "train" psychoanalysis for the rational tradition, for all the above reasons, in his last work, Freud is "incorruptibly honest"[107] in allowing difference to arise. In *Moses and Monotheism*, the struggles and the dilemmas are out in the open. The internally conflicting theoretical positions emerge in the last part of the book, in a section meant to be the last, serious, and careful theoretical investigation of the fundamental advantages of the renunciation of the human drives. It was supposed to be a final analysis of the importance of ethical and rational life, in which Freud tested the superiority of reason over drive; to find out "why an advance in intellectuality... should raise the self-regard both of the individual and of a people."[108] But this mini-incursion ends with a conflict that only great last works can offer. Freud's book, seemingly "composed by Freud for himself," as Said mentions, disturbed Freud's conscious agenda and acted as a late countermovement in his thought:

> Thus we are faced by the phenomenon that in the course of the development of humanity sensuality is gradually overpowered by intellectuality and that men feel proud and exalted by every such advance. But we are unable to say why this should be so. It further happens later on that intellectuality itself is overpowered by the very puzzling emotional phenomenon of faith. Here we have the celebrated "*credo quia absurdum*," and, once more, anyone who has succeeded in this regards it as a supreme achievement.[109]

These lines evince an undeniable and captivating candor precisely because they admit to an essential contradiction in psychoanalysis. In his final years, Freud was searching for a conclusive theoretical grounding, or "a definite standard of value,"[110] that will ultimately prove that the Jewish renunciation of instincts is a preferable outcome in history. Not coincidently, Freud registered this urgent dilemma of both his Jewish identity and his science as a question of the meaning of historical progress. Freud is interested here in the "development" of civilization. He wants to know if it is possible to impose the rational (Jewish) trajectory on history; to substantiate one element of reality over the other. What he discovers, however, is that there is no final goal that can direct history. Freud's search for an ultimate meaning of history amounts to a *credo quia absurdum*.[111] History only repeats itself within the bounds of reason and sensuality; in the end, intellectuality is "overpowered" by faith, and sensuality and reason are conflated in a "puzzling" arrangement.[112] Freud aimed to find the final proof for his insistence on reason, but this, ironically, only magnified the movement of repetition to other human dimensions. In this last note, the historical repetition reflects on another structural dichotomy of Western culture. This time, the *credo quia absurdum* projects the impossibility of the eternal dichotomy of secularity and religion. The sharp opposition of sensuality and reason, secularity and faith, collapsed in Freud's last theory of history.

In effect, Freud's book is a meditation on the power of repetition. For Freud, as I have shown, the oscillation between guilt and pleasure, reason and sensuality, religion and secularity truly represents the human condition. This oscillation also captures the radicalness of Freud's vision of the eternal return of the repressed. Bluntly stated, there is no way out of this historical repetition, which structures the limits of history. Yet reading Freud's book as subverting the logical opposition between sensuality and guilt that informs Western civilization, I ask whether there is a sense in which the messianic is operative within *Moses and Monotheism*. Can we assign a weak messianic power to the psychoanalytic project of Freud? Not in terms of an apocalyptic end of history, not in the hope of a messiah charging from the gates of heaven, and certainly not in terms of an overarching telos of history. But thinking of Freud's model of history, I argue that in the Freudian framework, history entails a peculiar kind of revelation. *Moses and Monotheism* offers more than a description of history. The book aims to intervene in history. In Freud's book, we are not given a truth but are instead healed from the need for an absolute truth. The intellectual search for absolute knowledge is counteracted in it. In psychoanalytic terms, history understood according to Freud's model of dynamic repetition offers liberation from one of our deepest dreams. It frees us from the power of truth by allowing us to recognize the fragmentation of eternal truths. In terms of the tale of the Messiah at the Gate of Rome, which opens this work, it is the repetitive waiting that is so important; it is the waiting that offers a revelation, not the coming of the Messiah.

In *Moses and Monotheism* there is no place for a messiah. But here, in his last great work, Freud calls for the awakening of the present from the forces of eternal truths via historical practice. I wonder how Benjamin would have defined such a project.

Notes

Introduction: Scenarios of Repetition

1. *T. Sanhedrin* 98a.
2. This follows the well-known entry in Malachi 3:23: "Now I am sending to you Elijah the prophet, Before the day of the Lord comes, the great and terrible day."
3. Psalms 95:7.
4. My reading draws on Emmanuel Levinas's *Difficult Freedom*. Levinas (1990), 72. In his reading, Levinas also focuses on notions of suffering and mourning and their interrelations with Jewish messianism that the story provocatively illustrates.
5. By German Jewish world, I refer not only to the modern German state but also to the German language speaking world, which includes various nationalities in Central Europe.
6. For a representative sample of publications on Jewish messianism in the last two decades, see Braiterman (2007); Bouretz (2010); Dubbels (2011); Idel (2010); Liska (2008); Kavka (2004); Löwy (1992); Mosès (2009); and Seeskin (2012). For recent edited volumes, see Frankel (1991); Morgan and Weitzman (2015); and Rashkover and Kavka (2013).
7. Aschheim (1996), 34.
8. Rabinbach (1997), 28. As Michael Löwy notes, "Theirs was a generation of dreamers and utopians: they aspired a radically other world, to the kingdom of God on earth, to a kingdom of spirit, a kingdom of freedom, a kingdom of peace." Löwy (1992), 2.
9. As Virgilius Haufniensis, Kierkegaard's pseudonym in *The Concept of Dread*, declares. Kierkegaard (1957), 16.
10. *R*, 19.
11. DeHart (2015), 92.
12. Wolin (1994), 31.
13. *SW*, 4: 392.
14. *AP*, 475 [N10a,2].
15. *SR*, 324.
16. Deleuze (1994), 55.
17. *AP*, 842 [G,17].
18. *OT*, 35.
19. Deleuze (1990), 287.

1. Notes to Chapter 1

1. Nietzsche (1999), 9: 11.
2. Nietzsche (2007a), 35, § 10.
3. Young (2010), 318.
4. For an introductory reading on Eliade, see Allen (1998); Deprez (1999); and Idel (2014).
5. Eliade (2005), 34. For more on Eliade's position here, see also *The Sacred and the Profane* (1961).
6. Eliade (2005), 28.
7. Ibid., 35.
8. See also Eliade (1975), 5–6; Eliade (1961), 95–99. Many critics of Eliade noted that in his description of myth as ahistorical, Eliade disregarded the historical nature of myth (and other religious facts) as a product of human imagination. See Allen (1998), 225–31.
9. Eliade (2005), 105.
10. Ibid., 35.
11. Ibid., 75.
12. Ibid., 89. Eliade is very impressed in this context with the practice of yoga. The practitioner of yoga, he believes, is an example of a person who completely renounced history for the mythical time. Eliade (1958).
13. Eliade (2005), 123.
14. Hahm (1977).
15. Löwith (1970), 9.
16. Augustine (2008), 12: 269.
17. 1 Thessalonians 4:17, emphasis mine. Augustine says: "If . . . the soul passes to its beatitude without ever again returning to its former misery, then, in that case, something new takes place in time, which, nevertheless, does not end in time. If this be true why cannot we say the same of the world? And, also, of the creation of man?" Augustine (2008), 12: 268. For Augustine, the pagan idea of *circuitus temporum* was grounded on the inability to comprehend infinity, forcing the pagan world to "close the circle" of time. The Christian, however, revered God, who was "eternal and without beginning." Ibid., 12: 270.
18. For the differences between Christian and Greek models of history, see Oscar Cullmann's influential *Christ and Time* (1964); and Brandon (1951).
19. Eliade (2005), 102–12.
20. Exodus 20:2.
21. In *Zakhor* (1982), Yosef Yerushalmi has canonized this understanding of Jewish history in a now famous claim: "If Herodotus was the father of history, the fathers of meaning in history were the Jews." Yerushalmi (1996), 8.
22. In this sense, German historian Reinhart Koselleck has been one the most important figures in recent scholarship, notably the claim in his volumi-

nous lexicon of *Begriffsgeschichte* that "the possibility of repeatable events" informed premodern historiography up to the seventeenth century. Koselleck (2004), 114. For a review of cyclicality and repetition in Western history, see Trompf (1979); Lynn Thorndike's classical *A History of Magic and Experimental Science* (1923–1958); and Momigliano (1996), 6: 1–23. Going back to Greek historiography, some in fact have questioned the attribution of cyclical time to Greek society. See, for example, John Van Seters's remark that "no cyclical view of time is evident in the Greek histories, whatever the philosophers might say." Van Seters (1983), 8.

23. Vico's *New Science* (1725) analyzes the mythical roots of civil society in an attempt to define an ideal form ("ideal eternal history," in Vico's terms) that explains the course of development and decline which all nations must pass: "Our Science therefore comes to describe at the same time an ideal eternal history traversed in time by the history of every nation in its rise, development, maturity, decline, and fall." Vico (1984), 104, § 349.

24. Ricœur (1995), 179. Peter Steensgaard similarly argues, based on several passages in Psalms and Deuteronomy on Jewish festivals, that ancient Judaism had an archaic concept of time according to which "life was renewed annually in connection with the new year." Steensgaard (1993), 69. For more on repetitive and cyclical structures in the Torah, see Chilton (2002) and Barr (1969).

25. Krochmal (2010).

26. Shmitta is the sabbatical year in the seven-year agricultural cycle that applies to the Land of Israel in the Torah. On the Doctrine of *Shemittot*, see Weinstock (1969), 153–248; Pedaya (2003), 213–411; and Scholem (1987), 460–74.

27. Scholem (1987), 462. Evidence of this doctrine, which dates back to the Book of Hanoch, the older sections of which date to 300 BC, and later in Philo of Alexandria, may suggest that the Jewish idea of cosmic cycles was in fact influenced by a wide variety of notions of eternal return in the archaic world. Weinstock (1969), 187–90.

28. David ben Judah heHasid (1982), 32.

29. Scholem (1987), 463–64.

30. Ibid., 471. The Messiah, others believed, comes repeatedly in the sixth millennium of each cycle. "And in the year of Messiah, namely, in the year whose secret is 358 of the sixth millennium, which is the year (*shannah*), then the Messiah will arrive. [However,] in an occult manner he has already arrived during the several cycles of the worlds which have already passed before the present one in which we are." From *Sefer ginat beitan*, chapter 52. Cited in Idel (1998), 169.

31. Rabbi Moshe ben Nahman, commentary on Leviticus, 25:2.

32. Idel (1998), 163.

33. Ibid., 179. According to Idel, the repetitive cycle of profane and divinity

infused meaning and order into what was perceived as a chaotic flux of endless time. Ibid., 93. In "Sabbath: On Concepts of Time in Jewish Mysticism," Idel expands on this claim and gives an example of a specific cycle of time in Jewish rituals—the Sabbath. Idel (2004).

34. Wolfson (2006), xi.

35. Wolfson (2015a), 113.

36. Wolfson (2006), 59.

37. Wolfson (2015a), 116.

38. Wolfson (2015b), 32.

39. Wolfson, to give an example to his argument, builds, in *Alef, Mem, Tau* (2006), on the famous precept of Babylonian Talmud that "the Torah be cherished by those who *study each day as the day it was given from Mount Sinai*" (Babylonian Talmud, Berakhot 63b, emphasis mine), as mandating that those who study the Torah must experience their *actual* present moment as a "recurrence of the Sinaitic theophany, a reiteration of the past that induces the novelty of the present." Wolfson (2006), 64. That is, for Wolfson, the study of the Torah produces not only a long series of interpretations of the Torah but an actual repetitive experience of the Sinaitic revelation. These revelations restructure the mode of time of the student. His or her immediate experience is a re-experience of the past. Further, in line with the insistence in Kabbalistic hermeneutics that each interpretation of the Torah is different, each revelatory experience is different as well: the student, in comprehending the present as a repetition of the past, experiences the present as always different. The rabbinic imagination, which infuses "time and text, revelation and interpretation," asserts, in short, that "each interpretive gesture [is] a reenactment of the revelatory experience, albeit from its unique vantage point, *each moment a novel replication of the past*." Ibid., 64–65, emphasis mine. Put in general terms, Wolfson identifies in the Kabbalistic tradition a structure of repetition that is not modeled on the return of the same, but on the return of the different: "repetition and novelty [are] not antinomical; what recurs is precisely what has been that which will recur as what has never been." Ibid., 65. See also the prologue to Wolfson (2005).

40. My reading follows Safranski (2002), 221–22. For Nietzsche's letter, see Nietzsche (1986a), 6: 112, Aug. 14, 1881.

41. Agamben (2004), 315–16.

42. Heidegger was the first to offer a metaphysical explanation of the eternal return in volume 2, "The Eternal Recurrence of the Same," in *Nietzsche* (1984). For the eternal return as existential exercise, see Hatab (2005); Magnus (1978); and Seung (2005). For Nietzsche's eternal return as "a new mythos," see Bertram (2009), 294.

43. Nietzsche (1968b), 549, § 1066.

44. Nietzsche believed that the eternal return is "the most scientific of all pos-

sible hypotheses." Ibid., 36, § 55. Later in the same book, he writes: "The law of the conservation of energy demands eternal recurrence." Ibid., 547, § 1063. One of the first to engage with and then rebuke the cosmological argument was Georg Simmel in *Schopenhauer und Nietzsche* (2001). For a recent discussion of the cosmological argument, see Danto (2005). Jorge Luis Borges offers a fascinating rebuttal of the cosmogonic argument in his 1934 essay "The Doctrine of Cycles," in which he reverts to the modern theory of entropy as a possible response to Nietzsche's eternal return. Borges (1999).

45. Nietzsche (2001), 194, § 341. Jaspers shared Löwith's interpretation, claiming that the eternal return finalized the "God is dead" statement by revoking the possibility of all kinds of transcendence. Jaspers (1979), 365–66.

46. Nietzsche (2006), 174.

47. Ibid., 177.

48. Ibid.

49. Nietzsche (2007a), 35, § 10. In *The Will to Power* Nietzsche writes: "Such an experimental philosophy . . . It wants rather to cross over to the opposite of this—to a Dionysian affirmation of the world as it is, without subtraction, exception, or selection—it wants the eternal circulation: the same things, the same logic and illogic of entanglements. The highest state a philosopher can attain: to stand in a Dionysian relationship to existence—my formula for this is *amor fati*." Nietzsche (1986b), 536. In *The Gay Science* this was introduced in aesthetical terms. Nietzsche (2001), 157.

50. Nietzsche (2007a), 13 § 6.

51. "Heraclitus philosophy knows no 'ethical imperative,' no 'Thou Shalt,' but also no mere 'I will.'" Löwith (1997), 118.

52. For the suffering in Nietzsche's theory of the eternal return, see Kain (2007), 49–63.

53. Löwith argues that in this formulation Nietzsche's eternal return retains a theological form. The willing of the eternal return promises personal redemption by inserting into Nietzsche's anti-Christian philosophy an eschatological arc that was never there in the original archaic formulations. Löwith (1997), 120. For an alternative reading of the eternal return as an attack on Christian values, see Rosen (1995).

54. In Löwith's book, the emphasis on the present caused Nietzsche's downfall. In his reading, Nietzsche continuously strove to work out the impossible contradiction between the fact of eternal return and his own ethical imperative of self-affirmation. According to Löwith, this was the contradiction through which "the astonishing unity and logical consistency of Nietzsche's train of thought breaks asunder." He even claimed that with this contradiction, "Nietzsche's reflection ends in insanity." Löwith (1996), 10.

55. Ibid., 121.

56. Nietzsche's focus on the present, it is important to note in the context of the main argument, was interconnected with his critical assessment of linear history, as Hayden White reminds us in "The Burden of History" (1966). Much like the concern with history in Kierkegaard and Heidegger, which I detail below, the widespread conceptualization of history as a succession of predetermined events proved dangerous to his life project. "Nietzsche hated history even more than he hated religion. History promoted a debilitating voyeurism in men, made them feel that they were latecomers to a world in which everything worth doing had already been done." White (1966), 116.

57. This wave of revolutionary readings was partly inaugurated in the 1964 Royaumont colloquium on Nietzsche.

58. For a good introduction to Deleuze's model of repetition, see Ansell-Pearson (1999); De Beistegui (2004); and the traditional introduction to the book in Williams (2013).

59. Deleuze (1994), 55–56.

60. Hegel, Deleuze says, was unable to think pure difference, as for Hegel, every difference had to be subsumed under the identity of a higher order.

61. Deleuze (1956), 79–112.

62. Deleuze (1994), 1.

63. Ibid., 24.

64. Deleuze (1990), 287.

65. Deleuze (1994), 24.

66. On Deleuze's reading of Nietzsche, see Ansell-Pearson (1997); Pecora (1986); and Perry (1993). For a pushback against this line of interpretation, see Malabou (2010).

67. "Eternal return cannot mean the return of the Identical because it presupposes a world (that of the will to power) in which all previous identities have been abolished and dissolved. Returning is being, but only the being of becoming." Deleuze (1994), 41. The conclusion on the origins of Nietzsche's eternal return in archaic myth is immediate: "We must understand that Nietzsche does not recognize his idea of eternal return in his predecessors of antiquity." Deleuze (1983), 29. See also Deleuze (2005), 87–88. In *Anti-Oedipus* (1972), Deleuze and Guattari go on to completely reject Eliade's argument that archaic society was governed by repetition of the same: "The idea that primitive societies have no history, that they are dominated by archetypes and their repetition, is especially weak and inadequate. This idea was not conceived by ethnologists, but by ideologists in the service of a tragic Judeo-Christian consciousness that they wished to credit with the 'invention' of history." Deleuze and Guattari (1983), 150–51.

68. Deleuze (1994), 55, emphasis in text. Derrida echoed Deleuze's reading in his own interpretation of Nietzsche: "The eternal return is selective. Rather than a repetition of the same, the return must be selective within a differential relation of forces." Derrida (1985), 45.

69. Deleuze (2005), 89.

70. Ansell-Pearson (2005), 16.

71. Deleuze (2005), 55. For the Spirit of Gravity, see Nietzsche (2006), 153–56.

72. Ibid., 87, emphasis in text.

73. Jameson (2015).

74. *R*, 19.

75. Kierkegaard notes this quality in the opening lines of the book, in the context of the notion of immobility of the pre-Socratic school of the Eleatics: "When the Eleatics denied motion, Diogenes, as everyone knows, came forward in protest, actually came forward, because he did not say a word, but simply walked back and forth a few times, with which gesture he believed he had sufficiently refuted the Eleatic position." Ibid., 3.

76. The diverse and frequently opposing interpretations of Kierkegaard's book *Repetition* led some, like Roger Poole in *Kierkegaard* (1993), to conclude that there is "no Kierkegaardian doctrine of repetition." Poole (1993), 82. Arne Melberg claims: "It is not easy to decide what sort of text this is: a narration or a philosophical essay or perhaps an ironic mixture of both." Melberg (1990), 71. Caputo offers wonderful introduction to the topic (1987, 11–35), as does Eriksen (2000). For more, see Cain (1993); Crites (1993); Bârliba (2014); Reimer (1968); Mooney (1998); and Poole (1993), 61–82. For the place of repetition in Kierkegaard's poetics, see MacKey (1971), 1–33, and Harrison (1986).

77. *R*, 80.

78. Ibid.

79. Ibid., 107.

80. Ibid., 3. "This is repetition," declares Constantin, "I understand everything, and existence seems more beautiful than ever." Ibid., 74.

81. Ibid., 76.

82. Ibid., 80.

83. Ibid., 79.

84. *FTR*, 306.

85. See also Müller (1980).

86. "Have you read Job?" Constantin asks the young man: "Read it. Read it again and again." *R*, 63.

87. Ibid., 104.

88. "Job continues to maintain that he is in the right. He does this in such a way that he demonstrates noble human boldness, which knows what a person is, that he, though delicate and quickly withered like the life of a flower, from the perspective of freedom is something great, has a consciousness that not even God, though He gave it, can wrest from him." Ibid., 105.

89. Ibid., 79.

90. "He would then have acted with an entirely different iron-like consistency and firmness. He would have gained a fact of consciousness he could have

stuck with, . . . because he would have established it himself by virtue of a relationship to God. In the same instant the whole question of finitude would become insignificant; genuine actuality would, in a deeper sense, make no difference to him." Ibid., 80.

91. In his words, repetition is a "task of freedom, in which the question becomes that of saving one's personality from being volatilized and, so to speak, in pawn to event." *FTR*, 315.

92. Caputo (1987), 29.

93. Ibid., 21.

94. John Caputo notes Heidegger's debt in *Radical Hermeneutics*: "Heidegger's dependence on Kierkegaard . . . is more decisive at this point, in my view, than in any other place in *Being and Time* . . . Heidegger not only restates his dependence on Kierkegaard, he misstates it. In borrowing upon Kierkegaard's theory of repetition—without knowledge—he invokes Kierkegaard at the most crucial ontological juncture in the published text of *Being and Time*." Caputo (1987), 82–83. See also Quist (2002); McCarthy (2011); and Caputo (1993).

95. My reading of Heidegger will emphasize the ontological and historical aspects of repetition to introduce the reader to the various dimensions of repetition in modern philosophy. John Caputo's *Radical Hermeneutics* offers a wonderful introduction to Heidegger's repetition. Caputo (1987), 60–119. For different aspects of repetition in Heidegger, see Miguel de Beistegui's chapter "The Politics of Repetition" in his *Thinking with Heidegger* (2003); Henning (1982); and Schrag (1970).

96. Heidegger (1962), 164.

97. Ibid., 394.

98. Ibid., 374. Heidegger connects this to Dasein's awareness of its own death. In its awareness of death, Dasein recognizes its finitude, and therefore the importance of the decisions it makes in the present. Heidegger investigated this structure vis-à-vis the mood of anxiety. Ibid., 356.

99. Ibid., 388. The other, inauthentic relation to the past is conceptualized as a form of forgetting (*Vergessen*): "If Being-as-having-been is authentic, we call it 'repetition.' But when one projects oneself inauthentically towards those possibilities which have been drawn from the object of concern in making it present, this is possible only because Dasein has forgotten itself in its ownmost thrown potentiality-for-Being." Ibid.

100. Ibid., 311. To note, Joan Stambaugh translated *Augenblick* as "moment." For the history of the idea of *Augenblick* in modern philosophy, see Ward (2008).

101. George Seidel puts this eloquently, when he writes that in authentic repetition "one dredges tradition as one might dredge a river in order to widen the channel of its possibilities for future navigation, in order also to get to the bottom of it." Seidel (1964), 122.

102. Heidegger (1962), 437–38. I have chosen an earlier translation by John Mac-quarrie and Edward Robinson over a recent translation by Joan Stambaugh, since the former select the English word "repetition" for Heidegger's *Wie-derholung*, while the latter chooses "retrieval." Recollection might have been another solution, even though it over-emphasizes the epistemolog-ical understanding of Heidegger's concept. The term is also problematic because of Kierkegaard's principal distinction between repetition and recollection in the opening pages of his *Repetition*.

103. *R*, 19.

104. Derrida (1962), 203.

105. Heidegger applies his concept of repetition differently a few years later in *Kant and the Problem of Metaphysics* (1929). He reintroduces repetition in the opening lines of the fourth section of the book, where he revisits the prob-lem of metaphysics and finds in the history of thought certain previously concealed "primordial possibilities." Heidegger writes, "By a repetition of a fundamental problem we understand the disclosure of the primordial possibilities concealed in it. The development of these possibilities has the effect of transforming the problem and thus preserving it in its import as a problem." Heidegger (1990), 211. In *Contributions to Philosophy* (composed in 1936–38 and published posthumously in 1989), Heidegger reiterates the following understanding of repetition: "*Solely what occurs only once stands in the possibility of re-petition* ... Here re-petition does not mean the stupid superficiality and impossibility of the mere occurrence of the same for a second and third time. Indeed the beginning can never be apprehended as the same, since it reaches ahead and thus encroaches differently each time on that which it itself initiates. Accordingly, it determines its own re-petition." Heidegger (2012), 45, § 20, emphasis in text. Repetition here allows Heidegger to think of origins that do not counter or oppose the first origin of philosophy but are concealed in it; philosophy must disclose them in its repetition of these beginnings. Ibid., 146–47, § 94.

106. Caputo (1987), 60.

2. Notes to Chapter 2

1. *SE*, 4: 194.

2. Ibid.

3. Goldstein (1992), 71.

4. *SW*, 3: 326.

5. Brenner (1998), 12.

6. The literature on the modern German Jewish world is immense. George Mosse's *German Jews Beyond Judaism* (1997) is the canonical entry point. For other good discussions on the subject, see Katz (1973) and Sorkin (1987). Paul Mendes-Flohr's *German Jews* (1999), with its focus on Rosenzweig's perspective of this reality of German Jews, is also helpful.

7. I use the term *assimilation* in the widest sense, to include all forms of assimilation, acculturation, and naturalization.

8. Aschheim (1982), 5, emphasis in text. The harshest report of this impossible condition is still Gershom Scholem's "Jews and Germans" (1976). Sander Gilman's *Jewish Self-Hatred* portrays how assimilation led to the internalization of antisemitic discourses by the Jews. Gilman (1986).

9. According to Jacques Le Rider, the crisis unfolded against the backdrop of a wider crisis of identity in *fin-de-siècle* Europe. Le Rider (1993).

10. Scholem (1980), 10.

11. Ibid.

12. Eiland and Jennings (2014), 46.

13. *SW*, 2: 630.

14. For a more detailed illustration and analysis of the impact of this generational crisis on Scholem and Rosenzweig, see Brenner (1993).

15. Kafka (2015), 74.

16. Ibid.

17. Ibid., 76.

18. Ibid., 78.

19. Freud's *Moses and Monotheism* is the site where this ambivalence is perhaps most noticeable. In *Freud's Moses* (1991), Haim Yosef Yerushalmi says it is "something of commonplace to regard both the content of *Moses and Monotheism* and its convoluted gestation as symptoms of Freud's deep 'ambivalence' about his own Jewishness." Yerushalmi (1991), 6. Note that Yerushalmi feels the book represents Freud's alliance with Judaism.

20. I address some of the literature on Freud and Judaism in the chapter on Freud's *Moses and Monotheism*. For a famous description of Freud's negative evaluation of Judaism and religion, see Gay (1987). For contributions to the discussion of Freud's relations to Judaism, see Oring (1984); Rice (1990); Robert (1976); Yerushalmi (1991); and more recently in Slavet (2009). For an attempt to reconnect Freud with Judaism and Jewish mystical traditions, see Bakan (1958).

21. As Freud notes in a letter answering Max Graf's question on whether he should raise his child (the famous little Hans) as a Jew. See Graf (1942), 473.

22. *SE*, 13: xv.

23. For Sigmund Freud's relations with his father, see Krüll (1986).

24. *SE*, 4: 197.

25. In the words of Marthe Robert in *From Oedipus to Moses* (1976), "The father who cut his ties from a small rural community, preserved within himself enough living Judaism to save him from being dangerously uprooted, but, since all he could pass on to his children was snatches of folklore seasoned with humiliating memories, they were left with a dead past, an uncertain future, and a present that had to be created out of the whole cloth." Robert (1974), 21.

26. *L*, 288–89, June 1921. For more on Freud in this context, see Hezser (2001). Scholem, in an essay on Benjamin, concurred with Kafka. He believed that Benjamin, Kafka, and Freud were important examples of writers who had no illusions about their place in the German world: "Freud, Kafka, and Benjamin belonged to those few...They wrote in full awareness of the distance separating them from their German readers. They are the most distinguished of the so-called German Jewish Authors, and it is as much their lives that bear witness to that distance, its pathos and creative quality of potentiality, as their writings in which things Jewish figure rarely if at all." Scholem (1976), 191. Harold Bloom similarly grouped Freud with Scholem and Kafka to claim that they are the most important representatives of Jewish tradition, who are "already larger figures in the ongoing tradition of spirituality than are, say, Leo Baeck, Franz Rosenzweig and Martin Buber... because of [the former's] cultural achievements." Bloom (1985), 14.

27. Hans Baron's classical study *The Crisis of the Early Italian Renaissance: Civic Humanism and Republican Liberty in an Age of Classicism and Tyranny* (1966) offers a wonderful analysis of this crisis.

28. Buber (1999), 31.

29. In the words of Michael Brenner: "Jewish culture in Weimar Germany was characterized neither by a radical break with the past nor by a return to it. Indeed, it used distinct forms of Jewish traditions, marking them as authentic, and presented them according to the demands of contemporary taste and modern culture forms of expression." Brenner (1998), 5. See also Meyer and Brenner (1996).

30. Myers (2003), 30.

31. Ibid., 31.

32. For Rosenzweig's *Lehrhaus*, see Mendes-Flohr (1997).

33. Rosenzweig (1965), 28. Elsewhere, Rosenzweig puts it in general terms: "Emancipated Jewry lacks a platform of Jewish life upon which the bookless present can come into its own." Ibid., 61.

34. Ibid., 98–99.

35. The revival of Jewish scholarship and education was complemented by Rosenzweig's Hebrew translations, as discussed in chapter 4.

36. Brenner (1998), 7.

37. Ibid., 158.

38. The influence of Yiddish theatre on Kafka is a notable example. See Beck (1971).

39. "By speaking a Jewish language, being well-versed in religious traditions, and proudly displaying their Jewishness, the [East European Jews] symbolized a direct link with their ancestors." Brenner (1998), 130. John Efron in his recent *German Jewry and the Allure of the Sephardic* (2016) identifies a parallel cultural phenomenon in the glorification of eighteenth- and nineteenth-century German Jewish communities of Sephardic Jews and the Jewish

Golden Age in Spain. Like the East European Jews, the Sephardim, claims Efron, "served a utilitarian value as a foil for those who had sought to return Ashkenazic culture in a uniquely German key." Efron (2016), 231.

40. Cohen (1980), 54.

41. Ibid., 55.

42. Ibid.

43. Ibid., 56.

44. Ibid.

45. Ibid., 57.

46. "In a new context and used for different purposes, traditional texts, artifacts, and even songs attained a new meaning and thus became new traditions themselves." Brenner (1998), 4.

47. In the following lines, I focus on what we may call the "formal" narrative of Zionist ideology, that is, the position that Zionism essentially called for an establishment of Jewish nation-state in the Land of Israel. It is not my intention to argue for this line of interpretation. Rather, I am interested in investigating how this widespread understanding of Zionism reflects some of the principles of return and repetition I identified earlier in the chapter. For an important critique of this line of interpretation, see Shumsky (2018).

48. A good introduction to the intellectual history of Zionism is offered by Avineri (1981). For a general historical survey of Zionism, see Walter Laqueur's comprehensive *A History of Zionism* (1989). For Zionism in Germany, see Poppel (1976).

49. Pinsker (1906), 1.

50. For an introduction to the place of history in Zionism, see Almog (1987).

51. Eliezer Schweid's "The Rejection of the Diaspora in Zionist Thought: Two Approaches" (1996) offers a good entry point to the Zionist doctrine of *shlilat ha-gola* (negation of the diaspora).

52. The commemoration of Jewish antiquity emphasized national rather religious themes. When Zionism returned to the war of the Maccabees, this was to remember a period in which the Jewish nation was strong and united and capable and willing to fight against the invasion of Rome. The fact that these events also depicted a struggle of Jewish religious fanatics against pagan influence was oftentimes more hidden away. For Zionism's reappropriation of the Bar Kokhba myth, for example, see Ben-Yehuda (1995) and Harkabi (1983).

53. For Zionism and messianism, see Ohana (2017). For the messianic vision of Zionism in orthodox Judaism, in figures such as Rabbi Zvi Hirsch Kalischer and Rabbi Abraham Isaac Kook, see Ravitzky (1996). Scholem was famously cautious of the messianic trajectory of the Zionist movement, and a December 1926 letter to Rosenzweig on the Hebrew language expresses his concerns: "This country is a volcano, and language is lodged within it. People here talk of many things that may lead to our ruin, and more than ever of the Arabs. But there is another danger, much uncannier than the Arab

nation, and it is a necessary result of the Zionist enterprise: what of the 'actualization' of the Hebrew language? That sacred language on which we nurture our children, is it not an abyss that must open up one day? The people certainly don't know what they are doing." Scholem (1990).

3. Notes to Chapter 3

1. Glatzer (1998), x.
2. For a recent study of Rosenzweig's transformative experience, see Pollock (2014).
3. Mendes-Flohr (1988), xiii.
4. *GSR*, I: 556, letter 525 (May 9, 1918), emphasis in text.
5. *SR*, 352.
6. *SR*, 308.
7. Mendes-Flohr (1988), xxvi. Karel Barth was formative of the Kierkegaardian revival of the early 1920s. Rosenzweig references Kierkegaard in a letter to Buber—one of the few places he mentions the Danish philosopher—in the context of Barth's theology. *GSR*, 2: 876. For more, see Herskowitz (2017). Despite the significant similarities between Rosenzweig's work and Kierkegaard's philosophy and theology, there are relatively few comparative works on Rosenzweig's knowledge and reception of Kierkegaard. Most commentators focus on their conceptualization of love; some engage with their respective theories of death and subjectivity or their critique of Hegel's idealistic formulation of the All. For a recent detailed discussion of the secondary literature on the subject, see Welz (2011). David Groiser references the concept of repetition in Rosenzweig and Kierkegaard in "Repetition and Renewal: Kierkegaard, Rosenzweig and the German-Jewish Renaissance" (2011). His work, however, focuses on Rosenzweig's notion of repetition as renewal and in the context of Rosenzweig's argument about the place of Jewish education in the renewal of Jewish life and, as such, lies outside the scope of the chapter's argument. Zachary Braiterman references Derrida and Kierkegaard's theory of repetition in "Cyclical Motion and the Force of Repetition in the Thought of Franz Rosenzweig," in *Beginning/Again: Toward a Hermeneutics of Jewish Texts* (2002).
8. This to such an effect that, as in Zachary Braiterman's unequivocal words, "'repetition' defined Rosenzweig's understanding of Jewish life." Braiterman (2002), 216.
9. *SR*, 348.
10. Ibid., 348.
11. Ibid., 320.
12. Ibid., 321.
13. As Peter Gordon writes in *Rosenzweig and Heidegger* (2003), "at his best, Rosenzweig confirmed exile as irremediable. But he also considered it the mark of Jewish redemption." Gordon (2003), 308.

14. *SR*, 349.

15. Ibid.

16. See Hermann Cohen's chapter "The Idea of the Messiah and Mankind" in Cohen (1972).

17. *SR*, 351.

18. Ibid., 237.

19. Ibid., 351–52. For more on the uncanniness of the Jewish existence in the midst of time, see Blond (2010), 27–58.

20. *SR*, 323.

21. Ibid., 324.

22. Gibbs (2005), 199. See also his claim elsewhere that Rosenzweig's "eternity... is not simple atemporality. Eternity for Rosenzweig is not the reality that is out of time; rather, it is the intensive possibility of completeness in each moment of time." Gibbs (1992), 108; and in Gibbs (2006), 127. Peter Gordon makes a similar claim: "For Rosenzweig, time and eternity are mutually inclusive. Indeed, the only possible notion of eternity available for the new philosophy is not something to be sought beyond time. Rather, it is discovered within time—it is, or at least can become, a modification of time." Gordon (2003), 189.

23. The characterization of the Jewish people as eternal people was connected to a larger discussion of Jewish chosenness. Rosenzweig elaborates on this notion of Jewish eternity vis-à-vis his concept of blood-community (*blutgemeinschaft*) by claiming that the Jewish people "'are eternal'" because they represent "a community of the same blood." Rosenzweig's *blutgemeinschaft* has been criticized for its political and ethical connotations. In recent years, however, several have attempted to rescue Rosenzweig from the racist implications of the term. Batnitzky (2000), 73–76; and Hollander (2008), 118–23. Peter Gordon similarly claims that blood, "a fluid rather than static medium," expresses a dynamic, rather than essentialized category of identity. He further argues that "the circulation of the blood" corresponds to Rosenzweig's ideal of repetition. Gordon (2003), 213.

24. *SR*, 319.

25. Ibid., 320.

26. Ibid.

27. See Löwith (1942), 72–74.

28. *SR*, 307.

29. Ibid.

30. Ibid., 310.

31. "This moment must have more as its content than the mere moment... not a moment that flies away, but a 'fixed' moment." Ibid., 307.

32. Ibid., 308. Pollock rightly points out that, for Rosenzweig, the hour, the week, and the year are all human inventions. There is nothing natural or objective in their repetition; "rather, such natural determination of time

first become cycles when human beings transform them." Pollock (2009), 278. Kierkegaard, to shortly note, rejects any naturalistic explanation of his repetitions as well.

33. "The circle alone, without the fixed point of beginning and end, would still be nothing other than the mere succession of moments; only through the fixing of that point, the holiday, does the repetition that takes place in traversing this circular path become noticeable." *SR*, 308.

34. The cycle, insists Rosenzweig, has to have an *end* to reflect repetition. The end curves time into a cycle: it produces a story that we can repeat as a whole. When the story has no end, it is incomplete, and the temporal cycle is transformed back into linear time, or a series of moments or beginnings.

35. *SR*, 333. Shabbat is a full cycle of repetition by itself: from the evening of Shabbat symbolizing creation, through the morning of Shabbat celebrating revelation, to Shabbat afternoon representing redemption.

36. Rosenzweig's claim is certainly debatable; the Christian holy day was changed in the first, second, and third centuries for several reasons. Christ's resurrection on Sunday was only one. See especially Eusebius's reasoning in *Commentary on the Psalms*.

37. *SR*, 380.

38. Ibid.

39. Ibid., 380–81.

40. Ibid., 336.

41. Ibid., 344.

42. Ibid., 336.

43. Pollock (2009), 282. Pollock, drawing on German Idealism's theory of intellectual intuition, even adds that "communal cyclical mirroring of the course of the All in the liturgical year would appear to serve the role, in Rosenzweig's system, of the 'objectified' intellectual intuition, which is filled by art in Schelling's *System of Transcendental Idealism*." Ibid.

44. "[Sukkot] is a holiday of Redemption only within the frame of the three holidays of Revelation and therefore Redemption is here celebrated only as hope for and certainty of the future Redemption, whilst it of course, as a neighbor in the same month, borders on the holidays of Redemption prevailing in real eternity." *SR*, 339. And later, "Redemption is not present in this holiday of Redemption [Sukkot]; it is only hoped for, it is awaited in the wandering." Ibid., 340.

45. Mosès (1992), 174.

46. "Through the commemoration of the mythical date of its foundation and the great events of its collective existence, each people constitutes its own sacred time ... thus conferring to it the appearance of eternity." Ibid., 186–87.

47. *SR*, 390.

48. Ibid.

49. Ibid., 391.

50. Ibid., 392.

51. Fackenheim (1982), 95.

52. Ibid., 35.

53. Eliade (2005), 52.

54. Ibid., 76.

55. *GSR*, 3: 68.

56. "The phenomenon had been the crux of idealism, and thus of all philosophy from Parmenides till Hegel; idealism could not grasp it as 'spontaneous,' because with this it would have denied the omnipotence of the logos; idealism had never done it justice and had had to falsify the sparkling plenitude of the many and present it as the dead chaos of the given." Ibid., 55.

57. Ibid., 98. Rosenzweig reiterates his claim that "the world is becoming" in his discussion of redemption in book 2. *SR*, 235.

58. Ibid., 52–53.

59. Ibid., 55.

60. Ibid., 50. Rosenzweig's overt non-essentialism is clearly demonstrated in his definition of Judaism: "There is no essence, that is a 'concept,' of Judaism. There is only '*Höre Israel*.'" *GSR* 3: 601.

61. *SR*, 239–40.

62. For the importance of Dilthey and *Lebensphilosophie* for Rosenzweig, see Gordon (2003), 85–91; 174–82.

63. *SR*, 231.

64. Rosenzweig's "world as life" formulation grounds and even secures his notion of the "world as becoming." He is very clear about this when he declares: "We were seeking an infinite lasting quality that could serve as a foundation or a support for existence that is always *confined to the moment*." Ibid., 239, emphasis in text.

65. *R*, 80.

66. *FTR*, 305.

67. Ibid., 104.

68. *R*, 69.

69. As Clare Carlisle notes, "repetition is an inward movement, an intensification; it is an actualizing movement, expressing a power of becoming." Carlisle (2005), 529.

70. Kierkegaard (1957), 16.

71. *SR*, 329, translation modified.

72. *JH*, 183. See also Braiterman's "Cyclical Motion," 223. Braiterman agrees that Rosenzweig's cycle of the year does not "signify the monotonous repetition of the same." Ibid., 216.

73. Rosenzweig argues that his New Thinking must be grounded in time: "The new thinking knows, just like the old-age [thinking] of common sense, that it cannot know independently of time—which was the height claim to glory that philosophy up to now assumed for itself." Rosenzweig (1999), 83.

74. *SR*, 306.

75. At this point, a deeper and unexpected meaning of Rosenzweig's insistence on beginning-to-end, or creation-to-redemption narratives should be recognized. Unlike the Christian cycles that portray one returning feature of the year or the week—the same return to the event of creation—the Jewish year and week narrate a diversified series of events with different symbolic meanings and thus portray manifold differences *within* the cycles of time. The Christian week presents the believer with *one* event, that of creation, while the Jewish week has a separate religious meaning for the days of week and for Shabbat. In this sense, the Christian year is a representation of a homogeneous empty time. To echo Benjamin's analysis of the modern experience of the eternal return, which I will discuss in greater detail in chapter 5, the fact that Christian time represents only one event reflects a logic of sameness. Since there is nothing on the Christian liturgical stage except a singular event, time is not experienced as a series of different events, but as a repetition of the same event again and again. Paradoxically, as in Benjamin's later work on history, the notion of linear history entails the logic of the eternal return of the same.

76. *SR*, 348.

77. It is here that Rosenzweig's theory reminds Wolfson's theory of cyclical linearity in Kabbalah: as for medieval Kabbalists, for Rosenzweig repetition unveils a dynamism of change and sameness, an eternity marked by differences. Wolfson makes note of that, claiming, "For Rosenzweig, the temporal mode has ontological status only by virtue of its theological correlates. His theology, therefore, may be labeled a metaphysics of temporality whereby the traditional distinction between time and eternity is transcended in the eternalization of time through the temporalization of eternity: in the fullness of the moment, one encounters the perpetual coming-to-be of what has always been." Wolfson (2006), 50.

78. *SR*, 352.

79. Ibid., 353.

80. Ibid., 352.

81. Ibid., 358.

82. Ibid., 352. Rosenzweig's theory of epochs offers a criticism of Hegel's theory of history. For Hegel, spirit progressed within history through a series of well-defined stages, or periods, organized under specific applications of the idea of freedom. Yet this concept of history, as is now apparent, horribly perverted time: Hegel's epochs constructed world history as a history of epochs, but in so doing violently repressed the natural flow of time and reality. Hegel (1988), 19–23. I will return to the notion of epochs or periods in the discussion of Freud's theory of history in the seventh chapter.

83. The transition from the old law to the new law forms a false cycle: the state "encircles in each the contradiction of old and new by the violent

renewal of the old, conferring upon the new the lawful force of the old."
SR, 353–54.

84. Ibid., 354.

85. Ibid., 348.

86. Ibid., 361.

87. Ibid., 358.

88. Ibid.

89. Ibid., 361.

90. Ibid., 357–58.

91. "[The Christian] himself is always only on the track, and his real interest is only that he is still always on the way, still always between departure and goal . . . If he wonders where he is just now at this moment . . . the answer that he gives to himself is always only: on the way. . . . Not as moment therefore does the moment become the representative of eternity for the Christian, but as central point of Christian world time." Ibid., 359.

92. *FTR*, 314.

93. Ibid., 315.

94. In Kierkegaard's ironic words, "If one knows something about modern philosophy . . . repetition is really that which has mistakenly been referred to as mediation. . . . the Greeks' development of the doctrine of being and nothing, the development of 'the moment,' 'non-being,' etc., beats everything in Hegel. 'Mediation' is a foreign word. 'Repetition' is a good Danish word, and I congratulate the Danish language for its contribution to philosophical terminology." *R*, 18.

95. *FTR*, 312.

96. *R*, 50, emphasis mine.

97. *FTR*, 308. See also: "Now freedom breaks forth in its highest form, in which it is qualified in relation to itself." Ibid., 302. According to Louis Reimer, this notion of freedom translates into revelation in Kierkegaard. Reimer (1986), 20.

98. *FTR*, 315.

99. "But no! Repetition was not possible here," Kierkegaard's writes at the start of the description of the trip. *R*, 21.

100. Ibid., 69.

101. God, Kierkegaard insists, "wants only the single individual, wants to become involved only with the single individual, no matter whether the single individual ranks high or low, is eminent or wretched." Kierkegaard (1993), 127.

102. Batnitzky (2000), 70.

103. For the social dimension of Rosenzweig's work, see Gibbs (1992), Chapter 5. Rosenzweig's prioritization of the community, however, does not entail a theoretical or practical disinterest in the individual. In the words of Eric Santner, Rosenzweig's community reflects a "logic of the remnant." In

opposition to Hegel's ideal society, Rosenzweig promotes an ethical community of love based "on the opening to and the acknowledgment in the Other qua stranger." The Jewish community both celebrated individual differences and grounded the possibility of its members' redemption. Santner (2001), 116.

4. Notes to Chapter 4

1. Scholem (1971), 318.
2. Ibid. In a letter to Buber years earlier, Scholem criticizes not the utopia they envisioned but the quality of their work: "*What fills me with doubt* is the excessive *tonality* of this prose, which leaps out almost uncannily from the particular wording... If I search in the original for what your translation gives, I can succeed only by singing—that is, 'reciting'—it; the mere text without music does not yield it." Buber (1991), 338–39, letter 343, April 27, 1926, emphasis in text.
3. *GSR*, 4: 2.
4. Rosenzweig (1920).
5. The first edition of Rosenzweig's Halevi translation from 1924 was published with Wöhrle publishing house and included only 60 poems and hymns. Rosenzweig (1924). In the second edition from 1927 (Lambert publishers), Rosenzweig collected 95 poems. Rosenzweig (1927). The title of the book, however, admitted to only 92 poems, since three were translated and discussed only in the commentaries. In Raphael Rosenzweig's afterword to the third edition of the book in 1983 (published in Rosenzweig's *Gesammelte Schriften* by Martinus Hijhoff), he notes that his father intended to publish a third edition with 103 poems, but never fulfilled this wish. *GSR*, 4: xxii.
6. See Buber's lecture "From the Beginning of Our Bible Translation," in Buber and Rosenzweig (1994), 176–78.
7. Rosenzweig (1999), 75–76.
8. "'The nothing' must not mean for us an unveiling of the essence of pure being, as it did for the great heir of two thousand years of the history of philosophy. But wherever an existing element of the All rests in itself, indissoluble and permanent, the main thing is to presuppose a nothing for this being, its nothing." *SR*, 27. For a discussion of the place of the Nothing and the All in Rosenzweig's ontology and their relation to German Idealism, see Pollock (2009), 120–80.
9. *SR*, 174.
10. Ibid., 170.
11. Ibid., 125.
12. "Love for God must be externalized in love for the neighbor." Ibid., 230.
13. *JH*, 74.
14. *JH*, 169.
15. Rosenzweig was especially outraged by a popular translation of Halevi's

Diwan by Emil Cohn that had been published a few years earlier, as he confessed to Joseph Prager in 1923. *GSR*, 2: 878, letter 843, Jan. 12, 1923.

16. *JH*, 170.

17. Ibid.

18. Ibid., 171.

19. Ibid., 176.

20. Ibid., 175. The alienation of Halevi had biographical aspects as well. Rosenzweig's *Nachwort* did little to inform his readers of the life and work of the poet. See more in Benjamin (2009), 71–72.

21. Seidman, to be clear, is critical of this tradition. Seidman (2006), 157.

22. Admittedly, Rosenzweig's personal lifestyle was not as radical as he professed in his magnum opus. Scholem mentions this in a 1975 interview to the Israeli journal *Shdemot*: "Rosenzweig thought he wouldn't be able to go on living if he should have to choose between Germanness and Jewishness." He therefore wanted to create a "Jewish-German synthesis." Scholem (1976), 20–21.

23. Benjamin (2009), 80. On translation as a process of distancing and defamiliarization (in the context of the Buber-Rosenzweig bible), see also Batnitzky (2000), 106–12.

24. Scholem (1976), 90.

25. Rosenzweig envisions Germany as a *Zweistromland* (lit., "land of two rivers"), referencing biblical Babylon at the intersection of the rivers Euphrates and Tigris. This image evokes his belief that Jewish life in Germany had the potential to flourish and ascend to the heights of Jewish cultural production in Babylon. As Paul Mendes-Flohr notes in *German Jews* (1999), "in Germany, Rosenzweig affirmed, the modern Jew also stands by two nurturing sources, German humanistic culture and a Judaism challenged and revalorized by the modern experience. Rosenzweig voiced the hope that what would emerge from the meeting . . . would indeed, be a New Babylon." Mendes-Flohr (1999), 23–24.

26. Ibid., 82.

27. *JH*, 171. Rosenzweig further explains this point in his essay "Scripture and Luther": "In the roots of words the severed areas lie together; and still deeper, at the roots of meaning, the roots of physicality, there is, apart from questions regarding some possible original relatedness of languages, that unity of all human speech which the surfaces of words only let us dimly intuit. The translator must dare the descend to these lower layers. How else is he to locate for the words composing a conceptual circle in the source language an analogous group in the target language." Buber and Rosenzweig (1994), 65.

28. *SW*, 1: 255.

29. *JH*, 171.

30. *SW*, 1: 262.

31. Ibid.

32. Truth be told, Rosenzweig's notoriously indigestible translations manifest his theory of translation much more than Benjamin's relatively commonplace attempt at translating Baudelaire's *Tableaux Parisiens*. Most works on Rosenzweig's and Benjamin's theories of translation are written in the context of the Buber-Rosenzweig Bible translation controversy, to which Benjamin contributed indirectly—Benjamin took ownership of Kracauer's line of criticism of the Bible translation in a famous letter to Scholem. *C*, 303, letter 156, May 29, 1926. For more, see Britt (2000); Jay (1976); and Rosenwald (1994). For Rosenzweig's and Benjamin's theories of language and translations, see Galli (2000). For possible influence of Rosenzweig on Benjamin's work, see Mosès (1989).

33. "The deeper (that is, the more existent and real) the mind, the more it is expressible and expressed . . . in a word, the most expressed is at the same time the purely mental. This, however, is precisely what is meant by the concept of revelation." *SW*, 1: 67.

34. Buber and Rosenzweig (1994), 40. In the same way, for Rosenzweig, redemption (as the reconnection of the individual with his world) meant a return to a universal harmonious language. *SR*, 388.

35. Benjamin would probably agree with Rosenzweig's assertion: "Nothing teaches more clearly that the world is not yet redeemed than the multiplicity of languages." But for Benjamin, the end point of Rosenzweig's argument would be inconceivable: "But between different languages only the stammered word mediates, and the gesture ceases to be immediate understanding, as it was in the silent glance of the eye, and is reduced to the stammering of gestural language, this poor temporary bridge for understanding." *SR*, 313.

36. *SW*, 1: 72.

37. Rosenzweig (1999), 88. For a discussion of the notes, see Galli (1995), 399–433.

38. *GSR*, 2: 875, letter 841, Dec. 20, 1922.

39. *JH*, 182–83.

40. Samuel David Luzzatto published two collections of Halevi's works in the nineteenth century that include 130 poems and hymns from the Diwan of Jehuda Halevi.

41. At first, he admits, the poems were "chosen quite accidentally." He omitted the "worldly poetry" soon after, and then decided to focus on the poems that would present a "collective picture of the poet." However, in the end, even this plan was "'overstepped.'" *JH*, 182.

42. Ibid., 183.

43. Ibid., 185.

44. Ibid., 182–83.

45. *GSR*, 2: 938, letter 900, Jan. 8, 1924.

46. *JH*, 184, emphasis mine.

47. Ibid.

48. Ibid., 182.

49. Ibid.

50. Rosenzweig's *The Star of Redemption* has a similar structure: the book opens with the words "from death" and ends with the words "into life." This transition founds the book's circular structure—the book offers not progress or a linear narrative from life to death, but a reverted cycle—from death to life. As Elliot Wolfson observes in *Giving Beyond the Gift* (2003): "This circularity is not simply going back to where one has been, a mere repetition and recycling of patterns, but it is rather a reverting to where one has never been and indeed where one can never be, which is precisely the mode of eternality that interrupts and intersects with time." Wolfson (2014), 44.

51. *GSR*, 2: 938, letter 900, Jan. 8, 1924.

52. Ibid.

53. *SR*, 354.

54. *GSR*, 4: xxii.

55. This issue is reflected in the translations of Rosenzweig's book: the English translation by Galli was based on the second edition of Rosenzweig's book and kept the original structure. The Hebrew translation of Rosenzweig's Halevi book was based however on the third edition: interestingly, it inserted the notes into the body of the book, but kept the *Nachwort* at the end. Rosenzweig (2011).

Intermezzo: Abrahamic Variations in Kafka and Kierkegaard

1. Kafka (2009), 58.

2. Ibid., 62.

3. Ibid.

4. Ibid., 63.

5. "Where there is only repetition, there is no progress in time. In fact, all of the situations in Kafka's novels are paralyzed images." Anders (1960), 34.

6. Corngold (1973), 57.

7. For the literature on Kafka and Kierkegaard, see Šajda and Stewart (2017), 23–29.

8. *D*, 1: 298, August 21, 1913.

9. Ibid.

10. In Richard Sheppard words, "Kierkegaard's [*Fear and Trembling* and *Either-Or*] must have touched Kafka on a very raw nerve, confronting him with what he knew he had had to do even while reminding him of the difficulty he had experienced in doing it." Sheppard (1991), 279. On Kafka's and Kierkegaard's Abraham, see David (1980); Powell (2012); Butin (2000); and Edwards (1966).

11. Jean Wahl, in a piece on Kafka and Kierkegaard, thus claims: "Kafka does

not say: Kierkegaard. He repeatedly speaks of Abraham. We know that the first book of Kierkegaard's with which he became acquainted was *Fear and Trembling*. This is why he saw Kierkegaard in the image of Abraham. Here and there, however, Kafka thinks of himself rather than of Abraham and of Kierkegaard." Wahl (1946), 282.

12. *L*, 190, January 1918.

13. Ibid., 200, March 1918.

14. Ibid., 199. One of Kafka's last diary entries was in December 1922; in the entry, sick as he is, he still notes his fascination with Kierkegaard: "All this time in bed. Yesterday *Either-Or*." *D*, 2: 232, Dec. 18, 1922.

15. Adorno (1983), 268.

16. *L*, 285–86, June 1921.

17. Robbins (1991), 91.

18. See Chris Danta's chapter "Sarah's Laughter: Kafka's Abraham." Danta (2011), 67–99.

19. Derrida (2007), 3.

20. See Derrida (1992). Benjamin, in his 1934 essay on Kafka, sees in those tactics a mark of Kafka's narrative form: "In the stories which Kafka left us, narrative art regains the significance it had in the mouth of Scheherazade: its ability to postpone the future . . . The patriarch Abraham himself could benefit by postponement, even though he may have to trade his place in tradition for it." *SW*, 2(2): 807–8.

21. Elsewhere translated as "Attunement" or "Tuning Up."

22. For Kierkegaard's diary entries, see the Hong and Hong translation of *Fear and Trembling*, FTR, 239–71.

23. *FTR*, 10.

24. Ibid., 13.

25. For good introductory readings, see Carlisle (2010), 46–50; Lippitt (2016), 22–29; Mooney (1991), 25–31; and Williams (1998).

26. Carlisle (2010), 46.

27. Kierkegaard notes that Johannes de Silentio, the man telling the stories of Abraham, "was not a thinker," nor "an exegetical scholar." *FTR*, 9.

28. Mooney (1991), 29, emphasis in text.

29. *Attunement* is the term Alistair Hannay used to translate Kierkegaard's title to the opening pages of the book.

30. *FTR*, 35. Lippitt (2016), 28.

31. Carlisle (2010), 48.

32. *FTR*, 14.

33. Ibid., 15.

34. Ibid., 20, emphasis mine.

35. Ibid., 21.

36. Ibid., 9.

37. *L*, 199.

38. This appears throughout *Problema* 3; for example, *FTR*, 115, emphasis in text. In several recent works, this singularity is understood in terms of negative theology. In line with Christian apophatic discourses, in the moment of his union with God, Abraham is emptied of any substantial content or signification. See Kangas (1998); Kline (2017); and Law (1993).

39. Caputo (1987), 21.

40. Kafka (1954), 103, aphorism 109.

5. Notes to Chapter 5

1. Scholem (1980), 63.

2. Scholem (2007), 44, Dec. 4, 1914.

3. Ibid.

4. For Benjamin's theory of myth, see Menninghaus (1986) and Mali (2003), 228–83.

5. For a good introduction to Benjamin's *Passagenwerk*, see Buck-Morss (1989); Missac (1995); and the following edited volumes: Hanssen (2006); and McLaughlin and Rosen (2003).

6. In his words, "method of this project: literary montage. I needn't say anything. Merely show." *AP*, 460 [N1a,8]. Elsewhere: "This work has to develop to the highest degree the art of citing without quotation marks. Its theory is intimately related to that of montage." Ibid., 458 [N1,10].

7. To follow Michael Löwy's argument in *Fire Alarm* (2005), in *Passagenwerk* "[Benjamin's] thinking forms a whole, in which art, history, culture, politics, literature, and theology are inseparable." Löwy (2005), 1.

8. As far as I can tell, Benjamin was unaware of a similar but much more rigorous work by his contemporary, French historian of science Abel Rey on the idea of cosmic eternal return. Rey (1927).

9. See, for example, Benjamin's insights on the interaction of walking with dreaming in "One Way Street" (1928).

10. Susan Buck-Morss notes that the first working title of *Passagenwerk*, "Paris Arcades: A Dialectical Fairyland," alludes to Benjamin's fascination with the story of Sleeping Beauty. Buck-Morss (1989), 34.

11. The epigraph to convolute N comes from Marx's 1843 letter to Ruge: "The reform of consciousness consists solely in . . . the awakening of the world from its dream about itself." *AP*, 456.

12. For a biography on Freud and Benjamin, see chapter 7. For a detailed study of Benjamin's reception of the psychoanalytic theory in the context of his theory of dreaming collective, see Wiegmann (1989); Gelley (2015); Müller-Farguell (2000); and Pile (2011).

13. While crediting Surrealism for instructing his insight of the dreaming collective, Benjamin was critical of the Surrealist overemphasis on dreaming exactly because they underemphasized the place of awakening from this dream. *AP*, 391 [K1a,6].

14. Ibid., 389 [K1,3]. Here as well: "the economic conditions under which a society exists not only determine that society in its material existence and ideological superstructure; they also come to expression. In the case of one who sleeps, an overfull stomach does not find its ideological superstructure in the contents of the dream—and it is exactly the same with the economic conditions of life for the collective. It interprets these conditions; it explains them. In the dream, they find their *expression*; in the awakening, their *interpretation*." Ibid., 855 [M,14].

15. In Susan Buck-Morss's influential reading of *Passagenwerk* in *The Dialectics of Seeing* (1989), this project of dream interpretation was deeply connected with the passages of Paris: "The covered shopping arcades of the nineteenth century were Benjamin's central image because they were the precise material replica of the internal consciousness, or rather, the unconscious of the dreaming collective. All of the errors of bourgeois consciousness could be found there (commodity fetishism, reification, the world as 'inwardness'), as well as (in fashion, prostitution, gambling) all of its utopian dreams." Buck-Morss (1989), 39.

16. For Benjamin, boredom is an experience that we have in a state of waiting; as change never happens, and "we don't know what we are waiting for." *AP*, 105 [D2,7]. Benjamin connects boredom to his model of dream: it manifested the ordeal of life in a state of dreaming; "a warm gray fabric [in which] we wrap ourselves when we dream." Ibid., 105–6 [D2a,1]. In a different formulation, boredom is "the external surface of unconscious events." Ibid., 106 [D2a,2]. (Such comments are repeated throughout the project. See, for example, F°,8; K°,6; and C°,2). In Joe Moran's words, boredom is "not simply crucially related to modernity . . . but [is] perhaps the quintessential experience of modern life." Moran (2003), 168. For more, see Benjamin (2005).

17. *AP*, 546 [S2,1]. Deleuze echoes Benjamin's basic intuition about the deep connection between the eternal return and dreamlike reality and the experience of boredom as "this fabric [in which] we wrap ourselves when we dream" when he says: "And following the Bergsonian hypothesis, the bare repetition must be understood as the external envelope of the clothed: that is, the repetition of successive instants must be understood as the most relaxed of the coexistent levels, matter as a dream or as mind's most relaxed past." Deleuze (1994), 84.

18. "For the 'Eternal Return of the Same,' as it stonily prevails over the most intimately varied feelings, is the sign of fate, whether it is self-identical in the life of many or repeats itself in the individual." *SW*, 1: 307.

19. *OT*, 134.

20. First signs of this formative intuition in Benjamin's corpus were in a work from the same period, *Fate and Character* (1921).

21. Interestingly, Freud briefly addresses the experience of eternal return in the same period, in his 1919 essay "The Uncanny," a year before his more

detailed exploration of the compulsion to repeat in *Beyond the Pleasure Principle* (1920). In his investigation of uncanny experiences, he refers to Hoffmann's "The Sandman." Freud focuses on the theme of the "double" which, he argues, produces such experiences. In this context, Freud notes, in a Benjaminian key: "The factor of the repetition of the same thing [*der Wiederholung des Gleichartigen*] will perhaps not appeal to everyone as a source of uncanny feeling. From what I have observed, this phenomenon does undoubtedly, subject to certain conditions and combined with certain circumstances, arouse an uncanny feeling, which, furthermore, recalls the sense of helplessness experienced in some dream-states." *SE*, 17: 236–37.

22. *AP*, III [D5,6]. This insight on the correlation between the eternal return, the always the same and the new, is one of the core trajectories of *Passagenwerk*, as Benjamin wrote in a letter to Horkheimer in September 1938 in which he reported on his new Baudelaire project: "The basic theme of the old Arcades Project, the new and the always-the-same [*das Neue und Immergleiche*], comes into its own only here; it appears in the concept of the *nouveauté*, which goes to the core of Baudelaire's creativity." *C*, 574, letter 303, Sep. 28, 1938, translation modified.

23. *AP*, 842–3 [G°,17]. In the last entry of convolute D, Benjamin claims more about the interdependence of the eternal return with the idea of progress: "The belief in progress—in an infinite perfectibility understood as an infinite ethical task—and the representation of eternal return are complementary. They are the indissoluble antinomies in the face of which the dialectical conception of historical time must be developed." Ibid., 119 [D10a,5].

24. In a fragment on Baudelaire from early 1938, Benjamin explains: "This devaluation of the human environment by the commodity economy penetrates deeply into the poet's historical experience. What results is the 'ever-selfsame' [*immer dasselbe*]." *SW*, 4: 96.

25. *AP*, II.

26. Put in slightly different terms, the new was, in essence, an old product sought by modernity in a traumatic compulsion to repeat, as Adorno summarized in a section on Baudelaire in *Minima Moralia* (1951): "The new, sought for its own sake, a kind of laboratory product, petrified into a conceptual scheme, becomes in its sudden apparition a compulsive return of the old, not unlike that in traumatic disorder." Adorno (2005), 236.

27. Benjamin writes, "'Primal history of the nineteenth century'—this would be of no interest if it were understood to mean that forms of primal history are to be recovered among the inventory of the nineteenth century. Only where the nineteenth century would be presented as originary form of primal history—in a form, that is to say, in which the whole of primal history groups itself anew in images appropriate to that century—only there does the concept of a primal history of the nineteenth century have meaning." Ibid., 463 [N3a,2], and 864 [O°,79].

28. *C*, 497, letter 263, Aug. 2, 1935.

29. *C*, 495, letter 263, Aug. 2, 1935. Adorno notes Benjamin's affinity to Jung in the same letter: "Therefore the collective consciousness is invoked and, indeed, I fear that in the present version it cannot be distinguished from the Jungian one." Ibid., 497, letter 263, Aug. 2, 1935.

30. *AP*, 894. In the final version of the 1935 exposé, Benjamin explains it in a Marxist register: "Corresponding to the form of the new means of production . . . are images in the collective consciousness in which the new is permeated with the old. These images are wish images; in them the collective seeks both to overcome and to transfigure the immaturity of the social product and the inadequacies in the social organization of production." Ibid., 4.

31. Ibid., 894.

32. "Here it is a question of the dissolution of 'mythology' into the space of history. That, of course, can happen only through the awakening of a not-yet-conscious knowledge of what has been." Ibid., 458 [N1,9]. Richard Wolin, in *Walter Benjamin: An Aesthetic of Redemption* (1994), claims this was "Benjamin's unique and brilliant research program of the 1930s: a secular redemption of modern mythology." Wolin (1994), xxxviii.

33. On the fundamental importance of the concept of tradition to Benjamin's theoretical perspective, see John McCole's instructive study *Walter Benjamin and the Antinomies of Tradition* (1993); Britt (2016); and Witte (2007).

34. *SW*, 3: 326.

35. Ibid., 4: 254.

36. *SP*, 3: 146.

37. In Benjamin's words, it was "a concomitant of the secular productive forces of History." Ibid.

38. Ibid., 3: 143.

39. Ibid., 3: 153.

40. Benjamin relates this dynamism to memory: "*Memory* creates the chain of tradition which transmits an event from generation to generation. It is the muse-derived element of the epic art in a broader sense, and encompasses its varieties." Ibid., 3: 154, emphasis in text.

41. Benjamin hints at this when he writes: "The momentum of primal history in the past is no longer masked, as it used to be, by the tradition of church and family—this at once the consequence and condition of technology. The old prehistoric dread already envelops the world of our parents because we ourselves are no longer bound to this world by tradition. The perceptual worlds [*Merkwelten*] break up more rapidly; what they contain of the mythic comes more quickly and more brutally to the fore; and a wholly different perceptual world must be speedily set up to oppose it. This is how the accelerated tempo of technology appears in light of the primal history of the present. || Awakening ||" *AP*, 461–62 [N2a,2]

42. Ibid., 116 [D8a,2]. The term *phantasmagoria* took the place of Benjamin's

notion of dream image in the exposé of 1939 and became a key concept of Benjamin's project in its later days. For Benjamin's phantasmagoria, see Cohen (1989).

43. Benjamin, to note, addresses elsewhere the idea that the form is the only meaningful remnant in modernity. In a famous letter of Benjamin to Scholem on Kafka from 1938, in which Benjamin elaborated on the problem of the decay of tradition in Kafka's oeuvre, Benjamin notes that while many authors were "clinging to truth, or what they believed to be truth, and, heavyhearted or not, renouncing its transmissibility . . . Kafka's genius lay in the fact that he tried something altogether new: he gave up truth so that he could hold on to its transmissibility, the haggadic element." *SW*, 3: 326. Unlike so many who aimed to rediscover traces of a long-lost truth, Kafka recognized the loss of tradition. He focused on the transmission of truth, or the form of tradition, rather than on its content, as the only meaningful trace of tradition. I identify a similar theoretical move in Benjamin's focus on the eternal return. His explorations of the horrific experience of eternal return uncovered the form of primal history.

44. The manuscript's working title was *Charles Baudelaire: Ein Lyriker im Zeitalter des Hochkapitalismus*; the work was to have three parts: (1) Baudelaire as Allegorist; (2) The Paris of the Second Empire in Baudelaire; and (3) The Commodity as a Poetic Object. Benjamin submitted the second essay for publication in 1938. The essay was rejected, forcing Benjamin to stop his work on the book and focus on revising the essay's central section, The Flâneur, which he published as "On Some Motifs in Baudelaire."

45. Howard Caygill offers a clear and insightful description of Benjamin's work on modern experience in *Walter Benjamin: The Colour of Experience* (1998). For a short list of contributions, see Benjamin and Osborne (1994); Beasley-Murray (2007); Jay (1998); Meiffert (1986); and Wolin (1982).

46. *SW*, 4: 317. See *SE*, 10: 25.

47. *SW*, 4: 319.

48. Ibid., 4: 327. Benjamin's Baudelaire is, in this context, a "secret agent—an agent of the secret discontent of his class with its own rule." Benjamin (1997), 104, fn 1. His poems explore urban capitalism and express the sufferings it produces. Furthermore, for Benjamin, Baudelaire is unique in his attempt to recreate in his readers the same shock effect that the city-crowds experienced.

49. As Rainer Nägele notices, in eternal return, "time is not a smooth, continuous sequence from past to present to future, but a conflictual configuration of fragmentary moments." Nägele (2005), 4.

50. We should differentiate between repetition's interruptions and distraction (*Zerstreuung*). The latter had positive value for Benjamin in series of works, most prominently in "The Work of Art in the Age of Mechanical Reproduction."

51. *SW*, 4: 319.

52. Ibid., 4: 336.

53. Ibid., 4: 329.

54. Ibid., 4: 330. See also a quotation Benjamin documents in *Passagenwerk* from Friedrich Engels's 1845 book, *The Condition of the Working Class in England*: "The miserable routine of endless drudgery and toil in which the same mechanical process is repeated over and over again is like the labor of Sisyphus. The burden of labor, like the rock, always keeps falling back on the worn-out laborer." *AP*, 106 [D2a,4].

55. Benjamin intimates this vision when he writes that "the idea of eternal recurrence transforms the historical event itself into a mass produced article." Ibid., 340 [J62a,2].

56. This appears mostly in essays such as "The Work of Art in the Age of Mechanical Reproduction" and "Experience and Poverty."

57. *SW* 4: 314. See also Benjamin's claim that "another reason for the isolation of information from experience is that the former does not enter 'tradition.'" Ibid., 4: 316.

58. Ibid., 4: 314.

59. Ibid., 4: 329.

60. *C*, 549, letter 293, Jan. 6, 1938. On the role of Blanqui in Benjamin's *Passagenwerk*, see Abensour (2013) and Dommanget (1972).

61. McFarland (2013), 233. As Tyrus Miller rightly points out, "the thought of the eternal return (of Nietzsche and Blanqui) redoubles and heightens the very forms in which reality is already immediately experienced as an ideological phantom, and in so doing, it offers purchase on the phantasmagoric character of the real." Miller (2008), 292.

62. Buck-Morss (1989), 238.

63. Spitzer (1957), 34.

64. *AP*, 113 [D7; D7a] and in the conclusion of the exposé of 1939, Ibid., 25.

65. Ibid., 112 [D6,2].

66. Ibid. [D6,1]. Similarly, the modern idea of progress was an illusion, if understood correctly: "What we call 'progress' is confined to each particular world, and vanishes with it." Ibid., 115 [D6a,1].

67. Geffroy (2015), 506.

68. *C*, 549, letter 293, Jan. 6, 1938. Benjamin added this insert to the *Passagenwerk*. *AP*, 112 [D5a,6].

69. Bernstein (1971), 340.

70. *AP*, 26. In convolute J, which was dedicated to Baudelaire, Benjamin returns to Blanqui. Here, Blanqui is recognized, again, as the one who failed, referring this time, to Benjamin's earlier work on the tragic hero: "Blanqui succumbed; Baudelaire succeeded. Blanqui appears as a tragic figure; his betrayal has tragic greatness; he was brought down by the enemy within." Ibid., 375 [J84a,2].

71. Ibid., 25.

72. Benjamin's reading of Blanqui became prevalent among his vast readership and friends. Adorno, for example, noted that Blanqui's work was written with "accents of absolute despair" in *Prisms* (238).

73. In his opening remarks to a recent English translation of Blanqui's book, Frank Chouraqui emphasizes Blanqui's optimism: "From within the infinite Blanqui sees a purely democratic world surging forth, an extrapolation of his dear human brotherhood and solidarity, where not only men of a class, but all becomes brothers; where not only mankind, but all objects become brothers." Chouraqui (2013), 17–18. In his preface to a recent publication of *L'éternité par les Astres*, Jacques Rancière, like Benjamin, ties Nietzsche with Blanqui and agrees: "The hypothesis of repetition is proposed for those who refuse all providence, as the only alternative to mortal equilibrium. . . . Repetition does not entail resignation. . . . Faced with the eternal return of mediocrity (Nietzsche) or oppression (Blanqui), each return of the dice must be bet again for [the prospect of] the regenerative shock [*le choc régénérateur*]." Rancière (2002), 24.

74. *AP*, III [D5a,2].

75. *SW*, 4: 166.

76. *AP*, 15.

77. In a letter to Strauß he asks: "Do you know Zarathustra? . . . In school, for many reasons, I did not dare approach him . . . In the last weeks, I read Zarathustra." Benjamin (1995–2000), 1: 7, letter 25, Nov. 21, 1912.

78. James McFarland, in his extensive study of these relations in *Constellation* (2013), argues that "casual mentions, quick references, brief citations of the philosopher move through Benjamin's prose; one catches, as it were, glimpses of Nietzsche, or what looks like Nietzsche, echoes of Nietzsche, or what sounds like Nietzsche, through the thickets of Benjamin's sentences." McFarland (2013), 4. In *The Story of a Friendship*, Scholem testifies to an affinity between Benjamin and Nietzsche's worldview during their time in Bern. Scholem (1981), 54. For more on Benjamin and Nietzsche, see Ponzi (2017); Pfotenhauer (1985); Reschke (1992); Mosès (2015); and Richter (2013).

79. *AP*, 115 [D8,6], emphasis mine.

80. Mosès (2015), 212.

81. See also Nietzsche (2006), 173.

82. Tiedemann (1989), 199.

83. *SW*, 4: 175. See also: "The heroic bearing of Baudelaire is akin to that of Nietzsche. Though Baudelaire likes to appeal to Catholicism, his historical experience is nonetheless that which Nietzsche fixed in the phrase 'God is dead.' In Nietzsche's case, this experience is projected cosmologically in the thesis that nothing new occurs any more. In Nietzsche, the accent lies on eternal recurrence, which the human being has to face with heroic

composure. For Baudelaire, it is more a matter of 'the new,' which must be wrested heroically from what is always again the same." *AP*, 337 [J60,7].

84. For more on Benjamin's admiration of Nietzsche's heroism and its relations to the figure of the dandy, see Helmut Pfotenhauer's claim: "What the eccentric gesture of the immoralist achieves with Nietzsche, would, according to Benjamin, be for Baudelaire the pleasure of the shock effect of aesthetic and political unreliability." Pfotenhauer (1985), 121.

6. Notes to Chapter 6

1. Scholem (1981), 125.
2. Ibid., 124.
3. Ibid., 125.
4. Ibid. Scholem's language is slightly softened in the next sentence, when in a circumvented manner he seemingly grants Benjamin's *Trauerspiel* the kind of authority Kafka's *Trial* has.
5. Benjamin (2013); Caygill (1998); Friedlander (2012); and Fenves (2001).
6. The resemblance between Benjamin's work on repetition and modern philosophy of repetition is addressed only sporadically in literature. Tim Flanagan's "The Thought of History in Benjamin and Deleuze" (2009) focuses on the role of allegory in Benjamin's vision of history in the *Trauerspiel* and its reverberation in Deleuze; Marc Katz's "Rendezvous in Berlin: Benjamin and Kierkegaard on the Architecture of Repetition" (1998) also addresses the topic inadvertently. See also Chowdhury (2014), 87–120.
7. Missac (1995), 112.
8. As Irving Wohlfarth notes: "Proust is concerned solely to salvage his own past; its salvation is, [Benjamin] keeps intimating, his 'private affair' (*GS*, 1: 643). For the author of 'Über den Begriff der Geschichte,' on the other hand, salvation has come to assume, on the eve of the Second War World, world-historical dimensions." Wohlfarth (2005), 1: 178.
9. Gibbs (2005), 197. It has become a commonplace to note the transition in Benjamin's oeuvre from his metaphysical/theological thought to his Marxist theory. My take on this is straightforward. I take the hunchbacked dwarf/automaton metaphor in thesis I to represent a new kind of relations between historical materialism and messianic theory of history. That is, theology produces visions of redemption that are missing in a period swallowed by boredom and with which the revolutionary classes can enact a radical change in history. My argument here echoes Wolin (1994), xlviii. The literature on Benjamin's messianism is naturally extremely vast. Gershom Scholem's "Walter Benjamin and His Angel" is still a canonical contribution (1976). Alongside Richard Wolin's *Walter Benjamin* (1994), I find the following most useful: Wohlfarth (2005); Habermas (1988); Jacobson (2003); Löwy (2005); and Bouretz (2010), 165–223. For non-messianic readings of Benjamin's theory of history, I'd recommend Caygill (2005) and Tiedemann (1989).

10. *OT*, 50.

11. Ibid., 33.

12. Ibid.

13. Ibid., 39.

14. Ibid., 44, emphasis mine.

15. Ibid.

16. Ibid., 46.

17. Ibid., 44.

18. Ibid., 40.

19. Ibid., 44.

20. Adorno (1990), 37.

21. At the time of writing the prologue, Benjamin has in mind the Italian thinker Benedetto Croce, known to have condemned any attempt to slot art into groups, genres, or periods. Benjamin, while accepting Croce's basic position of the irreducibility of works of art, still insists art forms are valuable and meaningful to art criticism: "[Tragedy or comedy] are themselves structures, at the very least equal in consistency and substance to any and every drama, without being in any way commensurable." *OT*, 44.

22. Deleuze (1994), 25.

23. *C*, 223–24, letter 126, Dec. 9, 1923, emphasis mine.

24. Benjamin qualifies his point a few lines later: "for in interpretation, relationships among works of art appear that are timeless yet not without historical relevance." Ibid., 224.

25. Ibid., emphasis mine.

26. "As essences, truth and idea acquire that supreme metaphysical significance expressly attributed to them in the Platonic system." *OT*, 30.

27. For Benjamin's reception of Leibniz, see Fenves (2001); Ferber (2013), 163–94; Nägele (1997); and Schwebel (2012).

28. *OT*, 28.

29. Benjamin defines truth as that which is "bodied forth in the dance of represented ideas" (Ibid., 29), and truth's method as "self-representation." Ibid., 30.

30. Ibid., 34.

31. Pizer (1995). For a good introduction to the *Ursprung* in Benjamin, see Hanssen (2000), 24–48; and Urbich (2012).

32. *OT*, 45.

33. Ibid.

34. In an earlier version of the prologue, Benjamin writes, "An idea takes on a number of historical manifestations," and also, "origin is entelechy. Becoming [*das Werden*] is established in entelechy." *GS*, 1: 946.

35. This duality is, as Stéphane Mosès notes in *The Angel of History* (2009), the "paradox of historical time according to Benjamin: the primordial data that constitute it (events, periods, works, or structures) are unique and

archetypal, irreversible and recurrent, at the same time." Mosès (2009), 96.

36. *OT*, 35.

37. Benjamin resorts to theological idiom to explain the relation between an individual work of art and the idea: "There is no analogy between the relationship of the individual to the idea, and its relationship to the concept; in the latter case it falls under the aegis of the concept and remains what it was: an individuality; in the former it stands in the idea, and becomes something different: a totality. That is Platonic 'redemption.'" Ibid., 46.

38. Ibid., 46.

39. The introduction of temporality and repetition to Benjamin's theory of knowledge encouraged a shift in the methodological approach of the philosophical investigation. The task of the philosopher was to discover the footprints of exemplary works *within* history. If previously, philosophy arrived at truth in logical, ahistorical manipulations, Benjamin insists on the need for a new kind of consciousness: a "philosophical history [*philosophische Geschichte*]" that focuses on original, authentic phenomena in their historical actuality. Instead of individual, separate reality, Benjamin is interested in "past and subsequent history [*Vor- und Nachgeschichte*] of such a being." Ibid., 47. This insight on fore-history and future-history became crucial to his work in *Passagenwerk*.

40. Ibid., 35, emphasis mine.

41. "In the leaf lies the true Proteus who can hide or reveal himself in all vegetal forms. From first to last, the plant is nothing but leaf, which is so inseparable from the future germ that one cannot think of one without the other." Goethe (1962), 366.

42. Goethe's mother metaphor and the epigraph of the prologue are the only places Goethe is mentioned in the prologue. Benjamin admits Goethe's influence only later in one of his notes on *Trauerspiel* (later added to *Passagenwerk*). *GS*, I: 953–54. For more, see Pizer (1989).

43. In his 1810 *Theory of Colours* Goethe says, "With light poise and counterpoise, nature oscillates within her prescribed limits, yet thus arise all the varieties and conditions of the phenomena which are presented to us in space and time." Goethe (1997), xxxix.

44. Goethe (1995), 156.

45. Friedlander (2012), 67.

46. Friedlander explains: "Merely comparing and contrasting the two figures would be pointless, given their extensive differences, but polarizing them would make them both partake in the presentation of a unity of spirit otherwise unrecognizable." Ibid.

47. *AP*, 475 [N10a,3], emphasis mine.

48. *OT*, 47, emphasis mine.

49. For more on the structure of "ideas as extremes," see Wiesenthal (1973), 35–74.

50. Deleuze (1994), 41.

51. *AP*, 160–61 [F4a,2], translation modified.

52. *C*, 224, letter 126, Dec. 9, 1923, emphasis mine.

53. Ibid.

54. *AP*, 470 [N7a,1].

55. *OT*, 46.

56. As Anson Rabinbach eloquently notes: "The historical search for origins is a form of secular redemption: the salvation of phenomena lost to recognition." Rabinbach (1979), 7.

57. As Howard Caygill argues: "Benjamin's text marks a point of collision between the various tendencies which were working themselves through in Benjamin's thought; it raises a stage on which the aesthetic, the philosophical, the religious, and the political continually interrupt each other, occasionally achieving dialogue but more often mutual destruction." Caygill (1998), 51.

58. *OT*, 36.

59. Ibid., 37. In one of his notes to the prologue, which he later filed in the *Passagenwerk*, Benjamin further explains the Jewish context of his work. Origin is a "theologically and historically vivid [*lebendige*] concept of the original phenomenon [*Urphänomen*] brought from the pagan natural context into the Jewish context of history. 'Origin'—that is the original phenomenon in a theological sense." *GS*, 1: 953–54. For a shorter version of this note in *Passagenwerk*, see *AP*, 462 [N2a,4]. Despite Scholem's testimony, as noted in the opening lines of the chapter, Benjamin in fact wrote to Scholem already in 1925 about this affiliation: "This introduction is unmitigated chutzpah— that is to say, neither more nor less than the prolegomena to epistemology, a kind of second stage of my early work on language (I do not know whether it is any better), with which you are familiar, dressed up as a theory of ideas. To this end, I also plan to read through my work on language once more." *C*, 261, letter 140, Feb. 19, 1925. For the Jewish origins of Benjamin's idea, see also Stéphane Mosès's claim that "for Benjamin the doctrine of ideas is only a veil behind which there appears the theological vision of his first writings on the philosophy of language." Mosès (2009), 181. Richard Wolin similarly observed that "nowhere is Benjamin's undying concern with the idea of redemption more evident than in the Prologue." Wolin (1994), 91. Charles Rosen alternatively claimed that Benjamin's notion of idea "derives most immediately from the aesthetics of early Romantics, above all, that of Schlegel and Novalis." Rosen (1988), 155.

60. *OT*, 56. Adorno articulates this problem in his discussion of coherence and meaning in music in his posthumously published *Aesthetic Theory* (1970): "Music analyses, for example, show that even in those works most diffuse and hostile to repetition, similarities are involved, that many parts correspond with other in terms of shared, distinguished characteristics, and

that it is only though the relation to these elements of identity that the sought-after nonidentity is achieved; without sameness of any sort, chaos itself would prevail as something ever-same." Adorno (1997), 141.

61. *OT*, 46.
62. *SW*, 2(2): 451.
63. *AP*, 473 [N9,7], translation modified.
64. *SW*, 1: 65.
65. Ibid., 1: 69.
66. Ibid., 1: 65.
67. Ibid., 1: 66; translation modified. *Geist* denotes both "mind" and "spirit" in German. Edmund Jephcott chooses to use "mind," and thus assigns Benjamin's argument to the philosophical tradition, while I believe Benjamin's essay should be connected to the religious debate on spiritual revelation.
68. Ibid., 1: 67, emphasis in text. Benjamin informs Scholem of the Jewish sources of the work in a November 1916 letter: "I do attempt to come to terms with the nature of language in this essay and—to the extent I understand it—in its immanent relationship to Judaism and in reference to the first chapters of Genesis." *C*, 81, letter 46, Nov. 11, 1916. Eric Jacobson claims in *Metaphysics of the Profane* (2003) that "for Benjamin the link to the language of creation was not simply a halfhearted attempt to work theoretically with Judaic material but also an attempt to find a basis for his own philosophy—a philosophy in itself as much as it was a philosophy of Judaism. The origin of language is, in this sense, not only the basis of Judaism but also at the heart of Benjamin's thinking on epistemology, law, and aesthetics." Jacobson (2003), 87. Jacobson adds that Benjamin probably learned about the role of language in creation from *Bereshit Rabbah*, which may have come to him from the Christian Kabbalist Franz Molitor or from a collection of midrashim by August Wünsch. Ibid., 85–86. For recent discussion of Molitor's possible influence on Benjamin's theory of language, see Mertens (2007), 133–68. On Benjamin's theory of language and Christian scholasticism, see Kohlenbach (2002), 1–60. Michael Löwy goes against the above reading to argue that at the time of the completion of his essay on language, Benjamin was unfamiliar with Jewish Kabbalah. Benjamin, consequently, had to be working within the contours of the theory of language of German Romanticism, following Novalis, Hamann, Schlegel, and Herder. Löwy (1992), 99. Scholem was also clearly aware of the importance of the Romantic theory of language to Benjamin. In a letter to Benjamin, he declares Benjamin is "the legitimate continuator of the most fruitful and genuine traditions of Hamann and Humboldt." Scholem (1976), 241. See also Scholem (1981), 48–49. For more on Benjamin's debt to early Romantic theory of language, see Menninghaus (1980), 22; and, more recently, Stern (2018).
69. *SW*, 1: 68. "[God] brought them to the man to see what he would name

them; and whatever the man called each living creature, that was its name."
Genesis 2:19.

70. *SW*, 1: 65.

71. Ibid., 1: 70

72. Ibid., 1: 67.

73. Ibid., 1: 65–66, emphasis mine. It is important to observe Benjamin's terminology in his description of the act of naming. He refers here to "the intensive totality of language" as a marker of the Adamic language. This intensity echoes the intensity he finds in the *Ursprung* where it grounds the possibility of revelation of the idea.

74. "The deeper (that is, the more existent and real) the mind, the more it is expressible and expressed, and it is consistent with this equation to make the relation between mind and language thoroughly unambiguous, so that the expression that is linguistically most existent (that is, most fixed) is linguistically the most rounded and definitive; in a word, the most expressed is at the same time the purely mental. This, however, is precisely what is meant by the concept of revelation." Ibid., 1: 66–67.

75. Ibid., 1: 71.

76. Ibid.

77. Ibid., 1: 72. In "On Language as Such," Benjamin describes the Fall in emotional terms, claiming that after the Fall, nature mourned the ruin of the Adamic language. For more, see Ferber (2013), 118–51.

78. For a clear analysis of Benjamin's by-now foundational "translation as revelation" theory, see Handelman (1991), 15–61. For alternative readings, see Paul de Man (1986), 73–105; and Weber (2008), 3–130.

79. *SW*, 1: 255.

80. Ibid., 1: 257. Benjamin decisively restates this in his notes to the prologue: "The presentation of ideas in concepts of origin [*Ursprungsbegriffen*] contains crucial instructions for the formation of concepts themselves. It must be historic. After all, everything original appears only as a double-determined being: Everything original is incomplete restoration of revelation." *GS*, 1: 935.

81. *OT*, 37.

82. *SW*, 1: 69.

83. Benjamin understands this "unique union" of conception and spontaneity to reflect an act of translation: "For conception and spontaneity together, which are found in this unique union only in the linguistic realm, language has its own word, and this word applies also to that conception of the nameless in the name. It is the translation of the language of things into that of man." *SW*, 1: 69. This dualism is developed in "The Task of the Translator." *SW*, 1: 261.

84. *OT*, 35–36, emphasis mine. A few pages earlier, he says: "The relationship between the minute precision of the work and the proportions of the sculp-

tural or intellectual whole demonstrates that truth content is only to be grasped through immersion in the most minute details of subject-matter." Ibid., 29.

85. Bram Mertens in *Dark Images* (2007), for example, claims intentionlessness designates an "epistemology [in which] the subject does not remain a discrete entity, but voluntarily immerses himself within truth, and appears even to become part of its sphere." In this form of knowledge, he adds, "the disappearance of the subject within [tradition] serves as the consummation of his initiation into its mystical doctrine." Mertens (2007), 179.

86. "Name as the heritage of human language therefore vouches for the fact *that language as such* is the spiritual being of man." *SW*, 1: 65, emphasis in text, translation modified.

87. Ibid., translation modified.

88. Ibid., emphasis in text, translation modified.

89. See Habermas (1988), 114.

90. *AP*, 462–63 [N3,1].

91. Ibid., 388 [K1,2], emphasis mine.

92. *SW*, 4: 395.

93. Ibid.

94. Žižek notes this similarity in *The Ticklish Subject* (2008): "As for Heidegger's notion of authentic choice as a repetition, the parallel with Benjamin's notion of revolution as repetition elucidated in his 'Theses on the Philosophy of History' is striking: here also, revolution is conceptualized as a repetition that realizes the hidden possibility of the past." Žižek (2008), 20. Andrew Benjamin in "Time and Task" reframes this similarity in different terms. For both, he claims, the present, which he terms the "*epochal present*," gives "rise to a specific task—where that specificity is itself molded and determined by the construal of the present." A. Benjamin (2015), 147, emphasis in text.

95. "It is the present that polarizes the event into fore- and after-history." *AP*, 471 [N7a,8].

96. Ibid., 470 [N7a,1].

97. Ibid., 476 [N11,5], emphasis mine.

98. Ibid., 474 [N9a,8].

99. "Resolute refusal of the concept of 'timeless truth' is in order. Nevertheless, truth is not—as Marxism would have it—a merely contingent function of knowing, but is bound to a nucleus of time lying hidden within the knower and the known alike." *AP*, 463 [N3,2].

100. On Heidegger and Benjamin, see Benjamin and Vardoulakis (2015). For their theories of tradition, and in the context of their models of repetition, see Caygill (1994).

101. *C*, 365, letter 196, April 25, 1930.

102. Ibid., 359–60, letter 193, Jan. 20, 1930. And as late as 1938, Benjamin com-

plained to Gretel Adorno that he was perceived "as a follower of Heidegger on the basis of a section of my essay on Goethe's Elective Affinities." Ibid., 571–72, letter 302, July 20, 1938. Benjamin was more daring in his criticism of Heidegger in 1920, when Heidegger did not yet have a prominent position in the German philosophical world. Incidentally, Benjamin briefly addresses Kierkegaard's philosophy in 1933, in a review of Adorno's *Habilitationsschrift* on Kierkegaard. This short text, however, focuses mostly on Adorno and does not mention Kierkegaard's repetition. *SW*, 2: 703–5.

103. *SW*, 4: 395.

104. In his later work, Heidegger thought of repetition in terms of the history of being, yet in *Being and Time* this idea is limited. In the later work, repetition is fundamental to locating different possible histories to being. In *Being in Time*, this is foreshadowed in his attempt to define his whole project about the question of being in terms of repetition. Heidegger (1962), 22.

105. *AP*, 470 [N7,7]. Benjamin describes this "messianic" opportunity further in addendum A to "On the Concept of History": "Historicism contents itself with establishing a causal nexus among various moments in history. But no state of affairs having causal significance is for that very reason historical. It became historical posthumously, as it were, through events that may be separated from it by thousands of years. The historian who proceeds from this consideration ceases to tell the sequence of events like the beads of a rosary. He grasps the constellation into which his own era has entered, along with a very specific earlier one. Thus, he establishes a conception of the present as now-time shot through with splinters of messianic time." *SW*, 4: 397.

106. Ibid., 3: 305. Scholem dated the fragment to the early 1920s, claiming it aligned with Benjamin's early metaphysical framework, while Adorno claimed Benjamin wrote it in either 1936 or 1937.

107. *GS* I: 1242. This quality of interruption of repetition applies to more than historical reality. When Benjamin thinks of the investigation from the side of the subject, he defines it in similar terms: "Where thinking comes to a standstill in a constellation saturated with tensions—there the dialectical image appears. It is the caesura in the movement of thought. Its position is naturally not an arbitrary one. It is to be found, in a word, where the tension [*Spannung*] between dialectical opposites is greatest. [The dialectical image] is identical with the historical object; it justifies its violent expulsion [*Absprengung*] from the continuum of historical process." *AP*, 475 [N10a,3].

108. Harry Harootunian, in "The Benjamin Effect," notes this quality of Benjamin's repetition, claiming that for Benjamin, "the act of reading and writing history [is in a] mode of repetition whose performance would produce an effect of difference." Harootunian (1996), 75. This "moment of difference," which serves as a "point of resistance" (Ibid., 80), he adds, "resembles" (Ibid., 70) Deleuze's later theory of difference.

109. Habermas (1988), 124.

110. *AP*, 462 [N2a,3].

111. Ibid., 475 [N10a,1]. For an alternative reading of Benjamin at this point, see Buck-Morss, who suggests "the conception of 'dialectical image' is over-determined in Benjamin's thought," Buck-Morss (1989), 67. See also Rolf Tiedemann, who, in his afterword to *Passagenwerk*, claims "the meaning of the dialectical remained iridescent; it never achieved any terminological consistency." Tiedemann (1999).

112. *AP*, 475 [N10a,2].

113. Richard Wolin puts this eloquently, when he argues that Benjamin "searches against the flow of historical progress for those moments of 'Messianic cessation of happening,' the rare instances of monads, or now-time, into which images of reconciled life are compressed." Wolin (1994), 58.

114. Wohlfarth (2005), 173, 942.

7. Notes to Chapter 7

1. Freud and Pfister (1963), 109–10, Oct. 16, 1927.

2. *SE*, 21: 17.

3. Freud and Zweig (1970), 91, letter 47, Sep. 30, 1934.

4. Ibid., 92.

5. Freud (1972), 205, Jan. 6, 1935.

6. Antisemitism is addressed in passing in several different places in Freud's large corpus: in a few of his dreams in *The Interpretation of Dreams* (1900); in *The Psychopathology of Everyday Life* (1901); in reference to Jung betrayal in *On the History of the Psychoanalytic Movement* (1914); in his Little Hans case study, *Analysis of a Phobia in a Five-Year-Old Boy* (1909); in connection with the accusations of psychoanalysis as a Jewish science in *The Resistances to Psychoanalysis* (1925); and in the context of his disappointment with Austrian discrimination, in *An Autobiographical Study* (1925).

7. *SE*, 23: 91.

8. Ibid., 23: 7. Jewish Austrian author Stefan Zweig reports Freud's concern that *Moses and Monotheism* was published "in the middle of the most terrible hour in Jewish History." Zweig (2009), 451.

9. See, for example, Trude Weiss-Rosmarin's (1939) response to the book, published in the same year.

10. Buber (1958), 7, fn. 1.

11. For introductory reading on *Moses and Monotheism*, see Gilad Sharvit and Karen S. Feldman's introduction to *Freud and Monotheism* (2017). The list of important contributions includes Assmann (1997); Bernstein (1998); Boyarin (1997), 189–220; Caruth (1996), 11–25; Derrida (1998); Grubrich-Simitis (1997); Paul (1996); Said (2004); Santner (2001); and Yerushalmi (1991).

12. For Freud's fascination with the figure of Moses, see also Grubrich-Simitis (1991); and Maciejewski (2006).

13. Schwartz (1998), 282.

14. Said (2004), 28.

15. Rice (1990), 128.

16. Said (2004), 28.

17. *SE*, 13: 100.

18. Ibid., 13: 131.

19. Ibid., 13: 143.

20. Ibid., 13: 142.

21. Ibid., 13: 145, emphasis mine.

22. Ibid., 13: 152, emphasis mine.

23. For further reading on the intersection of psychoanalysis and history, see Mazlish (1971); Friedländer (1978); Wolman (1971); and, more recently, Straub and Rüsen (2010).

24. Erich Fromm consistently attacked Freud for his "scientific self-misunderstanding" and his overzealous "biological orientation." Fromm (1941), 288. For an introduction to the relations of Freud with the Frankfurt School, see Jay (1996), 86–112; Robinson (1969); and Whitebook (1995).

25. See an early remark in a letter to Lou Andreas-Salomé: "I have already said this in *Totem and Taboo*." Freud and Andreas-Salomé (1972), 205, Jan. 6, 1935; see also his second prefatory note to the third essay: "I acquired that a quarter of a century ago when in 1912 I wrote my book about Totem and Taboo, and it has only grown firmer since." *SE*, 23: 58.

26. Ibid., 23: 18.

27. Ibid., 23: 47.

28. Ibid., 23: 19–20.

29. Ibid., 23: 47.

30. "There is no doubt," Freud notes, "that it was a mighty prototype of a father which, in the person of Moses, stooped to the poor Jewish bondsmen to assure them that they were his dear children." Ibid., 23: 110. For more, see Sharvit (2018).

31. *SE*, 23: 34.

32. Ibid., 23: 115.

33. Ibid., 23: 80.

34. The term appears in Freud's second paper on *The Neuro-Psychoses of Defence* (1896), and even earlier in a draft Freud sent to Fliess in January. Freud (1985), 165, Jan. 1, 1896.

35. *Beyond the Pleasure Principle* contains many examples of repetition: "dreams occurring in traumatic neuroses have the characteristic of repeatedly bringing the patient back into the situation of his accident"; "patients suffering from traumatic neurosis are much occupied in their waking lives with memories of their accident"; and the much-publicized fort-da game, in which his grandson repeated the disconcerting experience of his mother leaving him alone. *SE*, 18: 12.

36. Ibid., 18: 22.
37. Ibid., 18: 29.
38. Ibid.
39. Ibid., 18: 34. Freud uses similar terms in his essay "The Uncanny" from the previous year. *SE*, 17: 238.
40. Ibid., 18: 36.
41. Ibid., 18: 37.
42. Ibid., 18: 36.
43. As Deleuze eloquently puts it in *Difference and Repetition*, "we repeat because we repress . . . Freud was never satisfied with such a negative schema, in which repetition is explained by amnesia." Deleuze (1994), 16.
44. *SE*, 23: 80.
45. Freud (1972), 205, January 6, 1935.
46. Yerushalmi (1991), 10.
47. Freud conspicuously reverted to a Lamarckian theory of transgenerational transmission of psychical characteristics to explain the survival of the traits inflicted on the next generations by the return of the trauma. *SE*, 23: 99–100. Freud's argument reminds in its essentialism Rosenzweig's idea of *blutgemeinschaft*. However, as in Rosenzweig, some attempted to rescue Freud from an essentialist theory of Jewish identity. See, for example, Bernstein (1998), 27–74.
48. *SE*, 23: 86.
49. Ibid., 23: 86.
50. Ibid., 23: 87.
51. Ibid., 23: 90.
52. Ibid., 23: 85. "It is worth specially stressing," Freud claims, "the fact that each portion which returns from oblivion asserts itself with peculiar force, exercises an incomparably powerful influence on people in the mass, and raises an irresistible claim to truth against which logical objections remain powerless: a kind of 'credo quia absurdum' ('I believe because it is absurd')." Ibid.
53. Ibid., 23: 81.
54. Ibid., 23: 88, emphasis mine.
55. Ibid.
56. Freud's reduction of Judaism and Christianity to intellect and sensuality at this point is historically wrong and conceptually unwarranted. Jewish Hasidism's emphasis on emotional religious experience and Thomistic rational philosophy are but examples of this bias in *Moses and Monotheism*.
57. Freud always insisted on reconnecting his new theoretical constructs to his previous systems (even in much more fundamental revolutions in his psychoanalytic theory, such as the introduction of life and death instincts in 1920). In *Moses and Monotheism*, the ambivalence between rebelliousness and guilt that structured history in *Totem and Taboo* finds a renewed

function. It structures the specific manifestations of the religious phenomenon: the return of the repressed is materialized by the interaction of guilt and rebelliousness at a certain point of history: "The ambivalence that dominates the relation to the father was clearly shown, however, in the final outcome of the religious novelty." *SE*, 23: 87.

58. Ibid., 23: 89.
59. Grubrich-Simitis (1997), 60.
60. Robert (1976), 160.
61. *SE*, 23: 77, emphasis mine.
62. Ibid., 23: 80, emphasis mine.
63. Ibid., 23: 129.
64. Ibid., 23: 77.
65. Lacan (2007), 115.
66. See Michael Roth's observation: "Sublimation is the psychic stuff of the ideology of progress." Roth (1987), 111.
67. *SE*, 23: 40.
68. In Michel de Certeau's *L'écriture de l'histoire* (1975), Freud's theory of history is the "means of thinking and practicing a new kind of elucidation." De Certeau (1988), 299. De Certeau depicts a fragmentation in history in which a basic "primitive prototype" breaks "into a thousand facets ... decompose *and* camouflage a primitive 'clear' conflict." Ibid., 295. He also envisions a crucial place for the Freudian praxis in the interpretation of history as an "ever-finished *act* of elucidation." Ibid., 304. Freud, according to de Certeau, submits a special kind of *Aufklärung* (Ibid., 297), one that is as far as possible from a positivistic formulation of knowledge, but, an inherently endless project, disruptive in nature, it still aims at an (endless) interpretation.
69. Nietzsche (2007b), 4 § 3.
70. Foucault (1984), 78.
71. *SE*, 17: 143.
72. Ibid., 23: 115.
73. *AP*, 388 [K1,1].
74. *C*, 495, letter 263, Aug. 2, 1935.
75. Adorno and Benjamin (1999), 93, letter 33, June 5, 1935.
76. It is commonly assumed that Benjamin learned of psychoanalysis in 1918 at the University of Berne, during Haeberlin's lecture course in which Freud's case studies were introduced as part of a discussion of the psychology of suggestion and the occult. In his biography of Benjamin, however, Scholem indicates that Benjamin's attitude to Freud at that time was mostly "negative." Scholem (1981), 57. Diary entries of Benjamin and Scholem from that period note their mocking reaction to the scientific presumptions of Freud. This changed in the 1920s, partly due to Benjamin's growing attraction to Surrealism which brought him closer to psychoanalysis. This was a "first bridge to a more positive assessment of psychoanalysis," in Scholem's own admis-

sion. Ibid., 134. There are nonetheless only few references to Freud in Benjamin's work, so we cannot easily ascribe an *influence* of Freud on Benjamin. Laurence Rickels claims their relations were like "a long distance love affair" in which "Benjamin (like Kafka) admired Freud from the distance of total following." Rickels (2002), 149. Others use "intertexuality." Roff (2004), 116.

77. For other sites of connection between Freud and Benjamin, see, for example, Angelika Rauch's work on Benjamin's theory of history and the unconscious (2000). For Benjamin's debt to Freud's archeological model of memory, see Weigel (1996), 118; and also in Martens (2011).

78. Müller-Farguell (2000), 293.

79. Rainer Nägele defined their relations in terms of "a constellation," which "is not a question of influence." Nägele (1991), 57. Elizabeth Stewart, in *Catastrophe and Survival* (2010), 151–89, outlines the principles for a "Benjaminian psychoanalysis."

80. *OT*, 46.

81. Ibid.

82. Ibid., 45.

83. Quoted in Yerushalmi (1991), 17. German origin in appendix I of Yerushalmi's book (101–3).

84. Bernstein (1998), 69.

85. A third kind, the pious truth applies to the domain of religion. One such truth is "the existence of a supreme Being." *SE*, 23: 121. Evidently false in Freud's eyes, the pious truth nevertheless contains a grain of truth (historical truth) that has been distorted over the years. In *Moses and Monotheism*, to continue the example, the pious truth of God is a distortion of the Jewish admiration of Moses as a godly figure. Ibid., 23: 128.

86. Ibid., 23: 68–69.

87. Ibid., 23: 267.

88. Freud's insistence on this sort of retrieval of a psychoanalytic historical truth was the main reason he was so dismissive of the many counterarguments anthropologists mounted against his thesis of the primal father. Indeed, at times it seemed that there was no historical fact—or material fact, in Freud's terminology—that could have refuted his arguments (based on a different category of truth). Ibid., 23: 130.

89. In a now classical note from his introductory lectures of 1916, he explains, "It will be a long time before [the patient] can take in our proposal that we should equate phantasy and reality and not bother to begin with whether the childhood experiences under examination are the one or the other. Yet this is clearly the only correct attitude to adopt towards these mental productions. They too possess a reality of a sort.... *The phantasies possess psychical as contrasted with material reality, and we gradually learn to understand that in the world of the neuroses it is psychical reality which is the decisive kind.*" Ibid., 16: 368, emphasis mine.

90. I thank Yvan Vivd (Chris Shaver) for bringing this to my attention.

91. *SE*, 16: 368.

92. See Lewkowicz, Bokanowski, and Pragier (2011).

93. Richard Bernstein notes this shift in his *Freud and the Legacy of Moses* (1998): "there is a reversal of the presumed explanatory force of the appeal to 'origins.' Freud is not really explaining the historical fact of the Jewish religious tradition by an appeal to 'events' which presumably occurred in the shadowy historical past. Rather he is projecting what allegedly happened in the past—'the historical truth'—on the basis of our understanding of the dynamical conflicts of the human psyche." Bernstein (1998), 72.

94. Freud notes this in regard to his concept of pious truth: "To the extent to which [the idea of God] is distorted, it may be described as a *delusion*; in so far as it brings a return of the past, it must be called the *truth*." *SE*, 23: 129, emphasis in text.

95. For Freud and Deleuze in this context, see Somers-Hall (2017) and Rölli (2012).

96. Deleuze (1994), 16. Jacques Lacan explains in *The Four Fundamental Concepts of Psychoanalysis* (1973): "The function of return, *Wiederkehr*, is essential. It is not only *Wiederkehr* in the sense of that which has been repressed—the very constitution of the field of the unconscious is based on the *Wiederkehr*." Lacan (2004), 47–48.

97. Ansell-Pearson (1999), 104–13.

98. Deleuze (1994), 16.

99. Ibid., 17

100. Grubrich-Simitis (1997), 11.

101. *SE*, 23: 43.

102. Sharvit (2016).

103. Laplanche (1999).

104. *SE*, 20: 91–92.

105. Freud and Zweig (1970), 92, Sep. 30, 1934.

106. Goldstein (1992), 130. In "Why War?" Freud writes: "The ideal condition of things would of course be a community of men who had subordinated their instinctual life to the dictatorship of reason. Nothing else could unite men so completely and so tenaciously, even if there were no emotional ties between them. But in all probability that is a Utopian expectation." *SE*, 22: 213.

107. Zweig (1962), 355.

108. *SE*, 23: 116.

109. Ibid., 23: 118.

110. Ibid., 23: 116.

111. These lines captured the imagination of Daniel Boyarin, Eric Santner, and others. However, while Santner finds a clue to the Lacanian *Jouissance* (2001, 97–104) and Boyarin argues that Freud was faced here with the unimag-

inable proof of a "Jewissance," the rabbinic feminine forbidden pleasure (1997, 256), I find the context of Freud's dilemma to be its source. Here, Freud finds the basic *Aporia* of history.

112. A few pages later, Freud rediscovers his critical flair. Aiming at the eternal truth of the *pious believer*, he argues, "it had not been possible to *demonstrate* . . . that the human intellect has a particularly fine flair for the truth or that the human mind shows any special inclinations for recognizing the truth" (*SE*, 23: 129, emphasis mine). Abstract truth is not only an impossible purpose for history. By itself, it is meaningless and empty.

Bibliography

Abensour, Miguel (2013). *Les passages Blanqui: Walter Benjamin entre mélancolie et revolution* (Paris: Sens & Tonka).

Adorno, Theodor W. (1983). *Prisms*, trans. Samuel and Shierry Weber (Cambridge, MA: MIT Press).

Adorno, Theodor W. (1997). *Aesthetic Theory*, ed. Gretel Adorno and Rolf Tiedemann, trans. Robert Hullot-Kentor (Minneapolis: University of Minnesota Press).

Adorno, Theodor W. (1990). "Einleitung zu Benjamins 'Schriften,'" *Über Walter Benjamin: Aufsätze, Artikel, Briefe*, ed. Rolf Tiedemann (Frankurt am Main: Suhrkamp).

Adorno, Theodor W. (2005). *Minima Moralia*, trans. E. F. N. Jephcott (New York: Verso).

Adorno, Theodore W., and Walter Benjamin (1999). *The Complete Correspondence, 1928–1940*, ed. Henri Lonitz, trans. Nicholas Walker (Cambridge, MA: Harvard University Press).

Agamben, Giorgio (2004). "Difference and Repetition: On Guy Debord's Films," in *Guy Debord and the Situationist International*, ed. Tom McDonough (Cambridge, MA: MIT Press).

Allen, Douglas (1998). *Myth and Religion in Mircea Eliade* (New York: Garland).

Almog, Shmuel (1987). *Zionism and History: The Rise of a New Jewish Consciousness* (Jerusalem: Magnes Press).

Anders, Günther (1960). *Franz Kafka*, trans. A. Steer and A. K. Thorlby (New York: Hillary House).

Ansell-Pearson, Keith (1997). "Living the Eternal Return as the Event: Nietzsche with Deleuze," *Journal of Nietzsche Studies* 14: 64–97.

Ansell-Pearson, Keith (1999). *Germinal Life: The Difference and Repetition of Deleuze* (London: Routledge).

Ansell-Pearson, Keith (2005). "The Eternal Return of the Overhuman," *Journal of Nietzsche Studies* (30): 1–21.

Aschheim, Steven E. (1982). *Brothers and Strangers: The East European Jew in German and German Jewish Consciousness, 1800–1923* (Madison: University of Wisconsin Press).

Aschheim, Steven E. (1996). *Culture and Catastrophe: German and Jewish Confrontations with National Socialism and Other Crises* (New York: New York University Press).

Aschheim, Steven E. (2007). *Beyond the Border: The German-Jewish Legacy Abroad* (Princeton, NJ: Princeton University Press).

Assmann, Jan (1997). *Moses the Egyptian: The Memory of Egypt in Western Monotheism* (Cambridge, MA: Harvard University Press).

Augustine, Aurelius (2008). *The City of God, Books VIII–XVI*, trans. Gerald G. Walsh and Grace Monahan (The Fathers of the Church, Volume 14). (Washington, DC: Catholic University of America Press).

Avineri, Shlomo (1981). *The Making of Modern Zionism: The Intellectual Origins of the Jewish State* (New York: Basic Books).

Bakan, David (1958). *Sigmund Freud and the Jewish Mystical Tradition* (Princeton, NJ: Van Nostrand).

Bârliba, Ionuț-Alexandru (2014). "Søren Kierkegaard's Repetition: Existence in Motion," *Symposion* 1(1): 23–49.

Baron, Hans (1966). *The Crisis of the Early Italian Renaissance: Civic Humanism and Republican Liberty in an Age of Classicism and Tyranny* (Princeton, NJ: Princeton University Press).

Barr, James (1969). *Biblical Words for Time* (Edinburgh: Clark).

Batnitzky, Leora (2000). *Idolatry and Representation: The Philosophy of Franz Rosenzweig Reconsidered* (Princeton, NJ: Princeton University Press).

Beasley-Murray, Tim (2007). *Mikhail Bakhtin and Walter Benjamin: Experience and Form* (New York: Palgrave).

Beck, Evelyn T. (1971). *Kafka and the Yiddish Theater* (Madison: University of Wisconsin Press).

Benjamin, Andrew (2005). "Boredom and Distraction: The Moods of Modernity," in *Walter Benjamin and History*, ed. Andrew Benjamin (New York: Continuum).

Benjamin, Andrew (2013). *Working with Walter Benjamin: Recovering a Political Philosophy* (Edinburgh: Edinburgh University Press).

Benjamin, Andrew (2015). "Time and Task: Benjamin and Heidegger Showing the Present," in *Sparks Will Fly: Benjamin and Heidegger*, eds. Andrew Benjamin and Dimitris Vardoulakis (Albany, NY: SUNY Press).

Benjamin, Andrew, and Dimitris Vardoulakis, eds. (2015). *Sparks Will Fly: Benjamin and Heidegger* (Albany, NY: SUNY Press).

Benjamin, Andrew, and Peter Osborne, eds. (1994). *Walter Benjamin's Philosophy: Destruction and Experience* (New York: Routledge).

Benjamin, Mara H. (2009). *Rosenzweig's Bible: Reinventing Scripture for Jewish Modernity* (Cambridge: Cambridge University Press).

Benjamin, Walter (1997). *Charles Baudelaire: A Lyric Poet in the Era of High Capitalism*, trans. Harry Zohn (New York: Verso).

Benjamin, Walter (1995–2000). *Gesammelte Briefe*, 6 vols. eds., Christoph Gödde und Henri Lonitz (Frankfurt am Main: Suhrkamp).

Ben-Yehuda, Nachman (1995). *The Masada Myth: Collective Memory and Mythmaking in Israel* (Madison: University of Wisconsin Press).

Bernier, Mark (2015). *The Task of Hope in Kierkegaard* (Oxford: Oxford University Press).

Bernstein, Richard J. (1998). *Freud and the Legacy of Moses* (Cambridge: Cambridge University Press).

Bernstein, Samuel (1971). *Auguste Blanqui and the Art of Insurrection* (London: Lawrence and Wishart).

Bertram, Ernest (2009). *Nietzsche: Attempt at a Mythology*, trans. Robert E. Norton (Urbana: University of Illinois Press).

Blond, Louis P. (2010). "Franz Rosenzweig: Homelessness in Time," *New German Critique* 37(3): 27–58.

Bloom, Harold (1985). "The Masks of the Normative," *Orim: A Jewish Journal at Yale* 1: 9–24.

Borges, Jorge Luis (1999). "The Doctrine of Cycles," in *Selected Non-Fictions*, ed. Eliot Weinberger, trans. Esther Allen, Suzanne Jill Levine, and Eliot Weinberger (London: Penguin Books).

Bouretz, Pierre (2010). *Witnesses for the Future: Philosophy and Messianism*, trans. Michael B. Smith (Baltimore: Johns Hopkins University Press).

Boyarin, Daniel (1997). *Unheroic Conduct: The Rise of Heterosexuality and the Invention of the Jewish Man* (Berkeley: University of California Press).

Braiterman, Zachary (2002). "Cyclical Motion and the Force of Repetition in the Thought of Franz Rosenzweig," in *Beginning/Again: Toward a Hermeneutics of Jewish Texts*, ed. Aryeh Cohen and Shaul Magid (New York: Seven Bridges).

Braiterman, Zachary (2007). *The Shape of Revelation: Aesthetics and Modern Jewish Thought* (Stanford, CA: Stanford University Press).

Brandon, Samuel G. F. (1951). *Time and Mankind: An Historical and Philosophical Study of Mankind's Attitude to the Phenomena of Change* (London: Hutchinson).

Brenner, Michael (1993). "A Tale of Two Families: Franz Rosenzweig, Gershom Scholem and the Generational Conflict Around Judaism," *Judaism* 42(3): 349–61.

Brenner, Michael (1998). *The Renaissance of Jewish Culture in Weimar Germany* (New Haven, CT: Yale University Press).

Britt, Bryan (2000). "Romantic Roots of the Debate on the Buber-Rosenzweig Bible," *Prooftexts* 20(3): 262–89.

Britt, Bryan (2016). *Postsecular Benjamin: Agency and Tradition* (Evanston, IL: Northwestern University Press).

Buber, Martin (1958). *Moses: The Revelation and the Covenant* (New York: Harper).

Buber, Martin (1991). *The Letters of Martin Buber*, ed. Nahum N. Glatzer and Paul Mendes-Flohr, trans. Richard and Clara Winston and Harry Zohn (New York: Schocken).

Buber, Martin (1999). *The First Buber: Youthful Zionist Writings of Martin Buber*, ed. and trans. Gilya G. Schmidt (Syracuse, NY: Syracuse University Press).

Buber, Martin, and Franz Rosenzweig (1994). *Scripture and Translation*, trans. Lawrence Rosenwald and Everett Fox (Bloomington: Indiana University Press).

Buck-Morss, Susan (1989). *The Dialectics of Seeing: Walter Benjamin and the Arcades Project* (Cambridge, MA: MIT Press).

Burgess, Andrew J. (1984). "Repetition–A Story of Suffering," in *International Kierkegaard Commentary: Fear and Trembling and Repetition*, ed. Robert L. Perkins (Macon, GA: Mercer University Press).

Cain, David (1993). "Notes on a Coach Horn: 'Going Further,' 'Revocation,' and 'Repetition,'" in *International Kierkegaard Commentary: Fear and Trembling and Repetition*, ed. Robert L. Perkins (Macon, GA: Mercer University Press).

Caputo, John D. (1987). *Radical Hermeneutics: Repetition, Deconstruction, and the Hermeneutic Project* (Bloomington: Indiana University Press).

Caputo, John D. (1993). "Kierkegaard, Heidegger, and the Foundering of Metaphysics," in *International Kierkegaard Commentary: Fear and Trembling and Repetition*, ed. Robert L. Perkins (Macon, GA: Mercer University Press).

Carlisle, Clare (2010). *Kierkegaard's Fear and Trembling* (New York: Continuum).

Carlisle, Clare (2005). "Kierkegaard's Repetition: The Possibility of Motion," *British Journal for the History of Philosophy* 13(3): 521–41.

Caruth, Cathy (1996). *Unclaimed Experience* (Baltimore: Johns Hopkins University Press).

Caygill, Howard (1998). *Walter Benjamin: The Colour of Experience* (New York: Routledge).

Caygill, Howard (1994). "Benjamin, Heidegger, and Tradition," in *Destruction and Experience*, ed. Andrew Benjamin and Peter Osborne (London: Routledge).

Caygill, Howard (2005). "Non-Messianic Political Theology in Benjamin's 'On the Concept of History,'" in *Walter Benjamin and History*, ed. Andrew Benjamin (New York: Continuum).

Chilton, Bruce (2002). *Redeeming Time: The Wisdom of Ancient Jewish and Christian Festal Calendars* (Peabody: Hendrickson Publishers).

Chouraqui, Frank (2013). "At the Crosswords of History," in *Eternity by the Starts*, trans. Frank Chouraqui (New York: Contra Mundum Press).

Chowdhury, Aniruddha (2014). *Post-Deconstructive Subjectivity and History* (Leiden: Brill).

Cohen, Hermann (1972). *Religion of Reason Out of the Sources of Judaism*, trans. Simon Kaplan (New York: Ungar).

Cohen, Hermann (1980). "The Polish Jew," in *The Jew: Essays from Martin Buber's Journal, Der Jude, 1916–1928*, trans. Joachim Neugroschel (Tuscaloosa: University of Alabama Press).

Cohen, Margaret (1989). "Walter Benjamin's Phantasmagoria," *New German Critique* 48: 87–107.

Corngold, Stanley (1973). *The Commentator's Despair* (Port Washington: Kennikat Press).

Crites, Stephen (1993). "The 'Blissful Security of the Moment': Recollection, Repetition, and Eternal Recurrence," in *International Kierkegaard Commen-*

tary: *Fear and Trembling and Repetition*, ed. Robert L. Perkins (Macon, GA: Mercer University Press).

Cullmann, Oscar (1964). *Christ and Time: The Primitive Christian Conception of Time and History*, trans. Floyd V. Filson (Philadelphia: Westminster Press).

Danta, Chris (2011). *Literature Suspends Death: Sacrifice and Storytelling in Kierkegaard, Kafka, and Blanchot* (New York: Continuum).

Danto, Arthur C. (2005). *Nietzsche as Philosopher* (New York: Columbia University Press).

David, Claude (1980). "Die Geschichte Abrahams: Zu Kafkas Auseinandersetzung mit Kierkegaard," *Bild und Gedanke: Festschrift für Gerhart Baumann*, ed. Günter Schnitzler et al. (Munich: Fink).

David Ben Judah heḤasid (1982). *The Book of Mirrors*, trans. Daniel C. Matt (Chico: Scholars Press).

De Beistegui, Miguel (2003). *Thinking with Heidegger: Displacements* (Bloomington: Indiana University Press).

De Beistegui, Miguel (2004). *Truth and Genesis: Philosophy as Differential Ontology* (Bloomington: Indiana University Press).

De Certeau, Michel (1988). *The Writing of History*, trans. Tom Conley (New York: Columbia University Press).

De Man, Paul (1986). *The Resistance to Theory* (Minneapolis: University of Minnesota Press).

Deleuze, Gilles (1994). *Difference and Repetition*, trans. Paul Patton (New York: Columbia University Press).

Deleuze, Gilles (1956). "La conception de la différence chez Bergson," *Etudes bergsoniennes* 4: 79–112.

Deleuze, Gilles (1983). *Nietzsche and Philosophy*, trans. Hugh Tomlinson (New York: Columbia University Press).

Deleuze, Gilles (1990). *The Logic of Sense*, ed. Constantin V. Boundas, trans. Mark Lester with Charles Stivale (New York: Columbia University Press).

Deleuze, Gilles (2005). *Pure Immanence*, trans. Anne Boyman (Cambridge, MA: MIT Press).

Deleuze, Gilles, and Felix Guattari (1983). *Anti-Oedipus: Capitalism and Schizophrenia*, trans. Robert Hurley, Mark Seem, and Helen R. Lane (Minneapolis: University of Minnesota Press).

DeHart, Paul J. (2015). "'The Passage from Mind to Heart is so Long...': The Riddle of 'Repetition' and Kierkegaard's Ontology of Agency," *Modern Theology* 31(1): 91–122.

Deprez, Stanislas (1999). *Mircea Eliade: la Philosophie du sacré* (Paris: Harmattan).

Derrida, Jacques (1962). *Heidegger: The Question of Being and History*, ed. Thomas Dutoit, trans. Geoffrey Bennington (Chicago: Indiana University Press).

Derrida, Jacques (1985). "Otobiographies," in *The Ear of the Other*, ed. Christie V. McDonald, trans. Peggy Kamuf (Lincoln: University of Nebraska Press).

Derrida, Jacques (1992). "Before the Law," in *Acts of Literature*, ed. Derek Attridge (London: Routledge).

Derrida, Jacques (1998). *Archive Fever: A Freudian Impression*, trans. Eric Prenowitz (Chicago: University of Chicago Press).

Derrida, Jacques (2007). "Abraham, The Other," in *Judeities: Questions for Jacques Derrida*, eds. Bettina Bergo, Joseph Cohen, and Raphael Zagury-Orly, trans. Bettina Bergo and Michael B. Smith (New York: Fordham University Press).

Dommanget, Maurice (1972). *Auguste Blanqui au début de la IIIe république (1871–1880): Dernière prison et ultimes combats* (La Haye: Mouton).

Dubbels, Elke (2011). *Figuren des Messianischen in Schriften deutsch-jüdischer Intellektueller, 1900–1933* (Berlin: De Gruyter).

Edwards, Brian F. M. (1966). "Kafka and Kierkegaard: A Reassessment," *German Life and Letters* 20: 218–25.

Efron, John (2016). *German Jewry and the Allure of the Sephardic* (Princeton, NJ: Princeton University Press).

Eiland, Howard, and Michael W. Jennings (2014). *Walter Benjamin: A Critical Life* (Cambridge, MA: Harvard University Press).

Eliade, Mircea (1958). *Yoga, Immortality, and Freedom*, trans. William R. Trask (New York: Pantheon Books).

Eliade, Mircea (1961). *The Sacred and the Profane: The Nature of Religion*, trans. William R. Trask (New York: Harcourt).

Eliade, Mircea (1975). *Myth and Reality*, trans. William R. Trask (New York: Harper and Row).

Eliade, Mircea (2005). *The Myth of the Eternal Return: Cosmos and History*, trans. William R. Trask (Princeton, NJ: Princeton University Press).

Eriksen, Niels Nymann (2000). *Kierkegaard's Category of Repetition: A Reconstruction* (New York: De Gruyter).

Fackenheim, Emil L. (1982). *To Mend the World: Foundations of Future Jewish Thought* (New York: Schocken).

Fenves, Peter (2001). *Arresting Language: From Leibniz to Benjamin* (Stanford, CA: Stanford University Press).

Ferber, Ilit (2013). *Philosophy and Melancholy: Benjamin's Early Reflections on Theatre and Language* (Stanford, CA: Stanford University Press).

Flanagan, Tim (2009). "The Thought of History in Benjamin and Deleuze," in *Deleuze and History*, eds. Jeffrey A. Bell and Claire Colebrook (Edinburgh: Edinburgh University Press).

Foucault, Michel (1984). "Nietzsche, Genealogy, History," in *The Foucault Reader*, ed. Paul Rabinow (New York: Pantheon Books).

Frankel, Jonathan, ed. (1991). *Jews and Messianism in the Modern Era: Metaphor and Meaning* (New York: Oxford University Press).

Freud, Sigmund (1972). *Letters*, ed. Ernst Pfeiffer, trans. Elaine and William Robson-Scott (New York: Norton).

Freud, Sigmund (1985). *The Complete Letters of Sigmund Freud to Wilhelm Fliess*, ed. and trans. Jeffrey Moussaieff Masson (Cambridge, MA: Harvard University Press).

Freud, Sigmund, and Lou Andreas-Salomé (1972). *Letters*, ed. Ernst Pfeiffer, trans. Elaine and William Robson-Scott (New York: Norton).

Freud, Sigmund, and Arnold Zweig (1970). *The Letters of Sigmund Freud and Arnold Zweig*, ed. Ernst L. Freud, trans. Elaine and William Robson-Scott (New York: Harcourt).

Freud, Sigmund, and Oskar Pfister (1963). *Psychoanalysis and Faith: The Letters of Sigmund Freud & Oskar Pfister*, ed. Heinrich Meng and Ernst L. Freud, trans. Eric Mosbacher (New York: Basic Books).

Friedlander, Eli (2012). *Walter Benjamin: A Philosophical Portrait* (Cambridge, MA: Harvard University Press).

Friedländer, Saul (1978). *History and Psychoanalysis: An Inquiry into the Possibilities and Limits of Psychohistory*, trans. Susan Suleiman (New York: Holmes & Meier).

Fromm, Erich (1941). *Escape From Freedom* (New York: Holt).

Galli, Barbara Ellen (1995). *Franz Rosenzweig and Jehuda Halevi: Translating, Translations, and Translators* (Montreal: McGill-Queen's University Press).

Galli, Barbara Ellen (2000). "Translating is a Mode of Holiness," in *Cultural Writings of Franz Rosenzweig*, ed. and trans. Barbara Ellen Galli (Syracuse, NY: Syracuse University Press).

Garb, Jonathan (2007). "Moshe Idel's Contribution to the Study of Religion," *Journal for the Study of Religions and Ideologies* 6: 16–29.

Gay, Peter (1985). *Freud for Historians* (New York: Oxford University Press).

Gay, Peter (1987). *A Godless Jew: Freud, Atheism and the Making of Psychoanalysis* (New Haven, CT: Yale University Press).

Geffroy, Gustave (2015). *L'Enfermé* (Coaraze: L'Amourier).

Gelley, Alexander (2015). *Benjamin's Passages: Dreaming, Awakening* (New York: Fordham University Press).

Gibbs, Robert (1992). *Correlations in Rosenzweig and Levinas* (Princeton, NJ: Princeton University Press).

Gibbs, Robert (2005). "Messianic Epistemology: Thesis XV," in *Walter Benjamin and History*, ed. Andrew Benjamin (New York: Continuum).

Gibbs, Robert (2006). "Eternity in History: Rolling the Scroll," in *Liturgy, Time, and the Politics of Redemption*, ed. Randi Rashkover and C. C. Pecknold (Grand Rapids: Eerdmans).

Gillman, Abigail (2018). *A history of German Jewish Bible translation* (Chicago: The University of Chicago Press).

Gilman, Sander (1986). *Jewish Self-Hatred: Anti-Semitism and the Hidden Language of the Jews* (Baltimore: Johns Hopkins University Press).

Glatzer, Nahum N. (1998). *Franz Rosenzweig: His Life and Thought* (Indianapolis: Hackett).

Goethe, Johann Wolfgang (1962). *Italian Journey*, trans. W. H. Auden and Elizabeth Mayer (London: Penguin).

Goethe, Johann Wolfgang (1995). *Scientific Studies*, ed. and trans. Douglas Miller (Princeton, NJ: Princeton University Press).

Goethe, Johann Wolfgang (1997). *Theory of Colours*, trans. Charles Lock Eastlake (Cambridge, MA: MIT Press).

Goldstein, Bluma (1992). *Reinscribing Moses: Heine, Kafka, Freud, and Schoenberg in a European Wilderness* (Cambridge, MA: Harvard University Press).

Gordon, Peter E. (2003). *Rosenzweig and Heidegger: Between Judaism and German Philosophy* (Berkeley: University of California Press).

Graf, Max (1942). "Reminiscences of Professor Sigmund Freud," *The Psychoanalytic Quarterly* II: 465–76.

Groiser, David (2011). "Repetition and Renewal: Kierkegaard, Rosenzweig and the German-Jewish Renaissance," in *Zur Gegenwärtigkeit deutsch-jüdischen Denkens*, ed. Julia Matveev and Ashraf Noor (Munich: Wilhelm Fink).

Grubrich-Simitis, Ilse (1991). *Freud's Moses-Studie Als Tagtraum* (Frankfurt: Verlag Internationale Psychoanalyse).

Grubrich-Simitis, Ilse (1997). *Early Freud and Late Freud: Reading Anew Studies on Hysteria and Moses and Monotheism*, trans. Philip Slotkin (New York: Routledge).

Habermas, Jürgen (1988). "ConsciousnessRaising or Rescuing Critique," in *On Walter Benjamin*, ed. Gary Smith (Cambridge, MA: MIT Press).

Hahm, David E. (1977). *The Origins of Stoic Cosmology* (Columbus: Ohio State University Press).

Handelman, Susan A. (1991). *Fragments of Redemption: Jewish Thought and Literary Theory in Benjamin, Scholem, and Levinas* (Bloomington: Indiana University Press).

Hanssen, Beatrice (2000). *Walter Benjamin's Other History: Of Stones, Animals, Human Beings, and Angels* (Berkeley: University of California Press).

Hanssen, Beatrice, ed. (2006). *Walter Benjamin and the Arcades Project* (New York: Continuum).

Harkabi, Yehoshafat (1983). *The Bar Kokhba Syndrome: Risk and Realism in International Politics*, ed. David Altshuler, trans. Max D. Ticktin (Chappaqua: Rossel Books).

Harrison, Robert P. (1986). "Heresy and the Question of Repetition," in *Textual Analysis: Some Readers Reading*, ed. Mary Ann Caws (New York: MLA).

Harootunian, Harry D. (1996). "The Benjamin Effect: Modernism, Repetition, and the Path to Different Cultural Imaginaries," in *Walter Benjamin and the Demands of History*, ed. Michael P. Steinberg (Ithaca, NY: Cornell University Press).

Hatab, Lawrence (2005). *Nietzsche's Life Sentence: Coming to Terms with Eternal Recurrence* (New York: Routledge).

Hegel, Georg Wilhelm Friedrich (1988). *Introduction to the Philosophy of History*, trans. Leo Rauch (Indianapolis: Hackett).

Heidegger, Martin (1962). *Being and Time*, trans. John Macquarrie and Edward Robinson (Oxford: Blackwell).

Heidegger, Martin (1984). *Nietzsche*, trans. David Farrell Krell (San Francisco: Harper & Row).

Heidegger, Martin (1990). *Kant and the Problem of Metaphysics*, trans. James S. Churchill (Bloomington: Indiana University Press).

Heidegger, Martin (2012). *Contributions to Philosophy (of the Event)*, trans. Richard Rojcewicz and Daniela Vallega-Neu (Bloomington: Indiana University Press).

Henning, E. M. (1982). "Destruction and Repetition: Heidegger's Philosophy of History," *Journal of European Studies* 12: 260–82.

Herskowitz, Daniel (2017). "Franz Rosenzweig and Karl Barth: A Chapter in the Jewish Reception of Dialectical Theology," *The Journal of Religion* 97(1): 79–100.

Hezser, Catherine (2001). "Freud's Oedipus-Complex and the Problems of Jewish Assimilation in the Writings of Franz Kafka and Philip Roth," *Jewish Studies Quarterly* 8(3): 248–78.

Hollander, Dana (2008). *Exemplarity and Chosenness: Rosenzweig and Derrida on the Nation of Philosophy* (Stanford, CA: Stanford University Press).

Idel, Moshe (1998). "Some Concepts of Time and History in Kabbalah," in *Jewish History and Jewish Memory*, eds. Elisheva Carlebach, John M. Efron and David N. Myers (Hanover, NH: Brandeis University Press).

Idel, Moshe (2004). "Sabbath: On Concepts of Time in Jewish Mysticism," in *Sabbath—Idea, History, Reality*, ed. Gerald J. Blidstein (Beer Sheva: Ben Gurion University of the Negev Press).

Idel, Moshe (2010). *Old Worlds, New Mirrors: On Jewish Mysticism and Twentieth-Century Thought* (Philadelphia: University of Pennsylvania Press).

Idel, Moshe (2014). *Mircea Eliade: From Magic to Myth* (New York: Peter Lang).

Jacobson, Eric (2003). *Metaphysics of the Profane: The Political Theology of Walter Benjamin and Gershom Scholem* (New York: Columbia University Press).

Jameson, Fredric (2015). "The Aesthetics of Singularity," *New Left Review* 92(2): 101–32.

Jaspers, Karl (1979). *Nietzsche: An Introduction to the Understanding of His Philosophical Activity*, trans. Charles F. Wallraff and Frederick J. Schmitz (South Bend, IN: Regnery/Gateway).

Jay, Martin (1976). "Politics of Translation: Siegfried Kracauer and Walter Benjamin on the Buber-Rosenzweig Bible," *Leo Baeck Institute Yearbook* 21(1): 3–24.

Jay, Martin (1996). *The Dialetctical Imagination* (Berkeley: University of California Press).

Jay, Martin (1998). "Experience Without a Subject: Walter Benjamin and the Novel," in *The Actuality of Walter Benjamin*, eds. Laura Marcus and Lynda Nead (London: Lawrence & Wishart).

Kain, Philip J. (2007). "Nietzsche, Eternal Recurrence, and the Horror of Existence," *The Journal of Nietzsche Studies* 33.

Kafka, Franz (1954). *Dearest Father: Stories and Other Writings*, ed. Max Brod, trans. Ernst Kaiser and Eithne Wilkins (New York: Schocken Books).

Kafka, Franz (2009). *The Trial*, trans. Mike Mitchell (Oxford: Oxford University Press).

Kafka, Franz (2015). *Letter to the Father/Brief an der Vater*, trans. Ernst Kaiser and Eithne Wilkins (New York: Schocken Books).

Kangas, David (1998). "Kierkegaard, the Apophatic Theologian," *Enrahonar* 29: 119–23.

Katz, Jacob (1973). *Out of the Ghetto: The Social Background of Jewish Emancipation, 1770–1870* (Cambridge MA: Harvard University Press).

Katz, Marc (1998). "Rendezvous in Berlin: Benjamin and Kierkegaard on the Architecture of Repetition," *The German Quarterly* 71(1): 1–13.

Kavka, Martin (2004). *Jewish Messianism and the History of Philosophy* (Cambridge: Cambridge University Press).

Kierkegaard, Søren (1957). *The Concept of Dread*, trans. Walter Lowrie (Princeton, NJ: Princeton University Press).

Kierkegaard, Søren (1993). *Upbuilding Discourses in Various Spirits*, eds. and trans. Howard V. and Edna H. Hong (Princeton, NJ: Princeton University Press).

Kline, Peter (2017). *Passion for Nothing: Kierkegaard's Apophatic Theology* (Minneapolis: Fortress Press).

Kohlenbach, Margarete (2002). *Walter Benjamin: Self-Reference and Religiosity* (New York: Palgrave).

Koselleck, Reinhart (2004). "Representation, Event, and Structure," in *Futures Past: On the Semantics of Historical Time*, trans. Keith Tribe (New York: Columbia University Press).

Krochmal, Nachman (2010). *More Neboche ha-Zeman* (Jerusalem: Carmel).

Krüll, Marianne (1986). *Freud and His Father*, trans. Arnold J. Pomerans (New York: Norton).

Lacan, Jacques (2004). *The Four Fundamental Concepts of Psychoanalysis*, ed. Jacques-Alain Miller, trans. Alan Sheridan (New York: Routledge).

Lacan, Jacques (2007). *The Other Side of Psychoanalysis*, trans. Russell Grigg (New York: Norton).

Laplanche, Jean (1999). *Essays on Otherness*, ed. John Fletcher (London: Routledge).

Laqueur, Walter (1989). *A History of Zionism* (New York: Schocken Books).

Law, David R. (1993). *Kierkegaard as Negative Theologian* (Oxford: Oxford University Press).

Levinas, Emmanuel (1990). *Difficult Freedom: Essays on Judaism*, trans. Sean Hand (Baltimore: Johns Hopkins University Press).

Lewkowicz, Sergio, Thierry Bokanowski, and Georges Pragier, eds. (2011). *On Freud's "Construction in Analysis"* (London: Karnac).

Lippitt, John (2016). *The Routledge Guidebook to Kierkegaard's Fear and Trembling* (New York: Routledge).

Liska, Vivian (2008). *Giorgio Agambens leerer Messianismus: Hannah Arendt, Walter Benjamin, Franz Kafka* (Wien: Schlebrügger).

Liska, Vivian (2017). *German-Jewish Thought and Its Afterlife* (Bloomington: Indiana University Press).

Löwith, Karl (1942). "M. Heidegger and F. Rosenzweig or Temporality and Eternity," *Philosophical and Phenomenological Research* 3: 53–77.

Löwith, Karl (1970). *Meaning in History* (Chicago: University of Chicago Press).

Löwith, Karl (1997). *Nietzsche's Philosophy of the Eternal Recurrence of the Same*, trans. J. Harvey Lomax (Berkeley: University of California Press).

Löwy, Michael (1992). *Redemption and Utopia: Jewish Libertarian Thought in Central Europe*, trans. Hope Heaney (Stanford, CA: Stanford University Press).

Löwy, Michael (2005). *Fire Alarm: Reading Walter Benjamin's 'On the Concept of History,'* trans. Chris Turner (New York: Verso).

Maciejewski, Franz (2006). *Der Moses des Sigmund Freud: Ein Unheimlicher Bruder* (Göttingen: Vandenhoeck and Ruprecht).

MacKey, Louis (1971). *Kierkegaard: A Kind of Poet* (Philadelphia: University of Pennsylvania Press).

Magnus, Bernd (1978). *Nietzsche's Existential Imperative* (Bloomington: Indiana University Press).

Malabou, Christine (2010). "The Eternal Return and the Phantom of Difference," *Parrhesia* 10: 21–29.

Mali, Josef (2003). *Mythistory: The Making of Modern Historiography* (Chicago: University of Chicago Press).

Martens, Lorna (2011). *The Promise of Memory: Childhood Recollection and Its Objects in Literary Modernism* (Cambridge, MA: Harvard University Press).

Mazlish, Bruce, ed. (1971). *Psychoanalysis and History* (New York: Universal Library).

McCarthy, Vincent (2011). "Martin Heidegger: Kierkegaard's Influence Hidden and in Full View," in *Kierkegaard and Existentialism*, ed. Jon Stewart (Farnham: Ashgate).

McCole, John (1993). *Walter Benjamin and the Antinomies of Tradition* (Ithaca, NY: Cornell University Press).

McFarland, James (2013). *Constellation: Friedrich Nietzsche and Walter Benjamin in the Now-Time of History* (New York: Fordham University Press).

McLaughlin, Kevin, and Philip Rosen, eds. (2003). *Benjamin Now: Critical Encounters with the Arcades Project* (Durham, NC: Duke University Press).

Meiffert, Torsten (1986). *Die enteignete Erfahrung: zu Walter Benjamins Konzept einer "Dialektik im Stillstand"* (Bielefeld: Aisthesis Verlag).

Melberg, Arne (1990). "Repetition (In the Kierkegaardian Sense of the Term)," *Diacritics* 20: 71–87.

Mendes-Flohr, Paul (1988). "Introduction," *The Philosophy of Franz Rosenzweig*, ed. Paul Mendes-Flohr (Hanover, NH: University Press of New England).

Mendes-Flohr, Paul (1997). "The 'Freies Jüdisches Lehrhaus' of Frankfurt," in *Jüdische Kultur in Frankfurt am Main von den Anfängen bis zur Gegenwart*, ed. Karl E. Grözinger (Wiesbaden: Harrassowitz).

Mendes-Flohr, Paul (1999). *German Jews: A Dual Identity* (New Haven, CT: Yale University Press).

Menninghaus, Winfried (1980). *Walter Benjamins Theorie der Sprachmagie* (Frankfurt am Main: Suhrkamp).

Menninghaus, Winfried (1986). *Schwellenkunde: Walter Benjamins Passage des Mythos* (Frankfurt am Main: Suhrkamp).

Mertens, Bram (2007). *Dark Images, Secret Hints: Benjamin, Scholem, Molitor and the Jewish Tradition* (Oxford: Peter Lang).

Meyer, Michael, and Michael Brenner, eds. (1996). *German-Jewish History in Modern Times: Renewal and Destruction, 1918–1945*, 4 vols. (New York: Columbia University Press).

Miller, Tyrus (2008). "Eternity No More: Walter Benjamin on the Eternal Return," in *Given World and Time: Temporalities in Context*, ed. Tyrus Miller (Budapest: CEU Press).

Missac, Pierre (1995). *Walter Benjamin's Passages*, trans. Shierry Weber Nicholsen (Cambridge, MA: MIT Press).

Momigliano, Arnaldo (1966). "Time in Ancient Historiography," *History and Theory* 6: 1–23.

Mooney, Edward F. (1991). *Knights of Faith and Resignation* (Albany, NY: SUNY Press).

Mooney, Edward F. (1998). "Repetition: Getting the World Back," in *The Cambridge Companion to Kierkegaard*, eds. Alastair Hannay and Gordon D. Marino (Cambridge: Cambridge University Press).

Moran, Joe (2003). "Benjamin and Boredom," *Critical Quarterly* 45(1–2): 168–81.

Morgan, Michael L., and Steven Weitzman, eds. (2015). *Rethinking the Messianic Idea in Judaism* (Bloomington: Indiana University Press).

Mosès, Stéphane (1989). "Walter Benjamin and Franz Rosenzweig," in *Benjamin: Philosophy, Aesthetics, History*, ed. Gary Smith (Chicago: University of Chicago Press).

Mosès, Stéphane (1992). *System and Revelation: The Philosophy of Franz Rosenzweig*, trans. Catherine Tihanyi (Detroit: Wayne State University Press).

Mosès, Stéphane (2009). *The Angel of History: Rosenzweig, Benjamin, Scholem*, trans. Barbara Harshav (Stanford, CA: Stanford University Press).

Mosès, Stéphane (2015). "Benjamin, Nietzsche et l'idée de l'éternel retour," *Walter Benjamin et l'esprit de la modernité*, ed. Heinz Wismann (Paris: Les éditions du Cerf).

Mosse, George (1997). *German Jews Beyond Judaism* (Cincinnati: Hebrew Union College Press).

Müller, Hans-Peter (1980). "Welt als 'Wiederholung': Sören Kierkagaards Novelle als Beitrag zur Hiob-Interpretation," *Werden und Wirken des Alten Testaments*, eds. Rainer Albertz, Hans P. Müller, and Hans W. Wolff (Göttingen: Vandenhoeck).

Müller-Farguell, Roger W. (2000) "Awakening Memory: Freud and Benjamin," in *Methods for the Study of Literature as Cultural Memory*, eds. Raymond Vervliet and Annemarie Estor (Amsterdam: Rodopi).

Myers, David N. (2003). *Resisting History: Historicism and Its Discontents in German-Jewish Thought* (Princeton, NJ: Princeton University Press).

Nägele, Rainer (1991). *Theater, Theory, Speculation: Walter Benjamin and the Scenes of Modernity* (Baltimore: Johns Hopkins University Press).

Nägele, Rainer (1997). "Das Beben des Barock in der Moderne: Walter Benjamins Monadologie," *MLN* 106(3): 501–27.

Nägele, Rainer (2005). *Reading After Freud* (New York: Columbia University Press).

Nietzsche, Friedrich W. (1986a). *Sämtliche Briefe*, 8 vols., ed. Giorgio Colli. and Mazzino Montinari (Munich: Deutscher Taschenbuch Verlag).

Nietzsche, Friedrich W. (1986b). *The Will to Power*, trans. Walter Kaufman and R. J. Hollingdale (New York: Vintage).

Nietzsche, Friedrich W. (1999). *Sämtliche Werke: kritische Studienausgabe*, 15 vols., eds. Giorgio Colli and Mazzino Montinari (Berlin: De Gruyter).

Nietzsche, Friedrich W. (2001). *The Gay Science*, ed. Bernard Williams, trans. Josefine Nauckhoff (Cambridge: Cambridge University Press).

Nietzsche, Friedrich W. (2006). *Thus Spoke Zarathustra*, eds. Adrian Del Caro and Robert Pippin, trans. Adrian Del Caro (Cambridge: Cambridge University Press).

Nietzsche, Friedrich W. (2007a). *Ecce Homo*, trans. Duncan Large (Oxford: Oxford University Press).

Nietzsche, Friedrich W. (2007b). *On the Genealogy of Morality*, ed. Keith Ansell-Pearson, trans. Carol Diethe (Cambridge: Cambridge University Press).

Ohana, David (2017). *Nationalizing Judaism: Zionism as a Theological Ideology* (Lanham, MD: Lexington Books).

Orgen, Brian, ed. (2015). *Time and Eternity in Jewish Mysticism: That Which Is Before and That Which Is After* (Leiden: Brill).

Oring, Elliott (1984). *The Jokes of Sigmund Freud* (Philadelphia: University of Pennsylvania Press).

Paul, Robert A. (1996). *Moses and Civilization: The Meaning Behind Freud's Myth* (New Haven, CT: Yale University Press).

Pecora, Vincent P. (1986). "Deleuze's Nietzsche and Post-Structuralist Thought," *SubStance* 48: 34–50.

Pedaya, Haviva (2003). *Ha-Ramban* (Tel Aviv: Am Oved).

Perry, Petra (1993). "Deleuze's Nietzsche," *boundary 2* 20(1): 174–91.

Pfotenhauer, Helmut (1985). "Benjamin und Nietzsche," *Walter Benjamin im Kontext*, ed. Burkhardt Lindner (Königstein: Athenäum).

Pile, Steve (2011). "Sleepwalking in the Modern City: Walter Benjamin and Sigmund Freud in the World of Dreams," in *Companion to the City*, eds. Gary Bridge and Sophie Watson (Malden, MA: Wiley-Blackwell).

Pinsker, Leon (1906). *Auto-Emancipation*, trans. D. S. Blondheim (New York: Maccabaean).

Pizer, John D. (1989). "Goethe's '*Urphänomen*' and Benjamin's '*Ursprung*': A Reconsideration," *Seminar: A Journal of Germanic Studies* 22(3): 205–22.

Pizer, John D. (1995). *Toward a Theory of Radical Origin: Essays on Modern German Thought* (Lincoln: University of Nebraska Press).

Pollock, Benjamin (2009). *Franz Rosenzweig and the Systematic Task of Philosophy* (Cambridge: Cambridge University Press).

Pollock, Benjamin (2014). *Franz Rosenzweig's Conversions* (Bloomington: Indiana University Press).

Ponzi, Mauro (2017). *Nietzsche's Nihilism in Walter Benjamin* (London: Palgrave).

Poole, Roger (1993). *Kierkegaard: The Indirect Communication* (Charlottesville: University Press of Virginia).

Poppel, Stephen M. (1976). *Zionism in Germany, 1897–1933: The Shaping of a Jewish Identity* (Philadelphia: Jewish Publication Society of America).

Powell, Matthew (2012). "A Tale of Two Abrahams: Kafka, Kierkegaard, and the Possibility of Faith in the Modern World," *The Heythrop Journal* 52: 61–70.

Quist, Wenche M. (2002). "When Your Past Lies Ahead of You: Kierkegaard and Heidegger on the Concept of Repetition," *Kierkegaard Studies Yearbook* 2002: 78–92.

Rabinbach, Anson (1979). "Critique and Commentary / Alchemy and Chemistry," *New German Critique* 17 (Special Walter Benjamin Issue): 3–14.

Rabinbach, Anson (1997). *In the Shadow of Catastrophe: German Intellectuals Between Apocalypse and Enlightenment* (Berkeley: University of California Press).

Rancière, Jacques (2002). "Preface," in *L'éternité par les Astres* (Bruxelles: Les Impressions Nouvelles).

Rashkover, Randi, and Martin Kavka, eds. (2013). *Judaism, Liberalism, and Political Theology* (Bloomington: Indiana University Press).

Rauch, Angelika (2000). *The Hieroglyph of Tradition: Freud, Benjamin, Gadamer, Novalis, Kant* (Madison, NJ: Fairleigh Dickinson University Press).

Ravitzky, Aviezer (1996). *Messianism, Zionism, and Jewish Religious Radicalism*, trans. Michael Swirsky and Jonathan Chipman (Chicago: University of Chicago Press).

Reimer, Louis (1986). "Die Wiederholung als Problem der Erlösung bei Kierkegaard," *Kierkegaardiana* 7: 20–63.

Reschke, Renate (1992). "Barbaren, Kult und Katastrophen: Nietzsche bei Benjamin, Unzusammenhängendes im Zusammenhang gelesen," *Aber ein Sturm weht vom Paradiese her: Texte zu Walter Benjamin*, ed. Michael Opitz and Erdmut Wizisla (Leipzig: Reclam).

Rey, Abel (1927). *Le Retour éternel et la philosophie de la physique* (Paris: Flammarion).

Rice, Emanuel (1990). *Freud and Moses: The Long Journey Home* (Albany, NY: SUNY Press).

Richter, Gerhard (2013). "Das Kunstwerk in seinen formalen und genealogischen Bestimmungen: Benjamins 'kühle Stelle zwischen Kant und Nietzsche," *Benjamins Grenzgänge*, eds. Gerhard Richter, Karl Solibakke, and Bernd Witte (Würzburg: Königshausen & Neumann).

Rickels, Laurence A. (2002). "Suicitation: Benjamin and Freud," in *Benjamin's Ghosts: Interventions in Contemporary Literary and Cultural Theory*, ed. Gerhard Richter (Stanford, CA: Stanford University Press).

Ricœur, Paul (1995). "Biblical Time," in *Figuring the Sacred: Religion, Narrative, and Imagination*, ed. Mark I. Wallace, trans. David Pellauer (Minneapolis: Fortress Press).

Le Rider, Jacques (1993). *Modernity and Crises of Identity: Culture and Society in Fin-de-Siècle Vienna*, trans. Rosemary Morris (New York: Continuum).

Robbins, Jill (1991). *Prodigal Son/Elder Brother: Interpretation and Alterity in Augustine, Petrarch, Kafka, Levinas* (Chicago: University of Chicago Press).

Robert, Marthe (1976). *From Oedipus to Moses: Freud's Jewish Identity*, trans. Ralph Manheim (Garden City, NY: Anchor Books).

Robinson, Paul A. (1969). *The Freudian Left* (New York: Harper Books).

Roff, Sarah Ley (2004). "Benjamin and Psychoanalysis," in *The Cambridge Companion to Walter Benjamin*, ed. David S. Ferris (Cambridge: Cambridge University Press).

Rölli, Marc (2012). "The Story of Repetition," *Parallax* 18(1): 96–103.

Rosen, Charles (1988). "The Ruins of Walter Benjamin," in *On Walter Benjamin: Critical Essays and Recollections*, ed. Cary Smith (Cambridge, MA: MIT Press).

Rosen, Stanley (1995). *The Mask of Enlightenment: Nietzsche's Zarathustra* (Cambridge: Cambridge University Press).

Rosenwald, Lawrence (1994). "On the Reception of Buber and Rosenzweig's Bible," *Prooftexts* 14: 141–65.

Rosenzweig, Franz (1920). *Der Tischdank* (Berlin: F. Gurlitt).

Rosenzweig, Franz (1924). *Sechzig Hymnen und Gedichte des Jehuda Halevi* (Konstanz: Wöhrle).

Rosenzweig, Franz (1927). *Jehuda Halevi: Zweiundneunzig Hymnen und Gedichte* (Berlin: Verlag Lambert Schneider).

Rosenzweig, Franz (1965). *On Jewish Learning*, ed. Nahum N. Glatzer (New York: Schocken Books).

Rosenzweig, Franz (1999). *The New Thinking*, eds. and trans. Alan Udoff and Barbara Ellen Galli (Syracuse, NY: Syracuse University Press).

Rosenzweig, Franz (2011). *Perushe Frants Rozentsyaig le-tish'im ya-hamishah mi-shire Rabi Yehudah Halevi*, trans. Michael Schwarz (Jerusalem: Magnes Press).

Roth, Michael S. (1987). *Psychoanalysis as History: Negation and Freedom in Freud* (Ithaca, NY: Cornell University Press).

Safranski, Rüdiger (2002). *Nietzsche: A Philosophical Biography*, trans. Shelley Frisch (New York: Norton).

Said, Edward W. (2004). *Freud and the Non-European* (New York: Verso).

Šajda, Peter, and Jon Stewart, eds. (2017). *Kierkegaard Bibliography, Tome VII: Figures I to Z* (New York: Routledge).

Santner, Eric L. (2001). *On the Psychotheology of Everyday Life: Reflections on Freud and Rosenzweig* (Chicago: University of Chicago Press).

Scholem, Gershom (1971). *The Messianic Idea in Judaism*, ed. Werner J. Dann-hauser (New York: Schocken Books).

Scholem, Gershom (1976). *On Jews and Judaism in Crisis*, ed. Werner J. Dannhauser (New York: Schocken Books).

Scholem, Gershom (1980). *From Berlin to Jerusalem*, trans. Harry Zohn (New York: Schocken Books).

Scholem, Gershom (1981). *Walter Benjamin: The Story of a Friendship*, trans. Harry Zohn (Philadelphia: Jewish Publication Society of America).

Scholem, Gershom (1987). *Origins of the Kabbalah*, ed. Zwi Werblowsky, trans. Allan Arkush (Princeton, NJ: Princeton University Press).

Scholem, Gershom (1990). "On Our Language: A Confession," trans. Ora Wis-kind, *History and Memory* 2(2): 97–99.

Scholem, Gershom (2007). *Lamentations of Youth: The Diaries of Gershom Scholem, 1913–1919*, ed. and trans. Anthony D. Skinner (Cambridge, MA: Harvard University Press).

Schrag, Calvin O. (1970). "Heidegger on Repetition and Historical Understand-ing," *Philosophy East and West* 20(3): 287–95.

Schwartz, Regina M. (1998). "Freud's God," in *Post-Secular Philosophy*, ed. Phillip Blond (London: Routledge).

Schwebel, Paula L. (2012). "Intensive Infinity: Walter Benjamin's Reception of Leibniz and Its Sources," *MLN* 127(3): 589–610.

Schweid, Eliezer (1996). "The Rejection of the Diaspora in Zionist Thought: Two Approaches," in *Essential Papers on Zionism*, eds. Jehuda Reinharz and Anita Shapira (New York: New York University Press).

Seeskin, Kenneth (2012). *Jewish Messianic Thoughts in an Age of Despair* (Cam-bridge: Cambridge University Press).

Seidel, George J. (1964). *Martin Heidegger and the Pre-Socratics* (Lincoln: Univer-sity of Nebraska Press).

Seidman, Naomi (2006). *Faithful Renderings: Jewish-Christian Difference and the Politics of Translation* (Chicago: University of Chicago Press).

Van Seters, John (1983). *In Search of History: Historiography in the Ancient World and the Origins of Biblical History* (New Haven, CT: Yale University Press).

Seung, T. K. (2005). *Nietzsche's Epic of the Soul: Thus Spoke Zarathustra* (Lanham, MD: Lexington Books).

Sharvit, Gilad (2016). "Conscious Inhibitions: Freud, Anti-Semitism, and Hobbesian Imagination," *Journal of Modern Jewish Studies* 15(3): 349–65.

Sharvit, Gilad (2018). "Moses and the Burning Bush: Leadership and Potentiality in the Bible," in *Freud and Monotheism*, ed. Gilad Sharvit and Karen Feldman (New York: Fordham University Press).

Sharvit, Gilad, and Karen S. Feldman (2017). *Freud and Monotheism: Moses and the Violent Origins of Religion* (New York: Fordham University Press).

Sheppard, Richard (1991). "Kafka, Kierkegaard and the K's: Theology, Psychology, and Fiction," *Journal of Literature and Theology* 5(3): 277–96.

Shumsky, Dmitry (2018). *Beyond the Nation-State: The Zionist Political Imagination from Pinsker to Ben-Gurion* (New Haven, CT: Yale University Press).

Simmel, Georg (2001). *Schopenhauer und Nietzsche: ein Vortragszyklus*, ed. Klaus H. Fischer (Schutterwald/Baden: Wissenschaftlicher Verlag).

Slavet, Eliza (2009). *Racial Fever: Freud and the Jewish Question* (New York: Fordham University Press).

Somers-Hall, Henry (2017). "Deleuze, Freud and the Three Syntheses," *Deleuze Studies* 11(3): 297–327.

Sorkin, David (1987). *The Transformation of German Jewry, 1780–1840* (Oxford: Oxford University Press).

Spitzer, Alan Barrie (1957). *The Revolutionary Theories of Louis Auguste Blanqui* (New York: Columbia University Press).

Steensgaard, Peter (1993). "Time in Judaism," in *Religion and Time*, eds. Anindita Niyogi Balslev and Jitendranath N. Mohanty (Leiden: E. J. Brill).

Stern, Alexander (2018). "'The Mother of Reason and Revelation': Benjamin on the Metaphysics of Language," *Critical Horizons* 19(2): 140–56.

Stewart, Elizabeth (2010). *Catastrophe and Survival: Walter Benjamin and Psychoanalysis* (New York: Continuum).

Straub, Jürgen, and Jörn Rüsen, eds. (2010). *Dark Traces of the Past: Psychoanalysis and Historical Thinking* (New York: Berghahn Books).

Thorndike, Lynn (1923–1958). *A History of Magic and Experimental Science* (New York: Columbia University Press).

Tiedemann, Rolf (1989). "Historical Materialism or Political Messianism? An Interpretation of the Theses 'On the Concept of History,'" in *Benjamin: Philosophy, History, Aesthetics*, ed. Gary Smith (Chicago: University of Chicago Press).

Tiedemann, Rolf (1999). "Dialectics at a Standstill: Approaches to the Passagen-Werk," in *The Arcades Project* (Cambridge, MA: Belknap Press of Harvard University Press).

Trompf, G. W. (1979). *The Idea of Historical Recurrence in Western Thought: From Antiquity to the Reformation* (Berkeley: University of California Press).

Urbich, Jan (2012). *Darstellung bei Walter Benjamin: Die "Erkenntniskritische Vorrede" im Kontext ästhetischer Darstellungstheorien der Moderne* (Berlin: De Gruyter).

Vico, Giambattista (1984). *The New Science of Giambattista Vico*, trans. Thomas Goddard Bergin and Max Harold Fisch (Ithaca, NY: Cornell University Press).

Wahl, Jean (1946). "Kierkegaard and Kafka," in *The Kafka Problem*, ed. Angel Flores (New York: New Directions).

Ward, Koral (2008). *Augenblick: The Concept of the 'Decisive Moment' in 19th- and 20th-Century Western Philosophy* (Burlington, VT: Ashgate).

Weber, Samuel (2003). *Gershom Scholem: politisches, esoterisches und historiographisches Schreiben* (München: Fink).

Weber, Samuel (2008). *Benjamin's -abilities* (Cambridge, MA: Harvard University Press).

Weigel, Sigrid (1996). *Body and Image Space: Re-Reading Walter Benjamin*, trans. Georgina Paul, Rachel McNicholl and Jeremy Gaines (New York: Routledge).

Weinstock, Israel (1969). *Be-Ma'agley he-Nigle ve-ha-Nistar* (Jerusalem: Mossad Harav Kook).

Weiss-Rosmarin, Trude (1939). *The Hebrew Moses: An Answer to Sigmund Freud* (New York: The Jewish Book Club).

Welz, Claudia (2011). "Franz Rosenzweig: A Kindred Spirit in Alignment with Kierkegaard," in *Kierkegaard and Existentialism*, ed. Jon B. Stewart (Farnham: Ashgate).

Butin, Wernaa Gitte (2000). "Abraham—Knight of Faith or Counterfeit? Abraham Figures in Kierkegaard, Derrida, and Kafka," *Kierkegaardiana* 21: 19–35.

White, Hayden V. (1966). "The Burden of History," *History and Theory* 5(2): 111–34.

Whitebook, Joel (1995). *Perversion and Utopia: A Study in Psychoanalysis and Critical Theory* (Cambridge, MA: MIT Press).

Wiegmann, Jutta (1989). *Psychoanalytische Geschichtstheorie: Ein Studie zur Freud-Rezeption Walter Benjamins* (Bonn: Bouvier Verlag).

Wiesenthal, Liselotte (1973). *Zur Wissenschaftstheorie Walter Benjamins* (Frankfurt: Athenäum-Verlag).

Williams, James (2013). *Gilles Deleuze's Difference and Repetition: A Critical Introduction and Guide* (Edinburgh: Edinburgh University Press).

Williams, Linda L. (1998). "Kierkegaard's Weanings," *Philosophy Today* 42(3): 310–18.

Witte, Bernd (2007). *Jüdische Tradition und literarische Moderne: Heine, Buber, Kafka, Benjamin* (München: Carl Hanser Verlag).

Wohlfarth, Irving (2005). "On the Messianic Structure of Walter Benjamin's Last Reflections," in *Walter Benjamin: Critical Evaluations in Cultural Theory*, ed. Peter Osborne, 3 vols. (New York: Routledge).

Wolfson, Elliot R. (2006). *Alef, Mem, Tau: Kabbalistic Musings on Time, Truth, and Death* (Berkeley: University of California Press).

Wolfson, Elliot R. (2005). *Language, Eros, Being: Kabbalistic Hermeneutics and Poetic Imagination* (New York: Fordham University Press).

Wolfson, Elliot R. (2014). *Giving Beyond the Gift* (New York: Fordham University Press).

Wolfson, Elliot R. (2015a). "Kenotic Overflow and Temporal Transcendence: Angelic Embodiment and the Alterity of Time in Abraham Abulafia," in *Time and Eternity in Jewish Mysticism*, ed. Brian Orgen (Leiden: Brill).

Wolfson, Elliot R. (2015b). "Retroactive Not Yet: Linear Circularity and Kabbalistic Temporality," in *Time and Eternity in Jewish Mysticism*, ed. Brian Ogren (Leiden: Brill)

Wolin, Richard (1982). "Benjamin's Materialist Theory of Experience," *Theory and Society* 11(1): 17–42.

Wolin, Richard (1994). *Walter Benjamin: An Aesthetic of Redemption* (Berkeley: University of California Press).

Wolman, Benjamin B., ed. (1971). *The Psychoanalytic Interpretation of History* (New York: Basic Books).

Yerushalmi, Haim Y. (1991). *Freud's Moses: Judaism Terminable and Interminable* (New Haven, CT: Yale University Press).

Yerushalmi, Haim Y. (1996). *Zakhor: Jewish History and Jewish Memory* (Seattle: University of Washington Press).

Young, Julian (2010). *Friedrich Nietzsche: A Philosophical Biography* (Cambridge: Cambridge University Press).

Žižek, Slavoj (2008). *The Ticklish Subject: The Absent Centre of Political Ontology* (New York: Verso).

Zweig, Stefan (1962). *Mental Healers*, trans. Eden and Cedar Paul (New York: Ungar).

Zweig, Stefan (2009). *The World of Yesterday*, trans. Anthea Bell (London: Pushkin Press).

Index

Benjamin, Walter (*cont.*) mother metaphor, 171; Nietzsche, views on, 153, 157–60; nominalism, 166–68; oeuvre, 124; "On Language as Such and on the Language of Man," 107, 163, 180, 185, 186; "On Some Motifs in Baudelaire," 147, 148, 268n44; "On the Concept of History," 190–91, 226; *The Origins of German Mourning Play* (See *Trauerspiel*); power of modern repetition, 6; primal history (*Urgeschichte*), 141–43; problem of representation in art, solution to, 167, 273n37; relates dynamism to memory, 267n40; repetition and time, 9; "repetition of opposites," model of, 12, 43, 136, 165–79, 195–96; "Storyteller," 144–45; "The Task of the Translator," 106, 184, 276n83; technology, vision of, 151; theory of knowledge, 273n39; translation, theory of, 107; on translation and revelation, 106–8; truth and truth's method, 272n29; *Ursprung* (origin), 12, 170–75, 178, 227, 228, 231, 232

Bergson, Henri-Louis, 137

Bernstein, Richard, 204, 284n93

Beyond the Pleasure Principle (Freud), 148, 150, 212, 232, 280n35

Bialik, Hayim Nahman, 58

Bible, 53, 87, 128, 133, 134, 229; Buber-Rosenzweig, 97; translation of, 98, 99–100, 102, 103

Blanchot, Maurice, 32

Blanqui, Louis Auguste, 12, 135, 136, 153–60, 270n73; eternal return, theory of, 154; helplessness, 155; *L'éternité par les Astres*, 12, 153–60; as martyr, 154–57; as revolutionary spirit, 156; violence of, 157

The Blue Octavo Notebooks (Kafka), 120, 129

blutgemeinschaft, 254n23

B'nai B'rith movement, 51

Boyarin, Daniel, 284n111

Brauer, Isaac, 58

Brenner, Michael, 46, 251n29

Briese, Erwine, 133

Brod, Max, 105, 121

Brothers and Strangers (Aschheim), 48

Buber, Martin, 55, 57, 111; *Moses*, 204

Buber-Rosenzweig Bible, 97

Buch des Richters (Kierkegaard), 120

Buck-Morss, Susan, 264n10, 265n15

Caputo, John, 40, 42, 194, 248n94

The Castle (Kafka), 118

Catastrophe and Survival (Stewart), 283n79

Caygill, Howard, 162, 274n57

Central Park (Benjamin), 159

Certeau, Michel de, 282n68

Chouraqui, Frank, 270n73

Christ: death of, 23; return of, 23

Christianity, 8, 70, 76–77, 80, 216–18, 235; archaic eternal return in, afterlife of, 22–27; eternity to, 79; expansionism, 71; form of time, 23; Freud's reduction of, 281n56; Judaism transition to, 217. *See also* Judaism

chronos, 24

Clement of Alexandria, 24

Clermont Tonnerre, Count, 48

Cohen, Hermann, 56, 58, 59, 70, 71, 169, 236

collective unconscious, 141–43. *See also* consciousness

The Commentator's Despair (Corngold), 119

The Concept of Dread (Kierkegaard), 85

consciousness, 11, 21, 84, 134, 143, 146, 148–49, 190; aesthetic, 38; cyclical temporal, 26, 78, 98; Jewish national, 61

Greenberg, Uri Tzvi, 62
Guattari, Félix, 232

Habermas, Jürgen, 197
Halevi, Jehuda, 11; *Kuzari*, 102; poems,
13, 87, 108–10; "Praised Be He"
(yehe shime'cha), 109; Rosenzweig's
translations of, 87, 97–115; *shirei
qodesh* (devotional poems), 103
Hannay, Alistair, 263n29
Harootunian, Harry, 278n108
Hasidism, 57
Hegel, Georg Wilhelm Friedrich, 49,
83, 134; ideal of unity of being, 100;
logic of immanence, 94; ontology,
82; phenomenology, 33; system of
Spirit, 93, 94
Heidegger, Martin, 6, 10, 18, 27,
28, 32, 37, 38, 40, 124, 164, 169,
191–95; *Being and Time*, 10, 40,
191, 194, 278n104; *Contributions to
Philosophy*, 249n105; *Dasein*, 40–43,
193–95; *Kant and the Problem of
Metaphysics*, 249n105; "repetition-
as-recollection forward" model, 9,
18, 162; repetition *(Wiederholung)*,
40–43, 191, 192, 193, 194
Heraclitus, 22
Herodotus, 22
Hess, Moses, 61
Hessel, Franz, 134
Hibat Tsiyon movement, 60
*Historische Commission für Geschichte
der Juden in Deutschland*, 56
History and Class Consciousness
(Lukács), 140
*Hochschule für die Wissenschaft des
Judentums*, 56

Idel, Moshe, 26
Idolatry and Representation
(Batnitzky), 96
Institute of Social Research, 142, 147

The Interpretation of Dreams (Freud),
45, 52, 230

Jehuda Halevi, Rosenzweig's
translations of, 97–115; and alterity,
99–108; and cyclical time, 108–15;
messianism and translation,
114–15; model of translation as
foreignization, 102–6; *Nachwort*,
87, 102, 109, 110, 112, 113, 260n20,
262n55, overview, 97–99; and
revelation, 100–102; Rosenzweig's
notes, 111–14, 190
Jennings, Michael, 49
Jewish antiquity, 60–64
Jewish calendar, 108–10
Jewish cultural imagination, returns
and repetitions in, 54–64; search
for Jewish origins, 55–60; Zionism
and return to Jewish antiquity,
60–64
Jewish modernity, 4, 8; crisis of
tradition, 47–54; Jewish cultural
imagination, returns and
repetitions in, 54–64; messianic
thought in, 11, 13; tradition and
repetition in, 45–64
Jews, 10–11, 213; auto-emancipation
of, 60–61; East European, 11, 57, 58,
62; from Galicia and Lithuania,
58, 63; German-speaking, 46;
Polish, 58–59; rejected Christian
imperialism, 89; saved from
Pharaoh, 24
Judaism, 8, 24, 70, 216–18, 235, 236;
afterlife of archaic eternal return
in, 17, 22–27; Doctrine of *Shemittot*,
25; eternity to, 79; Freud and, 50–54,
281n56; marginal, 49; messianism
in, models of, 2; Muscular, 62;
Orthodox, 59; transition to
Christianity, 217; as *Volk*, 47. *See also*
Christianity

Jüdische Bücherei, 99
Jung, Carl, 137, 141

Kafka, Franz, 3, 7, 36, 46, 47, 52–53,
  63, 117–30, 196, 226; Abraham,
  122–23, 125–29; *The Blue Octavo
  Notebooks (Oktavhefte)*, 120, 129; *The
  Castle (Das Schloß)*, 118; dynamic
  repetition, model of, 11; letter on
  Abraham, 121–22, 123; "Letter to
  the Father," 48–50; members of
  young German Jewish community,
  45; messianic thought, 18; *The
  Metamorphosis (Die Verwandlung)*,
  118; model of repetition, 7–8;
  poetics, 8, 13; power of modern
  repetition, 6; remarks on *Fear and
  Trembling*, 121; repetition and time,
  9, 118–19; *The Trial (Der Process)*,
  117–18; version of biblical story, 122
kairos, 24
Kant and the Problem of Metaphysics
  (Heidegger), 249n105
Kant, Immanuel, 148, 190, 223
Kaufmann, Yehezkel, 62
Kibbutz Movement, 61
Kierkegaard, Søren, 5–6, 19, 27, 32, 69,
  119–29, 164, 180, 194, 247n75, 258n94;
  Abrahamic ideal, 119, 120–30; *Buch
  des Richters*, 120; *The Concept of
  Dread*, 85; *Fear and Trembling*, 5, 11,
  84, 119, 120, 121, 122, 123, 126, 127, 128;
  intersubjective realm, theories of,
  96; letter on Abraham to Klopstock,
  121; and model of dynamic repetition,
  8; religious existentialism, 125;
  repetition *(Gjentagelse)*, 5, 10, 11, 18,
  28, 37–40, 42, 84–86, 88, 95, 127;
  "repetition-as-recollection forward"
  model, 9, 18, 89, 124, 129, 162
Klages, Ludwig, 141
Klausner, Joseph, 62
Klopstock, Robert, 121, 124, 126, 196

Klossowski, Pierre, 32
Knights of Faith and Resignation
  (Mooney), 125–26
Köselitz, Heinrich, 27
Kraus, Karl, 181
Krochmal, Nachman, 24
Kuzari (Halevi), 102

Labor Zionism, 61
Lebensphilosophie, 83, 148
L'écriture de l'histoire (Certeau), 282n68
Leibniz, 168
L'Enfermé (Geffory), 155, 156
L'Entretien infini (Blanchot), 32
Les Fleurs du mal (Baudelaire), 147
Leskov, Nikolai, 144, 145
Le Tableau noir (Vaudal), 139
L'éternité par les Astres (Blanqui), 12,
  153–60
liturgy: and Halevi's poems, 108–10;
  repetition and, 76–77, 79–80
The Logic of Sense (Deleuze), 13, 33, 35
Löwith, Karl, 23, 28, 29, 30, 36; on
  formulation of Nietzsche's eternal
  return, 245n53
Löwy, Michael, 264n7
Lukács, György, 140
Luria, Rabbi Isaac, 26
Luzzatto, Samuel David, 261n40

Marcuse, Herbert, 137
McFarland, James, 270n78
Meaning and History (Löwith), 23
Mendelssohn, Moses, 98, 103
Mendes-Flohr, Paul, 67
Messiah, 243n26; arrival of, 1–3; at
  the Gate of Rome, 1–3, 6–7, 238;
  repetition, 2–3
messianism, 7, 13, 201; apocalyptic,
  2, 4; formulations of, 3, 6; gestures
  of, 127–30; Jewish, 1, 2, 3, 4, 18; and
  translation, 114–15; weak, 205,
  224–39